PASSING THROUGH

Passing Through

Exploring the Envelope, Part One

by

Manny Sousa, Captain US Navy (Ret)

XULON PRESS

Xulon Press
2301 Lucien Way #415
Maitland, FL 32751
407.339.4217
www.xulonpress.com

Printed in the United States of America.

ISBN-13: 978-1-5456-8182-4

TABLE OF CONTENTS

INTRODUCTION

Passing Through, Part One is my auto-biography from birth 1932 through 1971, the end of my fifth Vietnam tour and squadron change of command. Part Two, in progress, will complete PT, 1972-? Although leaving a legacy for descendants was a consideration, my primary purpose in writing PT is to share my spiritual experiences with Jean, who has been very prominently present in my life since my birth and following her death in 1949.

My facilitating narrative device is a 2027 interview by my son Michael, because it was useful to have a "devil's advocate" and an alternative to one-sided first person narration. Though adding the possibly confusing complication of a fictional story line in a factual memoir was a concern, chapter 2 will hopefully serve to introduce and clarify my strategy.

I attempted "whole truth" recollections, including negative aspects of my history, in the interest of credibility and confession, not justification. Though you will not find "divine inspiration" for some of my actions, I did my best to balance the gray areas of pros and cons in my choices as I saw them. Although Jean influenced my future in many indirect providential ways and regularly communicated with me through unspoken messages, omens, and agreements, she never interfered with my free will in any manner.

For such unique blessings in my life, I have often wondered 'why me?', for I am an unworthy sinner who has broken all the Commandments. Now, thankfully surviving at age 87, I have also wondered for what purpose I was saved. I now feel that my ministry is to publicly share my story as encouragement for others to acknowledge the Holy Spirit within us in whatever form Jesus deems appropriate in fulfillment of His promise.

I made an effort to condense PT with simple words and sentences, eliminating unnecessary filler. Nevertheless, because the events of PT entails many strands of woven interaction with those close to me throughout eight decades, I suggest reading PT beginning to end without skipping in order to keep track of people and events.

I highly recommend the therapeutic and nostalgic benefits of writing memoirs to all senior citizens. As a kind lady once chastised my wife when she objected to hearing one of my tales yet again said, "Let him tell his stories, That's all he's got." My prayer is that you are in contact with the Holy Spirit within you and will tell your stories too.

The Holy Spirit is given as a gift to live in
every Christian from the moment of salvation.
(John 3:5, Acts 2:38)

God gives each Christian gifts by His spirit to be used for
ministry in the building up the body of Christ
(Eph. 4:11-13)

I

1969: Introducing Jean

___

"Hello Manuel dear." Hamm-no one has called me Manuel since 1955. "Why are you speaking to me?"

"You need me."

"True perhaps, another difficult time was at hand "Where were you in 1955?", I asked facetiously.

"I was away. I'm sorry."

"Did you volunteer to be here, or were you assigned?"

"You need me."

"Are you someone I know?"

"Yes."

"What is your name?"

"Jean."

The light came on.

"My aunt Jean?"

"Yes."

The last time I saw her, 1949, I was sixteen and Jean was in her early twenties. Less than a year later, Jean was found dead in her Boston apartment with the unlit gas stove turned on. The police ruled it a suicide, but the family believed it was a homicide.

"Where are you?"

"Ether." defined as "an imaginary substance regarded by the ancients as filling all space beyond the sphere of the moon and making up the stars and planets."

"Will you remain there?"

"They will decide."

1

"Who are they?"

"I can't say."

"Did you know them when you were living?"

"Yes."

"Is your mother there?"

"Yes."

"Is she one of those who will decide?"

"Yes."

"Has God spoken to you?"

"Yes."

"What did He say?"

"I can't say, but He loves you all very much."

"Did you commit suicide?"

"No, it was an accident."

"Is there a possibility that you will return to earth in another life?"

"They will decide."

"Was I here before?"

"Stone Age, Crusades, and 1898."

"Can you see my future"

"Yes, but you can change it."

"Can you influence my future?"

"Yes."

"How?"

"If I told you, it wouldn't work."

Oh yes it would! As you will see, once I understood how her influence worked, it became increasingly easy to recognize Jean's hand in many significant events in my life. without ever once interfering with my free will.

This account of my conversation with Jean is condensed but factual as I recall it. My mother witnessed the event and wanted me to persist with more questions. "What does it all mean?" Mother asked. "Two simple truths", I replied, "God is with us and there is life after death. That is all we need to know."

I have spoken to Jean regularly since then to thank her for her watchful loving friendship, guidance, and help, but I had no further questions for some time. Nevertheless, her actions let me know very clearly that she was always nearby. Her messages, agreements, and omens were so undeniable, life for me is often a matter of "following The Yellow Brick Road" not always easy or without hazards, failures, sorrows, obstacles, and disappointments, but always great adventure.

As "God watches over fools, drunks, sailors, and children", so has Jean watched over me. She saved my life many times.

For those inclined to think I may be subject to hallucinations, I add this note: One day in 2010 I was seated at a table in the Quincy Florida airport terminal with Richard, a retired FSU oceanography professor who knew nothing about Jean. He suddenly asked, "Can you see the woman standing to your right with her left hand on your right shoulder?" "No", I said, "but I know who she is." Richard went on to describe her as pictured in this book and miming 'Mom', as she pointed up with her right index finger. Later, Richard reported that he regularly saw Jean walking with me at the airport.

I will further detail this event and the 1969 conversation in Chapter 25.

Jean 1940's

2

REUNION

THE YEAR IS 2027.

"Good morning. My name is Michael Sousa. I called yesterday. I am here to see Captain Sousa."

"Oh yes. Good morning Mister Sousa. You spoke with me. I am Georgina Estes, please call me Georgie. I told the Captain he was having a visitor today. As you asked, I didn't mention your name. He is outside on the grounds with his wheel chair. As you will see, we are fortunate to have very large grounds with a lake and wooded perimeter. We can't always keep track of the Captain, but he doesn't wander away so we don't get too concerned. He let's us know when he is 'Going to see the Wizard', as he says. I see you share the same surname, do you mind me asking if you are related? We like to keep track in case of an emergency."

"I am the Captain's oldest son, but please keep that confidential between us if you will, Georgie. We haven't communicated for many years and it might complicate matters for him to know who I am just now. I'm sure he won't recognize me with beard, glasses, bald head, plus extra pounds. I'm here to see if he will let me write his biography, so I'll need some time to see how it goes. I'm sorry to ask your cooperation in this deception, but I'll be using Sabino as my last name for now. Meanwhile, please call me Mike, alright?"

"Of course, I'll see to it, Mike. The Captain has seldom had visitors in his ten years here at Heritage Pines just a few old Vietnam squadron pals who call themselves the 'Pukin' Dogs'. I wasn't aware of any near relatives."

"Oh yes, I have two brothers and two sisters by a different mother. Plus, the Captain has ten grandchildren, not to mention several ex-wives."

"Goodness, Mike, I had no idea."

"Unfortunately, we have not been close or kept in touch, partly because his thirty one years in the Navy kept him moving, including six Vietnam tours. Then, three days after retiring, he

4

set sail for Europe aboard his sloop WINGS. He left my life just after I was born and I've seen him only several times. He and my mother were married only a year and a half and never lived together. So, as usual in these cases, he got the blame. But there are always two sides to the story, aren't there? I'm here to get his."

"Yes, Lord knows there are always two sides. What a shame. I do hope it goes well, for both your sakes. Will you be in town long, Mike?"

"That depends, Georgie. Perhaps several weeks. I have taken a room at the Waterman's Inn and hope to visit daily. How is he?"

"Oh quite well really, for all his 94 years. He is a bit frail, as you would expect, but trim and relatively fit. He uses the wheel chair around the grounds mostly as a walker and to have a chair with him. His eyesight and hearing are good. He is doing well on medication for a kidney condition and for slightly elevated blood pressure. He is on his third pacemaker for atrial fibrilation. Mentally, he is alert. His Pukin' Dog squadron pals affectionately say he is as grumpy as ever, though they do get on with some hell-raising here. One of them, Jaybee, tends to get a bit frisky with the ladies, but the girls easily keep their distance. I hope you don't mind searching the Captain out yourself. We are short-handed and I like to stay near the office. Just follow the yellow brick sidewalk to the edge of the woods. You'll find him as far into them as he can get with his wheel chair."

It was as Georgie said. There was the Captain, well into the tree line in his chair, covered with a scotch plaid blanket, obviously asleep. But there was something quite unusual about the scene. Either the wheel chair had a very high seat, or the Captain was floating motionless in midair nearly three feet above it! It was hard to tell which since the blanket hung down long enough on all sides to conceal the space beneath him. Not wishing to disturb the scene and to understand the sight, Michael stopped twenty feet away, remaining silent and motionless. But the Captain stirred, apparently aware of a presence nearby. Fighter pilot instinct perhaps. As he slowly awoke, so did the Captain slowly descend the space between himself and the chair. He had indeed been levitating! By the time he was fully awake, the Captain was normally seated.

"Who are you? Why are you sneaking up on me in my sleep, just when I was having a great flying dream?"

"Very sorry, Captain Sousa, I was just trying to avoid disturbing you. My name is Michael, but call me Mike. I am the visitor Georgie mentioned to you."

"Well Mike, do you have a last name?"

"Mike Sabino, sir."

"No need for sir, call me Captain, OK?"

"Yes sir er Captain."

"Am I supposed to know who you are?"

"No Captain."

"Then what do you want with me?"

"Well Captain, I am a writer doing research for a book about Vietnam."

"What's that got to do with me? You don't look like a writer. What have you written?"

"Nothing important, only job related stuff. I'm just getting started with serious efforts."

"Kinda' old to be starting, aren't you? Not your first career I take it. How old are you, Mike?"

"Yes, a late start. I'm 72."

"I have a son your age named Michael, a liberal lawyer with no sense of humor. I told him a joke about a Spic over thirty years ago and he hasn't spoken to me since, just because his mother's name was Rodrigues and he was raised to be in denial. Odd for him to think I'm biased since my father was born in the Portuguese Azores Islands which makes me sorta Spic myself—at least the Navy thought so. What's your daytime job?"

"I am a retired attorney Captain, but I enjoy writing."

"So let's start over, Counselor. What's this got to do with me?

"Well Captain. I wanted learn to fly but never took the time. I sometimes fly with my friend Philip, who has a 1948 Aeronca 'Champion' and he lets me fly it a bit, when he is with me, of course. Now I am interested in writing about Vietnam era Navy carrier pilots as a last of a breed since piloted conventional military airplanes and aircraft carriers are nearly history."

"Why carrier pilots, Mike."

"I've read that night carrier landings were the most dangerous and challenging thing ever done routinely with airplanes"

"True. Every night carrier landing was as hard as the first one. Nothing 'routine' about it for the guy in the cockpit. More tension than being shot at, the docs discovered. You say you *want* to fly but haven't done much about it. Obviously, you don't want to very badly. It's still not too late for you though. I flew my Ximango motor-glider until I came here. In fact, I still have it in my hangar at the county airport. As they say, 'It's all in the doin'. So tell me why I should spend time with a wannabe who says he *wants* to *write* about flying? Anyhow, who the hell cares to read more old war stories about Vietnam? You'll never sell it."

"You may have me there, Captain. Truth is, I have lived a very ordinary life one town, one job, one wife, three kids, and retired. Not much adventure. I always hoped to live aboard a sailboat and cruise the Islands. So I'd like to know more about what I missed. In fact, I am not so much interested in Vietnam as I am in the colorful naval aviators who lived it. I'll publish and peddle the book myself if I have to, if not your story, someone else's. However, if it can be your story, I suggest we co-author the book. You'll get the glory and we'll split the profit."

"Yeah sure, right, Mike, glory and profits. All I have to do is live another ten years and then figure out how to spend it all! One more time, Mike, without the bull, why me, and how did you find me?"

"OK, Captain, here it is. When I Google searched Vietnam Navy fighter squadrons, I got over four thousand hits on the 'Pukin' Dogs', even though it appears that the squadron never did anything historic—name and logo only.

"Why pursue it then?"

"Surely there had to be more than a name in bad taste, so I dug deeper on the internet. I finally found a reference to the Pukin' Dog DOGNET moderated by SECDOG, Jaybee Souder. I corresponded with him and wrangled an invitation to meet up with him and other San Diego Dogs at one of their occasional dinner get-togethers. I don't have to tell you how it went. I was told that Jaybee was in his usual fine form until the management, accompanied by a bouncer, asked us to please leave. One of the lady customers objected to his forward behavior. The San Diego Dogs have to change watering holes frequently. So I came to understand the old fighter pilot adage, which earn the Pukin' Dogs fame for epitomizing, 'If you can't be good, be colorful.' In fact, I would have chosen JayBee as my book subject, but he says he is writing his own, which I'm told he has been claiming to be doing for 50 years. Another Pukin' Dog who would have been an interesting subject was 'Engine Eddie' Davidson, but he shuns alcohol and has already written his own books of memoirs and poetry about Vietnam. Plus, I just thought a tee-totaling poet was too unheard of for an authentic fighter pilot, especially a Pukin' Dog, so I asked for Jaybee's recommendation.

Since you may be an elder survivor and you were back and forth to Vietnam for the entire eleven years, plus have some quite colorful personal history of your own I've heard about, here I am."

"Well then, Mike, you will be disappointed to hear that I have written some poetry myself—even had one published, but never a book. I'm not much of a colorful drinker either. Just how long do you think you can hang around this fancy old farts' farm for your project?"

"As long as it takes, Captain. I'm staying at the Watermen's Inn."

"This could take longer than I have left, Mike, so let's just give it a day or two and see what happens. Is that a recording gadget you have there?"

"Yes Captain, right here, ready to begin."

"There's a bench over there. Give me a push. Where do you want to start?"

"Tell me about the dream you were having when I arrived

"I told you, I was flying."

"What type of airplane?"

"No airplane, just me."

"How were you able to do it?"

"Willpower and concentration."

"How high did you go and how far?"

"Not very high or far, Mike, because it's difficult to keep my attention fixed on the focused concentration it takes when you're having that kind of experience. Even in a dream, I'm too old to take a fall when someone sneaks up on me, might scare me to death."

"My apologies, Captain. What if you could really fly? What if you actually perfected levitating yourself into the air anytime you wanted, without risk, and could fly as far, high, and long as you wanted to?"

"Awesome. Close, I think, to what astronauts feel on their space walks probably very similar to my dreams. No doubt, it surely would be the greatest adventure of my life. On the other hand, there very likely would be severe complications."

"How so, Captain?"

"Think about it, Mike. What if I strayed away from Heritage Pines? Georgie would have a fit. Worse still, what if I was seen in public an old guy floating around the countryside?"

"I see your point. It would be headline news around the world and the media would make your life a never ending nightmare. So, Captain, I hear you saying that you don't really want to fly badly enough to actually do it?"

"Up yours, Mike. Maybe you're enough of an ass to have been a fighter pilot after all."

"That's what my wife and oldest daughter tell me."

"Of course I want to fly, Mike. It has been the dream of my life, but I'm no closer to it than I was ninety years ago and there's no time left, so I guess the dreams will have to do, won't they?"

"But suppose you could *really* do it in a limited way in a secluded place with help from a trusted friend like Jaybee perhaps?"

"Jaybee! Good God, Mike, he'd write a book about it for sure, go on TV talk shows, and lecture tours probably with my pickled remains on stage with him. But of course he would very soon kill himself, or be killed, autographing the thighs of adoring women."

"Well then Captain, someone else thought it would be very hard to expect anyone to keep secret such an incredible feat, accomplished only once before in history."

"Yeah Mike, and look what they did to Him just for walking on water! Anyhow, it's only a dream. A good one though!"

Mike realized that there was going to be much more to this visit than getting to know his father and writing his story. He might help the Captain to consciously experience his miraculous feat. Perhaps divine inspiration would assist. Meanwhile, there was a long story to be heard.

"Have you dreamed of levitating before, Captain?"

"Many times. It began when I was four years old, though not exactly in dreams per se. I had frequent ear aches that kept me awake nights. I found that rolling my head back and forth on my pillow would put me half asleep and I could partially control my dreams. At first, from my bed I saw myself up in the far corner of the ceiling in a fetal position looking down at myself. I learned to elevate myself, not often successfully and not for long, but well and often enough that I came to believe I could actually do it if I believed strongly enough and practiced a lot. There was a special area of my consciousness that was difficult to find and hard to hold on to. To test my progress, I often stood on our bathroom scales and concentrated very hard on lifting myself, but awake I was never able to get to that special consciousness or budge the dial at all. When I was six, my tonsils were removed and the ear aches stopped, so there was no need to roll my head to sleep. Just the same, I kept it up for years because of the flying dreams I could create. Awake, I tried to imagine what it would be like to see clouds from above them, especially during intense summer night time thunder storms. Unfortunately though, a few years later I outgrew head rolling and lost the dream control ability. After all, appearing to be shaking your head 'no' is not the thing to do when you're in the sack with a young lady, is it?"

"No Captain that would certainly be counter-productive! So, did you also give up the possibility of actually levitating?"

"No Mike, even today I still strongly believe it's possible, but now I have to rely on random dreams. I feel that I lack enough willpower or confidence, otherwise I would have accomplished it. I was an insecure only-child and an obvious disappointment to my father who was a traditional "dog face" Army Sergeant. In his eyes, I was afraid of everything, a coward. One day Father stopped at an airport and said we were going flying in a friend's airplane. It was the first airplane I saw up close. As we walked toward it, I became enthralled with the prospect of my actual first flight. Of course Father had no idea who owned the airplane, nor did he have any intention of flying. He just wanted to scare me. Instead, it was just the kind of life-changing divine inspiration I needed."

"How did you feel toward your father about that?"

"Not much, one way or the other. It was the 30's, the Depression was on and a Buck Sergeant's pay didn't cover the bills. Mother was a professional seamstress, sewing nurse's uniforms at home. Besides playing trumpet in the Fifth Infantry Band, Father played with dance bands and the Portland Symphony. He was also a poker dealer at night, so we didn't see much of him. Still, I felt enormous tension in the house and believed that I was somehow the cause of it. I was already looking forward to my escape from home. Are you sure you really want to hear all this boring ancient history, Mike? None of it has anything at all to do with Vietnam, does it?"

"Please bear with me, Captain. It has to do with how you came to be a naval aviator. Were you soon able to get that airplane ride your dad promised?"

"No. In fact, it turned out that he was deathly afraid of flying himself! It was not until after the war when I was fourteen and had saved enough money from my morning paper route for a ten minute ride in a Piper 'Super Cruiser' at a small grass strip in Columbus Georgia."

"Until then, how was your interest in flying sustained?"

"Father sometimes took me to the band quarters at Fort Williams. The musicians had fun seeing if I could make sounds on various wind instruments. My first success was a note on a flute, earning me the nickname 'E Flat'. One of the men was a model airplane builder and Father brought many of them home for me. At first, they were small carved solid balsa models. Then there were larger balsa stick and tissue built-up rubber-powered flying models which I thought too much of to risk flight damage. Instead, I wound the propellers, got my eyeball as nearly inside the cockpit as possible, and pretended to fly inside the model around our small efficiency apartment"

"Tell me about your other interests besides flying, Captain."

"Girls, God, movies, and music, in that order, Mike."

"Girls? At that age?"

"Oh yes, I was fascinated by them. The first time I saw the nude figure of a woman I was astonished by her beauty. Her skin was as white as snow and faultlessly unblemished. I gazed at her entranced for a very long time. She was a statue of a Greek Goddess, I guess, about eight inches tall on the table in our front room bay window. I was about four years old. The day after admiring it, the statue disappeared. It was forbidden? I had done something wrong? Of course my curiosity was set ablaze. Searching for the hidden statue, I found a big thick hard bound library book in the hall closet with color cross section illustrations of the inside of a woman's belly with a baby in it! Wow! Fascinating! No doubt about *this* being forbidden fruit. I was sitting on the floor inside the closet, door closed, with a flashlight pondering the medical truth of creation when Mother opened the door. I don't know which of us was more embarrassed. Nothing was said to me or reported to Father, I think, but of course the book went the way of the statue, never to be seen again, which only further heightened my curiosity. It was time for some serious field study! The first time I recall getting out of that apartment, about age five, I ran across the street and found a five year old girl to play 'you show me yours and I'll show you mine' with. Amazing. Sure beat the hell out of statues and medical books! Soon, I found myself in a circle of five more similarly inclined sinister little boy and girl perverts. The highlight of our evil ways was when we found an abandoned fire-damaged apartment building nearby where we reveled in freeing ourselves of all garments and danced about in primal abandon. The end of it had to with the complexity of buttons on children's clothing in the 30's. Tops and bottoms with suspenders were hopelessly complex, interconnected with way more buttons than necessary and were primitive hindrances of free expression for a five year old to deal with to put ourselves back together for home re-entry.

Mine was an especially impossible outfit which defied re-assembly, so I came home all disarranged. Of course, as mothers always do, mine immediately recognized what had happened. But to her everlasting endearment, Mother simply re-buttoned me and said nothing about it to me. More than sixty years later, I told Mother the story to see if she noticed or remembered. She had a good laugh and held her index finger to her lips, 'Shhhh, don't say anything about it to your father'. Our little secret. There were few girls to play with for some time after that."

"What about God, Captain?"

"Father was an old world authoritarian, raised a Catholic in the Azores. Having married 'outside the church', he said he was no longer in good standing unless Mother and I converted. But Mother was a New England Seventh Day Adventist, which led to many very heated religious arguments since both church dogmas preached that their way was the *only* way to salvation. Mother endured a lot of mental abuse from Father, but she always held her ground on issues important to her. She took me to church Sundays, often read the Bible to me, and taught me prayers, one I still use: 'Dear God, please hear my prayer this evening. Thank you for a lovely day, For the tasks that I have finished and the time I had to play. Please take away my sins, dear God, and help me to be good for Thee. Bless my family and my friends, and tonight watch over me.' I was so well grounded in deep religious belief that I had an imaginary conversation with God when I was five. He asked what I wanted most in life. My response was 'Wisdom'."

"Have you had other imaginary conversations like that with God, Captain?"

"Three that were important, we'll get to those later, Mike."

"Sure. Were your parents able to adjust to their religious differences?"

"If you call not attending church or ever discussing it much after we went to Panama an 'adjustment', yes. Mother, however, never stopped reading her Bible. She even wrote notes in the margins, and composed several poems, Though she was far from being evangelical about her religion."

"How about school? Was it a welcome escape from home?"

"Lord no, it was 'from the frying pan into the fire' for me. It was awful. Right from the beginning, I hated it. I got off to a bad start with a hateful teacher the very first day in kindergarten, and because of my insecurity, I never adjusted well. Ever after it was 'them or me', with teachers and the school system seen as obstacles. Because of our frequent moves, I attended fourteen schools. Each move meant new curriculums and social challenges. I was an easy target for bullies and I was academically lost most of the time. I was a slow learner with a bad attitude - a C student. I still have nightmares about exams not prepared for."

"Tell me about that first day in kindergarten, Captain."

"As much as I wanted to be out, I was too insecure. Mother had to take me by my hand into the classroom and seat me at a desk. This did not go unnoticed by my teacher and classmates.

When the day finally ended with the sound of the dismissal bell, I leaped from my desk and started for the door. 'Be SEATED, children. *I* will say when you may leave, *not* the bell.' We obeyed teacher and the minutes dragged on. It seemed we were to be confined there for the night. It was more than I could bear and I began to cry. I guess Father had reason to be disappointed in me. Taking the opportunity to unite the other students on her side, the teacher led the class in singing 'Cry Baby Cry' to me. From then on I disliked school, teachers, women, and my peers. I had all the makings for being a paranoid sociopath. I believe that many kids like me suffer permanent humiliation and ego damage suffered from failure to adjust to the school system. There's no escape since school is compulsory, so the result is rebellious social behavior."

"Were movies an escape for you, Captain?"

"Yes, I suppose they were, Mike. I was allowed to go to Saturday matinees on my own. Usually, there were double feature cowboy films with cartoons and serials like Superman. I often stayed for two cycles. I liked the songs the 'Singing Cowboys' sang. At home we had a wind-up Victrola and a record of Roy Acuff singing 'She'll Be Coming Round the Mountain' which I played many times over."

"How long did you live in Portland, Captain?"

"In 1939, Father was transferred to the Panama Canal Zone. Mother and I moved in with a family in South Portland. There I was given a small black and white kitten to care for and began ice skating after school until dark on a pond with small trees growing through it, very picturesque. There were two gangs at school, but since I was a member of neither, I was bullied by both. I spent weekend afternoons at the movies watching films like 'Frankenstein' and 'Gulliver's Travels' over and over until Mother retrieved me. A few months later, we followed Father to Panama. There, the model airplanes re-appeared, but then started coming unfinished. That was the beginning of my life-long model-building hobby. I never knew who gave me those models, but he was a major influence on my life. At first, we lived so far off base that I missed almost a year of school, so I had to repeat the second grade. The Army still had some cavalry horses, so I took horseback riding lessons on base. Chubby, my first assigned horse, was short and stocky. The last time I rode him, Chubby laid down and tried to roll over on me, so I picked up on some Army stable language. One day, Father had an alarm clock apart on our dining room table when I left. When I returned from the stables, Father was still working on it when I casually asked, 'Are you still f—king around with that clock?' I swear, Mike, I have never seen a more shocked expression on a person's face. Of course, I had no idea what the word meant, but that ended my time around the Army stables. We finally settled into base housing, 'Skunk Hollow', at Albrook Army Airfield. At that time, Army was flying outdated P-26 'Pea Shooters' and the pilots were doing their best to bang them up. We could tell when there was another accident because cavalry's 'get-back-on-the-horse' thinking was to mass launch every plane and pilot on the base. The up side for me was the aircraft salvage yard where I went every afternoon after school to play in the wrecked airplanes -a big step up from pretending to fly models."

"How did you feel about the possibility that pilots may have been seriously injured or killed in those wrecks, Captain? Didn't the reality of mortal danger in aviation effect your desire to fly?"

"No Mike, fear of death never occurred to me in an airplane.except in the back end of airliners on low visibility landing approaches in rough weather, worrying if there might be some ex Naval Flight Officer at the controls."

"Is that fearlessness usual with aviators, Captain?"

"Yes Mike, not only usual but essential. If fear takes over the controls, that pilot should be grounded. Of course, that does not mean that risks are to be taken lightly. As they say, 'There are *old* pilots, and there are *bold* pilots, but there are no *old bold* pilots.' Flying teaches humility, since there are thousands of embarrassing ways to screw up. The survival trick beyond great gobs of luck is to always be aware of the risks and your own limits. The hair-on-fire cavalier 'hot' pilots don't last. One of the unique things about naval aviation was that night carrier landings are a great equalizer. Everyone had a bad night occasionally and all his squadron mates got to watch it on live television."

"Yes, Captain, I can see how the challenge and scrutiny would keep ego's in check. So, life in Panama wasn't so bad for you?"

"Not bad at all. My parents worked. It was the big band era. In addition to the Glenn Miller type classics, Latin music was increasingly popular with stars like Xavier Cugat and Carmen Miranda. Father led the Fifth Infantry Band's fourteen piece dance band, out front with his trumpet like Harry James two or three nights a week at the Officers Club. Mother went along to keep an eye on his female singer. I was glad to have the evenings home alone. By her own admission, Mother had little interest in being a homemaker and wanted to get a job. They had a hell of an argument about Mother going to work, but she won out and got a job selling jewelry at the Army Post Exchange. So, I didn't see much of my parents, day or night. It sure suited me, my escape was progressing! At night, I 'protected' myself with Father's late 1800's Colt 'Lightning' .41 caliber black powder long barrel six-shooter with which I fired caps. Father bought the Lightning when he first joined the Army in 1924 from a merchant sailor who said he got it in China. Supposedly, Lightnings were favored by Billy the Kid for its double-action and the fit of the grips in his small hands. It felt great in my small hands too! I still have that pistol."

"Let's see, Captain, you went to Panama in 1940. Were you still there when the Japs attacked Pearl Harbor?

"Oh yes, we were going for our Sunday drive off base when we were stopped at the gate and given the news. Father immediately reported for duty and was issued forty rounds of ammunition with instructions to 'make every one count because that's all you'll get. Since the Canal could be put out of commission with a single bomb, it seemed certain that the Japs would attack in order to slow replenishment of the Pacific Fleet which had just been decimated at Pearl Harbor. If the Canal were closed, East Coast shipping to the Pacific would have to sail far out of the way around South America's fearsome Cape Horn."

"What was Panama like then, Captain?"

"Amazing. Almost overnight, everything changed. All lights, including auto headlights, were blacked out. Hundreds of barrage balloons were put up and searchlights lit the sky. Thousands of Orientals or anyone with slanted eyes were rounded up and confined to tent cities. Soon, new P-40's replaced the aging Pea Shooters. Large rotary ditch diggers made trenches in the jungle for us to use as air raid shelters which soon filled up with Panama's mud, vegetation, cock roaches, malaria mosquitoes, boa constrictors, coral snakes, tarantulas, scorpions, iguanas, and every other kind of critter known to the tropics."

"Was there any enemy action?"

"One night at 1 AM the air raid siren sounded. We scurried off to our jungle 'shelters', but thought better of joining the critters in the ditches. I'm quite sure, however, that we would have quickly jumped into those 'shelters' had a bomb exploded. Fortunately, it was a false alarm and there were no other similar events."

"I guess you didn't get to play in the P-40's in the salvage yard?"

"No, but I drew hundreds of pictures of them. It is still one of my favorite warbirds. On dawn patrol takeoffs they flew so close to my bedroom window I could wave to the pilots and hear their radio transmissions on my AM radio. Boy, was I ever energized to be a fighter pilot. I strongly hoped that the war would last long enough for me to get into it. But I didn't get into that one or Korea, though I did eventually learn to 'be careful what I wish for'."

"How long did you remain in Panama, Captain?"

"Mother and I were evacuated by troop ship in February 1942 to New Orleans."

"Across the Gulf of Mexico, Captain? Weren't German submarines a threat?"

"If there were any Kraut submarines around, they surely heard us, hopefully noting that we were all women and children, and left us alone."

"Did you and your mother stay in New Orleans?"

"No. We took a long train ride back to Portland Maine."

"In February, after three years in Panama? That must have been quite a change!"

"You got that right, Mike The only winter clothes we had were what the New Orleans Red Cross gave us. Mother unraveled a huge wool scarf and knit a sweater for me. It was forty below zero for a week in Portland, so we hugged the radiators."

"It was just you and your mother on your own?"

"No, we were taken in by a family- the parents, daughter and granddaughter of one of Father's fellow band members. There were six of us in a small walk-up third floor two bedroom apartment. The granddaughter, Theresa, was a year younger than me."

"I'm an only child like you, Captain, so I expect that must have been quite an adjustment for you to move in on so many strangers."

"Not really. As you know, only-children get a boatload of attention and judgment from amateur adults who have had no practice or incentive to learn parenting. It was a relief and a blessing for me to blend into a crowd -an escape. Fortunately, the Guinards were a warm welcoming easy-going family. Best of all, Theresa and I became close friends."

"Was she your first girlfriend, Captain?"

"Yes, in a way she was, but I was only nine years old, so it never got past a one-time 'you show me yours and I'll show you mine'. Otherwise, it was just plain good friendship – a brand new and very valuable experience for me. I was quite a few years before I got close to another girl. But what the hell does any of this have to do with your book, Mike?"

"Please leave the book to me, Captain. If I intrude too deeply into your privacy, please say so and I'll back off. Otherwise, I'd like to hear your whole story and sort out the book later, OK?"

"Alright, I suppose so, Mike. I assure you that 'privacy' has never been an issue for me, especially now at my age. As my Granny said, *'Any* publicity is *good* publicity'. I just don't see why anyone should care."

"Everyone, no matter how uneventful their lives, has a story that should be told, if for no other reason than family history. Years ago, I saw a PBS TV series production of a very highly praised autobiography that went on for many episodes about a girl growing up on the plains of Africa. 'The Flame Trees of Thikka' seemed to have almost no plot at all, yet I enjoyed it very much. It's all in the tellin', *my* Granny says. Don't you agree, Captain?"

"I'll let you know after I read your book, OK?"

"Since it's your story, I don't expect you will have much criticism. Do you want to break for lunch?"

"No, I don't do lunch, but I'm sure Georgie will set you up in the dining room."

"I don't do lunch either, Captain. Will you let me take you out to dinner one night this week?"

"No thanks, Mike. It's too much trouble. They're well set up for me here and the foods suitable for an old salt who survived Navy grub, so why not join me?"

"I'd like that, but I'll take a rain check this evening. Since you have agreed to this, I need to unpack, set up my computer, and make some notes."

"OK Mike, Tuesday is steak night here."

"So, the food's OK and the grounds are nice, what's it been like for you here?"

"Honestly Mike, I can't complain. As places like this go, it's probably as good as it gets. They take pretty good care of me. Best of all, they leave me the hell alone when I wish it, which is most of the time. Of course, they make all these 'homes' look good to the folks who put their parents in them. Thank the Lord, I haven't been a burden to anyone. I'm sure life would have been unbearable hell for all concerned if any of my kids had taken me in. I was in another home for a short time before this place. It was a cross between a hospital and a jail .more like a jail. Of course, it all depends on good management and the people they are able to hire. For good reason, there are darned few people who are suited or willing to work in these places, especially for the low wages paid. I can understand their view. Who the hell would suffer the thankless frustration of working all day every day with crazy, decrepit, cranky, fussy, old bastards like us? Not me boy! We sure don't make it easy for them I can tell you. It takes a very extra special nurturing compassionate person to do it right. There just aren't many around, bless their hearts. Some of my fellow inmates are here because they want someone to do everything for them their way and then bitch about it. Some, like me, are here because they have no choice and bitch about it. It's the aging that's the *real* son of a bitch. Everything about your body craps out and hurts. Nothing is easy, and you have to rely on others a lot. Most of my life I expected sudden death, so I never planned on aging, not that a plan would have helped. The worst thing about being here for me is that I really don't care to be around all the activities and people so much, especially nosey folks who get in your face like wannabe writers who want to make a buck on your story. As you see, there are no hiding places."

"Hey, Captain, go easy on me!"

"OK Mike, sorry, just a sensitivity check to see if you were paying attention. Actually, I'm kinda glad to have you here for this. As a matter of fact, I am a wannabe writer myself, but like you with flying, I just never got around to it other than a few magazine articles and lots of DOGNET email. I began writing my 'Great American Novel' about the time Jaybee began his, but decided that while I could, *living* my story was more important than *telling* it. A good decision I guess, since now you get to do all the work."

"Suits me, Captain, that's why I'm here. I'm happy to meet you. I'm especially glad that you still dream of flying. As I hope you will see, in return for your story, I have one or two things to share which may be of interest to you. Perhaps an unexpected adventure."

Michael and Manny 2013

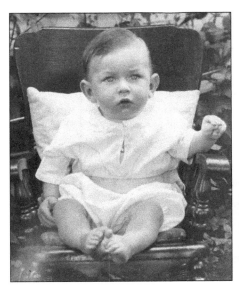

Future Fighter Pilot

Future Ensign

Father Manuel, Mother Ada & Junior, 1937

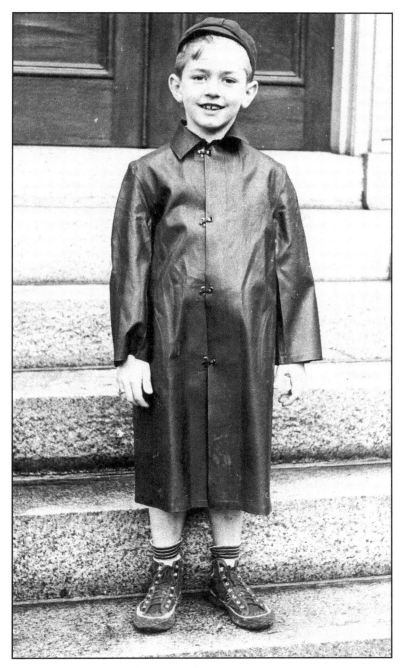

Junior in the rain, 1938

3

CAPTAIN KID

"What now, Mike?"

"Back to your story, Captain. OK with you?"

"Sure. Where was I?

"1942. How long were you in Portland and where did you go next?"

"The suicide rate among GI's in Panama was extraordinarily high, so before the war Army considered assignment there a 'Hardship Tour', limited to two years. Because Father could speak Portuguese, he was offered a direct officer commission as a Captain to be immediately reassigned to Embassy duty in Brazil. Father said he declined the offer because he couldn't take his family; however, I believe it also had to do with his lack of self-confidence to be an officer. Consequently, we rejoined Father less than a year later when he was transferred to a band at Camp Van Dorn, Mississippi, then publicly declared the worst Army base in the US. We lived in Liberty."

"Liberty? An odd name for a Mississippi town! I don't recall hearing of it."

"It was a tiny town twenty five miles from McComb, Mike, and you probably haven't heard of that town either. It probably still is a typical small southern agricultural town with a town square, a courthouse, small shops, and a large Baptist church-which I attended. We lived in a second floor apartment over a vacant store on the square that had been unoccupied for years. Our nightly ritual was to get out of bed, turn on all the lights, bring out the brooms, and swat down the bats swirling around the bedroom which we put in paper bags on the porch until morning."

"Coming to that small town in the deep South, with your big city Yankee 'down East' Maine accent, must have made adjustment difficult for you."

"Actually, Mike, the Liberty kids were friendlier than Maine kids. You're right about the accent though. That and my urban background combined to give some communication problems. In spelling class, for example, when asked to spell 'calf', I said 'c-a-f-e'. When asked to spell 'cow', I said 'c-a-r'. I needed speech correction class! We also learned, to our embarrassment, that Easter there was like Christmas for exchanging presents."

"What did you and your friends do together?"

"I learned to fish for perch with a pole at a pond, and cat fish with a trout line on Seven Mile Creek where I had a close-up with a water moccasin. My best memory was of my next door friend, Jason, and me playing with our combined large collection of toy lead soldiers and associated cavalry and artillery pieces. We re-enacted current European battles in my living room, with furniture and bunched up rugs for landscape. We convinced our eager' audience of kids, who paid one cent for admission, that we had personally witnessed these scenes by sailing to Europe nightly aboard the secret submarine we discovered in an underground waterway far below the basement of the old building I lived in. We called our expeditions 'The Secrets of SO-USA.' Our excited audience bought our show hook line and sinker."

"What great fun! What was your experience with Blacks there? I don't suppose you had seen many of them before then, had you, Captain?

"No I hadn't, and in fact I don't recall seeing many of them in Liberty either. The farms were small and poor, so there may never have been large plantations with slaves there. It's also probable that many blacks went north after the Civil War. I have only one memory of Blacks in Liberty. Jason and I sometimes pretended to be on a battlefield at a nearby gravel pit. We strategically located ourselves as lookouts at the edge of the cliff on the edge of the pit overlooking the scene. There was only one small wood building about twelve feet square with one door and no windows. One morning we saw a middle-aged stocky black man approach the shack. When he knocked, a black lady opened the door to him. The man entered and the door closed. It was pretty clear to us that these were enemy espionage agents sharing intelligence and planning an attack. We were sure that we hadn't been seen, so we held our positions and waited for their next move. After a half hour, the door opened, the man left, and the woman closed the door from inside. We waited another ten minutes before the door opened again and the black lady left in the opposite direction. We considered reconnoiter of the shack when they were gone, but it was time to go home for lunch."

"Aha, I see Captain. So you young spies had no idea what had actually happened?

"Oh yes, Mike, sure we did. It just wasn't a subject for discussion between ten year old boys in Liberty Mississippi in the forties. Home life was different too. Since Mother wasn't working or going to the O Club evenings, she went back to her sewing hobby. She and I were in the living room listening to the radio one afternoon during a thunderstorm when a bolt of lightning shot out of the speaker all the way across the room between us. Gasoline was rationed of course, so our weekend drives were curtailed. Father occasionally brought his trumpet home to practice and I was allowed to experiment with trying to play it in the evenings out on the porch. God knows what the neighbors thought of the racket blasting out across the square at night, but no one complained. Bless their hearts, I hope they didn't think it was my father playing!"

"How was your Southern Baptist Church experience there, Captain?"

"Excellent, Mike. I was sent off to Baptist Sunday school on my own, probably because my parents enjoyed Sunday mornings alone. I liked the atmosphere, the people, and the teachings. I fit right in and it all suited my own religious outlook so well that I stayed after Sunday School for the regular services. I was particularly inspired by those beautiful old Baptist hymns. In fact, contrary to the negative image that many people have of simple country farm folk in the South, life in Liberty was a very warm positive spiritual experience for me. But it was soon time to leave. Within a year, we were Colorado bound. Very different from Maine, Panama, or Mississippi for sure! Many thousands of troops were training at Camp Carson, now Fort Carson, in 1943. Consequently, family housing was so scarce that we lived in a two room efficiency motel apartment in Manitou Springs, at the foot of Manitou Incline and Pike's Peak, for the entire time. I even liked school! I was no longer a C student, because school grades were either 'Satisfactory' or 'Unsatisfactory'. I bad an outstanding teacher and I joined the school band. Trumpet, of course, though I truly was always a terrible musician to the point where Father justifiably did all he could to discourage me. 'There's no future or security in it,' he said. 'It's a bums life with alcohol, drugs, and drunks in bars and clubs. The only people who can stand being around drunks are other drunks. Only military or studio musicians can have normal lives.' Nevertheless, Mike, I love all kinds of music second only to flying. On to other things though. My friend David and I built many model airplanes. We launched some of our rubber-powered flying war planes on their first dramatic short flight with lit firecrackers in them. We also had BB rifles and played 'war' in the nearby rocky Garden of the Gods. My misfortune was having an authentic German helmet, so the kids shot at me! Then, we got bows and arrows and target practiced until we were ready to go 'big game' hunting in the Rocky Mountains. On our first hunt though, we encountered a big brown bear and decided that target arrows were not appropriate weapons for bear hunts! .At home, I was unhappy. It was a rougher than usual patch for my parents. Mother and I weren't getting along well either, though she was working at the Post Exchange. There were many harsh words escalating from Father until one afternoon he exploded in a rage and declared that he was leaving. To me he said, 'I wouldn't be married to her if it weren't for you.' Suspicions confirmed. Father then demanded to know who I wanted to go with. I chose Father. That did it boy, no more talk of divorce ever again from him! The lasting lesson for me was that all three of us would have been happier if they had divorced. I thought that staying married 'for the sake of the children' was a poor excuse."

"Does that explain some of your own marital history, Captain?"

"The issue did arise. Was it a factor in your history, Mike?"

"Yes, as it must be in all marriages with children. Judging by the high divorce rate, many parents agree with you. My experience was mixed. I didn't have a father since my mother never re-married. My mother did a good job raising me, but I think that a good male mentor and role model might have saved me some wasted time after high school as when your father steered you away from music and drinking. When the choice came to me as a parent in a failed marriage, I moved out into an apartment, but the wife and I remained married 'for the sake of the children' and tried to be good parents. I have no regrets, but I do see your point."

"It's a 'damned if you do and damned if you don't' matter, isn't it? Either way though, the biggest mistake would be to go through life with a burden of bitterness or guilt. We can only just keep on keeping on, doing the best we can."

"Well, it appears you kept on keeping on with your flying, Captain. Is the Ximango still flyable?"

"Yes it is. I have an excellent mechanic who keeps it in showroom shape."

"Can you still fly it, Captain?"

"Could if I had the strength to spread and fold the wings, the agility to get in and out of the cockpit, and a tail-dragger qualified pilot with me just in case. FAA classifies motor-gliders with gliders, which means you don't need a medical certificate to fly one, or even a driver's license since you can solo gliders at age fourteen. All you need is a pilot's license which are issued for life."

"So, strictly speaking, you're not actually required to have a qualified pilot with you?"

"Correct, Mike, that's a self-imposed condition. Remember what I said about old bold pilots? I'm a real old pilot for reasons other than sheer luck."

"Couldn't one of your Pukin' Dog buddies have flown with you?

"You gotta be kidding, Mike. Those guys are nearly as old as I am and they haven't flown in thirty years or longer. Besides, they weren't sober long enough while they were here to even drive a car. Jaybee is the most current pilot. He and I had a dogfight over Quincy Florida twenty years ago. I flew the Ximango and he flew my partner Jerry's Super Cub. He was whining 'This ain't fair!' as I had him like a grape in the fight. Then he bounced all the way down the runway on his landings and that's with him sober! At our dinner banquet, Jerry awarded JayBee a second place plaque for the dogfight and a Certificate of Completion for remedial flight training.

"Do you think I could fly with you, Captain?"

"Hamm.....there's a thought! It would depend on how much of a pilot you are. How long since you last flew the Champ with your friend, Mike"

"Two months. He let me land it three times."

"How'd you do, Mike honestly."

"Not perfect, Captain, but I didn't break anything. There was a sporty crosswind which made it challenging to keep a tail wheel airplane on the runway. Still, Philip was happy and said that if he were an examiner he would sign off on my license."

"Hamm....as I said, it has been ten years for me. I'd be rusty for sure, but safe–with perfect weather. As they say, 'flying is like riding a bicycle.'"

"Let's go out to the airport one day and have a look at your Ximango, Captain. Maybe even see how well I do with spreading and folding the wings, plus, whether I can get us in and out of the cockpit."

"I'll think about it, Mike, but don't get your hopes high. I may well chicken out on this idea of yours."

"Sounds good to me. Just say when, Captain."

"Most important, Mike, promise that you will not mention a word of this to anyone especially Georgie. She would be a nervous wreck."

"I'm sure you are right, Captain. Now, unless there's more to say about Colorado, let's break for the day and resume in the morning, alright?"

"That's it for Colorado on this tour, Mike. Father's next assignment was Fort Benning, Columbus Georgia. So this is a good stopping point for today. I'll stay here for a while longer. Please tell Georgie where I am."

"Will do. See you in the morning, Captain."

"God willing. Ten o'clock. Right here".

4

GEORGIA

"Good morning Mike."

"Top of the morning, Georgina. How are you?"

"Very well thank you. Did you get settled at Waterman's Inn?"

"Yes, What a nice place!"

"Oh yes, it has been a 'top ten' Chesapeake favorite for over a hundred years. The Captain is in a jolly mood. Your first meeting must have gone well."

"I'm glad to hear that, Georgie. So far so good. Has he gone to see the wizard this morning?"

"Yes, he said to send you to the same spot."

"Good. By the way, Georgie, would there be a problem for you if the Captain and I went into town sometime?"

"No problem, Mike. It would be good for him to get away. I only ask that you let us know when and how long you expect to be gone. Is that agreeable?"

"Certainly Georgie. I'll keep you advised."

Mike saw that the Captain was reading. "Good morning, Captain. I hope I'm not disturbing you?"

"Good morning, Mike. No disturbance, I was reviewing the Ximango Pilot's Handbook. How are they treating you at Waterman's Inn?"

"Excellent thanks. Nice place and excellent seafood."

"Ah yes, one of the best restaurants on the Bay for oysters, crabs, clams, or rock fish, Mike. Most of the local watermen are either related to Bob Waldschmidt or are good friends. So, you can be sure everything is fresh caught. Plus, Mark, Bob's uncle, is one of the best seafood chef's around. It ain't cheap, but shyster lawyers can afford it."

"Easy Captain, not all lawyers are bad guys!"

"Quite right of course, Mike. It's just the ninety nine percent who give the rest a bad name. Do you know why sharks won't eat attorneys?

"Professional courtesy. Very funny, Captain."

"Well Mike, you didn't have anything nice to say about the Pukin' Dogs yesterday, did you?"

"Touché, Captain. Glad to see you're reviewing your Ximango handbook, I hope it means there's a chance we'll be flying."

"There's a fifteen knot wind this morning and a thirty percent chance of rain this afternoon. Those outer wing panels weigh eighty pounds, so you don't want to practice spreading or folding them in a breeze or rain. It looks better for tomorrow, but don't get your hopes too high, Mike."

"Great, I'm looking forward to it very much, Captain. Shall we return to your story then? It's late 1943 and I believe you were about to move from Colorado to Georgia, right?"

"Yes, Columbus Georgia, near Fort Benning where the paratroopers were trained, so there was lots of testosterone flowing around town which brought them into conflict with the cops. No good reason for them being so macho though, the only requirement for being a parachutist is to be heavy enough to fall out of an airplane."

"What was it like for you to return to the South at age eleven, Captain?"

"Good in some ways, near disaster in other ways. At least we were no longer staying at a motel! For the first four years we lived in a two bedroom brick duplex on the perimeter of a playground, in a project called 'Baker Village', ten miles outside Columbus. Father went back to leading a dance band at the Officers Club three nights a week and Mother went to work at the Post Exchange. I was as glad to be more on my own again, as were they. I got a morning paper route delivering to a hundred and ten customers, on foot at 5 AM, then back in the afternoons to try to collect weekly bills. I walked the five mile route until I earned $17 for a bicycle. I was gaining ground toward facilitating my escape. A good part of my route was in a black neighborhood. It was a good experience, they were good customers and accepted me as a matter of fact. Later in my four years with the route, my pal Joe Davidson and I were welcomed in their small neighborhood bar where they sold us cigars and cheap peach muscatel wine which of course made us quite ill. I had a low digestive tolerance of alcohol for many years after that introduction."

"So, you had some insight of what life was like for the blacks there then, Captain?"

"Not really, Mike. Just a superficial impression from a white kid's perspective. Blacks were largely regarded as sub-human and were excluded from the white culture, except as a source of cheap labor. Everything including water fountains were segregated 'Whites Only' or 'Blacks Only'. Otherwise, blacks seemed to be pretty much left alone in the rural area where we lived and they appeared to be fairly well adapted to that. They seemed to find happiness in simple ways that white folks are never able to experience as well."

"Was your friend Joe an Army 'brat' too?"

"Joe was as much a real traditional southerner as it was possible to be. His family owned a huge plantation with thousands of acres on Esquiline Hill near Fort Benning which had been a working farm with many slaves before the Civil War. There were remains of the slave cabins and the family still lived in their declining 'Gone With the Wind' type mansion. Joe's father had passed away, so as 'the man of the house' he worked at their small grocery store near Baker Village. When we were old enough to own shotguns, Joe, Jerry, Max, and I often went on weekend camping and hunting trips on Joe's property. Though we said we were hunting rabbits and squirrels, we shot anything that moved, almost including each other on one occasion when a rabbit ran between us. I joined the Boy Scouts too."

"What was Joe's attitude toward blacks?"

"Good question, Mike. I saw no sign of bigoted prejudice in him. As I mentioned, he went with me to the black bar, plus we hung out at a small grocery store owned by an old black man named Henry who was quite a 'cracker barrel philosopher'. One day, for example, we got into a discussion about whether or not it was a sin just to think of sinning. His answer was, 'You can't stop the birds from flying overhead, but you can stop them from building nests in your hair'. Sorry to say though that Joe and I didn't always take Henry's wise counsel to heart. One night we lit a candle with rags and twigs at the base in the corner of one of his abandoned old slave cabins and went to the movies at the Village Theater for an alibi. When we came out and looked toward Esquiline Hill nothing was happening, so we assumed the candle had gone out and went home. About 2AM, however, I was awakened by sirens. There was the glow of a huge fire in the woods on the Hill, so I got dressed and rode my bike to the scene. Joe was already there as we watched the house burn to the ground."

"Were you caught?"

"No Mike, it was a 'perfect crime'. Joe and I never spoke of it, but I'm sure he felt even worse about it than I did. It might have been better for me if we had been caught. The consequences might have straightened out my sociopathic tendencies. Except for extreme good fortune, the thrill I got from taking dangerous anti-social risks very nearly got me into serious trouble at several points right up to the day I was commissioned. Not sure how much I want to discuss those events though. We'll see."

"Understood, Captain. How was school?"

"Terrible. The Baker Village Grammar School was a county school. Most of the kids were bussed in from farms, so there was little interaction. Georgia had an eleven grade system instead of twelve, no doubt reflecting the population's attitude toward education versus the need for the kids at home on the farms. Colorado had a twelve year system, of course, and grades were 'pass-fail'. So, Georgia had me skip the sixth grade, which put me back where I would have been if I hadn't been held back a year in Panama! Academics weren't much of a challenge, still, I was a C student. The consistent comments on my report cards were, 'Whispers too much' and 'Could do much better'. Neither of my parents had finished high school and no one on either side of the family ever attended college, so there weren't great expectations or encouragement of me at home. Girls mature early in the South. Several of my seventh grade female classmates had already been married or pregnant. Two others were sent to reform school. One of the 'boys' was an ex-marine who was bedding one of the three teachers we had that year. That teacher was fired, but the other two quit, literally ran out of the classroom under a barrage of spitballs we fired at them, sweet revenge for that kindergarten bitch I had in Portland. One academic anomaly for me was winning the school spelling competition, then placing fourth in the county finals."

"Sounds like total anarchy. Did you attend church, Captain?"

"Oh yes, the Baker Village Baptist Church a small church in a primitive building, but the messages and hymns were the same as in Liberty so I felt right at home at Sunday school and services. In spite of my anti-social nature, my faith ran quite deep. I didn't need Sunday morning pushes from my parents to attend. I even played a Sunday service trumpet solo of 'Onward Christian Soldiers' which didn't go well, so I was never asked again. I was entirely under my own steam when I 'answered the call' one Sunday morning at age twelve. Reverend Reed baptized me by immersion in the pool next to the pulpit as I smiled at my mother in the congregation, the only time she attended. A year later, Reverend Reed who was in his fifties, married to a most dignified lady, and a lovely daughter who sang church solo's married a Naval Academy graduate, ran off, never to be seen again, with our $70,000 church building fund and a thirteen year old girl. That's when I became a Methodist."

"Did you feel that nullified your baptism by the good reverend, Captain?"

"No, Mike, but it gave me a good story. I take it you are Catholic?"

"Not so much. What your Reverend Reed did was minor compared to the sexual abuses committed by priests, wasn't it?"

"Very true, Mike. The Catholic Church's denial of that conduct was disheartening. By ignoring the problem for ages, the church was complicit in making the priesthood a haven for homosexual child abuse which became a perk of priesthood and a recruiting attraction in a world where few men are willing to be celibate. Since there wasn't a mass exodus by the membership, one might argue that they were also complicit. But then, some other prior history of the Catholic Church was not exemplary, was it?

"Undeniably true, Captain. From the Inquisition to the Crusades to the Holocaust, the autocratic Vatican either engaged in, or looked the other way, on some of the cruelest atrocities in history. I'm not a religion scholar, but it seems that most church organizations have histories including less than admiral behavior by their administrators. It helps me to keep faith by separating my views of 'church' from 'religion'."

"Do you believe that Jesus was the Son of God, Captain?"

"Yes I do. After a slump from church affiliation I believe that Jesus was THE Devine son of God. I also believe that we are all God's children. Buddhist Dharma teaches that we are all 'Buddha's' within. Christ's life was a positive and hopeful message of love, forgiveness, salvation, and everlasting life through Him in baptism. Jesus became the most significant and effective revolutionary religious leader in history by leading the revolt against the dogmas and privileged practices of the established Jewish church of that time, and declaring that all individuals have direct access to God without the intercession of church authorities. However, during my absence from church affiliation I went through several variations in religious thinking. I once felt that one should resist accepting religion on faith alone. Psychologists' views of sudden evangelical 'born again' Christians as tending to be emotionally unstable had merit. Despite past close church association and dramatic spiritual experiences, I was skeptical of some Old Testament tales such as Jonah in the whale and I was confused by accounts of God's high profile harsh direct intervention with destructive wrath against man's follies which were in stark contrast to the New Covenant's testaments to God's and Jesus' unconditional love, forgiveness, and tolerance of free will. I wondered if God experienced a learning process in dealing with human frailty. If so, does that call His perfection into question? Still, I could not recall that God claimed to be perfect, so His human side was uplifting for me. Other passing 'deep thoughts' included a concept of God as the collective will of all intelligent life in the universe. I was also intrigued by the notion that modern human forms first appeared on Earth as space travelers who fell out of grace in the 'Garden of Eden' Earth by mingling with humanoid apes, thereby losing the capacity to return to the home planet 'Heaven.'"

"Didn't church Bible study help you bridge the gap?

"In my days of attendance I didn't challenge canned Sunday school lessons and preachers who put emphasis on fire and brimstone sermons. Consequently, it was easier for me to resolve those types of issues by regarding Old Testament and Psalms principally as finely crafted legends and poetry. Conversely, however, the New Testament consistent messages of compassion, plus my personal spiritual experiences, became the foundation of my Christian faith. If there were no New Testament, I might have been a Buddhist."

"So, weren't you also skeptical about the New Testament miracles?

"Well not skeptical as much as neutral which was once influenced by Barbara Thiering's theories about the true meaning behind the Bible stories and her interpretations of the limited translations of the Dead Sea Scrolls."

"How did the scrolls figure into the New Testament? Didn't they pre-date Christ?"

"Please consider Mike that I'm now over my pay grade in this discussion. As with all I have related in this project of yours, I am recalling my life from a ninety-four year old memory bank without the time or inclination for historical research. You may wish to do some homework. As I recall, the scrolls were discovered in caves near the present West Bank and were believed to have been written by monastic Jewish scholars, dated from the last three centuries BC to the first century AD. Thiering, however, challenged scroll dating on two counts. First, because of their environmentally protected locations in the dry desert caves where they were found, forensic evidence could not pinpoint the date of the Scrolls to within 200 years. Secondly, many paleographic scholars base their opinion of the earlier date on the prevalent hand-writing style in the Scrolls which pre-dated Christ. Thiering argued that was an invalid assumption because it is likely that the monks in remote mountain monasteries had retained the old hand-writing style as a tradition."

"So how did Thiering connect the scrolls to Christ?"

"Although written in a metaphorical style without specific names or dates, there is reference in the Scrolls to a power struggle in the Church initiated by a renegade revolutionary upstart `Dark Angel' among them which Thiering suggests documented the life of Christ's missing monastic years and his struggle against the established Jewish church. A significant road-block to translation and distribution of the scrolls was that they were closely held and very slowly translated. Some say the Jewish scholars wish to maintain their academic monopoly; moreover, perhaps they may not wish to further expose their dark side church history and Christ's persecution, just as the Catholic church might wish to limit public doubts about Christ's divinity, since a key factor in Thiering's proposition was that her enlightened studies of the Scrolls lent credence to her theory that the New Testament miracles were written with two academic levels of meaning: One, a literal meaning for uneducated mass consumption', pardon the pun, the other higher academic level, she theorized, gave a real history of what actually happened. For example, Thiering's historical explanation of the virgin birth was that the church allowed selected monks and nuns to cohabitate for one year. During that year the nuns were called `virgins' by the church. If pregnancy occurred, then the couple was permitted to marry, as she says may have been the case with Joseph and Mary."

"Hmmm, interesting food for thought. How about raising Lazarus from the dead? "

"Good question, Mike. To publicly bring a dead body back to life is a heavy duty miracle to explain away! Thiering proposed that there is another plausible historical level of meaning in that story. In the established church of Christ's time, as is still true in the Catholic Church, their path to salvation was proclaimed to be the only one forgiveness through confession to a church human go-between. Since church dogma declared also certain sins to be 'mortal', for which there was no forgiveness possible, the church had a monopoly on salvation and unilateral authority to excommunicate members, denying salvation and condemning a person to everlasting damnation in Hell. In the eyes of the Church, therefore, excommunicated persons were 'dead'. So it was with

Lazarus, who was excommunicated for following Christ's revolt. By welcoming Lazarus into His church, Jesus rescued Lazarus from the 'dead'."

"I like it, Captain! But what about Christ's resurrection and ascension into Heaven after His crucifixion? Isn't belief in that `miracle' central and critical to Christian faith in the Holy Trinity? What allegorical meaning could there be?"

"According to Thiering, the factual story of the resurrection and ascension miracle, may have been that when Christ was taken down from the cross, it was discovered that He was still living. Remember, the Roman soldiers had refrained from breaking Christ's legs, as required in Crucifixions. To assure the Romans that He was dead, Christ's followers proceeded with His burial. He was then rescued from the sepulcher, taken away into hiding, and nursed back to health. The few who saw Jesus naturally believed that He had risen from the dead. He had in fact `returned from the grave'. Since the Romans would surely make certain of His death if it was known that he was alive, it was necessary to keep the truth a close secret and get Jesus out of town to a place where He would never again be seen publicly. According to Thiering, Christ `ascended' back to the mountain monastery where He had spent His `missing years'. Therefore, no matter how the Bible story of the resurrection is viewed, the miracle is that God <u>did</u> in fact save Christ's life."

"So are you saying that the historical meaning in the stories are as relevant for you as the metaphorical?"

"For me, the most convincing truth of Christ's divinity is that by any measure, after two thousand years He stands as the greatest, most perfect and powerfully positive, influential, and consequential person who ever lived on this planet. His messages of love, forgiveness, and direct access to God, as well as His promise of salvation and everlasting life through Him, plus His willingness to suffer agonizing death on the cross for our sins are all the persuasion I need to emphatically believe that Jesus Christ is THE divine Son of God."

"Again Captain, how do the miracles figure in your faith?"

"Since I believe in God and Christ's fulfillment of His promise of the Holy Spirit, and as I consider the miracles of God's creations, and as I have had close personal experience with the Holy Spirit throughout my adult life, I surely believe with all my heart that anything is possible with God. Therefore, I do not harbor doubts about the New Testament miracles. Anticipating your next question, however, I will add that if Barbara Thiering's theories were to become proven facts, my faith would in no degree be altered."

"How were you able to settle your consideration of Christ's miracles?"

"Exposure to academic Bible-based sermons experienced beginning twelve years ago by non-denominational Christian church preachers. It was significant for me to be reminded, for example, that the Old Testament has over seven hundred precisely detailed and fulfilled prophecies of the Messiah's coming."

"How did it happen that you overcame your bias against churches to renew attendance, Captain?"

"Ten years ago I had a passionate affair with the widow of a squadron mate who happened to be a devout born again fundamentalist Christian who led me to attend a wonderful non-denominational Christian church in my neighborhood."

"A passionate affair in your eighties with a church lady? Goodness, how did that happen?"

"A providential series of events at a crucial crossroad in our lives. But let's not jump ahead now. There are many providential adventures to relate and little time to cover my story's next seventy years with Jean. We have gone astray on a discourse perhaps of little interest to readers; nevertheless, the topic is relevant to the aim of recording my biography."

"Understood, Captain. I have the feeling that we will cover more religious ground before we finish. Meanwhile, let's go back to Georgia in the mid-forties and a lighter topic. Did you continue building model airplanes?"

"Well, Mike, that is a lighter topic for sure! Not much modeling during the war. Balsa wood and related model materials were unavailable, so I worked on perfecting designs of kites and hand-launched folded paper airplanes. I tied a ten foot strings through holes in the wing tips of small recognition models and 'flew' them in a circle. When the war ended, I quickly got into gas engine powered control-line models, a natural step up from the recognition models. I had the encouraging success of winning first place in my first contest with my first control line model - fifty-five miles an hour in a tristate Class A speed event with a $25 engine as first prize! As it turned out, this was my beginning in life-long competitions in both model and full-size cars, boats, and airplanes."

"Wasn't that about the time of your first flight in the real thing, Captain?"

"Yes it was, Mike. One fine Sunday afternoon my friend Jerry and I biked to a small grass strip airfield where they were giving two dollar ten minute rides in a three-seat Piper 'Super Cruiser', as well as five dollar rides in a two place glider. When we bought our two dollar tickets for a Piper ride, we were told there would be a thirty minute wait. The glider was just being towed up, so we watched as it was released from the tow plane and soared peacefully. As it descended toward the airport, the nose of the glider dropped and it dove very steeply toward the runway. At the last second the nose came up and the glider rounded out at about ten feet above the runway. But the nose kept rising and rising until they went over the top of a loop and headed for the runway again for a second loop! As the glider recovered from the second loop, it made a tight circle to a graceful landing, rolling to a stop only a few feet away from us. When the pilot opened the canopy, we saw that his young soldier passenger was passed out cold in the back seat. Jerry and I were certainly impressed and damned glad we hadn't bought a ticket to fly with that pilot. After the passenger recovered enough to disembark, the pilot turned to us and asked, 'Are you next?' 'NO SIR, we have tickets for the Piper.' 'That's me!' he said, 'Let's go.' Jerry and I were stunned speechless, but it was too late to back out, so we climbed into the back seat noting that the door had been removed. It seemed that we had barely gotten off the ground before we began doing every imaginable stunt in the book – not that we recognized any of them. Jerry and I were thrown all over the cockpit and had no idea what was happening. We were pulled down into our seats at three times our weight. The sky and the ground swapped places over and over. We hung upside down in our seat belts as I saw my hat on the cabin headliner. The next moment I was sure we would be thrown out the side of the airplane through the missing door space. The pilot never looked back, but he must have been having a great old time trying to make us sick because it seemed like we kept up the aerobatics for eternity. Though the flight may actually have taken only the ten minutes we paid for, it was way more than we had bargained for! Thankfully, Jerry and I somehow maintained consciousness and didn't throw up, but we were damned sure glad to get back on the ground in one piece. I don't recall that we even looked at the pilot, much less thank him, as we beat feet to our bikes and made our getaway post haste"

"Quite an introduction to flying, Captain. Did it turn you off?"

"Not at all, Mike, but I was disappointed not to have had a chance to appreciate simply being in the air straight and level for a minute or two. Soon after that I had my second flight with another pilot in an Aeronca 'Champion'. He put me in the front seat and even let me have some stick time flying it which more than made up for what I missed on the first flight. Except for my dreams of levitation, flying was better than I had hoped it would be. Years before I 'flew' my father's car from the back seat on our weekend drives through the hills and around the curves with his bandleader's baton for a control stick. I had a small book by Piper called 'How to Fly a Piper Cub', so I knew what I was doing!"

"Great, Captain. Let's see, you were in Columbus for five years, from age eleven to sixteen. You said that girls matured early there and you had developed an infatuation for them at age four. So, how was your passage through puberty in Baker Village, if you don't mind me asking?"

"I don't mind at all. I already told you that I didn't actually 'get laid' for another ten years, so you know I couldn't have gotten into too much trouble. Actually though, Mike, I could not possibly have had a better introduction to intimacy. Baker Village teen social life in those days mostly consisted of informal soda fountain gatherings after school and movies at the Village Theater in the evenings or weekend matinee's. It was a great group of about twenty kids. We knew each other well, we were the same age, and we were at the same level of innocence. We felt little social pressure or undue self-consciousness, so we were quite relaxed with each other. No one was 'going steady'. I was financially independent and unsupervised. Then, spontaneously it seemed, we began having summer Saturday evening picnics at the clearing on Joe's plantation property at the very same clearing in the woods where we had burned down the cabin. Now, we set roaring bonfires instead. Refreshments were Nehi grape and orange soda's, hot dogs, marshmallows and watermelons. Sometimes we smoked 'indian cigars' which were long hard eight inch pods that grew on trees, or rolled 'rabbit tobacco', a pale weed leaf we learned about as Boy Scouts. Pretty naughty stuff, smoking 'weed', huh? So, after several of these gatherings, it seemed quite natural for the old 'spin the bottle' game to be introduced. Getting to kiss all the girls under such conditions was absolute heaven for me, but one girl stood out. Her name was Elaine. She lived only one block away after we moved to our new home several miles from Baker Village. She was Jewish and her parents owned a dress shop, so she wore a new dress every day. Elaine was tall, thin, a little awkward, and a bit plain. Like me, she was a mediocre student and an only child. She was cheerful and outgoing, but the kids mistook her innocence and malapropos for a lack of intelligence. Elaine and I clicked. Kissing literally took our breath away, so we did it a LOT. Looooooong slow light kisses with only our lips touching for hours, days, weeks, months, years. Well, not exactly true, but touching was added very gradually. We didn't need to go further faster. What we were doing was all the fun we could stand and there was no risk of ruining it. By the time I left Georgia four years later, we had progressed to being near nude in bed with advanced mutual touching, so of course there were times when the urge to proceed with the 'rough stuff' was strong. Fortunately, one or the other of us always backed off in time. Oddly, though we were a long term 'item', we did not 'go steady' or speak of lasting commitment. We both kissed others as well. In fact, Elaine was such a good kissing teacher that I became quite popular with other girls, in part I'm sure because I could be trusted not to push it too far."

"Sounds like you had a near perfect adolescence, Captain."

"Almost, Mike, except I hated getting up at five AM to deliver newspapers seven mornings a week. What little money I made was reduced by having to put some of it into a savings account. I desperately wished to quit, but the only way Father would allow that was if I found another job. Meanwhile, I spent my first earnings on a Whizzer motor-bike and two records; one was Tchaikovsky's First Piano Concerto, the other was Tex Ritter doing 'Rye Whiskey' on one side with 'Boll Weevil' on the other. Finally, when I was fifteen I altered my birth certificate to indicate I was sixteen so I could get a work certificate to take the job as usher at the Village Theater. I worked weekdays five-thirty to eleven-thirty with Wednesdays off, weekends one-thirty to eleven-thirty. Forty-four hours a week for seventeen dollars - thirty-nine cents an hour plus a free pass to other theaters for my night off! Obviously, my social life became limited and there was no time for homework, but I loved movies and there was a significant fringe benefit. Since the Village Theater was a social center for all my friends, it was a simple matter to let the girls in free and conduct backstage 'tours' where I demonstrated my well known watch that glowed in the dark. Our movie screen was made of material with thousands of small holes in it which we could see clearly through from backstage. The best part of my 'tour' was kissing and hugging behind the screen, unseen by the audience watching the movie but appearing to be watching us! The last time Elaine and I had alone before I left Georgia, she suggested that we end the way we began with long light kissing without the touching. It was a perfect end to a wonderful relationship. Fond memories to this day."

"How great for you both, Captain. Did you keep in touch with Elaine or ever see her again?"

"We did not correspond, but I did see her one time again when we returned from Germany three and a half years later. I'll get to that.

"OK. How did you feel about moving to Germany, Captain? You lived in Columbus longer than anywhere before and through your most important development years. Weren't you going to miss it?"

"Hell no. Leaving Columbus was the best move of my life, Mike, and just in time. Bad birds were building nests in my hair and I was heading down a dead end path. I seriously doubt that I would have made it to college or any of the rest to follow. Elaine would have gotten pregnant and we would have married. I would probably have been a truck driver. Moving meant a new opportunity to clear away the bird nests, re-invent myself, get back on track, and start over."

"A good stopping point for us today too, I think, Captain. Shall we resume tomorrow morning, same time and place?"

"Lord willin', Mike. Did you say anything to Georgie about my 'liberty pass' to the airport?"

"Yes but I didn't tell her where we might go. She just wants to know when we leave and plan to return."

"OK. take this Ximango handbook and look it over. I have another one, so you can hang on to that copy while you're here. And here's "Transition to Gliders", a training manual for power pilots. Aerodynamically, sailplanes are very sophisticated airplanes and soaring is an entirely unique and challenging sport. Next to levitation, it is as close to being a bird as you can get. Although gliders are so safe and simple to fly, you can solo at age fourteen, but it takes a lifetime to perfect the art and science of soaring. Every day and location is different, and no one knows all there is to learn about soaring. As gliders go, the Ximango is a relatively large, heavy and complex airplane. The wings unfold from thirty three feet to fifty nine feet about twelve feet more than most gliders whereas most gliders weigh about six hundred pounds and have a single wheel, Ximango's max is 1700 pounds and the conventional 'tail dragger' landing gear is manually retractable. It takes some muscle to retract the landing gear, so that will be one of your co-pilot jobs IF we fly. Of course, hanging an engine on a glider adds all the complexity of a power plane too, plus, the Ximango has a manually operated three-position propeller: climb pitch, cruise pitch, and feathered when the engine is shut down. So, the Ximango is a much more complex airplane than the Champ you've been flying, you're pretty busy on takeoff and climb out."

"Thanks for the books Captain, I'll read them carefully."

"No need to memorize, Mike. Just skim through the handbook. Procedures and limitations are highlighted. Read the transition manual at your leisure. Since my partner Jerry and I bought her in 2005, I have accumulated over two thousand hours in this bird. It's like a part of me when I strap in, so I'll keep you safe. I'll see you here in the morning."

Boy Scout Manny, 1945

5

MATERNAL KIN

"Good morning, Georgie"

"Good morning Mike. Beautiful day, isn't it?"

"Sure is, near perfect–clear skies, light winds, and the forecast high is seventy-six degrees. If he's up for it, I'll be taking the Captain for a drive later."

"Wonderful Mike, I'm sure he will enjoy that. He's waiting for you at the usual place."

"Good. We'll let you know when we leave. I'll have him home before dinner."

"Fine, I hope you both have a great day."

"Top of the morning, Captain. Looks like a decent day for an airport visit, doesn't it?"

"Let's see what it looks like in a couple of hours."

"Suits me, Captain. Did you get through the handbook?"

"More or less. Did you?"

"I skimmed through it for high points. Hopefully, my legal fast- reading experience will carry me through today."

"Well, we'll see. It's good to have confidence. Meanwhile, Mike, let's press on with this interview. Since you seem to want my entire biography, I am going to ask a favor. For the benefit my decedents who may one day be interested in family history and actually read your book, I ask to take this juncture to briefly tell what I know of my mother's immediate family. You can delete it later if it doesn't fit. Shall I proceed?"

"Lead the way, Captain."

Just as he had been deceptive about his identity, so had he been about a reason for this visit. This visit had much to do with self-identification. As far as his paternal family history was concerned, it was all news to him. The more the better.

"We drove to Portland before sailing to Germany to visit mother Ada's family her mother Grace and her husband Dan, plus Ada's six siblings–one older brother and five younger sisters and their families. As fate would have it, this was to be their final gathering of Grace's seven children, who were all born in Magalloway Plantation, Maine, where the only industry was the lumber company my grandfather worked for. Grandmother Grace Bennett, married Earl Hoyt at age sixteen and bore him seven children. Mother Ada, the second, was born April 28th 1911. Fifteen years later father Hoyt died on the operating table from an allergic reaction to ether during an appendectomy. Life in Maine was brutal in those days, especially during the harsh winters. Survival depended almost entirely on self-sufficiency. Grace did not fare well as a young widow and destitute mother of seven to the point where the farm was sold and her children were boarded out to foster homes, except for older brother Merton and Ada, who were old enough to be on their own. Merton married a local girl and the lumber company sent Ada off to a Boston girls' trade school to be trained as a seamstress. By the time I came along, grandmother Grace had recovered and worked at the B & M Bean factory, which greatly redeemed Portland's Back Bay sewage stench when the tide was out. The delicious odor of those eight hour baking beans pervaded the entire city. Grace had an endearingly husky voice and laugh. She resembled the great actress Ethel Barrymore and had similar commanding presence. She was warm, soft, and loving, yet highly intelligent and strong. She truly was the queen of the family. I remember her with great reverence and affection, As her oldest grandson, I was her favorite. Late in life, Grace married Dan Benwell, a fellow B & M employee, who had been an alcoholic to the point of having DT's. Grace refused his proposal unless he swore off. True to his word, Dan never drank again and I have never known two people more vigorously in love and happy until they passed away in the 50's. Everyone loved both of them. Lesson learned, it's never too late. Mother's brother and best childhood friend, Merton, was an oddball as are most 'Mainiacs'. Early on, he married a Magalloway farm girl. They had one daughter, but were soon divorced. During WW II Merton joined the Navy as a "SeaBee", as the Construction Battalion was known. He was reported "missing" when his ship was sunk in the Pacific, but thankfully turned up. After the war he became a career fireman in Portland and once made front page news for rescuing a baby from a burning building. Merton then married Tina, an attentive school teacher who was unjustifiably disliked by the family for her education, class, reserved ways, and pinched facial expression. They had one son, Leroy, who was still in jail last I heard. When Merton retired as a fireman, they moved to Naples Florida, where he had an outboard motor repair shop until he passed from cancer in the sixties. Mother's sisters, impressed me as exceptionally bright and independent women, each in their own way, yet very different from my mother who was labeled with an undeserved 'rich bitch' tag. It tells you something about Ada's sisters that they could consider an Army sergeant's wife a 'rich bitch', doesn't it? I could spend hours telling you just the little I knew about Ada's sisters. Briefly though, they were very colorful, earthy, salty, intelligent and strong-willed women, much like their mother Grace—only without her 'grace'. Francis had seven children, one stillborn, by her husband Tommy, a crude truck driver who stayed home only long enough to father Francis' next baby. They had a very stormy relationship, but an underlying everlasting bond. I admired both of them. Tommy and Father got along well, though they had little in common. In my teens I was proud to be allowed to play poker and go fishing with them at night off the piers in Portland harbor while they discussed women, comparing their relative traits to makes of automobiles - Cadillac's being tops, of course. It was a nice 'right of passage' for me. Tommy passed away in the sixties. Francis lived to a ripe old age and passed in the nineties, cared for by a devoted son who lived with her. Wilma was pale, thin, and frail, She also married a truck driver named Guppy who was as pale and thin as she was, so of course, they had three pale thin children. Wilma later got the family's attention when she abandoned her husband and children to run off with a man to Florida. Marjory was the sister most like her mother, and so was everyone's favorite. Stout, jovial, and bright, Marjorie, like Grace, was a commanding presence. Marjorie was married once, just long enough to get pregnant with her son Wayne before her Army husband shipped out to die on Normandy Beach during the D-Day landings. In the fifties, Marjory had an unhappy affair which resulted in the birth of her daughter. She worked mostly in hospitals as a nurse's aid and was living in a trailer when she died of heart failure in the seventies. Pearl was the saltiest, toughest, most fiery and temperamental of the sisters. She and Jean, the youngest sister, were very close, as were Pearl and Marjorie, who played guitar and sang country western music together. Pearl first married an abusive bartender and had her only child, Kenneth. Pearl's second husband was career Army. Her third husband, John, was a retired postal worker. They moved to Tallahassee in the eighties to be near her son Kenneth when John had a severely disabling stroke and passed away in the early nineties, a week before my father. Pearl passed away in a nursing home with Alzheimer's Disease. Jean was the youngest, prettiest and most glamorous of the sisters. She married the brother of Pearl's first husband, who was also an abusive bar tender, and had a baby girl. When Jean divorced, she asked my parents to take her daughter in. My father, agreed but only on the condition of adoption, his way of getting out of it since he knew it would be unacceptable to Jean. We never knew for sure, but believed that the daughter was raised by her ex's parents in Erie Pennsylvania. In 1949 Jean was working at a Boston night club as a cocktail waitress, cigarette girl, and photographer. With her during our 1949 visit was the owner of the club -an obvious mafia type figure. I always had a sort of 'crush' on Jean, though I rarely saw or spoke to her. Actually, it would be more accurate to say that I felt a unique spiritual connection with Jean, a recognition of her as someone I had perhaps known before. Less than a year later, Jean was found dead in her apartment with the unlit stove gas on. The police ruled it a suicide, but the family believed it was a homicide. Twenty years later,

Jean would reveal herself in my life in a very dramatic way. That Portland visit before sailing to Germany was important to me because I was old enough to be included as more than a child 'to be seen and not heard'. We all visited the old family homestead in Magalloway where the well-preserved farmhouse still stood. Several great photos exist of that trip two taken at a dam. One was of the entire gang face on, the other was of everyone's backsides as they leaned on the dam railing. Father titled that photo 'The American Can Company'. One Saturday afternoon we had a great clambake on the Back Bay beach with the tide out for clam digging fortunately with the wind behind us. Lobsters, 'Italian sandwiches' now called Subs, B&M beans, beer, and soft drinks complemented the menu. God knows how anyone survived eating those Back Bay clams. Soon, however, it was time to be off to New York City to board an Army transport ship for Germany. So that's it for Mother's folks in 1949."

"OK Captain. I'm glad you told me about your mother's family. Perhaps you will do the same on your father's side as well." "Sure Mike, we'll get to them too, but first let's go to the airport."

My mother Ada and her brother Merton, at the Hoyt family home, Magalloway Plantation, Maine, circa1915

Mother and her brother re-pose the photo at the same location thirty years later.

Mother, her mother Grace & Dan

Grandfather Hugh Hoyt

Great grandmother Viana Hoyt

Grandmother Grace Hoyt with 4 of her 7 children   20 years later - Wilma, Pearl, Margery, & Jean Hoyt

L-R- Dan & Grandmother Grace, Pearl & Wilma, Merton's Tina, Mom Dad & me, Wilma's Guppy, Uncle Merton

42

6

AIRPORT

"Shall we bring your chair along, Captain?"

"No, Mike, we won't be walking much, but you can give me a push to the lobby."

So they told Georgie they were leaving, and drove off.

"Which way, Captain?"

"Left out the gate. Stay on route four across the Patuxent River bridge into St Mary's County all the way to Leonardtown, about twenty miles."

"How did you come to be in this area, Captain?"

"All three of my sailboats were home-ported near here at Solomon's Island from 1972 to 88. Solomon's is technically an island only because there's a short bridge over a narrow inlet between it and the mainland. Basically it was a small fishing village, until the yachtsmen discovered it as one of the best and favorite ports on the western shore."

"Why Chesapeake Bay, Captain?"

"For me, the Bay is a uniquely outstanding place for a yachtsman–including old salts like me who long ago 'swallowed the anchor'. I even bought a lot on the edge of Calvert Cliffs in the seventies at the Chesapeake Ranch Club, just a few miles from here, but sold it along with everything else we owned when Susann-ex and I moved aboard WINGS."

"Only sixty five miles from DC and an easy drive down route four, yet this part of Southern Maryland seems quite remote, Captain."

"That's a feature I like, though Southern Maryland is much more developed and well-traveled than it was before this bridge was built in the seventies, very much against the wishes of the locals on this side. Actually, once outside DC's beltway in any direction except toward Baltimore, you soon find yourself in beautiful countryside and pleasant residential areas. We'll be taking the next right to cross the bridge. This area was first settled by Captain John Smith in 1639.

In fact, Saint Mary's City, near where we are going, was the first capital of Maryland. Hard to believe now, there's little there except Saint Mary's College, a few restored buildings, an Amish settlement, and a replica of one of Smith's vessels. The main event was the Patuxent River Naval Air Station, home of the Navy Test Pilot School and the Naval Air Test Center where all Navy airplanes underwent test and evaluation. These days, of course, the 'airplanes' tested are mostly UAV's, Unmanned Aerial Vehicles, Today's 'test pilots' are mostly ground-pounders playing video games with radio-conrtroled drones."

"Do you feel that your days in aviation were the best?"

"In some ways, yes. If flying is about higher and faster, as many fighter pilots believe, then there were no improvements to airplanes after us except in electronics and weapons. The F-4 Phantom was as good as they got. For the true romance and adventure of flight, however, I've always envied the generation of aviators before me who flew in the early days; World War One, the twenties and thirties, and World War Two when it was less about technology and more about personal skills, when wars were fought for clear good-against-evil causes, and we knew who the enemy was."

"I see your point, Captain. For me, flying the Aeronca 'Champion' is like turning the aviation clock back to the forties when the 'Champs' first flew. In fact, Philip's Champ is a restored Army World War Two L-16 liaison 'war bird'. As you know, it's as basic and simple as airplanes get only essential flight instruments and no electronics. There's not even a starter. We have to hand crank the prop to start the eighty-five horsepower Continental engine. There certainly is a special romance in flying that kind of an airplane low over the countryside at eighty knots -quite different than sitting in an airliner at forty thousand feet just under the speed of sound."

"Quite right, Mike. The guys who fly airliners shouldn't even log their flight time. All they do is sit there monitoring the electronics which do the actual flying and navigation from takeoff to landing. It was the great barnstorming aviators, like Lindbergh, who flew the rickety wood and fabric planes powered by unreliable engines with which they pioneered airmail and passenger routes day and night in all-weather without electronics or navigation aids. They appreciated the true 'romance' of aviation in ways we can never know. OK, here we are, turn right at the 'Saint Mary's County Regional Airport' sign, a pretentious name for a small country airstrip with only a four thousand foot runway, no control tower, and little traffic, but that's what I like about it simplicity. Just park to the left of that first hangar. I'll wait here while you slide the two hangar doors all the way to the side. The lock combination is twenty-five, twenty-five."

It was clear to see why the Captain needed help, the hangar doors were very heavy and screeched loudly on their bearings as they were opened. There she was, the Ximango, all pretty and snug in its clean 'T' shaped space with the wings folded and resting on the tips of their 'winglets' on boat seat cushions on top of the wings.

"OK, Captain, doors open. What a beautiful airplane!"

"Oh yes, she is. Much more so with her wings spread. Like sailboats, form follows function with sailplanes in an aesthetically pleasing way found nowhere else except in sailboats and nature. See that long handled dolly on the tail wheel, Mike? Just pick it up by the handles and push the bird straight out of the hangar, then swing the tail to the right to line her up on the taxiway. It'll take some muscle, max takeoff weight is nearly eighteen hundred pounds. Leave the tail wheel dolly in place, things can get exciting if the tail swings while you're spreading or folding the wings. Go ahead, I'll catch up."

With detailed instruction, close supervision, great care, and strenuous effort, Michael spread the eighty pound outer wing panels without incident.

"Good work, Mike. Spreading them is the easy part, folding them is more critical. If you lose it coming down, a winglet could go right through the top of the wing if the cushions slip out of place."

"I can sure see why. Lifting those wing panels is close to my strength limits and the angles are awkward, but I suppose it gets easier with practice. It would help if I were in better shape and twenty years younger."

"Yeah, tell me about it, kid. You sure got my sympathy."

After a brief walk-around inspection of wing locks, control surfaces, tires, and oil level, Mike helped the Captain into the left seat of the cockpit and got himself into the right seat.

"Well, this isn't the easiest airplane to get into, is it, Captain? Kinda' tight spaces, and the reclining seats tilted back even more by having the tail down with the open canopy partly blocking, makes it quite a twist and turn effort. I have to say that you managed quite well."

"Considering my decrepit age you mean, Mike? Couldn't do it without help though and as you'll see, getting out is even harder, a Ximango feature which most ladies are not willing to endure. Only five women have flown with me in this bird: my fearless mother at age ninety-six, my two daughters, an old Navy friend, Claudia; and Carin, who bless her heart, was always very supportive of my extravagant hobbies but subscribed to the Cole Porter lyric 'Flying too high with some guy in the sky is my idea of nothing to do.'"

"But I get a kick out of you?"

"Yup, that's the song, good for you! Now if you'll read that checklist to me, let's bring this machine to life. Put your rudder pedals all the way forward for leg room. You'll see that big guys' left knee gets in the way of the spoiler and prop shift levers."

After demonstrating the controls, engine starting, warm-up, and magneto checks, the Captain radio announced taxiing to runway two nine.

"You ready, Mike?"

"All set, Captain."

"OK, follow me through lightly on the controls. Saint Mary's traffic, motor- glider six two sierra x-ray rolling on two nine, west bound.' Tail up around forty knots and let her fly off. Brakes to stop wheel rotation, then gear up please, Mike."

"I see what you mean about the strength needed to get the gear up, Captain, but it's great that it's all manual, without electric or hydraulic systems involved."

"Yes, battery power is at a premium since I have averaged engine off for two thirds of the flight time. Even if the battery dies, however, it's possible to air start the engine by diving at 100 knots. Now we'll shift the prop to cruise pitch by throttling back to 3800rpm and pulling the prop lever part way. OK, now we'll cruise-climb at full throttle to 5,000 feet, generally on this heading across the Potomac River into Virginia. It's all yours, Mike, maneuver as you wish, I won't let you break anything. As you see on that placard before you though, no aerobatic G's."

"OK, I have the airplane, Captain."

"After reaching 5,000 feet, the Captain shut down the engine and demonstrated thermal soaring before turning the stick back to Mike.

"Wow, Captain, this is magic! I can't believe I'm climbing 800 feet a minute and looking at a feathered propeller. We've already gained over a thousand feet. Amazing. No wonder you love this airplane, it does everything. It glides so well, there's almost no feeling of descending, even when there's no lift. With no prop or engine noise, it's like having your own personal jet."

"You got it, Mike, and consider this with no lift or wind from where we are now at 6,000 feet with a 34 to 1 glide ratio and 160 feet per minute descent, if we had complete engine failure, we would have over thirty miles and thirty minutes to find a landing spot. We can easily make it home from here, as we'll see. On winter days with no lift, I climb out to 10,000 feet or so in less than twenty minutes, shut down and glide for forty minutes at 60 knots. If I'm in more of a hurry, this bird cruises under power at 110 knots for a 600 mile range, burning less than half the fuel consumption of other light planes and do it on much less expensive auto fuel. By the way, Ximango is the Portuguese word for falcon. They were built by Aeromot at the very southern tip of Brazil and flown for delivery to the USA, 5,000 miles across the Amazon to Daytona Beach. One was even flown around the world in the nineties."

"Amazing, Captain. I'm surprised I've never heard of Ximango's before. It does everything so well, it seems like the perfect recreational flying machine."

"You're right, Mike. Unfortunately, few folks have heard of them. Well, it's time to head back if we're going to make dinner time. There's just one seating so we'll be out of luck if we're late. I hope you don't mind, I told Georgie you are joining me. It's Tuesday, prime rib night, which is always a highlight of my week at Heritage Pines. They really do it right. OK with you?"

"I'll be honored, thank you, Captain. Good heavens, I had no idea we have been flying nearly two hours."

"Like they say, 'Time flies when you're having fun', Mike. Just point us east and see if you can find home field. I'll take it for the approach and landing when we get there, engine off unless there's a lot of traffic in the landing pattern."

"Do you always land 'dead stick', Captain?"

"Yes, if possible. It's a little easier than engine on and more fun to show off a little for the benefit of the power plane guys and the old-timer 'porch pilots' who hang around the field. The feature of gliders that makes them easy to land are the 'spoilers' which are very effective speed brakes used to control rate of decent and speed. So, you can lean toward the high fast side on approach and use the spoilers much as you would throttle, only in reverse. Of course, if necessary, it's a quick and simple matter to re-start the engine."

"Hmmmm, interesting. Seems like all planes should have spoilers, Captain."

"I agree, Mike. In fact some Mooney airplanes had miniature versions of them and all fighters have speed brakes. Since jet engines are a little slow on acceleration compared to props, most carrier landing approaches were once made with the brakes out, making more power immediately available for wave-offs or bolters by closing the speed-brakes as full throttle was added. OK, I have the airplane. Spoilers now."

"I see what you mean about spoiler effectiveness, Captain. Really throws you against the shoulder harness, don't they?"

"Yes, I have them full out now so we can descend rapidly, keeping the speed below the 80 knot max landing gear down speed. Gear extension is much easier than retraction, thanks to gravity, but I'll let you do the honors, now please. Good. 'Saint Mary's traffic, motor-glider six two sierra x-ray entering high downwind for runway two nine dead stick. Saint Mary's'. Half brakes now, thousand feet per minute descent, left turn. 'Saint Mary's traffic, motor-glider six two sierra x-ray left base, runway two nine, dead-stick.' Rolling out of the turn on runway heading, a little high and fast, more spoiler. 'Saint Mary's traffic, motor-glider six two sierra x- ray, on final for two nine, dead-stick.' Passing ten feet, begin the flare, spoilers in a little, touch down three point attitude, full spoilers out, prop lever to un-feathered, mags on, engine start, and turn off onto the taxiway. .Well we cheated death again, Mike. Take her to the barn, swing the tail wheel left to line us up for pushback and I'll read the shutdown checklist to you. Then you can exit and give me a hand getting out."

The disembarkation, wing fold, and push back into the hangar DONE, they were soon on eastbound on route four.

"Well, you done good, Mike. What do you think?"

"Thanks, Captain, it's still sinking in, but what an incredible experience. I can't thank you enough. Soaring is certainly an entirely different world to itself. A man in a simple machine, as close to nature as it gets, like sailing, with unmatched serenity. I feel as though I have been meditating for two hours, even though it keeps you busy. You have to pay attention to flying the glider all the time to react to all the subtle or dramatic changes in lift conditions, don't you? I was surprised by how tightly you have to turn, 45 to 60 degrees bank angle, to stay near the center of thermals. I was taught that you lose half your lift in tight turns."

"That's correct and that's why you carry extra speed in the turns, but the tradeoff makes it worthwhile since lift is so much stronger in the center of typical thermals. I say 'typical' because the greatest truth about soaring is that there are no 'great truths'. Every day is different. During the summer, when towering cumulus clouds develop, I often ventured into them. The base of cumulus clouds here averages four thousand feet and are formed by strong thermals below. When you first enter them, they seem quite benign. Often there is a smooth steady 300 feet per minute climb, but as you get higher the lift accelerates and it gets more turbulent. Then it often gets so cold and wet and turbulent I had to tighten my shoulder harness to keep from hitting my head on the canopy. I've seen nearly two thousand feet per minute sustained climb rate on the vertical speed indicator and visibility so limited I couldn't see the wings. It becomes difficult to keep airspeed under control, with the needle rapidly fluctuating between forty and a hundred knots, while keeping the lift centered. That's when I chicken out, pop the spoilers, and level the wings for the nearest exit. I've ridden these elevators to nearly thirteen thousand feet. Everything instantly goes back to peace and sunshine. When you leave the cloud you turn to look back to see the impressive sight of what you've just been in and how near you came to the top. Sometimes I was close, but never all the way out the top. Then you look out across the skyscape to an incredible sight of being high above many of the other towering cumulus clouds. The instant change from hanging on for dear life in a wild roller coaster ride with zero visibility, to the suddenly dramatic, peaceful and magnificent view, were simply some of the most breathtaking and satisfying adventures I ever had in an airplane."

"Cloud flying sounds like extreme soaring, Captain. Is that where the flying expression 'exploring the envelope' comes from?"

"Yes it is, Mike. The envelope refers to an airplane's performance diagram, a graphic chart of an airplane's limitations, showing how slow, fast, and high, with -other graphs of things like climb and turn rates, G limits, max range and speeds, etcetera. It's important for all pilots, but most especially fighter pilots, to explore and learn to fly his airplane most effectively to its limits by feel when the chips are down and the consequences final."

"So fighter pilots are special, Captain?"

"Oh hell yes, Mike, just ask Chuck Yeager or any of them and they'll look at you like you are the simplest sumbitch that ever walked. Truth is, the biggest difference is the size of their egos. Nevertheless, there is a difference in the nature of the fighter mission and the airplanes designed for it. As fighter pilots are fond of saying, there are two kinds of airplanes, fighters and targets.

As nasty as war is, there's the unique nobility of just one 'higher and faster' man in his machine against another in his machine in life or death aerial combat. There is a genuine lore that dates back to King Arthur and the Knights of the Round Table, so it goes with the territory that self-confidence can be as crucial to a fighter pilot as knowing his aircraft's performance envelope."

"How do other pilots regard fighter jocks, Captain?"

"Mostly with tolerant amusement, I think. They're seen as girl-chasing booze-hound braggadocio kids playing with expensive toys which have little practical value until they get bombs hung on them. The fact is that there has been almost nothing of the dog fights of World War Two. Ever after the US had unchallenged air superiority. So, who needed fighters taking up flight deck space? Still, there was an undeniable, though irrational, social and professional hierarchy within the pilot community which put fighter pilots at the top of the heap, followed by attack pilots and 'others', with multi-engine bomber, patrol or transport pilots at the bottom. Oddly, the pilot selection systems in military aviation reinforced this hierarchy. I was in carrier squadrons of all types and, in my opinion, there's not a nickels difference in the average level of pilot flying ability between squadron types."

"Well, Captain, we have safely arrived at Heritage Pines with an hour to spare. I'd like to go to the Inn to wash and change. May I meet you in the lobby in about forty-five minutes?"

"Good, Mike, see you then. Thank you for flying with me today. It truly meant a lot and I enjoyed your company. You're a good pilot. You should have been a naval aviator instead of choosing a life of crime."

"Thank you, Captain, the pleasure and honor was mine, I assure you. Don't know about that naval aviator part though. My Grampa told me that if I joined the Navy I might never be sure who the father of my children was."

"Mike, that applies to all fathers."

Manny's Ximango, Lake Iamonia 2010

7

REVELATION

In the time to prepare for dinner, Mike came to the decision that the time was at hand for confessing his true identity to his father, tonight after dinner"

"A great meal, Captain, thank you. What a beautiful dining room."

"Yes it really is nice, isn't it? This building was built in 1937 as a private lodge by a wealthy Baltimore millionaire with twenty-seven guest rooms on the second floor overlooking Swan Lake, now occupied by residents who prefer hotel style accommodations. The Heritage Pines folks have done a good job of maintaining everything in this building in its original configuration, condition, fixtures, furnishings, and amenities. The twenty foot high ceilings here in the lobby and dining room are all original local wood with a variety of other woods used to inlay Indian designs. That huge stone fireplace there is functional. There's always a big cozy fire going in it when the temperature warrants."

"Where do you live, Captain?"

"The rest of us live in the new quad facility down the street, which you haven't seen because it's hidden by a line of trees planted there for the purpose of preserving the original environment of this building. The building is in a square around a covered atrium. The ground floor is mostly game and meeting rooms, plus an office, small cafeteria, and nurse's station. There are a hundred and six single or two bedroom unfurnished apartments with small kitchenettes and living rooms. Housekeeping services are provided weekly. There are three sixteen passenger vans to haul us around to all kinds of activities, but many residents have their own vehicles. It all works out quite well. There's something for everyone. Would you like to sit awhile here in the lobby?"

"Sure. A very impressive place, Captain. I can see myself somewhere like this one day if I'm lucky."

"Lucky is the word, Mike. I have certainly had more than my share of it, for sure. Before we get back to talking about my life in Germany, let's talk about you for a change, alright?"

"There's little to tell, Captain. As I said, one town, one job, one wife, one family. What else can I tell you?"

"Well, let's go back to the question of why you are really here, Mike."

"The reasons I gave you were all true, Captain. I want to write your story."

"Yeah, Mike, I got that, but I'm having trouble wrapping my mind around why you want to do a book about a Vietnam era naval aviator. You have obviously gone way out of your way to be here. So my question still is—why me? Really Mike, is that the only reason you are here...the book?"

Thank God he had already decided to tell the whole truth, Michael thought. He would have been in a hell of a fix if he hadn't.

"To be truthful, Captain, not the only reason. Someone told me a lot about you and I wanted to meet you."

"Someone? Like your mother Emma or your wife Martha maybe?"

"When did you figure me out?"

"The day before you came here."

"How?"

"No stranger has been here to see me in years. So, when Georgie told me someone was coming, I got curious and called Bob at the Watermen's Inn to find out who had reservations. Guess whose name popped up before you changed it to Sabino? You're an old fart yourself now, but the Sousa mark on you would have given you away anyhow, despite the facial hair and glasses. Didn't you think it was odd that I didn't ask any probing questions about your family, hometown, or background? I was sparing you the eventual humiliation of confession. So why the charade, Mike, and what's your motive after all these years?"

"I sincerely apologize for the deception, Captain. I thought you might not want to see me. I guess the reason for coming was 'closure' .whatever that means, and I am serious about the book. I do want to tell your story, partly so I can try to understand you and myself better. What little I know about you is quite colorful. I sure hope you don't think I'm a buzzard circling for an inheritance."

"Inheritance? Now that's amusing. Obviously, you have no idea what these homes charge. In any event, I followed my Granny's advice and made myself worth more alive than dead. So, should I call you son?"

"Yes SIR."

"Touché, you got me there. 'Mike' and 'Captain' it shall be. We never got closely acquainted with the Dad-Son bit, did we? But if you have any axes to grind with me about that, go for it and get it over with. Note this, however, on balance I have no regrets. No one is putting me on a death bed guilt trip. Nevertheless, I promise to listen as patiently as I can and tell you anything you want to know."

"There will be no ax-grinding from me, Captain. Life with my mother, plus my own failures as a husband and father, long ago erased whatever blame I assigned to you in the past. No one can justly judge a marriage from the outside, can they? I am here to know you and myself better by writing your story. I hope that we can be friends. That's all."

"That's fine with me, Mike. So be it. Truly, I am happy that you are here. I'm not sure that telling my side of the story will accomplish anything positive. I have no wish to affect your memory of your mother. The important thing is that she seems to have done a fine job of raising you. History between me and her is of little consequence now. In any event, in the interest of keeping my story in context, I'd like to stay on some semblance of a time line. So, I'll say just one thing about your mother for now. We made our peace with each other several times. Over the years, during subsequent failed relationships, it occasionally crossed my mind that: everything considered, Emma and I might as well have made a better effort at making a go of it. At the time, however, that was not an option, as you will see. Early on, your Martha stayed in touch with my mother, so she had a positively biased source of information on me."

"I agree that it will be better to keep events in sequence, Captain. I don't have urgent questions now, but there's no need to be concerned about my image of my mother. Her version of your story was pretty transparent and I found her correspondence with the Navy about your marriage, so I already have a good idea what happened and why. She had a way of making life difficult for herself, pioneering single mother's rights. You are quite correct though, Emma was a very loving mother and she did her ultimate best to raise me right. I miss her very much."

"I'm sure you do, Mike. She was a special lady. Well, it has been a memorable day, hasn't it? Shall we call it a night and sleep on it?"

"It has been a perfect day, Captain, thanks to you for it all. The Ximango flight and dinner was fantastic. All along I felt guilty about my identity deception. I had already decided to come clean with you tonight, but feared the consequences. I can't express how relieved I am that you made matters easy for me."

"Since I knew all along, Mike, I share your guilt by not clearing up the matter right at the beginning. So, let's just call it even and move on. With regard to us moving on, one more thing while we're at it. I'm sorry we got so crossed up with our last communications forty years ago when I got fed up with Martha's inconsiderate behavior toward my mother on her Bermuda cruise, and you took Martha's side. After that I simply did not see how I could reach you. Then, when you separated, it seemed too much time had passed to fix it better to let sleeping dogs lie."

"I'm sorry about that too, Captain. All I can say is that those were difficult years. By the time I got back on track, it seemed too late to me too. So, can we call that even as well and move on?"

"Absolutely, Mike, let those matters rest in peace. It has been a perfect day for me as well. I'd like to ask you to bunk in my place to save you some money at the rate we're going you'll be here a long time but I'm in a one bedroom apartment and there simply isn't room, I'm sorry to say."

"Quite alright, I'm very comfortable and well settled at the Inn. Besides, I wouldn't want to risk wearing out my welcome, Captain."

"OK, then let's call it a night and resume same time and place in the morning."

8

GERMANY

Mike answered his phone at Watermen's Inn.

"Good morning, Mike. It's Georgie. I hope I didn't disturb you?"

"Not at all Georgie, is everything alright?"

"Oh yes. I just called to ask if you would stop by my office a little early, before you meet the Captain. There's a matter I'd like to discuss, if you have time."

"Sure, Georgie. Is nine o'clock OK?"

"Perfect. See you then."

Hmmmmm ...mysterious, Mike thought. What's this about? Maybe she heard about our Ximango flight and a butt-chewing is coming?

"Good morning, Georgie, how are you."

"Good morning, Mike, I'm fine thanks. Did you enjoy your flight with the Captain yesterday?"

"Uh oh, looks like I've been busted. Yes, it was a most enjoyable flight, Georgie. I hope you're not upset. We just didn't want to worry you. The Captain is very safe and competent. Plus, I have some pilot experience too. How did you hear about us?"

"Just teasing, Mike. I wasn't worried or the least upset. After all, the Captain is old enough to make those decisions for himself, isn't he? And he has been flying for some time, right? One of the busy-body 'Porch Pilots', as the Captain aptly calls them, called me last night. Small town you know, so it doesn't take much to make the news. Since the Captain's airplane is distinctively different, it's easily recognized. As far as I know, this is his first flight in a number of years, so I do admit that I'm relieved to hear it went well. I'll bet he is really happy to have you here now!"

"I think so, Georgie, and so am I. In fact, I took advantage of the good mood last night to confess my identity. It turns out that the Captain knew all along. He called Bob at the Inn the day you told him about a visitor to see who had registered. I had to use my real name to use my

VISA card, so it was easy for him to blow my cover. Anyhow, he says the score is even between us since he didn't say something earlier. Now we can drop the Sabino alias. Thank God."

"That's great, Mike, I'm so glad. I take it that you may be here longer than you thought then?"

"Yes, Georgie, possibly. So far in his story, the Captain is only sixteen years old. Now, with the flying and my identity resolved, this may be a long term effort."

"In that case, the reason I asked you to stop by this morning is that I may have some good news for you, Mike. As happenstance would have it, an upstairs room here has become temporarily available, one of the nicest, in the back overlooking the lake. The gentleman, Major Underwood, who lives there has accepted the pleas of his daughter to live with her in England. Since he is not sure that it will work out, he has retained the room by paying the rent a year in advance. He put his personal effects in storage, otherwise his is the only room with the original 1937 furnishings. I took the liberty of discussing your situation with the Major by email and he has very graciously offered the room to you rent free with the understanding that you may have to vacate on short notice should he decide to return. The only expense for you would be your meals in the dining room. How does that sound?"

"As happenstance would have it, Georgie, it sounds perfect. I just hope the Captain wouldn't feel that I'm closing in on him. I'd hate to wear out my welcome."

"Yes, he does value his privacy, I know, but I think you'll work it out. Your book project seems an ideal link. Flying will be a wonderful bond too. So, why don't you have a look at the room. If you like it, discuss it with the Captain, and we'll go from there. Here are the keys. You may take the stairs, but it's a bit of a climb with our high ceiling down here. So better still, ride the original Otis elevator up over there on the other side of the hallway by the desk. Its room number 103."

"Thank you so much, Georgie. I'll get back to you later today."

The room was gorgeously furnished in the style of the thirties with a massive carved mahogany cannon-ball bed with matching dresser and bedside tables, complemented by Tiffany lamps, an extravagantly ornate oriental carpet, rich colonial blue velvet drapes, crystal chandelier, and cheerfully patterned wallpaper. The large marble-tiled bathroom was fitted out with original style gold-plated fixtures, including a bathtub with lions' claw feet and a separate shower. The ambiance of the room, with the tranquil view of the lake and the woods beyond, gave Mike the feeling of having been transported ninety years back to the days when the lodge was built. It all seemed very fitting to Mike's mission of recording his father's past. After all, since levitation is possible, why not time-travel? Surely, some force was at work, call it what you wish -happenstance, providence, or divine intervention.

"Good morning, Captain. Sleep well?"

"Yes indeed. In fact, I had a Ximango flying dream last night. I saw your car out front early. What's up?"

"Georgie called to ask me to stop in to see her."

"Uh oh, I'll bet she got wind of our flight from one of those nosey porch pilots probably Peg Leg John."

"I don't know who called her, but you are correct. However, that wasn't what she wanted to talk about. Georgie seems fine with our flying. She says you're old enough to decide. The topic was Major Underwood's room."

"Oh yes, fine British chap. The Major left here three weeks ago to stay with his daughter at the family home in England. Her husband, who was titled nobility, passed away recently and left her to manage their home, which is something of a palace, one of those estates which are afford-able only if they are opened to public tours. George should fit in quite well as an authentic guide, he is a very agreeable and intelligent raconteur, as all Brits seem to be. He said he is keeping his room here, in case being a castle-keeper doesn't work for him. Don't tell me the room has been offered to you?"

"That's it, Captain. I just looked at it. It's perfect and the price is right - free! But I'm not sure I should take it. I wouldn't want you to feel I was crowding you."

"Crowding? Nonsense, Mike, makes great sense. By all means take it.

Heritage Pines is big enough for the both of us. If I didn't think so, I wouldn't be bashful about saying so, would I?"

"No, I don't think you would, Captain. I understand that 'bashful' is an unlikely trait to be found in fighter pilots right up there with 'humble' I hear. OK then, I'll take it. I do love this place and it will save me a bundle. I hope Major Underwood enjoys being a docent, because at the rate we are going, this book project may take a while. I'm glad you had another flying dream. Do you think our flight inspired it?"

"Yes I do, Mike. I had pretty much lost hope of flying the Ximango again.

None of those porch pilots will fly with me or anyone else for that matter. It would take a stick of dynamite up their butts to get any one of those tree-sittin' nose- pickin' turkeys airborne. All they do is hang around the Ready Room playing solitaire, pointing the scheming finger of scorn at everyone else, and convincing themselves they are the most enlightened intellectuals of the century. They're such screwballs they actually believe they invented a perpetual motion machine which they have somehow been unable to demonstrate for twenty years. I had all the fun I could stand with them early on, but when the Pukin' Dogs are in town, I set them loose on them. The Porch Pilots will never get over those episodes. Anyhow, as you said, let's get on with Passing Through. Where were we?"

"It's May 1949, Captain, you're sixteen and just passed through Portland Maine for a family gathering, enroute to Germany."

"Right. My parents and I boarded a troop ship in New York for a ten day passage to Bremerhaven. It was Mother's and my third ocean passage, but the first with Father. We saw little of him though, since the men and women were in separated berthing spaces. It was a smooth trip in fair weather all the way, after winter storms and before hurricane season. I loved being at sea again and spent every minute on deck watching the waves. From Bremerhaven we traveled south by train to Augsburg. It had been only four years since the end of the war, so there was still much evidence of the vast scope of destruction on the landscape, as well as in the faces of the people especially in the British and Russian zones where the victors' emotions ran deeper and their reconstruction interest did not. In the American Zone there were fewer signs of devastation, but it was difficult to adapt to the Germans' prolonged expressionless stares at us. Cities like Nuremberg were seventy-five percent destroyed, estimated from the evidence of aerial photos. Nevertheless, streets had been cleared of rubble and old ladies carried stones and bricks to rebuild the shells of cathedrals and downtown buildings. Old men had small children pick up GI's cigarette butts for them. The trains, busses, trucks, streetcars, and cabs were running, but there were few private vehicles except bicycles, motor bikes, and motorcycles. There were no signs of a functioning economy. The only 'business' operating was the 'black market', against a 'law' which was rarely enforced. Nearly all GI's and dependents, including us kids, sold or traded rationed Post Exchange cigarettes, coffee, candy, and food with the Germans. The most popular 'currency' was cigarettes, which were rationed one and a half cartons each week at the PX for one dollar per carton. We kept five packs to smoke and sold the carton on the black market for twenty dollars in Marks a very generous allowance for a kid over there in those days. Many families took advantage of the Market by trading for priceless antiques, but most GI's found other ways to spend their money. Beer and wine sold in the beer halls for twelve cents a liter and we're talking serious beer, Mike, up to sixteen percent! Then, consider the fact that there were eight million more German women than men after the war. The Jews were not the only ones killed in World War Two, nor for that matter the only ones to die in Nazi concentration camps."

"Captain, you're not suggesting that the Germans were victims are you?"

"Of course not, Mike. Except for children, there are no 'innocent civilians' in wars. All adults share the responsibility for their nations' acts. Hitler had good reason to believe that he was carrying out the will of the German people. But did you know that all the Nazi's in Germany had been killed? There was not a single one left alive anywhere. We knew that because all the kraut survivors proclaimed that they always hated Hitler and had never been Nazi's. Those hundreds of thousands of 'zieg heiling' civilians filmed at places like Nuremberg in 1939, plus the animals who ran the camps, all dead. Imagine that, Mike, all dead. And of course not a one of the survivors had any idea what was happening in the concentration camps until we rounded them all up and marched them through the camps immediately after the war with everything in place just as we found them, with thousands of stacked up rotting corpses shot in the backs of their heads when the bastards ran out of gas for the ovens. I'm simply pointing out the numbers, Mike. Millions of German women were aging widows with children, but without financial means or homes. Marriage and job opportunities for women were nil. The 'rich' GI's were obviously the most natural and attractive survival option."

"As a baptized Southern Baptist, Captain, how did you feel about such behavior by these women?"

"I found it difficult to believe in hell, Mike. Many German women were making survival choices in desperate situations that their American 'sisters' would never have to face. So German women would be damned, but American women saved? Everyone believes he acts on rational reasons for the choices he makes in life and death situations. Who's to judge?"

"What about the morality of the GI's, Captain?"

"Not for me to judge, Mike. Many young GI's were enjoying their first freedom away from home in a foreign land and did not handle the booze well, but I don't want to give you a one-sided impression. Historically, virtually all of our military men behaved admirably overseas in peace as well as war. By 1949, few of the GI's in Germany had experienced the war first hand, so they felt little animosity toward the Germans. Many GI's compassionately contributed to the survival of the elderly and children in the villages and on the farms. As in all wars, millions of GI's came home with 'war brides', sometimes much to the chagrin of their families. Imagine what it was like to take a girl from Munich home to the folks on the farm in Mississippi."

'1 expect there were many regrets and unhappy outcomes for all, Captain. War isn't the only possible hell on Earth, is it?"

"Indeed not, Mike. I had already seen many of these war brides married to guys in Fathers bands in the States before we went to Germany. German women were accustomed to the author-itarian oppression of European men and courts, but very soon learned their US 'rights' over their kinder gentler American husbands. It was a gruesome thing to witness. I should have learned that it is not possible to import a foreign wife into the US and not to expect her to change into an American, but I didn't."

"I look forward to hearing more about that, but how were the Germans governed and what was their attitude, Captain?"

"During that transition to self-rule, the American Zone was governed by the State Department's "HICOG" civilian government. The Army administered operation of many of the hotels and resorts. Army Military Police did a good job keeping the GI's out of trouble and the German police kept civil order. The Germans were compliant because they were just damned glad the war was over and that they were not in the Russian Zone. Their defeat was complete and there was no fight left in them. The closest thing to a German uprising was when they successfully stopped the Army from chlorinating the Munich water system, the prime ingredient in their beer. Still, the trains soon ran on time again, as they were famous for doing under Nazi rule. American dependents were housed in homes of owners who were generously compensated and resettled elsewhere. In the interest of boosting employment, each American household was provided a full time maid. US high schools were consolidated at major cities like Munich, Frankfurt, Nuremberg, and Heidelberg. I attended Munich High, a two hour train ride from Augsburg which meant the boys dormitory for me with most weekends at home. Hallelujah.escape! There were only two hundred of us in the entire student body at 'Dependents School Division for the High School Department, Munich Germany.' The boys 'dormitory' at 85 Harthauser Strasse was a three story private mansion, with a swimming pool and tennis court, in Harlaching, one of Munich's finest undamaged residential neighborhoods. Our Dorm Supervisor was an Episcopal Minister, who was on a sabbatical leave of absence from the ministry to dry out from drug abuse, apparently without success. He stayed in his room when we were there, even during meal time. We very rarely saw or heard from him. Consequently, we were on our own, without supervision. We came and went at any hour of the night, and there was no minimum drinking age in the Munich beer halls and night clubs. Free at last! The Gl's, who were under much stricter supervision and restrictions, hated us with a passion. Why should kids have so much more freedom than they had? Fortunately, we were smart enough to realize that if we didn't keep a lid on our actions, our fathers would be in trouble with the Army and our freedoms would quickly end. The Munich girls' dorm, on the other hand, was an entirely different matter. Security went to the opposite extreme of a near prison. They had a controlling middle-aged bitch, Mrs Mansur, known as Mrs "Man Sour", always visible, to the point of entering the girls' rooms unannounced at all hours. Bussed to and from school, the girls were otherwise allowed out only for supervised activities, such as our 'teen club'. Boys were allowed only in the living room after school, before dinner. German security guards, armed with automatic weapons, patrolled the dormitory grounds day and night and warned the girls sneaking a smoke, to go back inside off the balconies. So, compared to the kids of parents stationed in Munich and living at home, we dorm boys were far freer, while the girls living at home were much freer than the dorm girls."

"Quite a change from Georgia. Captain! But with all the availability of beer and German girls, wasn't there even more opportunity for those 'bird nests' in your hair?"

"No, Mike. Thankfully, the changes in Germany were all positive. We rarely interacted with Germans. It was May, near the end of my junior year, when we arrived, so I had only six weeks before summer vacation at home in Augsburg. Academically, I was way over my head, but the outstanding teachers made allowances for kids like me and I felt very thankful for the warm welcome of my classmates."

"Well that was a short 'escape' from home for you then. How did the summer go, Captain?"

"Surprisingly great, other than a curfew. Father said that if I lived at home until I was ninety, I would still have to be home by eleven o'clock. No doubt he was encouraging my permanent escape too. Initially, I sometimes hung around the Band Quarters with Father, who was now a Master Sergeant and acting band leader. I especially enjoyed rehearsals and started practicing on a baritone, but that ended in tears of frustration for me when I was unable to play a difficult passage well enough to satisfy Father's impatient rage. I didn't go back and did not touch another instrument for ten years. Otherwise, as always before, I was left to my own devices. My only school mate in Augsburg was Johnny Bell, a tall blond curly-haired blue-eyed slap-happy and agreeable pal a year younger. We rode our bikes for miles into the countryside and through the pristine Bavarian forests where trees were planted in rows and all undergrowth was cleared away. There was little traffic on the roads and bicycles were by far the most used vehicles, so bikes were safe to ride anywhere. On one outing we found a riding stable and rented horses, my first ride since Panama. We rode the horses into the woods, slowly because the horses weren't responding to our urgings. As soon as we turned around 'headed for the barn', however, we had a hell of a fast ride home! Augsburg was a relatively small city, noted during the war for being home to the Messerschmitt airplane factory which manufactured their most widely used fighter of the war, the Bf-109. Only the twisted steel beams of the factory remained and there were no signs of reconstruction interests at the site. About the only businesses open were gasthaus beer halls, where besides one liter mugs of beer, the fare mainly consisted of delicious breads, pickles, and wurst. At home, we had Elsa, our likeable, tough, hard-working, sinewy, middle-aged maid. Also with the house came a dirty all white cat with the shakes. 'Shaky' was dirty because she didn't groom herself. Except for that and being shaky, which we ascribed to shell-shock, she was normal. Then my parents bought a puppy. Not just any puppy, but Brando Von Der Maria, the son of the champion Schaeferhund of all Germany, Cralo Von Hounstetten! Brando and I got along beautifully. When he was small, his dog house was big enough for both of us and he loved to rough-house as hard as we could. He would bite without ever breaking skin, just hard enough to raise fast healing welts. Brando loved Shaky too. They ate from the same bowl and Brando often picked up Shaky by the scruff of her neck, vigorously shaking her back and forth with tail and legs a blur. Shaky took all this with good nature, but when she tried to walk away, Brando often flattened her with a big paw on her shoulder and picked her up again for more shaking. Mother feared for Shaky's survival as Brando grew. Then Shaky disappeared. Meat was hard to come by for Germans and it wasn't uncommon for them to eat dogs, so there weren't many running loose in the 'hood'. Boxers were rumored to be their favorites. Schaeferhunds were so revered and expensive, however, they hardly ever ended up in a stew. Finally, Mother confessed to having given Shaky to Elsa to dispose of to a hungry family! Tells you something about Maine farm girls, doesn't it, Mike? Anyhow, a few weeks later, as the song goes, 'the cat came back' and there was no more talk of eating Shaky. Brando was so happy to see her he gave her a good shake. One afternoon Johnny and I were walking down Main Street, when we noticed two girls looking in a shop window. The shop wasn't open, but there was a window display of women's clothes announcing the date of a grand opening. Language was not a problem for Americans since most Germans had been taught proper British English in school and spoke it better than we did. If a girl would not speak English, it was assumed that she did not wish to be seen with Americans. These girls appeared to be our age and were nicely dressed. One wore tight gray slacks revealing a most lovely round derriere. This was my first encounter with a German girl, so I was nervous. Still, bolstered by Johnny's courage, I approached. I was relieved that they didn't run away and they did speak English! Lola, the girl in slacks, looked as good from the front and was very charming. 'Whatever Lola wants, Lola gets?' I asked, quoting a popular song. 'Of course', she replied with a demure smile. I was in love. The four of us walked to the park and sat on a bench. It turned out that the girls were not German. They were Lithuanian displaced persons, DP's, living in a nearby compound. Lola's real name was Grarina Benevicus, perhaps the Lithuanian version of my middle family name Benevides? Finally, we asked them to dinner and we went to The Cave, the place to go in Augsburg, appropriately decorated with stalactites and stalagmites. Many GI's were there with young ladies from the same DP compound -which also had an eleven PM curfew for the girls. Unlike the Munich High girls' dorm, however, there were no set visiting hours at the compound and everyone stayed up late partying in the grand living room. So, Lola and I had little time alone except on long walks and chats in the park. To pass our time together, Lola often asked me to make up stories, which I accomplished from the plots of the hundreds of movies I had seen, some six times over while working at the Village Theater. As fate would have it, however, Lola was soon to leave. She was being sponsored by a farm family in Castana Iowa and therefore had to keep herself together, meaning no sex. That's what I meant in response to your birds nest question, Mike. Still, it was a wonderful experience. Our last night together I blew curfew. We went to Lola's room and I didn't get home until day-break. Nothing was said about it! It turned out that one of the band members was dating a girl at the compound too and he had been keeping my father informed about me and Lola. So I guess they cut me some slack that night."

"Did you hear from Lola after she left for Iowa, Captain?"

"Yes, I'm glad to say I did. I was highly honored when Lola wrote that she could be happily married to a boy like me. I hope she was. A boy like me would be lucky to be married to a girl like her."

"Great, Captain, a nice story. I guess your introduction to intimacy with Elaine was good training?"

"Yes, Mike, right on through the next seven years with four more girlfriends and two casual encounters with older German women! Was it my karma or Providence? Still, I rationalized that I was 'keeping my eyes on the prize' - flying. Besides, I further rationalized that intimacy might be the best part of loving for me, Perhaps to be lost after graduating to the 'rough stuff'."

"Quite a summer, Captain."

"Yes, but after Lola left, Johnny's older brother, Kay, arrived and I saw little of Johnny after that. So, I spent a good deal of time riding my bike alone. One day I stopped in the woods and sat on the ground next to my bike twirling a pedal. My thoughts turned to flying, wondering if it would come to pass for me. Soon I was in an imagined conversation with God. 'How badly do you want to fly?' He asked. 'More than anything', I replied. 'More than life?' He asked. 'Yes', I said. 'Suppose I tell you that if you fly, within ten years as a pilot you will have to sacrifice your life in combat to save a comrade. Would you do that?' God asked. "Yes I would, God' I said."

"Well, Captain, you did fly, and I see you are still living?"

"Thankfully yes, Mike, but the dramatic rest of that story will come. Summer was over and it was time to go back to school for my senior year. There was such a high turnover of students during the summer that I was something of an old-timer at the dorm, so I settled in quickly. Of course there was more cohesion among the local Munich kids since they had the summer together. Nevertheless, there was an open welcome and genuine camaraderie among all of us. Army 'brats' truly are a uniquely outstanding bunch of highly mature people, Mike. Since there were so many coming and going with such little time to get acquainted, the girls formed a society called the PPD's, 'Puky Peroxided Dames', named for the identifying streak in their hair pretty racy stuff for 1949! One of the PPD functions was to expedite pairing up girls with boyfriends. My PPD designated girlfriend was a lovely tall girl named Virginia 'Ginger' Carmichael, who suited me fine except that she was a dorm girl from Berchtesgarten, so we had little opportunity to get acquainted. Sound familiar? Our only private 'lights out' time together was during a gathering at one of the PPD's homes while the parents were away. Since we were virtual strangers, it was rather awkward. At the Winter Formal dance, December 21st 1949, I wrote in Ginger's dance card, 'Ginger, I will remember tonight and you the rest of my life. I think you're the swellest girl I've ever known and I like you very much.' A few days later, Ginger said that she would rather not 'go steady' any longer. Still, there is a photo of us together at the girls' dorm in the yearbook."

"Was that a word-for-word dance card quote, Captain?"

"An exact word-for-word quote, Mike. I wouldn't make up something so corny now."

"Very impressive memory, Captain. How is it that you recall it?"

"I have a good reason to, Mike, as you will see -much later."

"You must have been heart broken when Ginger dumped you."

"I didn't take the heave-ho too hard, Mike. Soon after there was a tug on my jacket sleeve in the school hallway. It was so dark I could barely see that it was Aurelie 'Winky' Jones, a PPD member who wrote the 'In Tune With The Teens' column in the Army's 'Stars and Stripes' newspaper. 'We're having a party at Joan's house Saturday night. Want to go?' she asked. 'I'm supposed to go home this weekend', I replied. 'Call your parents and tell them you're not coming', she said. And so I did! One of my serious flaws with women is that I am easy. All the PPD's except Aurelie were in established relationships. A few had 'gone all the way'. So, shortly after the party began, the other couples drifted off to various rooms and the lights went out. There I was, sitting on a couch in the dark, engaged in heavy petting with a stranger named 'Winky', my new 'steady'.

"Any port in a storm, Captain?"

"Yes, well there wasn't much of a storm, Mike, but it was a hell of a port! Aurelie, a Junior, was a town girl living with her mother, Helen, two younger sisters, baby brother, and step father Clayton, a high-ranking civilian Public Relations Director with the HICOG government who looked exactly like Teddy Roosevelt, in a two story Harlaching mansion. Helen was an exceptionally dynamic, intelligent and interesting woman. She had been a 'professional student' at the University of Chicago during the Depression. That is, she had eight years of college, without earning a degree because she only took courses which interested her. She had authored several published children's books. As it is still, the University of Chicago is regarded the capital of socialism. In Helen's time, intellectuals in many countries cited the Depression as a failure of Capitalism and embraced Communism as the alternative solution. They weren't promoting armed revolution, they just wanted change and were quite open about it. Wendell Wilke, a viable presidential candidate, represented the Socialist Party. Helen was one of those who supported him. After divorcing her husband Mackie, Helen moved to a Commune in Greenwich Village with the girls and came to know most of the famous people associated with the Communist movement. Many of them were later called before the infamous witch-hunt McCarthy Congressional Hearings. By then, however, Helen had married Clayton, bore his son, and moved to Munich. Helen was an avid antique collector and spent every dime to take full advantage of black market opportunities. She warehoused a huge collection of antique art, furniture, silver, crystal, statues, and two Steinway grand pianos enough for three later Vermont auctions to sell the things she didn't wish to keep. Reflecting the financial dedication of her efforts, as well as her past commune lifestyle, Helen reduced family expenses to a bare minimum to finance her black market activities. For example, Aurelie had a winter coat which was obviously made from a white Army hospital blanket. Compared to my quiet ordered existence, Helen's home was total chaos to me, but it seemed to work OK for them. Pretty, Aurelie resembled Audrey Hepburn, though not so thin as she. She was a standout in school society. I was no genius, but I was riding high too. I lettered in football and track, and I was elected President of the Student Council. Aurelie and I were a hot item. For the next three years we spent much of our time together. In the evenings, Aurelie's family retired to an upstairs living room and left us alone downstairs where we turned out the lights for hot and heavy sessions of petting. Aurelie was so passionate that she sometimes fainted. Still, no rough stuff. We were also such fast friends that we were virtually inseparable. Aurelie fit in so well with my friends that they voluntarily included her as one of the 'boys' in our activities. Dave Dickson, a senior Munich resident who seemed destined to be a Supreme Court judge, made a certificate proclaiming me and Aurelie as 'The Duke and Duchess of Harlaching'. The only disagreement Aurelie and I had was that she said she wished to have four children. I wanted no more than one because of the disarray I saw in her home. It was during this time I began sailing. Lake Starnberg, thirty-five miles south of Munich, is at the foot of the snow-capped Bavarian Alps. The yacht club was being used as an Army recreation center, but the Germans operated the marina where we were told that we needed a license to rent a sailboat. I had earned a Red Cross Life-Saving card that summer for a job as lifeguard teaching pre-school kids how to swim at the boy's dorm pool for fifty cents an hour. We successfully convinced the marina manager that my Red Cross card was my sailing qualification. 'Wanderer' was a beautiful thirty-five foot classic varnished wooden hull racer with no engine. So, it was miraculous that we land lubbers were able sail her out of and back into the marina without a scratch. After that, we spent many great summer days sailing Wanderer on the lake. One highlight was a going away party for Dan, who was leaving to attend Army Officer Candidate School. To celebrate the occasion, the five of us bought a forty liter keg of Maibach beer at the Hofbrau brewery, where I had an incident. When we came out of the brewery we found the gate locked where we had entered, so we decided to climb over the iron fence which was about ten feet high with iron spear-like spikes. As I jumped down, my class ring caught on a spike and stripped it off my finger along with a good bit of flesh. It looked so awful that we decided that a trip to the emergency room was in order. The German doctor on duty, who had obviously been through the war, looked at my finger and said 'Ach, superficial vound'. He simply wrapped it up, and told me to come back in a few days. When I did, the Army doctor was horrified when he unwrapped it. 'My God, who did this?' he exclaimed. Nevertheless, it healed well, but if that ring had been a little stronger, I would have lost the finger. Anyhow, the five of us set out to sea aboard Wanderer, provisioned with the forty litre keg, more than two gallons each for Pete, Chuck, Les, Dan and me with no food aboard. After several hours, Chuck noticed that we were sailing inside the course of a yacht race. When a girl on one of the boats waved back to him, we joined the race. We saw that we weren't gaining, so we began cutting inside the race course buoys. Even then, we fell so far behind that we gave up pursuit, tied the mainsheet to the tiller, and tacked and jibed around in circles with no one at the helm which was fortunate because on one circle we discovered Chuck in the water and hauled him back aboard. Since no one saw him fall over the side, Chuck would undoubtedly have drowned in the icy water if we had sailed a straight line. I still have photos of the event, but the only thing I remember after that was that each of us ordered two big hamburgers when we sailed back to the Club, whereupon Pete, Chuck, and Dan passed out cold, sprawled on the lawn, leaving Les and me to eat ten burgers, which of course made us very sick. American youth at our finest hour. One Sunday Aurelie and I found that someone had run Wanderer over an underwater piling and sunk, so we rented a row boat instead. We were more than a mile from the marina when a sudden vicious thunder storm swept down on us from over the mountains. In a flash we were in the midst of lightning and blinding rain driven by forty knot winds. It took all my strength on a single oar on one side to keep us pointed toward the marina. Still, we were being blown farther away as the waves built higher and higher. I waved to a passing motor boat which came by to toss us a tow line; however, our elation was short lived. We were towed at such high speed that our bow rose so high that water came in over the transom. When I went forward to try to level the boat and ask our rescuers to slow down, the entire row boat dove under water and broke the tow line. Aurelie went under with it, but I got a glimpse of her hair on the surface before she sank and pulled her up as the power boat circled back to help us aboard. After they dropped us off at the Club and just as we approached an iron bridge across the docks, it was struck by lightning. Some people came to help me get Aurelie to the bar. She was shivering hard and began to go into shock when she overheard that a five year old boy had been lost over the side from a sail boat in the storm. She soon recovered though when we wrapped her up in towels and blankets and got a few shots of brandy into her."

"Well, Captain, that was quite an introduction to life at sea. I see why you are so thankful for Jean's interventions. Did you live in the dorm the rest of your time in Germany?"

"No, Mike. The time line is fuzzy in my memory about my parent's movements in Germany, but briefly during my senior year, Father was transferred to Munich to take over a band from a drunk. Just a short aside about Father's leadership style. For six months in a row before he arrived, the Munich band had been awarded a live goat presented to the unit with the highest VD rate. In his first meeting with them in the Band room, Father stood before the men with a straight razor in his hand and announced that the next man to contract VD in his band would lose his dick. The following month the goat went to another unit and never returned. Father had a way of convincing men that he was dead serious and entirely capable of carrying out such threats."

"I see that your father did not subscribe to a 'theory Y' outlook on people as being honest, trustworthy, self-actualized, hard-working, and intelligent!"

"True, that's the way things were done in the Army then. Father was a 'theory X' person for sure which says people are basically stupid, lazy, and dishonest. He epitomized the old traditional 'tough but fair' dog-face sergeant. He was an always-right perfectionist disciplinarian. His approach to leadership was to make his bands so outstanding and successful, no matter how much ass-busting it took, that his men were proud to be in his bands. It didn't work that way for me. Though I admired and respected him in some ways, I felt no affection for him. If he stayed married to Mother for my sake, as he claimed, he blew that part of his life away."

"Frankly Captain, the way I see it, your father provided you with security, as well as strong valuable guidance and role model example at just the right times in your life."

"Quite true, Mike, as far as that goes. I was damned fortunate to have a good role model. So, I won't defend my feelings further now. How could I, you weren't there, were you?"

"Sorry, Captain. Honestly, I do not mean to be judgmental. Please understand that some questions are meant to draw out some deeper emotions. I guess it's my court room experience backing up on me. Sometimes it is necessary to bear down on witnesses when you're going for the truth."

"Come on Mike, that sounds good, but it's not about truth in a court room. It's about badgering a witness to win a case, isn't it?"

"Sometimes, but not always. I'll keep in mind that we are not in court."

"I've touched a nerve here, haven't I, Mike?"

"Alright, Captain, if you wish. I didn't arrive here with a high degree of either affection or animosity. How could I? I only saw you several times and you never did anything to cause me to believe you cared any more about me than your father did for you. So, I had reason for feeling the same about you. The revelation for me was when I had pretty much the same relationship with my own kids. Hopefully now you will find some benefit in telling your story. The most valuable possession to many of us old guys is our stories, but no one wants to hear them. This is different, I truly do want to hear them. Shall we move on?"

"Not quite yet Mike. I am long retired from tilting with windmills and those who do. As I told you, I have no regrets. One psychologist, who once wrote about men as fathers, relative to women as mothers, summarized it this way. Mother's love is constant, father's love is earned. Even the mother of a serial killer will always love and forgive her son unconditionally, no matter what. Not so the father who would more likely support execution of the s.o.b. One reason women were denied the vote for most of our history was the agreement that they tended to see the world through a kitchen window with the eyes of children, and are more likely to be ruled by irrational emotions. Women are genetically destined to bear and love children. Men, on the other hand, are designed to fight, hunt, and chase girls. Simple as that, just the way God created us. Marriage is a social invention mostly for the purpose of raising children. The awful truth is that once dad has done his impregnation and security duties, mother naturally turns her love and attention to her children and shuts down on the old man in the inevitably correct expectation that he will stray to other beds, thereby socially justifying herself in cleaning him out in court. In Latin countries where divorce may not be considered an option, and after good Catholic mothers bear all the children they can stand, it's not unusual for fathers to take a mistress. As long as he's discreet about it, mother gives tacit approval. So, Mike, I believe that infidelity and divorce is frequently not the husband's decision, though he may well not recognize it because of the guilt and punishment assigned to him. Another psychologist wrote that whereas boys once traditionally grew up alongside their fathers on the family farm or apprenticed in his profession, the industrial revolution resulted in separation between father and son, leaving boys in a female dominated environment at home and school. With less male identity, men tend to spend their lives with women like their mothers. But enough of that speech. I am grateful to have the opportunity to tell my story. I welcome your challenges too, Mike, as long as your expectations are realistic. After all, we are just two guys who happen to be related, trying to do our best in life. Now, where were we?"

"OK, Captain, I'm glad for your views, which may be typical of fighter pilots. Nevertheless, my sense of it is that is only the public side of you and that there is, or once was, a warmer side."

"If so, Mike, I lost touch with it. A saying in naval aviation is that 'everyone shits on the good guy'. There's no place for good guys in the cockpit of a fighter. The grizzly truth is that most aerial combat victories are won by pilots who sneak up on their victims and shoot them in the back without them even knowing there was someone behind them. I must admit, however, that one value of recalling my youth now does stir up innocent passions and dreams. However chauvinistic some of my views may sound, I did once strongly believe that there was no higher purpose in life than to achieve a lasting loving relationship. When I found myself in unhappy situations where that was not possible, I resumed the search. My own fault was in making wrong choices. I was too easy going into relationships, but too demanding in expectations once in them. The fact is, however, that there is no way to predict how a marriage will work until you're into it, is there? So I was married six times; however, note the fact that I averaged twelve years and tried not to repeat the mistake of marrying the same type of woman twice. As Elizabeth Taylor once said, 'At least I .was honest enough to marry them all.'"

"I can relate to that, Captain. Back to Munich in 1950, your senior year? You said that your father was transferred to Munich, so you had to leave the dorm to live with them. Back to captivity and an eleven o'clock curfew?"

"Yes, but since I had Aurelie in my life most of the time, it didn't seem bad this time. The days flew by so fast, I cannot recall details now, but it was a good year. Thanks to Clayton's position, we saw all the Munich Opera productions from Hitler's box. Our senior class trip was a voyage down the Rhine River aboard Hitler's yacht. Before graduation, however, Father was transferred back to Augsburg and I went back to the dorm. First, another story about Father. Although he was still a Master Sergeant, he had served as the Bandleader in his two previous assignments, which is a Warrant Officer's job. When Father checked in at Augsburg, he discovered that there was a Captain in another unit who had been assigned administrative command of the band. Father immediately went to General Abrams' office and demanded reassignment. If Father was not to be THE Commanding Officer, he wanted no part of it. After considering the demand, General Abrams dismissed Father with the promise to take care of relieving the Captain and went back to reading. When the General looked up again, Father was still standing there. 'I said I'll take care of it Sergeant. Dismissed!' Father replied, 'General, I'm not leaving until you tell the Captain he is relieved of responsibility for the band.' General Abrams called in his Orderly and told him to inform the Captain he had been relieved, and said to Father, 'I admire your spunk, Sergeant'. They became good friends. Abrams was determined to have Father promoted to Warrant Officer, but Father could not pass the bandleader physical exam because of an eardrum punctured in childhood. Father said he also didn't want the promotion because it would mean a sixty dollar pay cut. General Abrams took out his wallet and said he would make up the difference! It wasn't just about the pay though. Because Warrants were socially considered commissioned officers in the Army, promotion would entail all the mandatory social obligations for both of my parents. Father was uncomfortable with that prospect because of his Portuguese accent and his tenth grade education. Mother, in spite of her similar education however, was not so socially unsure of herself and loved the idea of moving up from 'enlisted men and their wives', to 'Officers and their Ladies'. Eventually, General Abrams was successful in Father's promotion. During that second time in Augsburg, Brando and I went to police dog training school at a field with bombed out buildings and craters. I was given bean bags with my scent which I left at various locations across the field and hid in a crater while Brando tracked me down. He learned to trot away from me as long as I pointed with my arm held out. When I dropped my arm, Brando stopped, turned and sat facing me until I put my hand on my chest, whereupon he ran to me and sat at my feet facing me. Of course, he also trained for the usual tasks like walking very close beside me without a leash. When I stopped, he sat in place for as long as I stood there. Brando was magnificent and we loved every minute of it, despite Brando's failure to complete the certification because of his fear of gunfire and a diagnosed blood anemia. I traveled a good bit that year too, but let's do the next chapter on that. It's too much to include in this one. Also coincidental that summer was the expansion of the University of Maryland Overseas Extension to a full-time junior college program in Munich. The Maryland overseas extension had been established because the Services were pushing officers without degrees to get one. Maryland conducted accelerated six week classes in non-lab arts and science courses at US bases from England to Africa. Maryland was able to attract outstanding professors because they could transfer from one base to another as often as every six weeks, expenses paid, living in Bachelor Officers Quarters, dining in the Officers Club, and with PX and commissary privileges. It was an outstanding opportunity for them to see Europe and get paid for it! The Munich program was expanded to a day program to accommodate dependents who had graduated high school and were remaining in Germany until their fathers were transferred back to the US. Although the Korean War was hot and heavy, dependent boys living outside the US were not required to register for the draft. Besides, like the faculty, out of town students were also dormitoried at the BOQ and then of course, Aurelie was still at home during her senior year at Munich High. So, there were lots of good reasons for attending UM Munich. It wouldn't be a financial burden to my parents either since I paid my tuition with the savings from my five years of working Georgia jobs. My escape was back on track better than I ever dreamed! Fifty five of us enrolled in that first class. Many had been out of high school more than a year and there were nearly the same number of men and women in the BOQ building we had to ourselves. The women had the entire second floor and we had the third floor, two to a room without supervision of any kind! For the most part, the women dated officers and the men dated German girls. Kenny, a pretty good trumpet player, got a running start at becoming an alcoholic. One evening we carried him to his desk before class and put a pencil in his hand as he stared unblinking off into space. Another classmate celebrated his birthday with nineteen shots of cognac. We were not sure he was still living when we deposited him on his bathroom floor next to the john. Things started to get out of hand when one of the men's rooms was furnished with wall-to-wall mattresses for group gropes with frauleins. One night my room-mate, Dick, woke me up with a nude girl standing next to him and he asked if I would care to have her which I politely declined, recalling Father's razor. One of our dorm mates was a fourteen year old black boy from Texas named Ulysses. His father was an education director with the HICOG government. Ulysses had been educated at home and had never attended public schools. His immaturity, education and cultural background had not in any way prepared him for us. He was so ignorant and superstitious that we called him 'Useless'. When someone got a rubber Frankenstein mask, an idea was born. One night we told Useless that a criminally insane and armed inmate had escaped and was last seen somewhere on base. I guess we overdid it because Useless wouldn't go to sleep. He came into the study room every few minutes in his pajamas with a steel pipe, scared to death. When it looked like he was going to stay up all night, we all gave up and went to bed. Later, someone came to wake me up Useless had finally gone to sleep. So I got into costume with the mask, trench coat, scarf, and gloves. We fired a blank pistol in the hallway and there was lots of shouting as I stomped toward Useless' room. Because he had the pipe and we needed some light, another guy ran into the room ahead of me with a flashlight. I threw open Useless' door and the flashlight provided perfect illumination for my mask. Useless froze with eyes wider open than I ever imagined possible. Then he jumped under his blanket and covered himself up, screaming at the top of his lungs. There were no repercussions from his father except that soon after Ulysses left school. There was one other mask event though. One night I wore it down the middle of a dimly lit street off base with a few of my buddies out of sight. As I approached a streetlight, a German on a bicycle came toward me. When he was close enough to see the mask, he did something I never saw another German bike rider do. With an expression of total horror, he stood up on the pedals and sped quickly down the street. Fortunately, sanity soon overcame the frivolity and life settled into a reasonable academic atmosphere. Dick and I even built a couple of model airplanes. His was an original free-flight model designed to resemble a hawk. It successfully flew out of sight on its first flight because we put too much fuel in it. The faculty and the courses were a great intellectual awakening for me. For lack of anything better, I was a history major. Many of the faculty stayed on at Munich rather than moving to other bases, so we were pretty much a big happy family. Several of them regularly dined with us and even week-ended with us at the Garmisch ski resort atop a two and a half hour tunneled cog rail ride inside the mountain to the top of the Zugspitz which had a hotel with the highest bar in Europe. It was operated for the Army, so rooms were a dollar a night, ski equipment was seventy-five cents a day, and drinks were a quarter. At that altitude, far above the tree-line four thousand feet straight down to the valley on the east side, it didn't take many drinks to do the job. Aurelie and I shared a room on these superb weekends and it was great to spend all night alone without her family nearby. Needless to say, there were times when our self-imposed celibacy nearly went by the board. The Zugspitz was a great place to learn to ski. The southwestern side was a shallow slope without rocks or trees. There was no lift, so we had to climb up to the edge of the cliff, point our skis down the slope and just go straight, fast as hell until we fell. Because of the altitude, we could still ski in May in shirt sleeves. By then there was a thick crust of snow on the surface which skis could not penetrate, so we really went fast as hell then. Problem was, if you fell on an elbow with your sleeves rolled up, the crust would badly scratch up an arm. One memory that stands out was the time the psychology professor and I braved a blizzard that was blowing so hard we had to crawl up to the top. Blowing snow so limited visibility that we came within a foot of crawling off that four thousand foot cliff. Hot buttered rums at the bar tasted especially good after that adventure. In February 1951 I went to Frankfurt to take the physical exam for the Navy ROTC scholarship, which amounted to tuition, books, fees, uniforms, and one hundred dollars a month to any of the fifty-five best universities in the US and a regular commission on graduation. I was so nervous about the eye exam that my armpits dripped sweat like a leaky faucet, even though I was sitting on a table in my underwear with the windows wide open. I flunked the exam because my blood pressure was over two hundred. I was convinced that my high blood pressure was due to a sympathetic nervous reaction, so I checked into Munich Army Hospital for a heart check where they documented my heart condition every hour for three days. Thankfully, it was normal. The following year I returned for another try. My pressure was still above normal, but I had a formal statement from an Army doctor to Navy summarizing my hospital checks. When I appeared before a review board I was asked why I wanted to join the Navy. I said that I wanted to fly. I was asked why I didn't join the Air Force. I couldn't very well say that it was because Air Force did not offer a scholarship, so I said that I also wanted to go to sea. I was selected as an Alternate, so I had little hope of continuing college when we returned to the US. My backup plan was to apply for the Naval Aviation Cadet, NAVCAD, program, which required only two years of college, but with my blood pressure problem I could no longer count on ever getting a pilot's license much less a Navy scholarship. I did not have the slightest idea of a backup career plan or ambition. My future looked bleak indeed. Aurelie's mother, Helen, must have believed I was no longer a viable prospect, and told my parents hat I was seeing too much of Aurelie. After all, I was only the son of an uneducated immigrant enlisted man and his 'wife'. My parents, bless their hearts, blew Helen off by telling her she should settle the matter with her daughter, they would not tell me who to see. This was the first indication I had of Helen's disapproval, though there were two related mysteries I did not understand until years later. Since Clayton was with the State Department, they had thirty day annual vacations in the US for which they rated trans-Atlantic passages aboard luxury liners like SS United States. Aurelie returned from her 1950 summer devastated. She cried a lot, but refused to say what had happened except that she had a very bad encounter with her father Mackie when she visited him in New York. Whatever had happened, the effects did not go away. I knew it was serious and I had a nagging feeling that it was important to our relationship, but Aurelie would not reveal it until 1968. The other mystery was my misgivings about Clayton's character, although I couldn't pinpoint any reason for it. Then, as the time for us to leave Germany approached, the sky brightened for me. A Navy letter arrived congratulating me for becoming a Primary Candidate for the NROTC scholarship. I was to go to the University of New Mexico at Albuquerque the coming school year on a four year scholarship. Father was so impressed that he actually shook my hand, congratulating me for doing it all on my own. Navy had accepted that my high blood pressure was not serious, so there was hope for the best. Thank God, I was back on track. A good stopping point before talking about travels in Europe, Mike. Don't you have to tell Georgie you are taking the Major's room?"

"Yes, Captain, and I want to start moving in this evening and checkout at the Inn after breakfast there in the morning. So, I'll see you at ten in the morning at your spot at the end of the yellow brick sidewalk?"

"OK, Mike, See you there.'

Puppy Brando, Augsburg 1949

Big Brando & Mom 1950

Me & Mom, Munich 1950

Carin "Ginger" Carmichael
Munich High 1950 year book

My first command at sea, with Pete, Dan & Chuck
Wanderer, Lake Starnberg, Bavaria, 1950

Lake Starnberg

9

OBSERVATION REVEALED

"Morning Mike, did you get moved into the Major's room?"

"Good morning, Captain, sorry I'm late. Yes I'm moved, but I have some settling in yet to do....Think it might rain"?

"Not according to the forecast, but the satellite picture shows a warm front approaching from the southwest, so an afternoon thunderstorm wouldn't be a surprise."

"Last night I dreamed of flying in one of those towering cumulus clouds you described, Captain, most likely inspired by our Ximango flight. What a wild ride and fascinating adventure. The popping out into the 'sky-scape' was priceless. Not much compared to your actual flights in them though, I suppose."

"I'd be the last to put down flying dreams, Mike."

"Ah yes, dreams can take us anywhere without limits, can't they Captain? Especially your flying dreams, and there's often such a thin line between them and reality."

"Yes Mike. After all, some of the most significant events of our lives occur entirely within our own minds. Our imaginations, inspirations, and dreams can become important realities."

"As with levitation, Captain?"

"I think so, Mike, but you might say I'm an eccentric to believe that."

"Not at all, Captain. Doesn't everyone strongly believe in many things they have never seen or experienced firsthand which defy scientific proof, God for example? Wouldn't life have much less meaning without dreams, aspirations, hopes, faith, and beliefs? Weren't many great scientific discoveries inspired, born, and nurtured inside scientists' heads? I happen to believe in levitation too, Captain."

"Have you dreamed of it, Mike?"

"More than that, Captain. I think I witnessed it."

"Really, Mike, you think you witnessed levitation? Tell me about it."

"I once saw a man appear to lift himself several feet out of his chair."

"What do you mean appear to, Mike?"

"Well, there was a blanket over him and I couldn't see the space between him and his chair."

"Was this some kind of carnival sideshow, magic act, or film?"

"No Captain. There was no one else around and I'm sure the man didn't know I saw him. There was no discernible reason I could see for him to be putting on an act."

"What happened then, Mike?"

"Nothing. I was so astonished I didn't know what to do. As a stranger, I didn't want to challenge him or intrude on his privacy, so I just watched and did nothing."

"Did you ever go back?"

"Yes, Captain, but that was the only time I ever witnessed the event. Nevertheless, I truly believe that what I saw was genuine levitation."

"Mike, does this have anything to do with what you meant when you said you had something to share with me when you first arrived?"

"Yes, Captain."

"There's more to it then, isn't there?"

"Yes Captain. That man was you. You weren't dreaming. You were actually flying, just as you described your dream to me."

A long silence followed.

"Well well, a good thing I didn't try to fly too far or too high, wasn't it, Mike? Why didn't you tell me this before, and how do I know you're not putting me on? After all, you were deceptive about your identity and there is no proof of your story."

"Captain, just as I have no proof, neither do I have any reason to fabricate it. I didn't tell you before because I hoped you might eventually trust me enough to help you learn to consciously achieve your lifelong goal of flying."

Another long curtain of silence fell between them. Instead of elation, as might be expected with such incredibly good news, the Captain seemed to be totally deflated. He just sat with his head bowed and his hands tightly clasped, perhaps in prayer.

"Mike, this just became a long day for me. I believe what you say, but I need a time out now to ponder this. I see that we can expect some weather through here this afternoon, so take the rest of the day off to get settled in your new quarters while I gather my thoughts and consider how to proceed from here, OK?"

"A good idea, Captain, I'll await your call for our next meeting."

When the Captain did not come to the dining room for dinner, Mike consulted Georgie.

"The Captain said he would have dinner in his room this evening, Mike. That's not unusual for him. He has a small kitchenette and he keeps several pots of spaghetti and stew he made in his freezer for such times as special events in the dining room in the evening, like birthday or anniversary frivolities. I hope there's nothing wrong?"

"No, Georgie. We were at a point in his story where he wanted to take a break. Plus, the rain was approaching and I needed to settle in and make some notes. I'm really happy with the room and this place altogether. You do an outstanding job managing it. In case he hasn't told you so, the Captain loves it here too."

"That's good to hear, Mike. I mostly have to judge how we're doing by the number of complaints. It goes with the territory in this business and I know the Captain wouldn't be bashful about offering 'suggestions' if he was unhappy with us. Like him, most of the men here achieved positions of authority in their professions. They were accustomed to being in charge, plus living in their own homes where things were done their way, so they are more than 'helpful' on occasion."

"I'm sure you get lots of 'rudder signals', Georgie, not to mention government regulations to deal with. Coming to a place like this may be one of the hardest adjustments a person ever has to make. I can see that it would be like being guest in a stranger's home and having nothing meaningful to do or contribute. Did you ever see the British comedy series about a retirement home, 'Waiting for God?'"

"Oh yes Mike, we have the entire series on DVD in our library. I love it, even though it portrays the home's manager as a greedy, selfish jerk, but the folks here mostly don't care for it. They complain about the British accents being difficult to understand, but I believe the scenes simply strike nerves too close to 'home' to be funny to them. As Garrison Kiellor would say about aging, 'It's not for the timid.' Especially now that medical science has given us a life expectancy of nearly a century. Our social systems haven't kept up, so we spend a third or more of our lives in retirement, with a sixty-five percent probability of our final three years in an assisted living, memory care, or nursing home. Before coming here, I worked at another retirement community operated by our parent company. which is a much grander scale facility than this one. There they have four types of accommodations, two and three bedroom duplex homes, full size apartments, smaller assisted living apartments, and nursing care rooms in what is virtually a hospital. Heritage Oaks has a single large buffet style dining room, which doesn't work very well for physically impaired seniors, however, there is another smaller sit-down dining room at the apartment building. The idea there is for seniors to begin easing into the assisted life style early on, rather than wait for drastic changes later. So, those communities prefer not to take in older folks and discourage them by charging an exorbitantly high, non-refundable, entry fee."

"Fenceless cul-de-sac retirement communities don't appeal to me. There's too much of everyone getting in each other's face. I guess they are OK for highly gregarious people though, who are the ones who adapt best to places like this. Like the Captain, I'd rather put it off as long as possible. He was retired from the Navy in 1986 with over thirty years active service when he was only fifty-three years old. His father enlisted in the Army in 1924 at age eighteen, and retired at age forty-eight. He passed nearly forty years later. So, both my father and grandfather spent close to half their lives in retirement. It's not easy for middle-aged band leaders and fighter pilots to begin new careers at age fifty, Georgie. Fortunately, the Captain saw the 'writing on the wall' after seeing his father flounder for a while before he went into his lawn mower repair shop at Pacific Beach, so he was well prepared for retirement with lots of interests and hobbies."

"Yes, Mike, the Captain seems to have maintained a more positive and optimistic outlook than most folks I know. At his age, he is extremely fortunate to be as alert and healthy as he is."

"Amen to that, Georgie. Naturally, I didn't know what to expect, so I am elated to find him in such good shape and with a clear memory of his past."

"Indeed, Mike, though I'm sure that writing his memoirs has helped a lot with that."

"Oh? He didn't mention that. He just said that he wanted to write his autobiography, but had been too busy living it.

"Oh dear, Mike, I'm afraid I may have spoken out of turn, though he didn't indicate that it was not to be mentioned to anyone."

"No problem, Georgie, I assure you. It makes me feel better about my identity deception. Besides, his writing has obviously made it much easier for him to tell his story and for me to 'co-author' it. The important thing is to get it into print. Hopefully, he will also agree to narrating it on CD or DVD."

"Good idea, Mike. That would especially benefit his children and grandchildren who barely know him."

"Gives him something to look forward to also, doesn't it? This project reminds me of an outstanding film, 'Little Big Man', starring Dustin Hoffman."

"Yes, we have that in our library too. It gets shown at least once a year. I think it's also one of the Captains favorites. The situation was much the same as yours, isn't it -a reporter interviewing the very old last survivor of Custer's Last Stand? The best therapy there is for old folks is to find an interested ear to tell their stories to. Unfortunately, that rarely happens, so we need to encourage more seniors to write their memoirs. We have had some success with volunteer student's assistance in recording oral histories, but it takes a special talent to be accepted and to do it well. Perhaps you should consider volunteering your services with others here after finishing the Captain's story."

"Georgie, at the rate we are going, I'll be lucky if I live long enough to finish the Captain's story!"

10

EUROPEAN TRAVELS & PATERNAL KIN

"Good morning, Mike, hope I didn't call too early. I wanted to catch you before breakfast."
"Not too early, Captain, I've been up for some time. Will you be having breakfast in the dining room?"

"Not this morning, that's why I called. I'm just having cereal and coffee here. Can we meet at the usual place about ten?

"Sure, Captain, see you there." Mike was relieved by the positive sound of his voice and arrived at their park bench ahead of the Captain, but soon saw him approach down the yellow brick sidewalk, pushing his wheelchair at a good clip, using it like a walker.

"Captain, you make good use of that chair!"

"Yeah, you should see me in Walmart with a shopping cart. I go through that place like shit through a goose. Listen, Mike, I've thought it through. First, it's a good thing that it was you to witness my flight and that no one else knows. I have been extremely fortunate to have a number of such providential events in my life. By the way, as you will see when we get to 1969, 'providence' in my life is a wonderful lady named Jean that's all I'll say about her for now. Second, knowing now that I have actually achieved levitation certainly gives new meaning to dreams come true; however, I don't see that I can do much more about it except await my next flying dream and hope that I can progress toward a transition to consciousness without losing concentration. Your part is to keep an eye on me as we press on with this interview and hope it leads to something."

"Sounds good to me, Captain. With Jean's help, I'm sure you shall succeed. Have you considered another try at returning to your childhood dream device of rolling your head back and forth on your pillow at night? It worked for you then to control your dreams, perhaps it could work even better now that you know what is possible."

"Good idea, Mike. I'll work on it, but my neck doesn't like that kind of exercise these days. I have a constant pain and restricted movement, I think caused when I relaxed too much on a carrier landing and my head snapped forward, aided by the weight of my helmet. Meanwhile, as I recall, we were going to talk about travels in Europe."

"Right Captain, the recorder is running."

"In the summer of '50 I rode with my parents to Paris. Father was going to the Paris factory for a Selmer trumpet because they were hard to find. Paris was incredible, Mike. Unlike Venice, brochures or travel documentaries could not describe it. You simply had to go there to experience the unique atmosphere, culture, spirit, ambiance, life-style, or whatever it's called. For me, the most notable feature of Paris, especially after Georgia and Germany, were the gorgeous high fashion women: fashion being bra-less very low neck lines virtually down to the waist. It was a common sight to see couples kissing and hugging on street benches. Several times I saw those couples apparently meet for the first time. The scene was stark contrast to Munich where women were typically stocky, without make-up, bundled up in drab tones of gray and brown, unshaved legs or underarms, and natural body odors in preference to perfume. The Selmer factory told Father they were making instruments for export only, so he set out to find a used one in a music shop. This occupied most of his time, leaving Mother and me on our own to tour the Eiffel Tower, Notre Dame Cathedral, museums, and art galleries. Of course we were not spared Father's frustration and impatience with his unsuccessful trumpet search, so Mother and I retaliated as a team to make life even more difficult for him. Looking back on a photo he took of Mother and me sitting on the cement steps of a museum, pouting, Father had more of a sense of humor about it than I gave him credit for. Needless to say, since I had no time on my own, my Paris adventure was limited to day tours. Nevertheless, I was able to visit Harry's New York Bar just long enough to join the International Bar Fly association to get the manual, directory, and famous fly-on-a-bar lapel pin so prized by everyone at Munich High. At that time, there was an IBF bar in many major cities on the planet, but it was twenty years before I found another one– and that turned out to be an embarrassing event I'll tell about later."

"I imagine the French were much friendlier to Americans following their liberation from the Nazi's than they are now, Captain?"

"I'd say they were only less unfriendly, Mike. The French have always been so stuck on themselves they can barely stand each other. Nevertheless, Paris was the most memorable city I ever visited. Frenchmen had some justification for their superior attitude, though no excuse for their unpatriotic history, I'd say."

"Where next, Captain?"

"My friend Pete Sell, was born in China. His father was a Lutheran missionary there until the Jap invasion was imminent. Since he spoke all twenty-six dialects of the Chinese language,

Pete's father received a direct officer commission into the Office of Naval Intelligence and served throughout the war. After the war, Pete went back to China on his own, working for the USO at the Yangtze River US Navy patrol boat base until the communist revolution. When Pete found his White Russian girlfriend shot dead in the woods, he decided it was time to leave China to rejoin his parents and sister in Munich where his father worked for the International Refugee Organization which was engaged in resettling Iron Curtain refugees. My father firmly believed, however, that Pete's father was actually a spy. I don't know why Pete latched on to me, but he was very idealistic about friendship. We once went on a week-long camping trip in the Bavarian Alps where, at Pete's initiative after consuming copious quantities of high altitude beverages, we sliced our forearms with a knife and mixed our blood in a 'blood brother' Roman hand shake ceremony and passed out. I still bear the scar. It was a bizarre experience for me, Mike, considering where I came from emotionally. I just went along with it, hoping I'd learn something about connecting with people. In the summer of '50 I was invited to ride with Pete and his family on a trip to Trieste and Venice. We over-nighted in Vienna where Pete's father attended a smoke-filled room meeting. The plan was to drive to Trieste through Yugoslavia which was still a communist country under Tito, but had recently opened its borders slightly to tourism. When we reached the frontier in a desolate area, however, we found only a formidable guard post and barrier. It was obvious that no traffic had passed this post in many years, as there were weeds growing out of large cracks in the road. We were adamantly refused entrance on the pretext that we did not have a carnet for the car as a bond against selling it. So, we drove to Trieste via Italy. At that time, the Free Territory of Trieste was an important sea port at the north end of the Adriatic Sea which was a hot spot of political stress because of contention for it between Italy and Yugoslavia. We were there only two days, but Pete and I covered most of the city by foot. I remember Trieste mostly for the drive down the cliffs surrounding the port, and a toothless old lady in a doorway who propositioned us and was greatly insulted when we declined. Next were three fascinating days in Venice, a uniquely beautiful city that I can say no more about than you already know from travel documentaries. The first night there we ordered chicken at a very posh Lido restaurant. Instead, they brought us a huge bowl of spaghetti. We didn't want to make a fuss by sending it back, so we stuffed ourselves then came the chicken! Spaghetti was the appetizer. On another night we went out in the harbor on a gondola where we joined many others lit up with lanterns for a concert by opera stars. Of course, Saint Mark's Cathedral and square was fascinating, but even more impressive to me was a museum collection of medieval armor which seemed alive and I felt strangely transported to those days. Jean offered a possible explanation in 1969. From Venice we stopped in Cortina, a charming Italian Alps ski resort. As Pete and I walked down this quaint city's sidewalk, a most attractive woman at least ten years my senior came toward us, so I smiled and said hello. As we passed, she raised her eyebrows, smiled broadly, and said hello very provocatively back to me over her shoulder. It was one of those 'be careful what you wish for' events, Mike. I didn't have a clue what to do next, so I just quickened my step. Had she stopped, I probably would have run. On the long climb up the Alps from Cortina, the car over-heated to the point we could hear engine oil sizzling like a frying pan, so we had to push it the rest of the way to the top of the Alps. Despite that, it was a wonderful trip. Now I want to comment further on my friendship with Pete. I'm at a crossroads choice about how much to tell in this story. There are things about me which may not serve good purpose to tell to people who would rather not know. Like the story about an evangelist revival where the preacher was encouraging the sinners in his congregation to come forward for salvation through confession. 'Tell it, brothers and sisters,' says the preacher, 'come forward now and confess your sins to the Almighty and all here that you may be saved. Tell it, tell it now brothers and sisters. TELL it.' So, this man comes forward, falls on his knees, and cries, 'Oh God, I am a miserable and unworthy sinner.' 'Yes brother, tell it now, tell it', said the preacher. 'Oh lord, I had sex with my neighbor's wife', said the sinner. 'YES, brother, tell it, TELL it!' said the preacher. 'And I had sex with my neighbor's teenage daughter', said the sinner. 'YES, brother, TELL IT, TELL IT.' 'And I had sex with my neighbor too', said the sinner. 'YES, YES, YES, brother, TELL IT, TELL IT' said the preacher.' And then I had sex with my neighbor's dog.' said the sinner. The preacher stopped and finally said, 'Brother, I don't believe I would have told that.'

"I see your point, Captain. Why tell your readers things about you they would rather not know? On the other hand, leaving out the negatives is dishonestly one-sided, isn't it? I guess it comes down to how far you want to reach out to your readers. Perhaps your kids would be disappointed, but considering your history in family relations, why should that really matter to you now? So what was it, Captain? Tell it, tell it, did you have sex with Pete's dog?"

"That's my boy, chip off the old block, aren't you, Mike?"

"Just comes natural, doesn't it?"

"For you maybe, but I had to work really hard at it. I came in second place in the '1984 Asshole of the Year' vote because I was not a quintessential asshole like the winner, but we'll get to that another time. To answer the question though, no, I didn't screw Pete's dog, but you might have thought I had as far as he was concerned. Our friendship jumped the track after our high school graduation train trip to board Hitler's yacht for the Rhine River cruise. One of the Pullman compartments was hosting a 'reception' with lots of booze. Big deal like we hadn't all had free access to alcohol all along. But this was a school sponsored event and the chaperone was Rex Gleason, our Principal. We called Rex 'Rote-A-Bean' which we understood was German for 'little red-headed fairy' entirely appropriate to his feminine and effete academic mannerisms. I believe Rex was disappointed that I had defeated his favored candidate in the vote for President of the Student Council, so he pursued the train drinking caper to boot me out, though he had no direct evidence. He had popped into the train compartment after Pete and I left, so he could only assume that we had been there too. When questioned, Pete confessed, being the idealistic citizen he was. Then Rote-a-Bean called me into interrogation with Pete present. I saw no gain for anyone in confessing, so I denied it, as Pete sat silent and stone-faced. So, Rote-a-Bean could only take satisfaction in breaking up Pete's friendship with me, for it was a long time before Pete spoke to me again. Personally, I didn't give a damn. If that's what 'friendship' was about, I was better off without it. So I just kept on keeping on."

"How do you feel about it now?"

"I wouldn't be recalling it now unless there weren't some sadness, but these are things we need to forgive ourselves and others for. There's no good in bearing baggage, is there?"

"Not if the learning experience was beneficial. I take it the matter didn't resolve itself between you?

"No it didn't. Soon after, Pete went to work for Radio Free Europe in Munich. Then he left for Muhlenberg College in Pennsylvania where he had been awarded a full scholarship by an anonymous sponsor. My father was right about Pete's father being a spy though, he returned to a Navy Admiral's uniform as the Director of the Office of Naval Intelligence."

"Did that surprise you, Captain?

"Yes it did, Mike, on two levels. First, that my father was so sure of it without knowing any more about Pete's father than what I told him. Second, that there was nothing about the Admiral's demeanor or appearance to cause me to think he was anything more than what he said he was-an ordinary paunchy rosy-cheeked middle-aged Lutheran minister doing missionary work."

"I guess he was good at spying, and that's why he was an Admiral?"

"True. One thing I enjoyed most about the Navy was the informality of plain folks dedicated to getting the job done with little regard for rank or regulations."

"Surprisingly different from the perception most people have of a rigidly authoritarian Navy, isn't it?"

"Yes, Mike, probably because of the public images remaining from the brutal life in the days of sail. Aboard eighteenth century Continental Navy ships like 'Old Ironsides'. For example, weapons were locked up until battle was imminent in order to prevent mutinous murder of the officers by the crew. Thankfully, Navy life has improved considerably since then.But, let's go back to travels."

"Where next, Captain?"

"A few weeks after the Venice trip with Pete's family, I was on the road again with my parents bound for Lisbon via northern France, Spain, and Portugal. From Lisbon we flew to San Miguel Azores for a three week visit with my father's relatives. First, some family history. In the mid nineteenth century, my father's parents immigrated from San Miguel, Azores, to Fall River,

Massachusetts, worked in the cotton mills, had thirteen children, became naturalized American citizens, and returned to the Azores to retire in the small town of Bretanha on San Miguel, one of nine Azores islands. There they raised horses and cattle on beautiful property on the edge of an extinct volcano, Sete Cidades, and built their prominent home, high in the center of town. Their retirement wasn't quite complete, however. My father, Manuel Benevides Sousa, was born May 28th 1904, the youngest of fourteen children in the family. Father's middle name, Benevides, was also a family name. The very common names 'Manuel' and 'Sousa', sometimes spelled Souza, are the equivalent of 'John' and 'Smith' in the US. There were twenty-two pages of Sous(z)a's in the Lisbon phone book in the '80's. Therefore, Benevides was the commonly used family name in the village. Since his siblings were either old enough to remain in the US, or died in child-hood, and his father died of injuries from being thrown from his horse when Father was ten, he was raised as a spoiled only-child. Because Father was the son of American citizens, he had dual American and Portuguese citizenship. To retain his US citizenship, however, he had to come to the USA before his eighteenth birthday. Father said his future in the poor and backward Azores was hopeless and he seemed destined to remain stuck in San Miguel to care for his widowed mother. As Father told it, his restricted romantic life in the Azores was painful. Courting, he explained, consisted of Sunday afternoon visits to a young lady's home, talking to her from the front yard wall while she leaned out her front room window. Matters heated up considerably for Father at age sixteen, however, when he jumped the fence for an affair with a married woman. He desperately needed to get out of town. Providentially, his bachelor brother Joe came to visit and Father sailed out aboard a merchant ship bound for Boston, supposedly for a short visit with his Fall River relatives to retain his US citizenship. In Fall River, however, Father soon felt his older brother Frank was being too interfering in his life. Then, one night Father severely beat up a fag who propositioned him. Believing he had killed the man, Father ran off to Portland, Maine, and joined the Army in 1924. Army still had horses and Father's intent was to be in the Cavalry, but the Army thought differently. John Philip Sousa, 'The March King', was at the height of his popularity in the twenties and Sunday afternoon military band concerts in the park were very popular family events. Wishing to enlarge the Fifth Infantry Band for the popular evening Retreat Parades, the Fort Williams Commanding Officer held an inspection and reassigned the men with the longest hair to the band, where they marched, holding instruments without playing them. Father had played valve trombone in his village band for religious processions, but never wished to make a career in music. Nevertheless, with infinite wisdom the C.O. assigned Father to the band simply because his name was Sousa. Thereafter, Father had virtually no contact with his Fall River family for nearly twenty years, at least partly out of guilt, but perhaps more because that's just the way he was."

"Didn't that cause severe strain in Sousa family relations, Captain?

"Not as far as I could tell. Everyone except Father seemed able to forget it and move on. For years Uncle Frank insisted that we come to Fall River for a visit, until we finally did in the forties. They couldn't have been more welcoming.

Frank was a dignified, respected, upright, and handsome man, who was a well-known checker champion whose games were a regular newspaper feature. One of Frank's sons had only one arm but was an Olympic World Champion soccer player on the Brazil team in a year that their victory was so famous that there was a feature film about him. Another fall River relative(?) was 'uncle' Joe Pavo who we visited at his beautiful home on Fishers' Island New York. Joe was a handsome, dark-skinned, muscular, curly haired, lady's man of the sea, a confirmed bachelor, and lobster fisherman with his boat which he took south to Florida in the winter for charter sword fishing. Had we not gone to Germany, I would have accepted his offer of a job on his boat for the next lobster season. Father's.brother Joe remained in Bretanha at the family home with Mother Alexandra, married and raised two boys and a girl. The girl Maria and one of the boys immigrated to Brazil, then to Canada. Last I heard, that boy was in jail. The other boy Joe married a school teacher and remained in the family Bretanha home until he died of cancer in his early forties. Our visit in 1950 was treated by the entire island as a major front page news event. Because returning successful 'immigrants' were regarded by everyone as wealthy heroes, Father was idolized everywhere and played the role well. Mother and I were overwhelmed and humbled with kindness, especially by Grandmother Alexandra, then in her nineties, severely bent by osteoporosis and less than five feet tall, but still walking three miles to church every morning. Every early morning Alexandra awakened me with a bowl of hot coffee and milk. I understood that the 'coffee' grounds were actually made from burned potato skins. Father taught me to say 'Thank you my Grandmother, very much'. Wherever Mother went, someone held an umbrella over her head and had a chair for her when they stopped. Of course everyone assumed Mother and I were Catholic, and there would have been upset feelings if the truth were known. So, Mother and I faked it for Father's sake and went to mass regularly, though we were so awkward with the rituals it must have been obvious that this was our first experience in Catholicism. There was one minor miracle, however. I was walking with Father and his childhood friend one day, as they spoke only Portuguese. When Father's friend said something to me in Portuguese, instead of translating Father said 'el falla nada', literal meaning, 'he says nothing'. It was obvious from the man's expression that he understood that I was a mute, but that went over Father's head, so I remained silent, biding my time as they went on with their conversation. Finally, when there was a brief lull, I spoke. The man was so startled by the 'miracle' that he became speechless."

"Good one, Captain, but how did you get by with the language the rest of the time there?"

"There was a man in the village in his thirties who had been raised in the US and spoke English. I don't recall his name, but bless his heart, he took time off from his work to translate for me the entire visit. While Father was with his friends and Mother was with Grandmother Alexandra, I was with the 'boys' who were mostly in their twenties. I had a hard time steering around answers to some of their questions about things like sexual promiscuity in Europe. I tried to be honest but vague in my short answers to conceal my own innocence. Things had changed in the Azores since Father's day, the boys were probably more experienced with sex in the city than I was. One day I was introduced to a pretty girl a bit younger than I who was a friend of Joe's daughter and perhaps sister to one of the boys. Later, one of the boys put me on the spot by asking if I liked the girl. Well Mike, I didn't know how to respond. I couldn't say no I did not like her, that might be taken as rejection and injured feelings. On the other hand, if I said yes I did like her, then that might mean we were engaged to be married."

How did you get through it?"

"I'm not sure, I just mumbled and smiled and hoped my translator would fix it up for me, which I believe he did, thank goodness. I did not see the girl again."

"What was life like in San Miguel?

"Simple, poor, and backward. The volcanic Azores Islands, named after their soaring birds, is a thousand miles west offshore from Europe. Except for the US Air Force Base at Terciera, the Azores was largely cut off and ignored by the mainland Portuguese government. I had the feeling that the clock had been turned back at least two hundred years. Few roads were paved, few villages had electricity, most homes were small primitive stone cottages, the women wore black mourning shawls, hospitals were crude, the government was oppressive, and few people were educated. Social life was largely centered around the Catholic church and religious festivals. The people seemed to be waiting to die, a trait I noted in all Catholic rural populations but more prominent with the Portuguese who are said to be 'happy to be sad'. Despite their poverty, however, people were very warm and friendly. At all the many homes we visited, we sampled their large variety of home-made wines and liquor, some very potent. By the end of the day after making the rounds of visits, we were reeling. Father said that as a child he always drank wine instead of water, perhaps the wine was more sanitary than the water supply. An example of oppressive taxes was the requirement to have a license for cigarette lighters and a high tax on matches. Since there was a cigarette factory and virtually all men smoked, necessity mothered invention. Men lit their cigarettes by striking steel on flint into corn silk and blowing it into flame-in their hands! The most revered and educated people in the villages were the priests. The Bretanha priest I met was well respected for being social and down to earth. One told me, 'The road to hell is paved with priests heads.' One day, however, I was presented to a group of five very young priests who were in agreement that Europe would be better off if the Nazis had won World War two."

"Amazing to hear such an outrageous statement from young Priests. To me, that implies approval of the Holocaust. Do you suppose they were taught that in Seminary?

"Possibly, but that view was not unique to Catholics. Many Europeans despised the Jews. For good reason, they feared Russia far more than the Nazi's. But enough of that, back to San Miguel. The Portuguese are known as men of the sea because so many are fishermen. But the fishing industry in the Azores was primitive. Since the islands are volcanic, the coast is steep, rocky, and open to the hostility of the Atlantic. There are few harbors. There was only one place near Bretanha where small boats could be launched and recovered. Each morning the fishermen manually maneuvered their twelve foot dinghy's down a steep narrow cliff trail to the water. Four to six men rowed the boats out to sea and fished with hand lines over the side all day, and then hauled the boats and their catch back up the trail in the evening. The Azores was the last place on earth where whales were hunted with rowed long boats and hand thrown harpoons. While we were there, two fourteen meter sperm whales were brought in, so I went down to the factory to see them when they were hauled ashore. I had my picture taken next to one holding a large bamboo fishing pole. I have never smelled anything else nearly as strongly offensive."

"Are they still whaling that way, Captain? Didn't the 'save the whale' folks object?"

"Because it was such a dangerous profession and so few whales were killed, Azores whaling was not on anyone's save the whales 'hit list'. Nevertheless, typical of Portuguese ways, whaling went by the boards because the government failed to renew their license. My guess is that the oversight occurred because the fishermen could not pay the required bribe. As in many Third World countries, government workers in the Azores were not paid living wages and it was understood that 'tips' were the common form of subsidy. Today, all that remains of the Azores whaling industry is a museum in Faial."

"No doubt not missed by the men who risked their lives going down to the sea in long boats after them. You mentioned volcanoes, are any still active?"

"Yes, but on a relatively small scale. In the early fifties one erupted on Faial which evacuated the Island for a short time. The result was a modest expansion of the shoreline. There is a region on San Miguel Island where the ground is so warm that the vegetation is tropical and the ponds and streams are quite hot. The locals bake some meals by burying them underground; however, there have been no active eruptions there in modern history."

"Sounds like a catastrophe waiting to happen."

"Perhaps, but less certain than the floods, fires, mud slides, and earthquakes of California, and there has been no mass exodus of the west coast."

"Is there anything more you'd like to say about that Azores visit?"

"Just that the greatest benefit to me was meeting my grandmother Alexandra. What a magnificently outstanding lady she was strong, intelligent, kind, and loving, even in her nineties. On the other hand, the most inexplicable aspect of the visit was Father's benign disregard for her. It was a long time later before I came to understand the Portuguese psyche, which also gave me insight into myself. But we'll get to that, Mike, there's a lot of Portuguese in you too. So, let's end this chapter here."

"OK, Captain, as you wish. May I join you for dinner?"

"Of course, I'll meet you there."

Father 1907

Father on chair, parents left, siblings behind, Azores `1905

Uncle Frank Souza and wife, parents and me, Fall River MA 1949

Father's home town, Bretanha
San Miguel Azores

Center Father & his mother, right brother Joe and family 1947

Cousin, Mother, Alexandra, Azores 1950

II

ALBUQUERQUE

"In July 1952 with Navy orders to the University of New Mexico, I returned to the US with my parents. Shall we pick up the story there, Mike?"

"Sure, 'Captain, the recorder is running."

"Our flight to New York from Frankfurt aboard a Flying Tigers chartered C-54 was memorable. We were routed via Ireland, but diverted to the Azores because of weather. The airplane was packed with soldiers and dependents. The lone stewardess had more than she could handle with kids crying and running up and down the aisles. We were well out over the Atlantic when a fat Tech Sergeant, who insisted on smoking cigars, called out loud enough for everyone on the plane to hear, 'Stewardess, Stewardess, come here. Look out on the right wing. There's oil all over it coming from number four engine.' Naturally, it became deadly quiet in the cabin as the stewardess looked out to confirm. Still loud enough for everyone to hear, the fat Sergeant demanded, 'Why didn't they fix that before we took off?' That was the last straw for the overworked and harassed stewardess, she stood up with her hands on her hips and snapped back, 'Sergeant, if they kept this plane on the ground for everything that's wrong with it, we never would get in the air.' And she stormed up the aisle to the cockpit. When she returned to the cabin she sat on the arm of a front chair and put her head own on her arm on the top of the headrest until we landed at Santa Maria, Azores. All remained still in the cabin. After landing it was announced that we would stay overnight for an engine change. The next morning, the word quickly went around that the Air Force had refused to give the Flying Tigers an engine -so we re-boarded and took off for Newfoundland anyhow, with new oil all over the right wing as before. We arrived at Newfoundland at night in a hellacious thunder storm to refuel and re-oil the leaky engine, and then took off right back into more thunder storms for the rest of the night into New York City. I had the window seat directly behind Father and could see that he was perspiring nervously. The turbulence kept everyone buckled to their seats. Frequent flashes of lightning made it appear that the propellers were stopped. Oh boy, oh boy, I thought, here's my chance to get even for the time in Portland when Father tried to scare me about flying. 'Look Dad, both engines on our side have quit. I wonder if the other ones quit too.' Father just froze and didn't say anything, but I could see his collar soaking in sweat. I wasn't the only coward in the family after all. Sweet revenge. Thank you God."

"Weren't you frightened too, Captain?"

"No, I was fascinated. I finally had the chance to see night thunderstorms from inside, between, and above them. Mother wasn't scared either, she was always fearless. We had Father's 'number'."

"See Captain, there was some compensation in having a father around after all, wasn't there?"

"I suppose so if you look at it from the dark side. Anyhow, this trip was to be the last of my time at home. Father had orders to the Army Band in DC, but didn't want to be in such a high profile job. Somehow he was successful in getting his orders changed to Fort Carson, Colorado Springs. On the drive west, we diverted to Columbus Georgia for a few days to put our home up for sale, so of course I called Elaine. She drove right over to pick me up in her shiny new black Buick sedan and handed me the keys! She had matured a lot and looked great. We drove around to visit our old gang. Now charming, graceful, and self-confident, Elaine outshone all those who had considered her dumb and awkward. Her parents had set her up 'in business with her own maternity boutique across the Chatahoochee River in Phoenix City, Alabama, and she was obviously doing very well. We also stopped at the Baker Village shop to say hello to her mother, who made it clear that she was not happy to see me back in town. That mattered little to Elaine, she was very glad to see me. I sensed that we could easily pick up where we left off; however, I felt compelled to tell her about Aurelie and there was no kissing or touching. She said that she had been engaged too, but ended wedding plans when she found she couldn't go through with it. Nevertheless, to my astonishment, Elaine announced that she would move to Albuquerque too! At this point, Mike, I should have taken more interest in the distinction between Elaine and Aurelie. Though it meant a four year separation and despite my protests, Aurelie chose to be an English major at the University of Vermont. Elaine, on the other hand, after a three and a half year separation with no expectation of ever seeing me again, plus knowing I was engaged now, was ready to leave her home and business to move to Albuquerque to be with me."

"What happened, Captain?"

"Nothing. I never wrote to Elaine or heard of her again – out of loyalty to Aurelie, I told myself."

"Ever regret it, Captain?"

"Not really Mike. Though I certainly retained fond feelings for Elaine and thought of her many times over the years, I believed that my nostalgia had more to do with lost innocence than love. After all, we grew up together through adolescence in a very successfully intimate way that I could never recapture with others. In retrospect, I see that Elaine was smarter than me in recognizing that was love. Perhaps I was blind to my own feelings. But that's the way it is with boys, isn't it?"

"Yes Captain. Some would call it immaturity, but women say that all men are out of touch with their feelings."

"Yes, Mike. I like the way a recently divorced actress once put it, 'Sure, women can fake orgasms, but men can fake whole relationships'.

"Next stop Albuquerque, Captain?

"Yes, Mike. As we drove west through Texas and into New Mexico I had a growing sinking feeling. As we descended from the Sandia Mountains on route sixty-six east of Albuquerque, it looked like we had landed on the moon. It was a clear dry day with unlimited visibility to the horizon a hundred miles west -without a tree or hill or any sign of life -just desert sand and sagebrush. Yet, the road sign said Albuquerque was only fifteen miles away. We knew that route sixty-six ran straight through the middle of it and we could see the road on the western horizon. But there was no city! As we approached, we began seeing a few run down gas stations, motels, gift shops advertising Indian turquoise jewelry, and a rattlesnake zoo. Nothing was said, we were totally speechless until Mother finally began laughing. Father and I joined in, but it was one of those laughing spells which comes from believing that nothing could be this bad. Finally, we saw that the reason we hadn't seen Albuquerque was that it was hidden in the valley of the 'mile wide and a foot deep' Rio Grande River. As we drove into town, it was more of the same type businesses we had seen approaching, just more of them. It was apparent the entire city was stretched out along route sixty-six and was literally little more than 'a wide place in the road'. The last straw was driving onto the University campus. Instead of an ivy covered community of scholars, the damned place looked like what I imagined a Navajo reservation would be. All the buildings were mud huts! Yeah, I know, Mike, 'adobe', how quaint. A big lump formed in my throat. Mother cried. She told me later that she cried all the way to Colorado Springs to have left me in such a dismal place. As excited as I was to be moving forward, I remembered how beautiful Bavaria was and what a great time that had been in my life. I missed Germany. Sorry, Mike, I know that it's your hometown I'm running down, and I know how it has changed into much wider place in the road since the fifties, but it's still no place I would choose to live."

"I don't get it, Captain. Everything was going your way just as you always hoped. You were far away from home on a full scholarship, sailing smoothly on toward a degree, a Navy commission, and flight training. You had it all in the palm of your hand. What was missing?"

"Quite right, Mike, I had no legitimate reason to complain. I simply felt depressingly lost and out of place. Germany had been so good, nothing could follow it. There, I was with a close group of classmates I loved and I was socially successful. I had lettered in sports, elected president of the student council, and declared the Duke of Harlaching. I had been raised above the self I had been before by wonderful people in a grand environment. In Munich I was a big fish in a perfect little pond. For certain, there was no hope for that in Albuquerque where I was doomed to remain a small fry in a very unattractive big desert."

"How did you cope with it then?"

"I worked. Not at academics where I did poorly, barely keeping my head above water, but at a series of part time jobs."

"Why did you work? Didn't the scholarship include tuition, books, and fees, plus $50 a month?"

"Yes, Mike, but it wasn't enough. My parents had to send $80 a month to cover my room and board. I was not happy to still be dependent on them."

"What jobs did you have?"

"The first semester I lived in the dormitory, a zoo with no chance to study amidst the calamity. The only good thing was that my roommate, Ernie Suazo, introduced me to Spanish culture and, against his will, to your mother."

"Against his will?"

"Ernie and I were at the campus book store when my breath was blown away by one of the most beautiful women I had ever seen. She was in tight jeans and turquoise sweater, silver belt, long black hair, and flashing dark eyes. Ernie knew her and spoke to her, but he didn't introduce me. Later, I asked Ernie to arrange an introduction, but he was reluctant. 'You don't want to know her, Manny. She is bad news.' He refused to elaborate but I persisted until Ernie finally included me in a family home social event with Emma Rodriguez attending. We dated on and off for the next three years, but she allowed little more intimacy than kissing, even though we sometimes spent the night at her apartment. My old karma in relationships remained unchanged. Just as well, I thought. I was being loyal to Aurelie and avoiding risks which could upset the future. As an NROTC Midshipman I was subject to the same regulations as the Naval Academy Midshipmen. Marriage or pregnancy was a Class A offense with mandatory expulsion."

"Ah, I see where this is leading, Captain. But what was Ernie warning you against?"

"He never said more than that Emma had once run away to be married. Her parents had them arrested on their wedding night and had the marriage annulled, so I assume she was under age. I never raised the subject further with Emma and she didn't offer the story, but she did admit to a prior marriage in the paper work for ours. Perhaps you can elaborate?"

"This is news to me, Captain, I know nothing about it. But it says something about your relationship that you didn't discuss it, doesn't it?"

"What it says is that we were not very close."

"Then why did you go on seeing each other for three years?"

"Good question, Mike. I can't speak for Emma. She was mysteriously exotic. I understood she was artistically gifted as a dancer and singer on stage, but I only saw impromptu dances at her apartment. She said she was a part time UNM student, but I didn't see evidence of that. I do know that she was working for an attorney. I enjoyed being with Emma because she was bright and eccentric. Mostly, I enjoyed her company and introduction to Albuquerque's Spanish culture. 'Castilian Spanish' she said, I suppose to distinguish herself from being Mexican or Indian, not that it mattered to me. The warm social gatherings of families and friends were uniquely special to me. Toddlers to grandparents contributed to the entertainment with songs, dances, or poetry. It was a great get away from superficial campus fraternity life into the kind of genuine warmth I had felt in the Azores. I was surprised to discover, however, that there were strong prejudices on both sides between Hispanics and Anglo's in Albuquerque. I had never thought of myself as Hispanic nor experienced any kind of bias. I discovered that I was 'passing' as either Hispanic or Anglo without being either one."

"Weren't you a fraternity member, Captain?"

"Yes. Ernie and I went through fraternity 'rush' just to confirm our negative attitudes against them, but to my surprise the Kappa Sigma's were different. Many of the members were Korean War veterans and football players. The atmosphere was genuinely informal and friendly, without the phony social attitudes of the other Houses. In any event, they were better than the chaos at the dorm, so I applied. I thought Ernie had also, but that didn't happen, so I rarely saw him again. Much later I learned he had been black-balled because he was Hispanic, and that I would have been as well except that someone checked with the Registrar to find out where I was from. I was OK, I was from Germany!"

"How did you feel about that, Captain?"

"I have little respect for fraternities. I learned that in those days most fraternities and sororities, including Kappa Sigma, also had membership restrictions against Blacks and Jews written into their constitutions. I believe the restriction against Hispanics was an informal Southwest add-on. In the early fifties Congress passed a law against racial or religious membership restrictions in private organizations or public facilities. If you saw or read 'Gentleman's Agreement' you recall that many Eastern resort hotels excluded Jews. The Masons would not admit Catholics. Within a year, any university with such affiliated organizations on campus would cease to receive federal funding. Any fraternity or sorority with those restrictions were to be disallowed. I attended the Kappa Sigma national conclave that year where, of course, constitutional changes were the major topic. I have to say that I was highly impressed by the impassioned eloquence of the opposing speeches by the representatives from Southern schools. The gist of their presentations was to mourn the demise of tradition as well as those chapters on southern campus, for if the restrictions were deleted, then no southern family would allow their children to join a club which had permitted Blacks or Jews, even if only in Northern Chapters. I don't know how it turned out in southern chapters, but of course the constitutional restrictions were removed in all Greek organizations. Even so, there were no Blacks, Jews, or Hispanics in our chapter."

"Did you go along with that, Captain?"

"As a matter of fact no. When I left the chapter it was headed for its financial demise and is no longer on the UNM campus. I never heard or asked what happened. Next time I visited, 1969, it was a vacant lot."

"What are your feelings about that now?"

"Nothing one way or the other, Mike. UNM had the reputation of being a 'playboy' school. Many students were East Coast kids, apparently judged unworthy by their parents of an Ivy League education and were banished to the West. Many of the others were veterans going to college on the GI Bill purely for the free ride and social life with no intention of graduating. The demise of Kappa Sigma was no loss to UNM."

"Were there no bright spots in fraternity life?"

"Actually yes, Mike, it's good you asked. I don't mean to be totally negative. Our initiation was a memorable hoot indeed. It began with us pledges locked up in one of two upstairs attics, the one called 'Hell', the other one was called 'Heaven'. There was a huge fire in the front room fireplace with red hot Greek KS branding irons. We figured they were going to fake branding us and weren't worried about it until they led the first pledge out of Hell blind-folded and we soon heard the very real horrifyingly painful scream of our new 'brother'. There was no doubt about the genuineness of the scream or its source. It became very quiet in Hell as one by one the event was re-enacted with each of us. Then it was my turn. I was led blind-folded and forced to kneel head down facing the raging inferno with my bare butt in the air. Several brothers on both sides firmly held me in place as ceremonial incantations were recited. The red hot branding iron was passed close enough to my face that I could feel the searing heat of it. I was told to brace as the branding iron was rammed directly to the right cheek of my bare ass and boy did I scream in pain as I heard the searing sound and smell of burned flesh, but wait, I definitely felt the heat of the red hot iron on my butt but there was no pain! At last the blind-fold was removed and the truth revealed. The iron applied to our rears was cold-soaked in dry ice. The freezing temperature had the same effect on the mind as heat. As the cold iron was applied, the red hot iron was pressed against a piece of meat nearby to complete the audio and odor effects, which were stunning, to say the least."

"Very clever. What other fun and games were there?"

"There were several ingenious 'winner-gets-a-prize' competitions. One had us in two lines sitting on the floor facing each other with a paper napkin between our feet. At the sound of 'go' we pulled as much hair off the legs of the pledge opposite us as we could and placed it on the napkin before us. The pledge with the most hair on his napkin at 'stop' won. My favorite though was the relay race. We divided into two teams at opposite ends of the room. Nude. At the sound of 'go', a contestant on each team picked up a raw egg off the floor with his butt, carried it to the opposite end of the room and placed it on the floor for his team mate to pick up for return and so forth. If a contestant broke an egg or dropped one he had to go back for another one. The winning team got a 'prize'. If you have never tried to pick up an egg with your butt and walk twenty feet with it in place without breaking or dropping it, you simply have never lived, Mike."

"Good grief. What did the sorority sisters do for initiation fun?"

"I have no idea, but it does spark one's imagination to consider their relay races, doesn't it? I never got close enough to a 'sister' to ask, but I'm sure they weren't as inventive as we were. In fact, I'm breaking an oath of secrecy in telling you what we did. However, the Kappa Sigs are no longer at UNM, so I might get away with this revelation seventy five years after the fact."

"I should think so, Captain, but even if they track you down, what could they do about it?"

"Who knows? They might really brand me this time!"

"What were fraternity social functions like?"

"Equally inventive. We had BYOB 'Pan Parties' at the Rio Grande. The Pan was a galvanized wash tub with blocks of ice into which whatever booze you brought - whiskey, rum, gin, brandy, beer, etc. was dumped into the mix for consumption by dipping fruit jars into the highly potent concoction. We also had a 'Poverty Party' where the House was boarded up and the electricity turned off. Entrance was down a coal chute into the dark and spooky cellar. Lit candles stuck in the tops of liquor bottles provided the only lighting. Campus regulations prohibited serving alcohol, so the liquor bottles were filled with booze. All you had to do for a drink was pull out the candle."

"Sounds like fun! What jobs did you have?"

"Well, let's see. First, I was a House Boy at the Kappa Kappa Gama sorority house where the sisters did their best to embarrass me. Then I drove a home delivery van for Smokey Joe's Restaurant, 'the best food deal in town', where the cook was said to blow his nose in whatever he was cooking if something upset him. A waitress there told me that if she had problem customers, she spit in their coffee. Then I arranged and delivered flowers for McKown's Flowers. Weddings, Easter, Mother's Day, etc. were major rat races. One day I was delivering seventy two orchid corsages to a convention downtown when I saw an eighteen wheeler with an EXPLOSIVES sign on its bumper in my rear view mirror bearing down on me at a stop light. The driver was looking in his rear view mirror and never even touched his brakes before rear-ending me, pushing me into the car ahead. When I called Kevin, the shop owner, he cried 'How are the flowers?' Finally, I became our fraternity Treasurer, House Boy, and House Manager which paid all my living expenses and released me from being dependent on my parents. Our cook was a large and wonderful black lady with a badly disfigured face who said she had been Frank Sinatra's cook during his first marriage. She thought they had been a wonderfully happy couple and was very saddened by their divorce. We became good friends and she insisted that I visit her at her home. When I arrived, the whole family was there, including an attractive young black lady my age. It was a set up. Apparently my 'passing' abilities knew no limits! Nevertheless, I did pass up this opportunity."

"I'm surprised, Captain, from what I know, yyou rarely passed up such opportunjties. So what was your academic experience like at UNM?"

"Bad start. I had enhanced my Navy scholarship application by saying I wanted to be an aeronautical engineer. UNM didn't have an Aero major though, so I signed up for Mechanical Engineering. As a consequence, none of the sixty-four credit hours I had earned in my two years at Maryland were applicable, so I was a freshman again. To add insult to injury, I did so poorly on the UNM math aptitude test that I had to take a no credit dumb-bell math course. One day in mechanical drawing class, the Polish professor looked at my work, then up at me and said, 'You don't really want to be an engineer do you?' So, I went to the counselors and took all their vocational interest tests which indicated a strong interest in music, but Navy would not permit majoring in theology or music. Next on the list was psychology. The counselor advised that a BA in Psych was worthless unless my parents could support me for life. Well, I thought, my parents couldn't support me but the Navy could!"

"So you switched majors then?"

"No, I struggled through the rest of the second semester. The last straw came during registration for my third semester. I had an unresolvable schedule conflict which would have put me in another math course with a professor I could not bear. So, I went to the Chairman of the Psychology Department for approval to switch majors and began the tedious registration process all over, complicated by having to sort out my engineering credits, as well as past credits at Maryland. I was overjoyed to discover that all of my credits from Maryland, plus the year of engineering had fulfilled all the course requirements for a BA in psychology except total number of credit hours. I had just gone from being a freshman to a senior! I had two years of scholarship remaining to do one year of academics – a sleigh ride if ever there was one. Thereafter, every Psych course I took was in graduate school, many with labs. One experiment I recall was testing nipple sensitivity to temperature changes. With three years of Navy scholarship remaining, I could even coast through to a Master's degree."

"But why psychology instead of another major, Captain?"

"Why not? Psychology was relatively easy and interesting, and like most Psych majors, I had a selfish motivation to understand myself better. So why not do it on Navy time? Moreover, I enjoyed writing' stream of conscious thought' short stories and had an underlying ambition to one day write 'the great American novel'. I believed that an understanding of human behavior would be more useful than a degree in English Literature. Coincidentally, I found it useful background as a leader and manager in the Navy, as well as in personal relations. There are greater benefits to higher education than job training, aren't there?"

"Yes indeed, life enrichment and disciplined thinking among them. Speaking of the Navy, what was the NROTC program like?"

"Academically, we took a Professional Development course each semester, such as Naval Orientation, Naval History, and Navigation. Once a week we formed up in uniform at the stadium for 'Drill'. For a good laugh, Mike, never pass up the opportunity to see a Navy unit trying to march, you'd think we were all on rolling decks at sea with no one marking time. Each summer we went on six week Navy cruises. Beyond that, the NROTC Unit was much like a fraternity, only better I thought. I was active in intramural sports competition. I ran in track events and won the Southwestern Conference Intramural foil and epee fencing championships. I was also team captain of our pistol team and ranked number one in aptitude evaluation in my first year. My best friends at UNM were fellow Midshipmen. Dave Sanchez and Max Sloan who were on the pistol team too. We had access to the Colt 'Woodsman' 22 caliber target pistols which we used to hunt jack rabbits on the Navajo reservation until we got bored with that and shot at each other from behind boulders just to hear the bullets ricochet over our heads a la the western movies. Dave Sanchez, who admitted he was the bastard son of a Tijuana prostitute, did a tour in the Marine Corps before getting his PhD in math from Cambridge and returning to the UNM faculty for a career as a Math Professor. Max Sloan quit smoking because his younger sister died of lung cancer in high school. He had a fatal crash one night flying a T-28 in flight training. The cause was carbon monoxide poisoning. Jim Weber, who I once heard from every Christmas, did a tour as Communications Officer aboard an aircraft carrier and then went on to a PhD and college teaching career, retiring as President of a Colorado college."

"If I have the dates right, Captain, you graduated in June 1955, five months before I was born, so you were at UNM only three years instead of four. Why didn't you use all of the Navy scholarship?"

"You have the dates right, Mike. No, I did not use the fourth year of the scholarship, nor did I go for the Master's Degree even though it would have been a relatively simple matter. My favorite professor, Doctor Keston, who taught all the child psych courses, was an exceptionally colorful, eccentric, and brilliant man. He had been a professional student at the University of Chicago during the depression and had three PhD's - psychology, chemistry and music and considered himself to be a concert quality pianist. He had given a battery of personality tests to UNM students and learned the music majors deviated the most from normal, followed by psych and sociology majors. He then designed a music appreciation test in cooperation with his friend Dimitri Metropolis, conductor of the Chicago Symphony. Each question on the test was an audio multiple choice on tape. Each question was four short selections of classical music which were to be ranked in order from best to worst. For example, one of the questions consisted of four selections from Beethoven's Sixth Symphony. He had given the test to thousands of people of all ages and backgrounds. Those who scored highest on his music test were then given the personality tests. His purpose was to learn more about the musical personality, but he hadn't yet analyzed his data. So far, the only observation he made was that you could as well give a monkey his music test as a pre-adolescent child. I had taken many of his classes and scored well on his test. In my third year at UNM I had fulfilled the course requirements for a Master's degree and had another year of scholarship remaining with nothing to do but analyze Doctor Keston's data for my thesis."

"Why did you decide against it, Captain?"

"There were several reasons. First, I would have had to take statistics courses in preparation for grinding out the numbers - hard and boring. Besides, a Masters in psychology wasn't worth much more than a Bachelor degree and I had no career ambition to be a psychologist. Second, I wasn't getting any younger and I wanted to get on with flying. Third, Aurelie was graduating. Most of all, I just wanted to get the hell out of town. I was simply sick of school and Albuquerque"

"Was I a factor in that last reason, Captain?"

"No Mike. My mind was made up the year before when I told Navy my intention to double up on Naval Science courses so I could be commissioned after my third summer cruise. There was a long spell that last year when I hardly ever saw Emma."

"Didn't you see Aurelie at all during those three years?"

"Very little, Mike. It's a long drive from New Mexico to Vermont, so the only brief opportunities were before or after six week Navy summer training cruises at her homes in New Jersey, then Vermont. Aurelie's mother Helen, and stepfather Clayton, kept me occupied with helping them with their hobby, restoring and remodeling classic New England homes for resale. One year I drove Bob's and my '41 Plymouth East. I was stopped by a cop in a small town who was very suspicious of a reprobate looking kid wearing a well weathered cowboy hat and an old corduroy barn coat full of holes driving an old black-primered sedan with New Mexico plates in Vermont headed for the Canadian border. All my luggage and the car seats were spread all over the road for search and lots of radio cop talk taking place. Finally, the bastard just drove off and left me to reload my stuff."

"Your cop karma wasn't working very well in those days, was it? Those infrequent visits with Aurelie don't sound like much to maintain an engagement on."

"We sustained the relationship on the strong bond we developed in the three years in Germany. In addition to the romance, we were truly good friends. In a way, Aurelie was like family to me. Besides, we both put college ahead of our marriage plans."

"Didn't Aurelie visit you in Albuquerque?"

"No Mike. Presumably, money was the obstacle. Still, it was a sore subject. I couldn't get over feeling that if she were truly serious about us, Aurelie would have come to UNM with me in the first place. After all, she was not going to be a rocket scientist or on a scholarship. She was an English major with the only stated ambition of having four kids. I guess I hung on because I made a commitment and hadn't come up with a better option. The truth was that marriage was not top priority for me either. It was easier to go along with a comfortable status quo for the time being. Nevertheless, a six year courtship and engagement was way too long. Prolonged absences do not make the heart grow fonder, as we later discovered."

"Didn't you see your parents at all while you were at UNM?"

"Oh sure. I drove to Colorado Springs for holidays, but Mother was working at the Post Exchange and they lived in a small two room apartment, so I didn't see much of them and slept on the living room couch. Two of the trips were memorable, however. One of my frat brothers, Bill Thompson, was from Pueblo, forty miles South of Colorado Springs, so I sometimes drove with him. There were four of us in a beat up Ford going home for Christmas '53 when one of the water pumps sprang a leak. The garages were already closed for the weekend, but we were able to get the owner of an auto parts store to sell us a pump, which we had to change ourselves. The two water pumps on flat head Ford V-8's were also engine mounts, so there was lots of grunting and cursing required to change one. In the process we lost all the anti-freeze and the temperature was forecast to go well below zero on our route through Raton Pass, but we figured we would be OK as long as we kept the engine running. In the long climb up the Pass, however, the engine got very hot. We assumed that the new pump was leaking, so lacking other available fluids, we all peed into the radiator -to no avail. What we failed to realize was that the water in the radiator had frozen which stopped circulation to the engine, so it was steaming hot. The engine finally quit altogether and we were stuck near the summit of Raton Pass at one AM with no traffic and temperatures which froze local thermometers at forty below zero. Our only hope was to bundle up as much as possible inside the car and hope for the best. Fortunately, several hours later, a good Samaritan stopped and gave us all a ride to Pueblo. Another trip was even more eventful. My roommate, Bob Bogan, had a 1932 Model B roadster hot rod which his girlfriend refused to ride in. So Bob and I bought a 1940 Plymouth two door sedan and I got to drive the roadster a lot, including one Spring Break trip home alone. It was one AM on the road between Pueblo with no traffic when I saw the headlights of a car pull onto the highway behind me and close the distance very rapidly to dangerously close behind me and just stayed there. My speedometer wasn't working, so I was guessing speed with the tachometer. I could probably have outrun the bastard, but something told me to just hold the 3300 rpm I had been cruising at. Finally, the car shot past me and I saw that it was a State Trooper. Not long afterward, I saw the headlights pull out again and the event repeated three times before the cop gave up on me. I got home about 2 AM. When I got up the news was all about a State Trooper who .was shot three times and killed at about 1:30 AM on the Pueblo Colorado Springs highway. There was only one witness who said he saw the cop on the side of the road behind an old convertible with a young male in a leather jacket in the cops' passenger seat and the interior lights on. I fit the description! Later, since my parents weren't home, I decided to go for a ride on the same route north toward Denver. A short way out of town, however, I saw a police road block ahead. There I was in a leather jacket driving an old convertible and had been on the road from Pueblo when the cop was shot, so I stupidly whipped a u-turn across the median and sped 'off south. Fortunately, I got away with it. Otherwise, God knows my picture would have been on the front page of every newspaper and the evening TV news would have had film of me in hand cuffs being led away to jail, and who knows what after that. They never did catch the killer, so I would have been the only suspect."

"How fortunate for you, Captain. Someone was surely watching over you that time."

"That time and many others, Mike."

"You have mentioned the Navy summer cruises. What were those like?"

"My 1953 summer cruise was aboard Shannon, a destroyer converted to a mine layer home-ported in Norfolk, Virginia. There were over a hundred of us Mids aboard, half were Fourth Class, the others First Class, that is, freshmen and seniors. Also, half of us were NROTC, the rest were Naval Academy. The Naval Academy Mids were tightly bonded and naturally looked down their noses at us amateur sailors. They knew how to spit shine shoes. We all displaced the lower rank sailors, so of course we lived and worked like them, bunked two feet apart in hot cramped compartments. Standing two separate four-hour watches a day as helmsmen, bridge lookouts, boiler and engine rooms, etc., we were otherwise occupied with scrubbing, mopping, and chipping paint, or conducting drills. There was precious little spare time and no place to hide. The officers, including the Captain, were aloof and kept their distance from us and the hostile crew. Much of the crew appeared to be waterfront rats who enjoyed taunting us. For example, several petty officers in the engine room had fun grossing us out by displaying their advanced cases of venereal diseases and dwelling on the morbid details of their disgusting sex lives. It was not a happy ship by any means. We were bound for Brazil and Trinidad in company with the carrier Saipan, cruiser Macon, and several other destroyers. Getting there, of course, meant crossing the Equator and all the traditional fun and games accompanying initiation of 'Pollywogs' in ceremonies conducted by the 'Shellbacks'. For this cruise that meant we could expect some serious physical abuse by the crew who were all Shellbacks reveling in the opportunity to dish it out to us lower-than-the-lowest-layer-of-whale-shit-on-the-ocean-floor future officers. In preparation, the Shellbacks rigged a framework on the gun deck to support a canvas lined pool with a high platform attached, as well as other ominous looking torture devices. We Pollywogs decided that the best defense was an offense and three days before crossing we revolted. Some enterprising Pollywog poured acid in the pool which burned large holes in the canvas. Then we stormed the gun deck to tear down the structures which resulted in some hand to hand engagements, ending when three inch fire hoses were turned on us. One Mid broke an arm when he was blasted off the gun deck to the main deck. Similar revolts were taking place on the other ships and one Pollywog was lost overboard. This was serious stuff, Mike, and it got worse. The Shellbacks finally put down our rebellion the day before crossing. All us Pollywogs were corralled into the mess hall with the lights and ventilation turned off, wearing just our underwear. The next day, the ceremonies began by taking us out of the mess hall one at a time, blind-folded, crawling on hands and knees on the steel decks with shocks administered by a bare electrical wire to ensure submissiveness before being forced to crawl through several two by six bottomless canvas laundry bags sewn together to make a tunnel lined with fuel oil and garbage. To speed us on our way, Shellbacks beat us with four foot lengths of flat three inch fire hose shilela's soaked in sea water with nicely cord-bound handles. From the tunnel, each Pollywog was lead to the Royal Court, Commanded by King Neptune himself and his 'queen', to face charges of grave misconduct and sentencing of punishment. Also present at Court was Davey Jones and the Royal Baby, who was the fattest, hairiest, ugliest, and grossest boiler room sailor aboard, dressed only in a diaper. Homage to the Court was paid by each Pollywog by kissing the Royal Baby's fat hairy greasy bare belly several times with a helping shove to the back of the head. Amazingly, all our revolt damage had been repaired, so the next station was in the stool at the top of the ten foot tower above the pool filled with fuel oil and garbage. Each Pollywog was pushed backward off the stool into the pool and then led to the Royal Dentist's chair where the Royal Medicine was administered down the Pollywog's throat with a grease gun. The Royal Medicine was a masterful concoction designed to cause projectile vomiting. Pollywogs were then led to another chair to be administered the Royal Antidote by the same means and with similar violent results. After more tunnel crawling and other stations I can't recall, the last obstacle was running the gauntlet down the line of Shellbacks swinging fire hose Shilela's before being washed down with fire hoses to clear away the oil, garbage, blood, and tattered remains of underwear."

"Good God, Captain, does the Navy still permit that?"

"Well, they still were in 1971 aboard the carrier America when we sailed from Cuba via Brazil, Cape Horn, and Australia to Vietnam, and then across the Equator again going the rest of the way around the world coming home. Thank God I had already done it. With the vast expanse of flight deck and more than six thousand sailors aboard, imagine what running the gauntlet was like for the Pollywogs on that cruise?"

"How do you prove that you are a Shellback, not a Pollywog? Do they just take your word for it?"

"Lord no. An official entry of the crossing is made in each Shellback's Navy service record. Plus, he is presented an 8 X 10 certificate from The Domain of Neptunus Rex for framing, as well as a wallet size replica. Anyone who could not provide absolute Shellback proof was assumed to be a Pollywog and made to go through the initiation again. I carried my Shellback card in my wallet for thirty years."

"For good reason, that's the most brutal ceremonial naval tradition I have ever heard of. What do they do aboard cruise ships?"

"It varies, but I believe the ceremony is little more than a cute costume party in the ball room."

"How do the merchant ships conduct the ceremony?"

"I don't know, Mike. There aren't many crew members aboard merchant ships and most have crossed many times. Still, given their usual multi-national mix of waterfront rats, I imagine that some Pollywogs get worked over in some grizzly ways best not contemplated. At any rate, only Navy Shellback records will get you out of doing it the Navy way."

"What was Brazil like in 1953?"

"A mixed bag. We were the first US Navy ships to visit in eleven years and we were told we might not be welcomed because of Communist leanings and anti-US sentiments. Half the Task Group went to the capital Rio de Janiero with the carrier Saipan and we went to Sao Paulo, Brazil's largest city. I'm glad to say that the natives were friendly. I met a tall gracious and lovely young lady at a 'command performance' Embassy reception who was coincidentally named Maria Rodriguez. She spoke not a word of English, nor I Portuguese. We dated very properly all ten days in port and I even met her parents, but the only advanced conversations we had were when we encountered my pal Dave Sanchez who did his best translating for us with his Spanish. After touring Maria aboard Shannon, one of the Chief Petty Officers told me that she was the most beautiful Brazilian girl he had seen, a very high complement considering the competition. In Dave's translation of our final conversation, Maria declared her intention to visit me in Albuquerque. I didn't take it lightly since her family approved and appeared to have the means to send her."

"What came of that, Captain?"

"We exchanged English-Portuguese letters, with Dave's translations, for several months. But when she confirmed her intention to visit, with proposed dates, I backed off. It was going to be way too complicated, expensive, and time consuming for me to host her properly, plus, for her and her parents it would probably mean we were engaged if we weren't already! So, I put off responding with polite regrets and never heard from her again."

"I guess that episode was similar in some ways to being presented with the young lady during your Azores visit."

"Exactly. Good training! While Portuguese romancing may advance slowly, it seemed that wedding plans proceeded at light speed! Scary business, Mike. As I was to learn the hard way, the Spanish culture can be similar."

"So, how did the 'old world' Portuguese match with the Brazilians?"

"From my perspective now, having visited Brazil three times, compared with four visits to the Azores and a year living in Portugal, and despite the fact that most of the Brazilian Portuguese descended from the Azores, my impression is that there is little similarity between Brazilians and other Portuguese. The traditional cultural and religious constraints imposed in the old world vanished and went to the opposite extreme in Brazil. Rio's lpenema Beach and Carnival are about as free and far removed from old world Catholicism and the traditionally 'happy to be sad' Portuguese image as it is possible to get."

"Are you saying that the Brazilians tend to be less moral by comparison?"

"Not really, just freer from artificial constraints. Underneath, I think most people want to have morally decent lives. The beaches and carnivals can give an exaggerated impression, whereas daily lives are conventional. For example, the first night ashore Dave and I went to a bar where there were several single girls who appeared to be prostitutes. One of our shipmate Midshipman was sitting with one until the girl erupted emotionally and drove the Midshipman away from her table. He came over to sit with us, confirming that she was a prostitute and confessed that he had insulted her. We could see that she was shedding tears. Finally, the Mid, feeling very remorseful returned to her table and apologized profusely. When we sailed out of Sao Paulo, I saw her on the dock crying and waving her handkerchief to that Midshipman. What he and I learned, and I saw in all countries outside the US, is that prostitution is a socially accepted profession, sometimes even honored as Geisha's are, and that those women, like all others, deserve to be treated with respect, whether or not you use or approve of their services. I'm reminded of a great line in an old movie you may recall. The story was about a socialite who is attracted to a professional assassin who only sleeps with prostitutes, so she poses as one to get him to bed. The next day at lunch she asks her older and wiser girlfriend why such a man would only date prostitutes. Her friend replies, 'Because he knows what their price is. He doesn't know what our price is.'"

"Are you suggesting that all women set a price for sex, Captain?"

"To some degree yes, but that's not as cynical as it may sound. Some Eastern cultures place very low value on women and allow no opportunities outside of marriage except prostitution. In general, Western women are much more practical about taking advantage of 'supply and demand'. Most often in women's marriage decisions, security is the price. After all, raising children requires it. So, women need a reason, but men only need a place. We suffer from a flaw in God's design which gave us a mind and a penis, but the blood supply to operate only one of them at a time."

"Too true, I fear. Pitiful, isn't it? So, where to next, Trinidad wasn't it?"

"Ah yes, Trinidad is a beautiful lush tropical mountainous island in the West Indies off the coast of Venezuela and at that time was still a British colony. Port of Spain, the capital, was the most colorful contrast to any place I had been. Populated mostly by Black decedents of slaves, plus American Indians and East Indians, Trinidad is the home of Calypso music, steel drums, and

Limbo dancing which were in their prime then. Max, David, and I went ashore mid-morning with bathing suits under our uniforms, intending to go to the beach. On the way, however, we stopped at a cabaret and had a fifteen cent 'rum and coca-cola' and another and then another. The only other customer was the youthful remains of an ex-patriot American who appeared to have spent the night on the floor, semi-revived for more debauchery. He was dancing with one of the bar girls to the calypso music of a three piece band. On my third rum and coke before noon, I could easily see myself as the wasted American if I stayed in Trinidad a week. During a break, the guitarist singer came to our table and sang verses describing each of us to a 'T'. It was dinner time when we left. So much for the beach. After a fine Indian meal, we followed the sounds of a steel band to another cabaret where the bar. girl 'waitresses' were taking turns dancing under the Limbo pole with a very thin guy who must have been nearly seven feet tall. More rum and cokes. The mood was magic. Several sailors ventured onto the floor and did the Navy proud with their performance. Three of the girls came to our table and stood behind us rubbing our shoulders. The girl behind me explained that though she was heavy, that was a good thing because the fat made her tighter and she offered to satisfy me for five dollars. Then she ran her left hand down my chest to my crotch where she was visibly shocked to find no trace of manhood which had been well compressed by my tight bathing suit. As she stood back, she said that if I could satisfy her she would give me five dollars. Thus ended my closest encounter with a Black girl. Not so for the sailors though. Even for the deep southerners, the color barrier quickly dissolved."

"Different attitudes in different latitudes, Captain?"

"Exactly right. Even in the fifties the differences were socially artificial. They always were, as we have learned more about the lives and loves of folks like Thomas Jefferson."

"So, was that the extent of your romantic adventures in Trinidad?"

"Not quite. The three of us returned to the Indian restaurant for lunch on the following day. Three attractive Indian girls were there so I invited them to join us and I introduced us as Tom, Dick, and Harry. Since they were married and just having a girl's day out, it was all quite innocent until one of the girls said her husband was traveling off the island, so if I came to her house the next day for lunch, she would cook me a real Indian meal. I accepted with every intention of going, but thought better of it after sleeping on it."

"Excuse me for saying so, Captain, but you were a twenty one year old 'cherry boy'. Either you were in masterful control or you were pretty damned shy."

"Just shy, I think. One of my ex's teased me about being a monk in a previous life. Maybe so, I have always been fascinated by Gregorian Chants. Still, I truly loved women and wanted nothing more than a close loving and lasting relationship. I just couldn't loosen up for one night stands with strangers and I was wary of getting girls I cared about into trouble. Foremost, I meant to observe at least one of the Ten Commandments, 'Thou shalt not commit adultery'."

"It sounds more like you were just scared, Captain."

"Have it your way, Mike. You may be right. Whatever the reason, as I said before, I felt that door would lead me to leaving behind important hopes and dreams of the future. I was correct."

"OK, we covered the ports, how was the rest of that cruise?"

"Awful. Without dwelling on it, it was by far the most negative Navy experience I ever had. The foul nature of the crew was exacerbated by the attitude of the officers, life at sea aboard Shannon was miserable. Destroyers never stop rolling, even in calm seas, so you have to hang on to something every step or risk injury on slippery decks. There were long lines for awful meals with an extreme shortage of silverware, so you had to take the dirty silver from a man leaving the table or eat with your hands. A deep dislike developed between the equally numbered Naval Academy and NROTC Midshipmen. One day when we all together in the cramped crews compartment below decks, we got word that the entire University of Oklahoma sophomore class of forty Midshipmen had been killed in a Navy plane crash. One of the Naval Academy Mids was overheard by an Oklahoma Mid to make the extremely distasteful observation 'Well, we all move up forty numbers.' There was very nearly a full-blown riot and it might have been better if we had cleared the air with one, for the bitterness did not diminish. Everything went sour as we were enveloped in hostility toward each other and the Navy. Another Mid and I intentionally disgusted the rest of the Mids by generating a phony discussion and survey of heterosexual oral sex, an unacceptable topic in those days. One of my jobs was First Loader on a four-gun forty millimeter mount, which meant feeding thirty pounds of four round clips into a cannon firing at a rate of about two rounds a second, which caused me to jump a foot every time it fired. Once during gunnery, practice with live ammunition firing five inch guns and forty millimeter anti-aircraft guns at a target sleeve towed by an airplane, we were steaming downwind at the speed of the wind, so gun smoke enveloped the ship and obscured the target from our view. Controlling the radar gun director, a First Class Mid called for a cease fire to wait for the smoke to clear. But in his zeal to commence firing again, he prematurely locked the gun director onto the tow plane and a number of rounds were fired at it before ceasing. Several rounds exploded near the tail of the tow plane fortunately without damage or injury."

"The Captain must have nearly dirtied his pants at the prospect of losing his command as he saw a Mid shoot at a tow plane."

"No doubt, but he surely would not have been missed by anyone aboard. He was a lousy officer and ship handler. To cap off the cruise, he stopped the ship dead in the water fifty feet from the dock and we had to haul it in by hand. I wasn't going to be missed either. In part as the result of our sex survey, I was ranked last in aptitude by my peer Midshipmen. So, in six weeks I went from number one in my class to dead bottom. Good for me. Screw the Navy."

"Kinda makes me wonder how you made it in the Navy, Captain."

"Me too, Mike, and you ain't heard nuthin' yet, though that cruise was the low point in my attitude. Father once told me that I was too rebellious to succeed in the military. Fortunately, however, Naval Aviation was more forgiving of leadership styles than the Army or Air Force was. I damned sure would not have succeeded as a 'Black Shoe' Destroyer sailor."

"I can see why you ended up loving the Navy so much then. Your second cruise was better?"

"Yes, for the Second Class cruise our six weeks was split between Amphibious Warfare orientation in Norfolk, Virginia, and Aviation Indoctrination at Corpus Christi, Texas. There was little worth noting, except that I got to drive a landing craft and had my first ride in a Navy single-engine SNJ trainer similar to what I first flew in flight training. One day at the Corpus Navy Exchange, Dave and I found a baby skunk all wet and abandoned in the bushes. Since it was too young to odorize us, we took it back to the barracks, dried it off and gave it some water. We decided to try to keep it as a pet so we took it to a veterinarian in a shoe box to have it de-odorized. On the way, however, we noted that our little 'flower' friend had begun to develop that capacity. Since it was Saturday, the vet put our Flower in an outside cage. When we called Monday, the vet said that Flower had passed away. We believed, however, that Flower bought himself a ticket to heaven by fully developing his defensive mechanism over that weekend."

"Too bad, I've heard that skunks make good pets, and they are cute little critters. So, that brings us to your last cruise?"

"Yes, Mike, but first I need to back up to early that year to tell about your mother and me. I will keep the account as factual as I can recall, without vindictiveness. I hope that you can accept that I'm relating this only because it's an event in my life and other's too consequential to pass over lightly. For you, some of this may be in the category of 'I don't believe I'd have told that'. We can delete later, but I want to tell it all to you this time. Plus, there were repercussions to others besides you, your mother, and me."

"Understood, Captain. I'll do my best to stick to my role as a reporter, and separate personal reactions."

"OK, I'll hold you to that. I hadn't seen Emma for months because of her barriers to intimacy. It was just too frustrating for me to spend the night fully clothed with her with little more than kissing permitted, and the balance of our relationship did not compensate. So, I was very surprised one Saturday afternoon at the House when I was told there was a girl out front who wanted to see me. There she was, long wavy black hair, tight white sweater, and riding jodhpurs breathtakingly gorgeous. After driving awhile in her car, I asked where she wanted to go. I was stunned when she said to a motel. There was little doubt what was coming, but I chose to go along, one step at a time. What man can ever understand what goes through a woman's mind when she makes these decisions? In the motel, barriers were lowered and whatever doubt I had about the extent of her intentions were quickly extinguished. Everything was happening way too fast for me. After all, this was to be my first time. Obviously, I was not her first. I panicked and told her I couldn't go through with it because, as she already knew, I was engaged to Aurelie and I was not in love with her. It was a bad scene, Mike. Emma collapsed in tears, humiliated. You know how women's tears work on us, I felt like a complete jerk, so I apologized profusely and tried my best to console her. In my view then, when a woman sincerely offers her body, it is a kind of sacred act which no man should reject cruelly. That's how naive I was. My consoling worked too well, however. Things heated up to the point where the main event was imminent. There was just one stipulation by Emma, I had to promise not to pull out. It had something to do with her being Catholic, but at that point I agreed. Afterward, I was remorseful and fearful of the possible consequences. A few weeks later I flew to Denver to take the Navy's aviation flight aptitude test and physical exam. I had two concerns. First, my high blood pressure history. Because the Army said it was just a nervous reaction to having it taken, I had daily readings done at the campus clinic to accustom myself to it. It worked, my pressure dropped to a consistent 110 for years after, but I couldn't be sure how I would react in this all important examination. Secondly, I wasn't sure of my eyesight. I had worn glasses for several years in Georgia. There was no remaining problem I knew about, still, there was cause for concern. Pondering the possibilities during the flight to Denver, I had my third imaginary conversation with God. 'Is flying still the most important goal of your life?' He asked. 'Yes it is', I replied. 'Would you sacrifice anything for it?' He asked. "Anything', I said 'Would you give up Aurelie?' He asked. That stopped me for a minute before I replied, 'Yes'."

"Wow, God asked you hard questions, didn't He? First your life and then Aurelie. What happened?"

"Everything went well in Denver. No problem with my eyes or heart and I had their first ever perfect score on the flight aptitude test. At that time, Navy's test, developed during World War Two, was the most accurate job aptitude test ever devised."

"Great, so you were on your way to flight training. Home free!"

"Not quite, Mike. When I got home, Emma came bouncing up to me with a broad smile and announced, 'Guess what, Manuel? I'm pregnant!'"

"So God was having you make good on your choice, wasn't He?"

"No doubt, Mike. That would surely end my relationship with Aurelie, but that was just the tip of the iceberg. Emma wanted to get married immediately, supposedly just to legally legitimize the birth. I explained that I could not be married until I was commissioned in September following my final summer Navy cruise, or I would be tossed out of the NROTC program and lose my entire Navy future. Emma wouldn't hear of postponing the wedding. Figuring that I would put it off and skip out on her after the cruise, Emma reported me to the Dean of Men and I was called into his office. Although the Dean had no authority in such matters, I was lectured on doing the 'honorable thing'. That wasn't so bad, but Emma's next act was a call to my parents to be the first to tell them they were going to be grandparents. The first I knew of the call was when Father showed up to intervene. After meeting Emma, his advice to me was to marry her and move in with her, and then tell Navy about it during the cruise before I was commissioned. He also advised me to tell Aurelie goodbye and never see her again. Otherwise, she would make me suffer for it the rest my life with her. Next, Emma threatened to report me to the C.O. of the NROTC with the attorney she worked for in tow. She was going for the throat and didn't give a damn about the consequences. The only concession she made was a promise that her attorney would take care of the divorce following the birth free of charge, no strings attached. Her only purpose, she insisted, was a legitimate name for the child. There was no realistic choice left, I was in a corner with no practical option remaining but to marry her and hope for the best with Navy. Needless to say, however, the only feeling I had for Emma was hatred, especially after her best friend confided to me that Emma told her the pregnancy was intentional. My parents, especially Mother, never believed that I was the father, though I never dwelled on it. Nevertheless, Ernie Suazo was right about Emma being bad news, I should have listened to him. Finally, Emma and I were married in a civil ceremony with a few of her friends attending. I kept my head down and mouth shut in what must have been among the most unhappy 'shot gun' wedding ever. The mood was sustained when a sand storm cancelled graduation exercises and diplomas were mailed out. It was a great relief to graduate and leave Albuquerque for summer cruise aboard the battleship Wisconsin from Norfolk bound for Scotland and Denmark"

"Would you have returned after the cruise for the marriage, Captain?"

"If Emma hadn't been so hatefully aggressive, yes. I suppose I might even have tried to make a go of it, given the chance. That option was never proposed until it was far too late. Looking back, it's obvious that Emma wasn't interested in marriage. After all, she never spent a day of her life cohabitating in one, did she?"

"No, but because she was Catholic, she felt she was always married to you."

"I know she said that, Mike, but do you really believe it? Even discounting her former annulled marriage, there is the fact that she and I were married outside the church, so it was never 'blessed' and we never lived a single day as a married couple. Whatever, it doesn't really matter. If that rationale gave her a socially approved crutch to lean on, I was a very happy camper to be leaving Albuquerque with Bob driving his new Pontiac sedan towing my '29 Ford roadster hot rod."

"What happened to the '40 Plymouth and Bob's '32 roadster?"

"Glad you asked, Mike. There are two more Albuquerque stories to tell involving the roadsters. When Bob's parents gave him the Pontiac, he sold his '32 roadster and we sold the Plymouth. I then owned a '40 Ford coupe for a short time but sold it to buy the '29 roadster. It was a beautiful classic hot rod which won first place at the state fair auto show that year. The father of the kid that owned it was a car dealer and the kid also had a classic canary yellow '51 Mercury coupe. When the kid was arrested on his second marijuana charge, the police told the father to get the kid out of the state or he was going to jail, so his father sent him to UC Berkeley! Since he could take only one car and preferred the Mere, I sold the '40 Ford and bought the roadster for $500. Bob was into drag racing so I tagged along by racing the '40 coupe and then the '29 roadster, but I didn't see much fun in that, so I just had fun driving around town and the open roads. I never came closer to death than one afternoon taking a mountain curve too fast and came within inches of skidding off to a two thousand foot embankment. Hey, that reminds me of another one I'll back up and throw in here. On a visit to Colorado Springs, I took Mother for a ride on a mountain dirt road in my '40 Ford coupe. When I took a curve too fast and the right rear wheel went off the road on a steep embankment, Mother stuck the heel of her right 'brake foot' shoe right through the floorboard - another one of our little secrets we never shared with Father. So here's the other '29 roadster story. While the whole family was in Munich I sometimes went to the Armed Forces Radio studio to watch Father's band record radio shows where I met the Sergeant announcer for `Hillbilly Gast Haus, the most popular radio show in all of Europe. The show came on at three PM after 'Outpost Concert' classical music show with the announcement. 'Now let's listen to some GOOD music'. Well guess who I ran into on campus one day? That announcer. He was out of the Army attending UNM, so we hopped into the roadster and went to a Mexican bar for a beer. He happened to have a pint of bourbon with him, so we got good and blitzed. Interestingly, before the Army, he had been a radio soap opera actor in New York. But when he followed me into the Men's room and stuck his tongue in my ear while I was standing at the urinal, I knew it was time to go home. I don't remember much about what happened except fighting him off as we rounded a curve. When I came to, I had busted out my two front teeth on the steering wheel after we had gone through a telephone guy wire and hit a large tree. The whole front end was bashed, the gas tank and battery in the rear had pushed the back of the seat forward, and my passenger was unconscious with his forehead into the windshield. Thankfully, he soon regained consciousness and we parted company never to meet again. I walked to the fraternity house and woke up Jim so we could tow the roadster home, but when we got there it was gone. By then I was sober enough to call the police to report it stolen. They had it towed. Their comment was that they didn't see how anyone had lived through it."

"Fools, drunks, sailors, and children, right Captain?"

"You got it Mike. I was damned lucky. Turns out that the roadster wasn't so badly damaged. I found a great body shop that straightened the frame, knocked out the dents, and painted it as good as new for only $200. My front teeth were another matter. After a dentist told me what needed to be done and what it would cost, I asked if he could patch me up well enough to last until I was commissioned in three months so the Navy would take care of me. He did some grinding and installed temporary caps for $40 and I was good as new for a while. One more Albuquerque roadster story. Since it was a classic hot rod, without fenders or bumpers, I bought two motorcycle fenders for the front wheels and two trailer fenders for the rear wheels. One of my pals, who drove for a mortuary, said I could use their paint booth and equipment if I came in at night while he was on duty. While I was painting, he had a call to bring in a body from the hospital. When he asked if I would like to see the embalming procedure, I reluctantly agreed. The body was a thin old lady in her eighties laid out on a tilted slab with her blood being drained down the side grooves while the mortician was beginning the cosmetic enhancements. I was surprised by my unemotional reaction. It's amazing how lifeless a dead body is and how impersonal the procedure is. There really isn't much to it."

"I'll take your word for it, Captain. You had some close-ups with life and death in Albuquerque, Didn't you?"

"Yes, and there's another one I almost forgot, perhaps because it falls in the 'I don't believe I'd have told that' category. I was sitting in my room one night talking to three friends when a brother who was a married photographer at Lovelace Clinic joined us. Since he didn't live in the house, we didn't see him often, but we had seen some photos he had taken at the clinic. The most spectacular one I recall was a series of the side vertical cross sections of a frozen still-born human fetus. On this occasion, however, he asked if he could speak privately to me and one other friend there. He had been asked to recruit two volunteers with our general physical features to be sperm donors for an artificial insemination attempt, a pioneering procedure at that time. They would pay us $25 each for each attempt for up to three monthly donations. We had no idea what the procedure was, but of course we agreed, $25 was a lot of money to us and such an interesting way to earn it. Sure beat giving blood! The doctor was a short round rosey-cheeked man who surprised me with his shyness. He explained that this was for a couple who were childless because the husband was sterile. Instead of adoption, they preferred this option. The procedure, it was explained, was simply to mix the sperm from two donors, for anonymity, on the back side of a diaphragm and insert it into the vagina at the precisely right time. I had to sign legal papers to declare that I would never attempt to learn the identity of the mother if we were successful. Finally, the doctor handed me a urine sample type plastic cup and directed me to a rest room down the hall where I was to deposit the sperm. That was it. Simple as that! So down the corridor I went with my little specimen cup to what was nothing more than a closet with a toilet and a sink -pretty sterile atmosphere for this kind of donation, not even any 'reading material'. So picture this Mike. There I am sitting on a toilet trying to inspire myself and an intern opens the door and stands there in shock as several nurses look in. It seemed like an eternity, of course, before the intern backed away closing the door. Good grief, Charley Brown. Now what?

It wasn't easy, but it worked. The wife got pregnant first try and that was the end of my professional sperm donor career. I was batting a thousand in those days."

"Is this a good stopping point for this chapter?"

"Yes indeed. It's nearly supper time. Let's go."

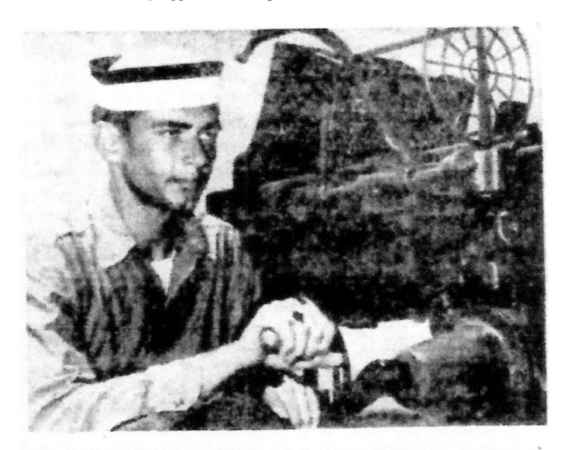

OPERATING GUN CONTROL — Midshipman third Class Manuel B. Sousa, son of Army Warrant Officer Junior Grade and Mrs. M. B. Sousa, Camp Carson, operates the Gun training control on a quadruple mount 40 mm anti-aircraft gun aboard the light minelayer USS Shannon as part of his FHTNC training in the Navy. He is a sophomore at the University of New Mexico.

USS Shannon, DM-25

12

PENSACOLA

Next morning at the lodge for breakfast.

"Good morning Captain. Sleep well?"

"Yes, darn it, too well. It's getting to be a long spell since my last flying dream."

"Have you tried rolling your head on your pillow at night?"

"Yes, but like I said, my neck is stiff and the pain is distracting. I may not be able to recall that talent."

"You got through the pain of ear aches as a child. Maybe your neck will limber up if you keep trying. Meanwhile, flying your Ximango might be inspirational."

"I've been thinking that too. I called a glider instructor I know, Sam Steel, to see if he might be willing to instruct you for your license. He flies an old Cub out of Salisbury on the Eastern Shore sixty miles east, so it would be fairly simple for him to fly here. He is willing, but it wouldn't be quick or cheap, Mike. What do you think?"

"I'm game if you are willing. Since I'm not paying room rent now, it would be affordable, I think. What are the requirements?"

"It's not too bad for a glider license which includes motor-gliders. No medical certification or even a driver's license required, and you can solo at age fourteen. You need only ten solo flights, which can be done in the landing pattern, before your flight exam. Of course there's also a written and oral exam on Federal Aviation Regulations. If you flew every day, you could finish up in a couple of weeks with my help. But there are always weather delays or aircraft and instructor availability which could stretch it out for months."

"That might take quite a chunk out of our time for the book too, wouldn't it?"

"Not necessarily. On those days you fly, which would require only a couple of hours, we could carry on with the book after dinner. If we finish the book and you leave before getting your license you would still be ahead if you got your license at the glider port east of Albuquerque."

"Sounds good, I'd love to do it. Very generous of you to trust your Ximango to me, Captain."

"Not really. Consider it compensation for doing the book. Besides, like us, it's not good for the Ximango to just sit idle, and I'll have an aerial chauffer into the bargain."

After breakfast at the end of the yellow brick sidewalk

"Where do you suppose they got these bright yellow bricks, Captain?"

"I don't know where the clay came from, but I'm told that the man who built this lodge in the thirties was a great fan of the Wizard of Oz film and had the resources to have bricks made any color he wished."

"What a great film, wasn't it? Its appeal to young and old alike never goes out of date. Why do you suppose?"

"For me, it's the universally wonderful gospel messages delivered in a most charming way. Although the 'Great Oz', like all 'wizards', turned out to be a fake, his simple lessons were the greatest gifts one could wish for. The only difference between the Straw Man and someone with a brain was simply the matter of a diploma. The only difference between the Tin Man and someone with a heart was a gold watch testimonial. The only difference between the Cowardly Lion and someone with courage was a medal. And finally, all Dorothy needed to find her way was to realize that there is 'no place like home'. During Vietnam, I saw many 'lions' scrambling for medals, doing dumb things or grossly exaggerating the truth to get them to prove their courage and ensure promotions. The thing was, Mike, we all knew that in many cases medals were awarded for phony events, so did nothing to prove courage or heroism. Same thing with degrees, gold watches, or ruby slippers. As the Dalai Lama said, 'We are all Buddha's within'. But I digress. We left off with leaving UNM and Albuquerque behind, didn't we?"

"Correct. Recorder running, Captain. You and Bob towing your roadster to New Jersey."

"Against Father's advice, I decided to face Aurelie for our farewell. We had been very close in Germany and we had been engaged for six years, so I wanted closure. I was not prepared for what happened. Aurelie had been in the care of a psychologist. There was nothing very unusual in that, everyone in Aurelie's family saw psychologists at every bump in the road. I was very surprised, however, that Aurelie was totally forgiving and declared she wanted to go to Pensacola with me."

"Goodness, Captain, God let you off the hook, didn't He? How did that strike you?"

"Strike is the word. I was highly elated that Aurelie was so willing to forgive and forget. On one hand I was still committed, but on the other, I had written off chances of our future together. Plus, I really wasn't sure I needed the added complexity in my life at this point. Just the same, I was cautiously hopeful that things might work out somehow. We wouldn't arrive in Pensacola until late September and your birth was due six weeks later. If Emma was true to her word, I could be free again as early as the end of the year. Aurelie and I could pick up where we left off as planned after getting to know each other again. At that point, any positive possibility in my personal life looked good to me, Mike."

"Sure, besides, you had more important priorities then, didn't you?"

"Flying, you mean? Hell yes, damn tootin' I did. Does it make me a bad guy because I held *my* priorities to be more important than your mother's or Aurelie's?"

"OK, shall we leave it and move on?"

"Listen, Mike, when you put yourself in the judge's seat with a rhetorical question like that, you're not getting by with 'Shall we leave it'. If you wave a red flag in my face, standby for a ram. We covered 'ax-grinding' at the beginning."

"Good call, Captain, quite right. I'll do better."

"OK. So I boarded the battleship Wisconsin. Norfolk to Edinburgh to Copenhagen and return in six weeks. What a magnificent city Edinburgh is. What wonderful people. I loved every minute there even though I was assigned to Shore Patrol duty. There was not a single incident. None of us could even buy a drink in the pubs without the Scots taking us in and picking up the check. There was a heat wave, seventy four degrees, warmest it had been in ten years and people were sitting in the parks with their faces into the sun like sun flowers, soaking it in. Afternoons in the park there were bag pipes with kilted dancers and crossed swords on the ground. We were pulled in to participate. While there, several sailors married women they met the year before. My impression of these wonderfully cheerful and feminine ladies was that a man could be happily married for life to any one of them. Of course, part of the picture was the reality of Scottish life. Because of family land ownership and economic conditions, men had to wait until their mid-thirties for their inheritance before they could afford to be married. American sailors had an advantage."

"Did you have a romantic adventure there?"

"Romantic adventure? Are you kidding? Wasn't I already in enough deep doo-doo?"

"You certainly were. Copenhagen next?"

"Yes, a wonderfully colorful city, but cold and unfriendly compared to Edinburgh. There were several Shore Patrol incidents. I was glad not to be involved."

"How did you feel about your second exposure to the 'Black Shoe' battleship Navy?"

"Pretty good, compared to the destroyer cruise. Our battleships were the all-time queens of the seas. Beautiful lines and a hell of a lot of fire power. When we fired all nine sixteen inch guns broadside, it moved the ship twelve feet sideways. Everything was first class compared to destroyers."

"So, you were commissioned immediately at the end of the cruise?"

"Not immediately. The Captain went ashore as soon as we docked and I had to sit on my butt for three days awaiting his return.2 September 1955, the tenth anniversary of the Jap surrender aboard Wisconsin's sister ship, USS Missouri. Ironically, on the next passage the CO ran the Wisconsin aground going up the river to the Philadelphia Naval Shipyard for decommissioning, thereby also decommissioning his career."

"Did you heed your father's advice to tell Navy you were married before you were commissioned?"

"Yes I did. During the cruise I asked the Chaplain what I should do. He said he would discuss it with the Officer in Charge of Midshipmen and get back to me. When he did, I was told to sign the papers saying I was single."

"Then what?"

"I picked up Aurelie and we reported for duty at Pensacola Naval Air Station, towing my roadster with the 1947 Ford 'woody' station wagon her parents sold me. The gate guards said I couldn't drive the roadster on base because it had no bumpers. I guess they had seen kids like me show up for flight training before."

"Quite an entrance, Captain. Did you and Aurelie live together?"

"No. She took an apartment in town and a job at Monsanto mills. I lived in the Bachelor Officers Quarters at Naval Air Station Pensacola during Preflight Training and then NAS Whiting Field twenty five miles away for Basic Flight Training."

"What was Preflight Training like?"

"Lots of aeronautical academics, plus physical fitness and survival training. The academics were interesting since it was directly related to flying. Physical fitness and survival training was grueling torture like the god awful 'step test', jumping off a twenty foot tower into the pool, the obstacle course, plus devices like the 'Dilbert Dunker' which was a cockpit on forty-five degree rails that dumped you into the pool and turned upside down sinking as you struggled to get free from chute and harness."

"What did you do with your hot rod?"

"Since I couldn't drive the roadster on base, I left it parked at the base hobby shop. Two fellow OI's, Officers under Instruction, we were called who saw the roadster asked if I might be interested in stock car racing. I said I would loan the roadster's engine if they furnished the car. So, Keith and George bought a '47 Ford coupe and we set about modifying it in the hobby shop garage for late model stock car racing on the local Five Flags half mile dirt track. We worked on it every night until 10 pm closing time. So Aurelie and I had little time together, except that she got pregnant."

"Whoa, hold up there, Captain. How did that happen?"

"In the usual way of course. What can I say? Totally stupid of us. Naturally, Aurelie felt somewhat left out of the sex picture and wanted to be included. It certainly was not my intent, but felt I couldn't deny her, so I went along with it. I was easy. After waiting so long, I guess my guys had their wings and track shoes on. Pulling out was not adequate birth control."

"This is getting better than the 'Officer and a Gentleman' film."

"Oh yes, Mike, and it keeps getting *much* better. For the sake of appearances, Aurelie and I got an apartment and told our friends that we were married. I went on to begin flying at Whiting Field and racing our coupe on weekends. Initially, we were to share the driving, but Keith was more interested in turning wrenches. Then George scared himself in an excursion off the track, so all the driving was left to me. What a blast, sliding around a half mile dirt track in our Navy blue and Gold polka-dot number '01' coupe. I won my second race, never placed lower than third, and never won more than forty dollars! This was literally a red neck junk yard sport. Since Navy didn't permit us to race because of the risk, I did not use my name. So, an announcer labeled me 'The Purple Mask' and it stuck. It was during this time that I met Dorothy. She drove up with George in his '38 Ford roadster. When she stepped out, I damned near fainted. It was not just that she was absolutely the most gorgeous woman I ever saw, before or after, there was an inner light so familiar in her I strongly felt that our destiny was entwined. Soon after, however, Dorothy too was pregnant. She and George were married and we all became close friends."

"So, considering the circumstances, it seems life wasn't going all so badly for you."

"Not for long though, Mike. Soon after you were born, one day just after a flight, a Marine with a sidearm walked up and asked, 'Are you Ensign Sousa, sir?' 'Yes, why?' 'Would you come with me please? Captain Williams, the JAG Officer at NAS Pensacola wants to see you. He will explain.' Emma had tried to call me at the BOQ and my ex-roommate told her I had gotten married and moved out. She immediately wrote the Bureau of Naval Personnel stating that we were married before I was commissioned, had a child, that I had not supported her financially, and that I had also married someone else. Captain William's informed me that I was being charged with non-support, bigamy, and making a false statement. I had a fifty percent chance of losing my commission."

"How did you respond?"

"I told Captain Williams the truth about what had happened. When we married, I told Emma I would send whatever allowance Navy paid me for being married, which amounted to $87 a month rental allowance. An Ensign's basic pay was $220 a month. Fortunately, I had receipts for the money orders I had sent Emma. The non-support charge was totally bogus. Initially, I didn't divulge my conversations with the Chaplain aboard Wisconsin in the hope of keeping him and the Officer in Charge away from negative consequences."

"How did Captain Williams react?"

"Great, but I'm going to digress before answering to tell you about this very special man. Captain Williams, I learned, had been a naval aviator in the Pacific during World War Two and was shot down over a Jap occupied island. He not only managed to evade capture, but over the next few months killed all forty Jap soldiers on the island and was subsequently awarded the nation's highest medal, the Congressional Medal of Honor. After the war, Williams left the Navy, went back to college for a law degree, and then re-joined the Navy in the JAG Corps.

"What's a JAG, Captain?"

"Judge Advocate General, the Navy's legal beagles. Which brings me back to your question. Williams was a Prince in the finest sense of the word. After finally confiding that I had told the Chaplain I was married, Williams located him and he confirmed my story. Then Williams came to our apartment to meet Aurelie and advised her to go home until the matter was cleared up, which she did. Then he got in my Albuquerque attorney's face to accelerate the divorce. He got written positive endorsements from my flight instructors and drafted a letter for the Admiral's signature to recommend no further official action. Before signing it, however, the Admiral called me in. It didn't go very well, Mike. I really did not need another morality lecture from a stranger at that point. Not even my father had done that. Nevertheless, the Admiral signed the letter, but with paragraph four deleted which would have been his personal endorsement of my great worth to the Navy as cannon fodder for another Korea."

"Bad attitude, Captain?"

"I was innocent of all charges. If that didn't satisfy them, I was in the wrong Navy. Williams was mildly disappointed and I'm sorry for that. He was a great benefactor and had surely walked the extra miles for me, but I had a line of self-respect that I wouldn't sacrifice. I sent Christmas cards to Williams every year until they were returned for unknown addressee. Anyhow, it took until June to get Emma to divorce court. She dragged her feet every step of the way, piling up bills. She had an expensive caesarean delivery solely because, as she told me later, she did not want to have a birth pass through her genitals. She said she couldn't work because she was breast feeding. Her attorney got fed up, fired her, and refused to represent her in the divorce. And so it went. Finally, I drove non-stop from Pensacola to Albuquerque for divorce court. It was June. Aurelie was seven months pregnant. The judgment was $100 a month child support, more than a third of my pay. 'For the sake of legitimacy' my ass, and this wasn't the end of her efforts to screw me by a long shot. On the way back to Pensacola, I met Aurelie in Pascagoula Mississippi, where there was no waiting period. We were married by a pastor in a small church the day after the divorce was final. To get past the embarrassment of being very pregnant, I told the minister that we had been married before I was commissioned and I needed another official date of marriage. Had I known the future complications, I wouldn't have made up that excuse."

"Quite a colorful picture, Captain. Two kids and two wives in a year, arrested for bigamy, driving stock cars, and going through flight training. You had all the makings for a fine Pukin' Dog, didn't you?"

"Yup, not even Jaybee could hold a candle to me and it does get better. Not that I was trying to be colorful, I just followed the Yellow Brick Road."

"How did Aurelie hold up through all this?"

"Magnificently well. She couldn't have been more positive and optimistic."

"There was never a harsh word between us or hint of recrimination from her about Emma. Nevertheless, there was an underlying toll on our relationship. Too much happened too fast for us to renew the bond. We simply made the most of the chaos and quietly hoped for better in our future."

"Didn't the pressures and distractions effect your flying?"

"No, but I was disappointed initially. I wasn't much better as a flight student than I had been in academia. No doubt about it, I was always a slow learner in everything except auto racing. I could understand why Navy flight training was all about procedures and precision which required rote memorization, but it took some of the romance out of flying in the early phase. Dirt track auto racing was easy for me and more exciting. However, as I progressed in flying and personal matters settled down a bit, it got to be fun. We started out flying SNJ's, the Navy version of the famous AT-6 Texan. The SNJ was used as an advance trainer in World War Two and became the most demanding primary trainer Navy has had. Its performance was nearly equivalent to some of our front line fighters in the early forties. There are many still flying. We flew in four plane divisions with an instructor chasing, through formation, aerobatics, air-to-air gunnery, dive bombing, and carrier qualification phases. It turned out to be more fun than any other airplane I flew in the Navy, especially tail chase aerobatics and carrier landings. There was one infamous instructor in the formation phase known as 'The Screamer' because he was inclined to lose his cool with his students. The Screamer was immortalized one day when four instructors replaced the Screamer's students and did everything wrong -much to the rage of the Screamer, whose tirades and rants were preserved for posterity on an audio tape which occasionally still makes the rounds on the internet. As you will see, I enjoyed the opportunity to fly with the Screamer five years later. The gunnery, dive bombing, and carrier qualification phases were flown at Barren Field, Foley Alabama -called 'Bloody Barren' because of the high accident rate. Dive bombing was done on offshore targets. Because it is difficult to judge altitude over water, plus the lure of 'target fixation', it was essential to keep track of the rapidly unwinding altimeter in forty-five degree dives. One of my classmates failed to pull out. Water depth was only thirty five feet, so he and the SNJ were recovered. Out of respect for my classmate and curiosity to see what a 250 knot impact with the water did to an airplane, I went to see the wreckage on a flatbed truck. There were no signs of body parts, of course, but the heavy seat belts and shoulder harness were broken and there was a clear imprint of the body's impact with the instrument panel. As I stood looking at the wreckage, a short, thin, elderly looking Commander walked up and asked about the crash. We stood silently for a few moments before he said, 'Sometimes, when I think about all the friends I have lost in plane crashes....' and he choked up in tears. I wondered if I would one day have that same experience."

"Did you?"

"No. I was lucky to lose no close friends to crashes or combat. The loss rate was much lower in my day than in the Commander's. On a lighter note, I should relate two night landing pattern stories about the Jap and Italian students in training with us. The pattern for our first night landings in SNJ's was four airplanes in the lower pattern doing touch and goes. Four more planes with a designated leader circled higher above the field until the lower pattern made final landings. A Runway Duty Officer, RDO, instructor was posted on the approach end of the runway to observe and control the lower pattern. Another instructor flew around the upper circle. To signal a final landing to others in the lower pattern, the RDO told students when to turn on their landing lights. One Jap student did not understand. 'Turn on your landing lights', the instructor said. Pause. 'Say again RDO?' 'Turn on your landing lights.' Pause. 'Uh, say again RDO?' 'TURN ON YOUR LANDING LIGHTS'. Pause. 'Ah SO! Randing Rights!" Later, the upper pattern instructor said, 'Leader of the upper pattern, you are too close to the field. Take it out.' No response. Minutes pass and the instructor says, 'Leader of the upper pattern, you are too far out now, take it in.' No response. Soon the agitated instructor .says, 'Leader of the upper pattern, I told you to take it in. ACKNOWLEDGE. In a heavy Italian accent the student said, 'First you tella me take it out, then you tella me take it in. Why don't you make uppa you mind?' After the flight, in the hangar, I saw the instructor giving the Italian holy hell, but the Italian couldn't have cared less, standing there holding his helmet with 'Que Sera Sera' stenciled across the back of it."

"Did the foreign students go through the entire flight training program?"

"No. They didn't carrier qualify. In fact, our little joke was that the Japs only had to be taught how to takeoff."

"What was carrier qualification like?"

"Well, three more classmates had accidents which totaled their SNJs. Fortunately, they were uninjured. One had an engine failure on takeoff and came down in a wooded area. Trees sheared off both wings, turned him sideways, and two more trees took off the nose and tail. The only sizeable part of the SNJ remaining was the cockpit with him sitting in it unscratched. Another classmate stalled and spun into the ground on a field practice carrier landing approach. As the pilot jumped out of the wreckage and ran full speed past the instructor Landing Signal Officer with his helmet on and parachute bouncing off the back of his legs, the instructor said, 'Broke your airplane didn't you? The third accident was aboard the carrier, USS Saipan, the same carrier that was in our Brazil cruise. Saipan was a small World War Two escort carrier with no angled deck landing area, which meant that if you didn't hook a wire there was no going around for another try. You were going into the barricade or worse. I was a 'walk aboard' which meant I was to hot seat another classmate's SNJ after he made his qualifying arrested landings. Meanwhile, I was permitted to observe the proceedings from the starboard catwalk abeam the landing area. One of the Chiefs said I was lucky to get to see my classmates do it before trying it myself. I assumed he meant good luck, but on his first approach another classmate leveled off high, flew into the barricade, and crashed into the island structure–uninjured. I was impressed by how fast the wreckage was cleared away. Obviously, the crew had done this many times before! Finally it was my turn. I was chewing gum so fast and hard after my first landing that the taxi director had a big laugh. What great fun, Mike. How glad I was to be Navy, the Air Force sure had nothing to match the thrill of this!"

"Better than auto racing, Captain?"

"Oh hell yes. The thing about racing on a half mile dirt track was that the thrill was sustained throughout the race. Although just the final phase of a flight, carrier landings top anything else you can do with an airplane, a quality thirty second crescendo of mounting unmatched excitement."

"You make it sound like sex!"

"Even better, Mike. Good analogy though, but speak for yourself on the thirty seconds timing."

"What next, Captain?"

"The final phase of basic flight training was instrument training in T-28's, a much higher performance airplane than the SNJ, but less fun. Flying blind on instruments under a hood is a difficult grind, very precise flying, demanding constant concentration on flight instruments to fight off false sensory signals which would otherwise result in complete spatial disorientation vertigo. The book work was tough too, with many flight rules to memorize. But it all seemed to pass quickly."

"So much for basic, on to advance training?"

"Yes, a very important step. Where you went next determined your entire flying career. There were separate programs for seaplanes, patrol planes, propeller driven carrier planes, and jets. Initially, I wanted to be an airline pilot, but whatever residual ambition I had along that line were washed away in basic training. Now, I wanted to fly carrier based jet fighters, period. Problem was, so did everyone else and there weren't many Navy jet fighter squadrons in the fifties. Then some enterprising personnel genius came up with the idea of taking advantage of the supply-demand situation by offering advance training of choice for extending obligated service one year. At first I decided to take my chances, but then it was obvious that so many were extending for jets there was no chance of getting them otherwise. I was almost too late. I literally ran all the way to the Admin office and was so out of breath I was barely able to make my preference known. But jets it was to be. Just one more hurdle, the checkout flight physical. I flunked it. Disqualifying astigmatism in both eyes."

"How could that be? You passed the Denver eye exam just the year before. Your eyes couldn't have gone bad that fast."

"That's what I thought. Obviously, Denver didn't catch it. Providence had interceded."

"Do you think providence had something to do with the choices made in your imaginary conversation with God?"

"I was willing to trade Aurelie for flying, and passed the tests, so now I had Aurelie back and flunked. What would be your answer?"

"No doubt about it, Captain. How did you get around it?"

"It was my great good fortune that the eye doctor was another Captain Prince like Williams. The doctor said that the Navy's standards on eyesight were based on getting twenty years of flying out of me. If I wore sunglasses, stayed out of the sun, and could read anything on the 20-20 line on the eye chart the next morning, he would recommend a waiver. So I did, and he did, and I was on my way to Corpus Christi for Jet Advance Training."

"You must have felt that God was putting you through the mill. How did you feel about that?"

"I did feel a strong hand in my life, I didn't know about Jean's influence then, but I was very grateful that matters kept turning out well. Reminds me of the story about God's sense of humor. One day He and Saint Peter were watching a Catholic Mass and God said 'Watch this'. He said 'Sit down' and everyone sat. 'Stand up" and they did. 'Kneel' and they did. 'Sit', 'Kneel', 'Cross yourselves', 'Stand', 'Kneel', 'Sit", and so on. God and Saint Peter had a jolly fine time."

"What about your racing pals, George and Keith?"

"Glad you asked. The divorce and settlement were a financial blow and Aurelie was no longer working, so I had to put the engine back into my roadster and sell it. The wagon's wood was rotted out, so that had to go too. I replaced it with a '53 Studebaker. My hot rod days were over. For the second racing season, Keith and George bought a '32 coupe and moved up to modified stock car racing Friday, Saturday, and Sunday at Pensacola, Fort Walton Beach, and Montgomery. I did the driving, but little mechanical work, though I attended the hobby shop every night until closing time. There was so little time for Aurelie that I totally missed her birthday. It was time to quit and I did."

"Did you lose touch with George and Keith when you moved to Corpus Christi?"

"Keith went to patrol plane training in Kansas, so I lost touch with him for a long time. George went to single engine propeller attack training nearby. He and Dorothy lived near us and we became even closer friends than we had been in Pensacola."

"Aurelie must have been close to delivery?"

"Very close, Mike. My last Pensacola T-28 flight was August 11th '56. David Alexander Sousa was born August 28th in Corpus Christi."

"How did it go?"

"No complications. The wives had been briefed about the importance of letting their Jet Pilots get full nights of rest and not keep them up with rocking the baby, diaper changing, and bottle feeding. Aurelie took it to heart, bless her, and was very stoic. The afternoon when it was time, she simply went to the base hospital and gave birth. By the time I was informed, it was all over."

"What were you feelings about fatherhood then?"

"Honesty, I must say that David was the most perfectly beautiful baby I ever saw, before or since. Otherwise, I have to admit that I felt detached. It had simply happened, with little will or contribution from me."

"Same about me?"

"Yes. In a normal family relationship, perhaps I would have felt more involved. Who knows? As it happened, two months later Aurelie was pregnant again. Christopher Lee Sousa was to be born July 13th '57 in San Diego. So, I had two wives and three children in twenty months. There was so much on our plates that there was little opportunity to contemplate the emotional significance of marriage or fatherhood."

"My my, Captain. Your forebodings about sex were certainly well founded, weren't they? Did you ever wish you had taken your father's advice to never see Aurelie again?"

"At the time, it wouldn't have been productive for me to dwell on that question, Mike. We just accepted events as being the nature of life and made the best of it. As it turned out fourteen years later though, as you will see, Father was correct. In Germany I disagreed with Aurelie's declared intention to have four children. Obviously, however, we were well on our way to that. You no doubt wonder why birth control wasn't employed, but these were the fifties remember, many years before 'the Pill', diaphragms, foams, or vasectomies. Condoms and the 'rhythm method' were about the only choices other than the good old Catholic solution the absurd 'rhythm method'. Then when the diaphragm came along, Aurelie said she couldn't use it because of her tipped uterus. I had a block against condoms, so I certainly do not hold myself blameless, Mike. In any event, ladies who want to have babies are an undeniable force and having five wonderful children turned out to be a great blessing and a joy. There have been a number of times in my life where events occurred counter to my wishes, but turned out to be better choices than I would have made for myself. As my good friend Ron Hess observed, 'Men are led through life by their penis.'"

"Sad but true, isn't it? But you were surely well compensated. You were a Jet Pilot in the hay day of jets."

"Absolutely, jet pilots were everyone's heroes then and we were pioneers on the cutting edge of aviation, only fifty years since the Wright brothers' flight. Navy was still flying our first generation of carrier jets and space programs were Buck Rogers dreams. Risky business too. After flying my first jet, the TV-2 under the hood for instrument training, I went to the final squadron before getting my wings to fly Korean War vintage F9F-5 'Panther' fighters. For our welcome aboard, the squadron CO, 'Tiger' Lewis, assembled us in the ready room. He sat on the edge of the desk and glowered at us individually for a very long time like Jack Balance in his worst crazy gunfighter role. Finally, he said that within three years one in five of us would have been killed in a plane crash. After letting that sink in, he lectured us that we had to want to fly more than anything else in life. 'If you wouldn't rather fly than eat, I'm going to find out who you are and boot your butt out of this program.' Someone had complained about being scheduled to fly during lunch time. As much as we all loved flying more than life, I think we each felt a touch of unworthiness. I did decide, however, that I'd better show some responsibility as a family man and get some life insurance. The John Hancock agent who came to our home was a very charming lady who kept buttering me up with 'Oh, you Jet Pilot you' and sold us a ten thousand dollar ordinary life policy for a whopping forty dollar monthly premium, nearly half of my flight pay! Our 'black shoe' peers, always jealous of flight pay, liked to ask, 'I know what you do to earn your flight pay, but what do you do to earn your base pay?' Our answer was, 'Look, we don't get paid more than you, we just make it quicker'."

"What was flying Panthers like?"

"Outstanding. Wonderful. Everything before this had been two seat trainers. Panthers were the real thing, single-engine single-seat front line carrier jet fighters flown in Korean combat just a couple of years before. Perhaps you saw them in the movie 'The Bridges of Too RI'. We flew in four plane flights, plus an instructor. Our instructor was very cool and near our age. He looked and acted like Elvis Presley. Since he was a duck hunter, he named us 'Pintail Flight'. Instead of checking in on the radio after startup or frequency changes by saying 'One up', 'Two up', etcetera, we quacked, once for number one in the flight, and so on down the line. Our first flight was to go off on our own to individually explore the Panther's envelope. Before the flight, another member of the flight and I had a discussion about what would happen if we pointed the nose straight up and rolled the airplane until it ran out of airspeed. Finally, we asked the instructor. His logical answer was that it would be very difficult to judge pointing straight up, so the nose would just fall off toward the closest horizon. We decided to test that answer and both had the same experience. We may not have had our noses pointed exactly straight up but the gyroscopic action of rolling kept us on track until the yaw string in front of the windscreen, used as a yaw trim indicator for air-to-air gunnery, shot straight out in front of our Panthers as we fell back down the way we came! Not for long, of course, the Panthers were smarter than we were in righting themselves nose down. Except for carrier landings, we did pretty much everything we had done in SNJ's formation, aerobatics, and gunnery. I have a vivid memory of my first Panther takeoff. First flights in a new type airplane were always similar for me, a feeling that I had no idea what I was doing. Since jets did not have ground level ejection seats then, we took off and landed Panthers with the sliding canopy open to facilitate exiting the cockpit in the event of a crash. We were briefed to land straight ahead if the engine quit on takeoff. Since there was family housing off the departure end of the normally used runway, someone asked if we shouldn't try to avoid them. The answer was 'No, land straight ahead there might not be anyone home. So, I was thinking about that during my first Panther takeoff when I closed the canopy and it got so deadly quiet I was certain that the engine had failed, but it hadn't, thank goodness. No one had mentioned that the Panther's pressurization system was the quietest ever made. I have never flown another airplane with near the silence in the cockpit not even gliders. I have several more flying tales in that phase to report. David had colic which kept us awake most of the night. One morning I slept through the alarm and was fifteen minutes late for a six AM briefing. To my horror, Tiger Lewis was replacing our instructor. Thankfully, I was spared with a brief comment on the importance of punctuality, but Tiger put me on his wing for some close formation work. Although his helmet and oxygen mask covered all but his gunfighter eyes, that was enough to cause a slight ripple through my controls when he looked at me. During another flight with our regular instructor I saw eight airplanes where I knew there were only four, a sure sign of anoxia, confirmed by the fact that my oxygen regulator was not blinking, and made further apparent when I tried to report it to the instructor with slurred speech. We immediately descended and returned to base. Trouble shooting revealed that the cockpit pressurization dump valve was open, so I'd had a double whammy coincidental failure which might have been fatal. On the next flight I found that the oxygen blinker on that airplane wasn't working either, so I had my mask checked. We carried our knee board checklists and oxygen mask in our helmets. It was discovered that a piece of checklist plastic binding had broken off and lodged in my oxygen mask exhalation flapper valve holding it open with the result that I had been inhaling cockpit air instead of oxygen. One weekend we had a mass cross-country flight of twenty Panthers to Dallas. The rumor was that Dallas girls were very attracted naval aviators, especially in dress blue uniforms. Navy 'Wings of Gold' were crassly called 'leg spreaders'. Our 'Pintail' flight wasn't scheduled to stay overnight, so we did not take along baggage. As fate would have it, however, the weather closed in and we were stuck for the night. So, we joined our classmates for a Saturday night at the Dallas Hilton in our sweaty flight suits. I will never forget the scene in the lobby. One enterprising young aviator had purchased a toy helicopter at the gift shop which flew at the end of a hand cranked cable to the rotor with a sign underneath reading 'Party in room 812. Free booze. Everyone welcome.' just as a black tie and furs reception party arrived. And it worked! Some of them showed up! Mike, I just can't express how proud I was to be in the company of such out-standing naval aviators."

"Wow, Captain, I'm beginning to understand. You were in the right place, weren't you?"

"Oh yes, I was a most fortunate man. December 19th 1956, the day I got my 'Navy Wings of Gold' was the proudest and happiest event of my life and the second of only two times I got so drunk I lost memory of the celebration. It was a long and hard row to hoe, but it happened and nothing could ever take it away from me, I was a Naval Aviator. Thank God."

"What about Dorothy and George?"

"Dorothy had cooked us a wonderful Christmas dinner and then excused herself to give birth to their daughter Anne. Inexplicably, George quit flight training, got orders to the Philippines, and left Dorothy and Anne behind. Dorothy returned to Pensacola and they eventually divorced. Having grown up with nine siblings on a Texas ranch, Dorothy was even more stoic than Aurelie. As a wise man once advised, 'A man should always marry a girl from Texas, because no matter what happens, she's seen worse.' This was far from the end of Dorothy in my life though, and I did see George again."

SNJ "Texan"

Span, 42 ft
Length, 29 ft 6 in
Height, 11ft &1 in
Wing area, 254 sq ft.
Wts: Empty, 4,158 lb-gross,
5,300 lb
Power plant: One 550 hp
Pratt & Whitney R-1340-AN-1.

Performance
Max speed, 205 mph at 5,000 ft
Cruising speed, 170 mph at 5,000 ft

**"OI", our '47 Ford Stock Car,
Five Flags Speedway, 1/2 mile dirt track, 1956**

ENS. MANUEL B. SOUSA, JR

T-28 "Trojan" - engine Wright R-1820-86, wingspan 40 ft, max wt 8,500 lbs,
max speed 343 mph, ceiling 35,000 ft

TV-2 "Shooting Star" - engine Allison J-33, wing span 37 ft,
max wt 15,000 lbs, max speed 600 mph, ceiling 47,000 ft

F9F-2 "Panther" - engine Pratt & Whitney J-48, wing span 38 ft
max weight 19,500 lbs, max speed 575 mph, ceiling 45,000 ft

13

WELCOME TO THE FLEET

"Good morning, Captain. Sleep well?"

"Yes, Mike, very well. I'll tell you about it after breakfast. I wouldn't want any of these old farts in the Lodge dining room overhearing."

"Old farts? Goodness Captain, at ninety four, aren't you the oldest fart at Heritage Pines?"

"Depends on what you consider old farts, I reckon. Some at Heritage Pines retirement home were old farts when they were fifty."

"I see, but it sounds like you have good news?"

"Nothing grand, but progress. Other news may interest you more. Sam Steele is flying his Cub over at two this afternoon to begin your flight training. Since you are both more experienced in Cubs and Champs, your first lessons will be in Sam's Cub. Sam is charging you $85 for travel expenses each trip and $100 an hour for instruction in his Cub. It's been awhile since Sam has flown a Ximango, so I will go around the patch with him for a few landings before he flies it with you. Sam's Ximango lessons will be $50 an hour. Pretty reasonable these days, I'd say. After you solo the Ximango, you'll be able to fly over to his strip for instruction and save the travel fees. We'll be late for dinner at the Lodge, so plan on dinner at the Food Barn near the airport. Sam won't be joining us. We should leave here at noon and have the Ximango ready to go before Sam arrives. Meanwhile, we can spend a couple of hours with the book after breakfast."

"Sounds great, Captain. Good day for it too. I'll tell Georgie we'll be away to the airport past dinner."

After breakfast, at their regular spot on the edge of the woods...

"So, tell me your news, Captain. Did you have a flying dream?"

"Not exactly, but there's progress to report. I've been working at limbering up my neck to roll my head on my pillow. I'm getting through the neck pains better and I've begun to regain the kind of self-hypnosis I did as a four year old trying to get past my earaches and put myself asleep, which led to controlling my dreams of levitation. Well, not really dreams, since I remained semi-conscious. Flights of fancy I suppose you could call them, or out of body experiences."

"How much progress have you made?"

"So far it's as I began ninety years ago. I saw myself curled up in a fetal position looking back down at me from the far corner of the ceiling of a large room."

"That's great. Anything else?"

"No, that's it. It didn't last long just a few seconds."

"Do you recall what the next steps were at age four, as your flights progressed?"

"Oh yes. The experience gradually lasted longer. Then I shifted to being on the shelf in the corner of the ceiling, looking back down at myself on the bed."

"What did you do? Was there any sound or motion? What did the room look like? Where was it?"

"No sound or motion. I remained still and in a fetal position, floating without support. The room was dimly lit and featureless -no doors, windows, pictures, light fixtures, or furnishings. Nowhere I had been before."

"How did you feel? Were you frightened?"

"It was very peaceful and calm and my ear aches left. I think I was reassured by seeing myself on the bed looking back up at me without alarm or fear. When you're four, the whole world is so new and full of wonders, it's easy to accept such events as common experiences. So, the dreams eventually progressed to flying freely, but required so much focused concentration that success was spotty and short-lived. Many times I failed altogether. Although I knew it wasn't real, I believed that it could be one day."

"Well, Captain, you were certainly right about that. I've seen you actually levitate -albeit you were asleep and didn't realize it! You didn't seem surprised when I told you. Why was that?"

"Partly because at my age, the surprise threshold is quite high, Mike. Besides, the dreams are so vivid and I've had so many of them over the years that I felt the experience was very close to reality. So when you said you saw me levitate, it was not a great leap of faith for me. Mostly, I felt nostalgia. When you have wanted to accomplish something so strongly for so many years, and finally get there, you realize that it was the adventure of the journey that mattered more than the destination itself. I felt the same when I earned my Navy Wings, and especially when I sighted the Cape Saint Vincent light house arriving in Europe after sailing Wings across the Atlantic in '86. Important phases of my life had ended and could not be repeated. Buddhists say that death is life's greatest adventure, and it may be. Meanwhile, I think the getting there is the best part. It was the same with sex and love too. What do you think, Mike?"

"I haven't thought about it much, but I see your view. I can relate it to earning my law degree. Graduation and passing the Bar didn't seem like big events after the effort that went into the achievements. Landmark ceremonies which come at the end of adventures, remind me of your thoughts about the Wizard of Oz's awards. I agree that sex itself is overrated. Of course, it's easy for us to say that at our age, but the best part of it was the romance and intimacy. And who knows what 'love' really is? Women, especially mothers, think they have an exclusive understanding and men just don't get it. But I think much of women's notion of love is self-satisfaction derived from manipulating men and children. That's why so many women are nurses and teachers -captive audiences."

"Right, Mike. On the other hand, men 'love' to do fun things with machines and organizations which become extensions of themselves."

"Like sailing and flying, Captain?"

"Exactly, Mike, or being a Commanding Officer...which brings us back to 'Passing Through'. We left off in December 1956. I had just gotten my naval aviator wings and six of us in my class received orders to VAH-6 at Naval Air Station North Island. We had never heard of a 'VAH' squadron. We knew that 'V' meant heavier than air, so we weren't going to a blimp squadron. We also knew that 'A' meant an attack squadron, so that wasn't bad because some had jets. But the 'H' was a mystery. The Administrative Yeoman could only suggest helicopters! Good grief, helicopters? Then we asked our bachelor instructor. He didn't know what 'H' meant either, but said he would fly anything to be stationed at North Island because Coronado's Mexican Village bar and restaurant was naval aviation's most famous 'body exchange'. Finally, someone told us about the directory of Navy squadrons where we found VAH-6 listed as Heavy Attack Squadron Six, assigned twenty four AJ-2 'Savage' 'aircraft. So, what was Heavy Attack and what were AJ's, we asked? Who knew? Finally, someone told us AJ's were carrier based bombers with two props and a jet, designed to deliver nuclear weapons. Our hearts sank. We had extended obligated service for a year to be jet fighter pilots, now we were going to be multi-engine prop bomber pilots? Good Lord, what a letdown. Then, someone told us that AJ's were being replaced with new twin jet A3D Sky Warriors. Hey, not so bad after all, we were going to fly the latest jets in the fleet! So, with high hopes, we set off for San Diego. I'll digress here to tell about North Island, on the west side of San Diego Harbor. San Diego was home port to a major portion of Navy's Pacific Fleet, carrier squadrons, and seaplanes. As many as four carriers were home-ported at Naval Air Station North Island with the pretty little town of Coronado attached. Besides the Mexican Village, Coronado was best known for the Hotel Del Coronado, a huge posh beautiful hotel built in the twenties, affordable only to the rich and famous. There was no connecting bridge across the harbor. Other than driving thirty plus miles around South Bay, auto ferries or 'nickel snatcher' passenger launches were the only way to get to North Island. Although Coronado residents were happy to be isolated from the San Diego riff-raff, the nickel snatchers were a hell of an inconvenience and bottleneck for the thousands of sailors and civilian workers commuting daily to the base. Finally, in the sixties, despite very strong resistance by Coronado, a major bridge replaced water transport across the harbor."

"Coronado sounds exclusive. Were you able to afford to live there or did you ride the nickel snatchers too?"

"We were very fortunate to find a nice affordable two bedroom apartment on the ground floor just a few blocks from the base. Looking back now, I can't imagine how we managed our finances, but we settled in quickly and comfortably, despite the fact that David was only five months old and Aurelie was five months along with Christopher."

"Fast start, Captain! Did it go as well for you at the squadron?"

"Unfortunately no, it was a depressing evolution from the first day we drove onto the squadron parking lot. It was a Sunday afternoon. Aurelie, David and I drove around the base to check out the locations of facilities and the squadron area. Our impression was that NAS North Island was a very old and cluttered major Navy seaport industrial site. Every square foot of it without huge warehouses, aircraft overhaul facilities, and machine shops was paved over with roads, parking areas, or runways. It seemed to be more a ship's facility than an air base. Naturally, Navy was very hardware oriented by virtue of operating subs, ships, and airplanes based at large seaport cities. There was little room at such bases, nor funds in the Navy budget, to accommodate dependents facilities or housing. With many husbands deployed to sea at any given time, there was little cohesion among navy wives, unlike the other services where many bases are remotely located with housing and facilities on base. So, Navy wives were independently on their own with little reason to feel attachment to the Navy or their husbands' jobs. Consequently, 'family separation' was the primary cause of low career retention and the high divorce rate. Eventually, we located aircraft hangars and a HATRON SIX sign and logo. Immediately on turning into the parking lot we were greeted by a guard shouting 'Halt' and leveling the muzzle of an automatic weapon into my face through my open passenger window, though there were no gates or signs to indicate it was a restricted area. Welcome to the Fleet! Strangely, when I reported to the squadron the next day, there were no armed guards, restrictions, or apparent security of any kind. Nor were there any signs of welcome as I checked in. The Duty Officer barely looked up and the Admin Chief simply handed me a list of offices to check in with. So it was everywhere I went. No 'welcome aboard', no handshakes, no introductions, no offers of help. The morale in this squadron had to be the lowest in the Fleet. It didn't take long to find out why. VAH-6, the only heavy attack squadron on the West Coast, was an unusually large squadron, at least three times the size of other carrier squadrons, with twenty-three AJ-2's assigned and over ninety flight crews, plus twenty ground officers, and over 600 enlisted men assigned to the Aircraft Maintenance Department. Every pilot came from multi-engine patrol plane backgrounds. Many were ex-seaplane pilots. None of them had less than five thousand flying hours compared to our three hundred hours. None of them had carrier experience before coming to AJ's, so they had little motivation to land airplanes larger than Doolittle's B-25's onto small World War Two flight decks especially at night. The AJ had no co-pilot, the right side had no flight controls, it was occupied by the Bombardier-Navigator, a 250 pound bombsight computer, radar scope, and optical bombsight. The Bombardier-Navigators '(BN's)' were all junior officers with Reserve commissions. Several BN's were naval aviators who had completed multi-engine flight training and had made one or two deployments as BN's, but never graduated to flying in the left seat as Heavy Attack Aircraft Commanders because they didn't accumulate the required minimum 1200 hours flight time before they were due for release from active duty which they all eagerly looked forward to at the earliest opportunity. The third seat of the AJ, behind the pilot, facing aft, was occupied by an enlisted Third Crewman, who actually did not have a job in the airplane. Each deploying attack carrier had a three plane AJ Detachment and four 3-man aircrews, so there were many men in the squadron coming and going who never met. We soon learned that the A3D Sky Warrior was several years away from fleet introduction and that the six of us, were to be trained and deployed as BN's like the junior aviators before us. To say that this did not sit well with us would be a gross understatement. The most vocal among us, Jack, wrote his Senator and Congressmen charging Navy with breach of contract because we had extended obligated active duty to be Jet Pilots, NOT bombardiers. A Congressional investigation followed which made all of us very unpopular in the squadron. 'PI', political influence bypassing the chain of command, was unacceptable in military service. In a heated exchange with Captain Charles, the HATWING Commander, Jack called the Captain a sonofabitch which he certainly deserved only earned Jack court martial charges, which were dropped after Jack's second letter to his Congressman."

"Were there any positive results of the Congressional Investigation?"

"None. Navy successfully defended itself with the old standby 'needs of the service' excuse, plus the technical 'catch twenty two' that we had extended for jet pilot training only, with no guarantee of assignment to jet squadrons. As Navy Recruiters are often quoted, 'If you can't take a joke, you shouldn't have joined up'. To make matters' worse, my collateral duty assignment was Assistant Maintenance Officer, which my BA degree in psychology did not qualify me for! My boss, Commander Jack Bolton, the Maintenance Officer, was a one-man-show jerk who had virtually nothing to do with me. The AJ was a highly complex airplane and a maintenance nightmare. The squadron's aircraft flight readiness status was often under ten percent. Reliability was so bad that crews routinely did not bother strapping in to their seats until the takeoff check list was complete at the end of the runway because chances were that grounding discrepancies would result in taxiing back to the line without flying. The files of thousands of maintenance instructions on the office shelves were so way over my head that I escaped by hanging out with the Chiefs and Petty Officers in the Line Shack, passing the time of day picking up pearls of wisdom like: 'the good thing about being married in the Navy is that you have a happy marriage half the time, no matter how you look at it–and that's more than most men can say.'"

"Weren't you flying at all?"

"Not in the squadron at first. While the Training Department was trying to invent a B/N syllabus for us, I bummed rides at Station Ops in the co-pilot seats of R4D's or SNB's, twin engine transports. When we finally began B/N training, it was in the ass end of P2V Neptune patrol planes, modified with AJ bombsights. During boring four hour flights, the six of us took turns dropping twenty five pound inert practice bombs from ten thousand feet on a radar reflector on the Salton Sea, north of El Centro. Since there were more of us than there were 'ditching stations' aboard P2V's, one of us had to sit at the unauthorized navigator's station for takeoffs and landings. One day, the Avionics Chief Petty Officer substituted for our regular instructor in order to get his monthly four hour flight time to qualify for flight pay. As we taxied out he abruptly ordered me to, 'Get in your ditching station.' When I tried to explain that there wasn't another ditching station and that we had been using the navigator's seat instead, the Chief exploded, 'Not when I'm here, GET IN YOUR DITCHING STATION!' I stayed put, I'd had all the fun I could stand. There was no further exchange on the subject until after we landed and I called the Chief aside to tell him what I thought of his disrespectful manner. He demanded to know what he said and I quoted him with the same tone he had used. 'That's what I said and just the way I said it. If you don't like it, tell it to the Ops Officer.' And he walked away! Well, well, my first leadership challenge. I did better than the Ops Officer though, I went to the Commanding Officer with the result that the Chief was permanently removed from flight pay status. Imagine the Chief's added chagrin, Mike, when it turned out that as the Assistant Maintenance Officer, I was his boss's boss. Having been raised by an Army Sergeant, I knew how to regularly get in that bastard's face in his office and in front of his men. In three months he threw in the towel and retired. That was the first time anyone had ever pissed me off to the point of getting revenge– quite a satisfying new experience! It set a line of self-respect that no one was going to cross again without vengeful consequences to them. Thank you Father."

"Good for you, Captain. Too many people would have let it slide and have it eat away at them ever after. Anyhow, what did the six of you do besides drop practice bombs and bitch about it?"

"We translated stereo photographs of targets into radar predictions by viewing them with stereoscopic magnifying glasses. To-scale pencil drawings the size of the radar scope, depicting predicted radar returns, were made for each five mile increment of the inbound track for what the B/N hoped to see on his radar during the run-in heading a laborious, tedious, and boring task. Using those radar predictions, we then made our early AJ flights on very high altitude practice simulated bombing runs on the Air Force's Radar Bomb Scoring site in downtown Los Angeles with the designated 'ground zero' being the southwest corner of the Sears Roebuck Building. Unless you've done it, there is no way to describe the difficulty of the B/N's task to consistently find a particular building on radar in a city the size of Los Angeles especially with no intrinsic motivation for the job. Another tediously boring job for B/N's was celestial navigation, using a periscope sextant to shoot and plot star sights for position fixes on long over water night flights. For two of us, staring for hours at aerial photos of Los Angeles, drawing pictures of radar scopes, and spending hours at navigation plotting boards was too much. This was not what we extended for. BN assignment in Heavy Attack with no pilot flying opportunity was entirely unrelated and inappropriate to naval aviators' training, and it certainly would have a negative impact on future promotions and assignments for those of us who remained on active duty. Since military flying is entirely voluntary hazardous duty and no one can be ordered to it, Mark and John took their only remaining protest option, they turned in their wings and quit flying. As punishment, they were immediately transferred to destroyers. We never heard of them again, but I expect that their punishment was suffered most by the crews on those ships who served under them. The whole affair was an incredibly stupid waste of time, dollars, and manpower by the Navy."

"What next for the four of you then, Captain?"

"We attended SWUPAC, Special Weapons Unit Pacific, for three weeks of highly intensive academic and hands-on instruction on the two actual nuclear bomb types carried by AJ's. Incidentally, since an FBI special personal background investigation was required for a Top Secret security clearance to attend SWUPAC, the question of my bigamy allegations were resurrected, probably during an interview with Emma. You'll recall that to explain Aurelie's obvious pregnancy, I told the minister who married us that we had been married previously and just needed a later date to satisfy Navy Regs. Unable to find evidence of bigamy, an agent finally asked me to sign a formal statement under oath declaring my innocence. I had good reason to suspect Emma because she was writing irrational letters to my CO complaining of my 'negligence'. After several of these letters, the Admin Officer finally just gave them to me to draft responses for his signature."

"How .long did that go on?"

"About once a month for more than a year. Emma was also writing newsy letters to me with pictures of herself and you as though we were still married and I was away on cruise. If Emma's motive was to upset Aurelie, it worked, but not to your benefit. There was no way I could ever agree to seeing or corresponding with you as long as your mother and Aurelie were in the picture."

"That pretty much goes along with my mother's portrayal of you to me as a youngster. She did date other men, but none of those relationships lasted long. I believe she scared men away because she was so strongly independent and eccentric, but I am certain that if she wanted to re-marry she would have made it happen. In any event, she was a devoted mother to me. Well Captain, what say we get back to a more pleasant topic. How was it for you to get up close and personal with atomic bombs at SWUPAC?"

"I was most impressed by their simplicity. Basically, a nuclear reaction is nothing more than putting two sub-critical parts together to form a single super- critical reaction. H-bombs use the heat and pressure of a nuclear reaction to initiate a secondary hydrogen reaction. The difficulty with building one of these monsters comes in processing the raw materials, but of course there were many other technical refinements developed in improving the efficiency of reactions. The smaller and older of the two weapons we carried was quite a Rube Goldberg affair. Because each of the two sub-critical parts were so close to being dangerously super critical, we had to assemble the bomb in the air, miles from the carrier and at altitude. The Rube Goldberg part was in the airborne assembly. The BN and Third Crewman went into the bomb bay with the core, which we launched with in the cockpit. The bomb, with its own battery, had two doors in the nose which opened with a push of a button, then a track extended down in front and a small trolley car ran out onto which the core was placed. When another button was pushed, the trolley retracted into the spherical pit in the belly of the bomb, the track folded up, and the doors closed. If the bomb battery was dead, we had a beautiful little box of shiny wrenches to accomplish the task manually. Then all that was left for us to do was set the two barometric fuses for the airburst altitude -and deliver the damned thing to the target."

"Amazing. What about the larger bomb?"

"The other was a very much more powerful and sophisticated multi-megaton hydrogen bomb. Even when nuclear bombs were so reduced in size and weight that they could be delivered by single engine light attack planes, the yield of our H-bomb was more powerful than the total of all the other bombs the Air wing could deliver. I'll have more to say later about launching with a real one."

"It seems the AJ and the heavy attack mission was a pretty big deal in keeping Navy carriers in the big picture during the operational introduction of nuclear weapons."

"Oh yes indeed, though I had little appreciation for my situation at the time. Remember, these were the Days of the Cold War when the US was facing an imminent all out nuclear exchange with the USSR. Conventional weapons were no longer an option. Every American cit- izen—man, woman and child understood the meaning of the terms Mutually Assured Destruction and Nuclear Holocaust. Our homeland would not be spared annihilation in World War Three. Fallout shelters were installed in the basements of many homes. School children were drilled in taking cover. Signs were posted in public places with shelter locations and instructions. One 'sign of the times' advised folks to curl up in the fetal position with their head between their knees and kiss their ass goodbye."

"Was it really that serious?"

"Worse. On top of everything else, there was the Korean War, the Berlin Airlift, and finally, the Cuban Missile Crisis, all of which nearly escalated into nuclear attacks. Most Americans believed that a nuclear war with the USSR was inevitable."

"So the Navy response to the threat was the AJ? How did it come about?"

"In the opening paragraph of Steve Ginter's book, 'North American AJ-1 Savage', he writes: *'The North American AJ Savage came into being as the direct result of the greatest Navy and Government controversy since Billy Mitchell and the Battleships. This controversy was over the future strike capability of the Navy, if any.'* At the end of World War Two, the Army Air Corps, which became the Air Force in 1947, had total control over all nuclear weapons and their B-29's were the only airplanes that could deliver them due to the bombs' size and weight. The Hiroshima and Nagasaki bombs each weighed over ten thousand pounds, the Nagasaki 'Fat Man' type bomb measured nearly six feet in diameter. Navy argued that the B-29 lacked long enough range, requiring launches from foreign bases to reach Soviet targets; however, there weren't many countries where the US was permitted or willing to store nuclear weapons. Navy argued that Air Force's follow-on B-36 and B-52 long range high altitude strategic bombers were vulnerable to early detection and attack, so would require fighter escort from foreign bases. The Navy's proposal was that it could launch strikes from carriers free to sail over two thirds of the Earth's surface without foreign bases or fly-over agreements. Consequently, Navy was allocated a grand total of three weapons and opened bomber design competition in August 1945, awarded to North American Aviation, for a fast medium range carrier based bomber capable of delivering a Fat Man. Meanwhile, Navy needed an interim carrier based nuclear delivery airplane. The only choice was the P2V Neptune land based patrol bomber, which was too large for normal carrier operations. Nevertheless, the Navy ordered twelve specially modified Neptunes which were to be hoisted aboard carrier flight decks in port, deck launched with rocket assist motors, and the crew recovered after ditching alongside rescue ships IF they returned."

"IF, Captain? Were survival odds that grim?"

"Yes, grim for everyone. Our role was retaliation, since politics did not allow for a preemptive attack. The Russians had the first strike surprise advantage. We'd be coming from behind at he outset - a bad position to be in for a nuclear exchange which might not last past round one because there would be little capability for follow-on strikes. Some scientists predicted that a radiation dust cloud would enshroud the planet and snuff out all life on the earth's surface. So, bomber crew survival was mostly a cosmetic consideration."

"Were P2V's ever deployed operationally aboard carriers?"

"No, but contingency plans for it were in place. To publicize the capability, however, a P2V with a dummy nuke aboard was deck launched from an offshore Atlantic Coast carrier and flown on a round-trip non-stop flight to the Pacific Coast, returning to an East Coast Naval Air Station."

"How did the AJ introduction pan out?"

"Quite well. The AJ-1 was ordered in June 1946, the first three prototypes flew in June 1948, and squadron deliveries of fifty five production AJ-l's began in September 1949. The improved model AJ-2's came along in February 1953. The Savage was the first naval combat aircraft to carry a nuclear weapon and the world's largest carrier based aircraft. All carriers deployed with four-plane AJ detachments. Because AJ's were usually in launch alert status and folding its seventy five foot wing span was a four hour manual operation rarely done, AJ's were a significant deck handling headache for aircraft handlers aboard small World War Two vintage carriers where they were always referred to as 'goddam AJ's'. But as far as we were concerned, AJ's were just damned bombers we had to ride 'shotgun' in. We believed that there are there were only two types of aircraft—fighters and targets."

"How did you hold up through all this?"

"I guess my Army upbringing and gratitude to be a Naval aviator, helped me to keep my head down and my mouth shut. I resolved to try to make the most of a bad situation which I had no control of. If 1200 flight hours was required to get in the AJ left seat, I was going to get it in record time. I volunteered for every flight with an available seat days, nights, weekends, cross-countries, test flights - anything. Even so, however, it was going to take at least three years to get out of the right seat and by then I would be out of the squadron. They threw us a bone by deciding that we could log BN flight time as co-pilot, but without ever being at the controls that was a total farce. We would have no opportunity whatever to maintain flying proficiency, so it was unlikely that I would ever fly as a Navy pilot."

"I know it didn't happen that way, Captain. What did?"

"I made friends with Bob Scully, the squadron Landing Signal Officer who was looking for two trainees, so another 'classmate', Hank James, and I volunteered. It was a good move. It was an outdoor job away from the squadron and got me out of the Maintenance Department assignment. Plus, controlling field carrier landing practice with paddles or radio was something like flying model airplanes. But the huge surprise benefit came with our next change of command. Our new CO was Commander Burly Grimes, a cigar-chewing General Lemay type fighter pilot whose favorite expression was 'horseshit'. When he discovered that he had two LSO's who weren't flying the AJ, he said 'horse shit', got a waiver of the 1200 hour flight time requirement, and put both of us in the left seat to be trained as Heavy Attack Aircraft Commanders! Glory hallelujah. Thank God. Three months later, Hank and I were on our way to the Western Pacific aboard the carrier Hornet as the first and only first tour junior officers ever to deploy as designated Heavy Attack Aircraft Commanders."

"Quite an incredibly favorable turn of events, Captain. What was it like to fly the AJ? Was it disappointing after flying jets?"

"Are you kidding? Hank and I had just jumped from the worst flying job in the Navy to the most prestigious; how could we possibly be disappointed? AJ's were unique in aviation history and a joy to fly. Sure, they were bombers, but with two props and a jet, sometimes referred to as 'two screws and a blow job', they were capable of speeds over 400 knots and could even be flown on the jet alone at light weights. The controls were hydraulically boosted and there was a respectable five G maneuvering limit which even made AJ's competitive in dog fights. Best of all, we flew off carriers, even at night when it was so challenging that the only other night flyers were the all-weather fighters. Even by twin engine bomber standards, AJ's were BIG airplanes, in part because the fuselage size was determined by the Fat Man bomb. It was a powerful experience for me to walk up to one sitting silently on the flight line and then climb aboard to breathe life into it as though I were Dr Frankenstein 'It lives, it lives!'. I never felt anything like that about any of the other twenty plus type airplanes I flew."

"So it was all smooth sailing, no screw ups?"

"Now that you mention it, Mike, four small incidents do come to mind. Hank was riding shotgun with me one day when we had to make a sharp left turn taxiing out of the chocks. There was an AJ up on jacks off the ground undergoing maintenance with its tail sticking out of the hangar in front of us. My attention was focused on signals by the taxi director for the turn when I felt us hit something as the taxi director frantically gave the crossed wands stop signal. We stopped with our right wingtip fuel tank under the hangared AJ's tail, dangerously close to lifting it off the jacks. Fortunately, the AJ did not fall off the jacks and there was only minor cosmetic damage. We were able to make the flight, but I knew that Skipper Grimes wouldn't miss the chance to embarrass me at the next All Pilots Meeting so I skipped it and Hank had to take the ribbing. Since he was acting as my co-pilot in the right seat, it was his responsibility to be sure our right wing was clear, plus there should have been a wing walker lineman at that wing tip."

"What about the taxi signalman's responsibility?"

"I don't know what was said to him, but I'm sure he felt as embarrassed as I did. I probably should have discussed it with him and Hank after the flight to ease our mutual pain, but it was more my style to let such sleeping dogs lie. The less said about it the better."

"Then what, Captain?"

"The second incident I recall occurred off Hawaii. We were operating there for the Hornet and Airwing Operational Readiness Inspection (ORI) by CINCPACFLT (Commander in Chief Pacific Fleet). In the rush to deploy us on this cruise, there hadn't been time for Hank

Welcome to the Fleet

and me to fill one small block for our HAAC designations, four night arrested carrier qualification landings - our first ever. So, one night in Hornet's flight schedule was set aside just for our command performance, our one and only chance before sailing on to the Western Pacific (WESTPAC). Now Mike, four arrested landings in one night is a formidable challenge. Lots of things can go wrong - bad weather and ship or aircraft malfunctions, not to mention considerable pilot stress and strain. Flying low in an inky black hole on the ocean, visually orienting on finding the ship and lining up on center line and the optical glide slope with no visual horizon reference or depth perception, while also keeping track of the cockpit instruments for altitude, airspeed, power setting, and attitude, combine to make night carrier landings the most difficult routine operational task performed in airplanes. Throw in some rain, a pitching deck in high seas, low fuel state, an electrical failure, a rough running engine, or food poisoning, and there's nothing 'routine' about it. On Hornet vintage carriers, there was only ten feet between the airplane and the aft blunt end of the ship, often referred to as the 'spud locker' or the 'ramp'. One and a half degrees of deck pitch reduced that clearance to zero. Add rolling and heaving, the vertical movement of the entire ship crossing waves, and it becomes extremely demanding white-knuckle flying.

"How were your firsts memorable?"

"It was January 23rd 1958. My total flight time was 592 hours, but only 165 hours as First Pilot. I had begun flying left seat in October, made seventeen day arrested landings in November, five more in January, including two landings earlier that day on Hornet. That night was a fairly clear and calm, but impressively dark. Since there was no reason for my BN, Jack Lancio, to be aboard, I launched with my Third Crewman in the right seat. I'm sorry I can't recall his name, but he was very young, pleasant, and fearless. It was good not to have three nervous people aboard. I didn't catch up with flying the airplane on the first approach. I felt like I wasn't in charge of the event. I wondered why in the hell I was doing this, or if I could. I wanted to stop the airplane and get off. Although the approach itself wasn't out of limits, the LSO either sensed my uneasiness or his own and I was waved off. My second approach was to a wave off as well, but this time it more the LSO's uneasiness than mine. On my third approach, just as I was turning onto final heading, with no warning whatever, my starboard engine suddenly and without warning quit cold. Of course, it took a second or two to comprehend what was actually happening. In twin engine aircraft it is important to be certain which engine has failed before taking corrective action which might shut down the wrong one. A great truth is, 'never turn into the dead engine'. Fortunately, I was in a left turn, away from the dead engine. Another great truth is, 'in an emergency, the most important thing is to maintain safe flight'. So the task at hand was to scan the engine instruments for clues while also flying the airplane on one engine at 500 feet on approach for my first night carrier landing."

"It makes my hands sweaty to hear it, Captain. What did you do?"

"Well, before I could do much of anything, all by itself the engine started again smooth as silk, just as before, so I continued the approach to a reasonably good landing. I guess the engine took my mind off worrying about the landing. As I taxied out of the landing area, the Air Boss said on the radio, 'Congratulations ...' I thought he meant for finally getting aboard ...'You just made the forty-nine thousandth arrested landing aboard Hornet.'"

"What a way to finish off the night!"

"Finish? I wasn't finished. I needed three more landings to be qualified and this was the last night to do it. Bad engine or not, I was going to press on if the engine ran-up OK before the next catapult launch. I also started the jet engine for back-up and went on for three more arrested landings with my very brave Third Crewman in the right seat and no further engine problems. Subsequent investigation revealed a crack across the top of one of eighteen cylinders between intake and exhaust valves requiring an engine change. Did I mention that I was the Detachment Safety Officer?"

"No, you didn't, but you obviously were not a very good one, were you?"

"Like my Granny always said, 'You can't argue with success.' However, I did give a stern speech in our Ready Room, warning everyone not to compromise safety for the sake of a readiness inspection. I had no idea how badly I was going to eat those words two days later during the NOREX."

"Do as you say, not as you do, Captain? What is a NOREX?"

"Nuclear Ordnance Readiness Exercise to test the carrier's ability to handle actual 'war reserve' nuclear weapons in a precisely timed sequence as part of SIOP."

"Lord, how do you keep track of all those acronyms. What's a SIOP?"

"Single Integrated Operational Plan, which was the schedule for all nuclear strikes, including Air Force and Navy bombers, as well as intercontinental ballistic missiles. Some targets were considered so strategically important they were designated for multiple weapons, so we might arrive on target to find a smoking hole. Also, it was possible that a bomber's track could take it into a fireball. SIOP was an attempt to coordinate the timing of strikes, thus the importance of adhering to the launch schedule timing in a NOREX."

"Interesting, Captain. How is it you knew so much about the targets?"

"Each of our assigned targets were laboriously planned during the weeks before deploying on cruise, using every available piece of intelligence. As BN's did with the Los Angeles RBS site photos, they again made pencil radar predictions from actual target stereo photos. Crews' highly detailed flight plans were then closely reviewed by the CO, Airwing Commander, and sometimes by the carrier's CO."

"What can you say about the nature of the targets?"

"Priority was assigned to destroying the enemy's offensive capability for a second strike, so they were military targets. Places like airfields, not people. Typically, our targets were long range bomber bases in remote locations, not population centers or industrial sites."

"Were all your targets in the Soviet Union?"

"No, and that's all I can say about targets, except to note that one of mine was such a great distance that we had to land for refueling to reach it."

"There couldn't have been much chance of getting there on that one, much less getting back!"

"Perhaps, however, we devoted a good deal of effort to planning how we would succeed alive. We were not in some goofy Jap Kamikaze frame of mind, I assure you. Nevertheless, our best hope of survival was to be so convincing to the Russians of our capability and determination to wipe them off the map too that they would be rational enough to decide against launching an attack. That's what 'Mutually Assured Destruction' (MAD) and 'Deterrence' were all about and it worked."

"But we couldn't use that rationale so well against insane Muslim terrorist acts without identifiable nationalities, could we?"

"Not to the degree we did against the USSR, but we convinced Arab nations that they would be held responsible and attacked with dire consequences to their political security if we were nuked by terrorists harbored by them. Muslim or not, all people are motivated to survive at some subterranean level, aren't they?"

"God, I truly hope so, but there's much evidence to the contrary when it comes to Muslims."

"Perhaps, but that is not nearly as politically viable nor militarily possible as it was in the Cold War. Invasion of Afghanistan and Iraq, for example, were only partial successes."

"Nevertheless, those actions sent strong messages to Saudi Arabia and the others that there could be major consequences to them for supporting terrorism. Some say Korea and Vietnam were not successful; however, they were only limited 'battles' in the Cold War which we won. Our determination in those conflicts was backed up with 'Do Not Cross' lines defending against forceful Communist expansion. They were effective military deterrents in the big picture which bought us time to succeed on the political and economic fronts. Truman had the guts to take sole responsibility for dropping the Bomb on the Japs. So, 'Bad Cop' Nixon credibly frightened Russia, China, and Vietnam into believing he was crazy enough to launch pre-emptive strikes against them and that 'Good Cop' Kissinger was the only one keeping him from doing it. Nixon had the strength to launch B-52's against Hanoi and force the North to talk peace. Reagan's brilliance was leading the US into outspending the USSR into economic and political oblivion to win the Cold War. Carter and Clinton should have been impeached for their damage to our credibility. Johnson was rightly run out of office for his irresponsible leadership failures in the Vietnam Conflict. But I'm getting ahead of myself again. Where were we?"

"You had recalled two of three AJ incidents you wished to relate and you were telling about the NOREX."

"Ah ha, yes. Good for you remembering a Navy acronym. My mission was to fly off a war reserve H-bomb to be downloaded at Barbers Point Naval Air Station. The real thing, Mike, three and a half megatons–fuse disarmed of course, but capable of a low order detonation in a crash or fire. Because of the size of the bomb and the low fuselage, AJ's had to be parked directly over the dedicated special weapons elevator straight up into the bomb bay. I was greatly impressed that the AJ was engineered to take the load of a ten thousand pound bomb on a single suspension point throughout a hydraulic catapult shot. Unlike the follow-on steam catapults with steady acceleration down the track, hydraulic cats were more like a cannon shot with most of the acceleration at the beginning. It was quite a jolt and one hell of a load to put on a bomb suspended by a single lug to launch a fifty two thousand pound airplane up to flying speed in a two second run down a hundred and fifty foot track. But back to my story. The bomb elevator was located so the AJ was also in position on the number two catapult directly in front of the Captain's bridge, wings spread, ready to launch without taxiing forward. The only other airplanes aboard capable of carrying much smaller weapons on this launch were the single engine AD Skyraiders which were spotted aft on the flight deck for deck launch on their own steam; however, since the AJ's port wing hung out across the flight deck too far to allow the AD's to deck launch, we had to go first. If I didn't get off, no one would and the NOREX would be a complete failure."

"I smell one coming, Captain?"

"Yes indeed, Mike. Everything was routine through the load, but interesting to note that though we were aboard a carrier at sea, there was an apron around the bomb bay to obscure the weapon from view, for even its size and shape was Top Secret, and the area was guarded by a half dozen Marines with automatic weapons. Jack, my BN, and I went through the bomb's lengthy check list with the Weapons Officer and an inspection observer. Although I had been hands-on with the cutaway training weapon, touching the real thing in the bomb bay of an airplane I was going to fly, having also been through the target planning process, brought the whole business home to me. Although I was much too busy and focused on the task at hand to ponder the experience, I was acutely aware of the reality of my job. This was no longer just a training exercise, this was as close to the real main event as we could get without going all the way. Actually, Mike, like so many complex events which sped by in rapid succession, there never was time allowed for deep introspection, nor anyone interested in hearing it. When I have recalled stories they were abbreviated, out of context, and impersonal, seeming to be things that happened to someone else or like a movie I once saw. The greatest benefit now in telling you these stories is for me to consciously relive them in sequence and put them in some kind of perspective. Until now, it never really struck me how much complete trust my country had put in me at a very inexperienced and tender age. But I digress too much. When I got to the magneto check on the port engine, the RPM drop was out of limits so I gave the thumbs down signal to the Catapult Officer. So much for the NOREX, the first tour Lieutenant JG in the AJ was blowing the whole thing. Without shutting down, I set the parking brake and Jack went back into the bomb bay to replace the bomb's safety pins. A mechanic came into the cockpit to help troubleshoot the engine, but it only got worse. After about ten minutes of this fruitless exercise and answering constant radio inquiries from the Air Boss, damned if my boss, Lieutenant Commander Marv Cooper, the Detachment Officer in Charge, didn't show up on the flight deck and signaled me with a thumbs up and launch signal to go anyhow! So, after we got the mechanic out and Jack back in after removing the safety pins again, I shoved the throttles up, saluted the Catapult Officer, and down the deck we went -with the parking brakes still set, digging four grooves in the teak flight deck and a rooster tail of splinters behind us."

"Oh my God, how awful. What happened?"

"You say oh my God. Imagine yourself as Hornet's skipper, Captain Tom Connolly, with ambitions to be the Chief of Naval Operations! There from his bridge, before him a first tour Junior Officer was going down the flight deck in an AJ with a bad engine and an H-bomb aboard with the brakes locked, falling out of sight off the bow heading for the Pacific Ocean, likely to be cut apart by Hornet's bow and perhaps sucked into the giant screws setting off a low order nuclear explosion under his fantail?"

"Gives new meaning to one's career going up in smoke, doesn't it, Captain? But I take it that did not happen. What did?"

"Well, the catapult paid no attention to the locked brakes and we fired off with plenty of flying speed. However, with the nose gear off the bow before the main landing gear, the effect of the locked brakes was to pitch the AJ's nose down enough for us to drop out of sight from the flight deck. So I took the only action open to me, I pulled the yoke back to get the nose up and climbed out heading for Hawaii. It was all over so fast that I had no emotional reaction. The only radio transmission to me was an unnecessary reminder to release my parking brakes before landing."

"What were the consequences for you?"

"Fortunately, we spent two days at Barbers Point before rejoining Hornet in port, so there was some breathing space for reflection by all. Obviously, I was embarrassed about the parking brakes, but there was no harm done by it. The worst was having held up the launch, plus the public humiliation of being told by my boss to go anyhow. It made me feel stupid and timid, even though seven bad spark plug leads were later found on that engine. I should have refused to launch, it had been a foolish risk. Nothing was said directly to me about the incident; however, a few weeks later Captain Connolly reviewed one of my targets with me on the bridge and the sonofabich lectured me about the courage needed to fly such missions. As it happened, we rarely flew because Connolly didn't want to risk accidents on his watch. 'We're just out here in case something starts', he said. I had only twenty three flights and only two at night, during the remainder of the six month cruise to WESTPAC. Connolly deservedly came to be called 'Captain Tuna, Chicken of the Sea'. Nevertheless, he later succeeded in becoming the Chief of Naval Operations."

"Quite an entrance you made there on Hornet, wasn't it? Reminds me of what you said before about the Pukin' Dogs, 'If you can't be good, be colorful'"

"Yeah, and what Ron Hess advised, 'Don't ever just fade into the woodwork, let 'em know you were there.' That's life, live and learn. There's a great truth for everything, isn't there?"

"Yes indeed, that's how they become cliché's. So, did the rest of your AJ flying on that cruise go without incident?"

"Almost, but not quite. Because AJ's were so large and difficult to handle on the flight deck, we were always last to land on a recovery. The only parking area large for us was behind the island structure on the starboard side of the flight deck. So the routine was to shut down AJ's in place after landing, hook up a tug on the nose gear and push us back into the parking spot as the ship turned out of the wind. One day as we were doing this the Officer of the Deck got too frisky with the starboard (right) turn out of the wind and Hornet heeled sharply to port at a ten to fifteen degree angle. It was more than the tug cold handle and we were sliding rapidly toward the port side. When the tugs brakes proved ineffective, the driver jumped off and ran up the deck and left me to try to stop both the AJ and the tug, rapidly accelerating toward the edge of the flight deck for a sixty foot drop into the Pacific. With the AJ's engines shut down, so were the hydraulic pumps which supplied brake pressure to the main landing gear, so my instinctive application of rudder pedal brakes was useless. Fortunately, the NOREX incident familiarized me with the AJ parking brake system which was operated by an air bottle independent of the hydraulic system. We so rarely used it it was easy to forget they were there. By the time I reached down to pull the brake handle, we were rolling so fast and so close to the deck edge, I believe another second or two delay would have been too late."

"What fallout from that incident was there?"

"Nothing. Not a word was said to me about it, though I'm sure the Officer of the Deck probably got an ear full from Captain Connolly. Hornet's turns out of the wind were much more tame thereafter."

"Didn't it seem strange to you that there wasn't much more said to you about those four AJ incidents?"

"Yes it did, Mike. I expected lots of hindsight chiding, as my critical Army father would have done; however, it was a consistent experience throughout my Navy career that, as long as no harm was done, we were given credit for being smart enough to learn through introspection. Silence can be a very effective leadership technique for developing young executives, especially applicable to the Navy where subs, ships, and aircraft operate far from direct supervision and where quick independent thinking is required by CO's. One of the aspects I enjoyed most about being in the Navy was the fact that we were given this latitude to do things our own way as long as desired results were achieved. At the same time, we very well understood that a single serious error could be career terminating. I doubt that there is any other organization, military or civilian, where this is so uniquely true. In that sense at least, we were like sole proprietors, it was up to us to learn to sink or swim on our own and that thinking extends to the lowest ranking Seaman. We were literally on the same ship together and any one of us could sink it if we didn't pay attention."

"With so much technology and ships scattered across the earth's oceans, I can see where the Navy has to operate with a looser chain of command than the other services. I found out the hard way about the downside of self-reliance as a sole proprietor of a law firm, as opposed to being a state office employee subject to comparatively close supervision, rigid regulation, and constant scrutiny. Navy life sounds like the best of both worlds, except at the great price of family separation with years at sea away from civilization."

'True, Mike. Nothing's ever easy or perfect. The choice is a matter of one's priorities. Perhaps this is a good place to stop. We can pick up with the Hornet cruise when we get back from the airport this evening, OK?"

"OK, Captain, let's go."

Naval Air Station North Island
Coronado-San Diego CA

AJ "Savage", Navy's first nuclear bomber, 1950

wingspan 72 ft - max wt 51,000 lbs - engines 1 x Allison J-33 & 2 × Pratt & Whitney R-2800, 2,400 hp - max speed 471 mph - Service ceiling 41,000 ft - bomb 12,000 lb

AJ-2 Savage, Naval Aviation Museum Pensacola. I had eleven flights in this one in 1957-58.

14

Hornet to the Western Pacific

"Thank you for a wonderful day, Captain."

"For what, Mike? All I did was have fun watching you humpty bump down the runway trying to land Sam's Cub."

"Yeah, well maybe I did oversell my flying abilities a bit to you."

"You did OK. I've known few pilots, including myself, who made consistently good three-point landings in a Cub. The Champ you flew no doubt had the landing gear modifications which made everyone look good. Nevertheless, as they say, Mike, the Piper Cub is the safest airplane ever built - it can just barely kill you. There are an unlimited number of ways to humiliate yourself in an airplane. Hopefully, you learn the lessons; otherwise, they will come back to bite you in the butt one day. In any event, after mastering the Cub, Ximango landings will be a piece of cake for you. How was Sam as an instructor?"

"Excellent, just right, couldn't be better. We are going to get along just fine."

"How was your flight in the Ximango with him?"

"No problem Mike, when he says you're up for it- perhaps in three more Cub flights you'll switch to the Ximango. Sam is a certified flight instructor in gliders as well as powered aircraft, so you're all set to go with him all the way for a Private Pilot certificate as well as a glider rating with a motor-glider endorsement. Any idea what you might do with that?"

"No, but it will sure improve the options. There's the glider club east of Albuquerque and then there's Philip's Champ, but 85 horsepower off a mile high runway on a hot day is a bit 'iffy'. After flying your Ximango, soaring would be more fun in the long run, I think, and there's probably lots of lift off the Sandia Mountains. We'll see. Meanwhile, I don't want to detract from pressing on with your book and it's early enough to put in another hour or two. Shall we adjourn to the Lodge lobby?"

"Sure. Let's finish the 1958 Hornet cruise."

"OK, there is someone on the porch, let's use this table. All set, Captain, recorder running."

"Although Hawaii is 2,500 miles off the US West Coast, there was another two weeks of sailing the wide Pacific Ocean to our next port call, the Philippine Islands and the largest naval base in the world then, Subic Bay. To maintain Hornet's speed of advance, there were no flight ops, so there was plenty of free time to just enjoy the fascination of being at sea again and settle into the routine of life on an aircraft carrier. I was in an all steel four-man bunk room smaller than a jail cell directly under the number one catapult. There were two bunk beds, one sink, four five-drawer chest-desks, and four hanging lockers. There was no port hole or air conditioning, just one vent blowing hot humid ambient air. My three room-mates were BN's, including Jack, all of whom were second tour Lieutenants who had made the previous Hornet cruise. Since I was junior, I got a top bunk directly under the catapult track. It was no place to be during a launch, but I was rarely in the room during flight quarters or any other time except to try to sleep. Our Detachment shared Ready Room Two with an FJ-4B Attack squadron which made no bones about letting us know we were inferior in their midst. Whenever it got too bad we'd remind them that though they were capable of carrying light nuclear bombs, they were not included in SIOP, that our bomb had more bang than theirs, and that we were Hornet's primary mission. Finally, we put up a heavy black curtain divider across the ready room to block out some of the sight and sound of them. We were also pretty much isolated from the rest of the air wing. The unpopularity of the AJ because of its size and being a prop powered multi-engine bomber, plus our small number, made us easy prey for bias."

"How did that effect your group?"

"Not much at all. Since squadron morale was so low at home and we were virtual strangers to each other before this cruise, we felt little loyalty to the Navy or each other. There was also a degree of distance between pilots and BN's. So, whereas Ready Rooms are normally the primary social and working hangout for squadrons, we didn't spend much time there."

"Tell me more about the distance between pilots and BN's."

"I don't want to overstate this, it's just that there was a degree of professional disconnect which overlapped socially. Some flight officers had been physically disqualified from flight training and were somewhat envious of pilots. Others were in the Navy to avoid the draft and were attracted to being Flight Officers by the extra pay and prestige. Naturally then, there was a tendency for them to be critical 'back seat drivers' with 'short-timer' attitudes. Add to that the fact that I was junior in rank and experience, yet in command of the aircraft and their fates, and you have the basis for a certain degree of distance between us which made each of us loners. Again I say, I don't want to exaggerate this. It was simply an undercurrent. Like most pilots, I was enough of a loner to begin with, so it all had little effect on me. At sea I spent time on deck watching the sky and the waves, on the LSO platform observing landings, or watching movies in the Wardroom. I even built a model of a World War One fighter which I never flew."

"How about when the ship was in port?"

"Good question, Mike. This was a fork in the road for me. Working hours aboard do not change in port, since the administrative machine grinds on as usual. So, unless you took leave and left the ship, or signed up for tours, it was still a nine to five job which left no time for sightseeing. One choice was to stay aboard for dinner and movie in the Wardroom, write a letter or read, and go to bed early. The other choice was to go ashore with the gang for happy hour and dinner at the Officer's Club, and then on to the bars downtown. Civilian seaport commercial waterfronts are pretty much the same all over the world–bars and women. So the evening downtown choice was inevitably bound to lead to inebriation, sex and the attached risky physical and emotional consequences. I was way ahead in experiencing the consequences, so I set out to be a monogamous 'straight arrow'. That was an easy choice for me in the Philippines. The naval base was huge and had every imaginable recreation facility. The Cubi Point Naval Air Station where carriers docked was far from the front gate and downtown. The 1950's Cubi Officers Club was the most unique and famous in Navy history. A short distance from the carrier pier and situated on top of a hill with a gorgeous view overlooking the entire primitive Subic Bay. The Club was a grass shack built of iron pipes on a cement slab with four foot bamboo sides and screens up to the grass roof. Needless to say, with several hundred pilots at happy hour in such an informal setting, behavior regularly got quite rambunctious, so the Cubi Club was not the place for the Navy families stationed there. Fortunately, the Subic Officers Club was a proper, new, modern, large, formal, air-conditioned Club with a dance floor, live music, regular night club acts, and excellent food. A good place for a couple's dining and dancing night out, but of little interest to us of course. I'll have more to say about the Cubi Club and the Philippines during Vietnam cruises when we made nearly all our port calls there. All in all, it was a lousy place to visit. Outside the base gate across 'Shit Creek', an open sewer into which children dove to recover coins tossed in by sailors crossing the bridge, was the town of Olongapo which made any of the worst parts of Mexican border towns look good. Sailors were regularly beaten, stabbed, and robbed. The girls mostly resembled monkeys and the VD rate was incredibly high with strains invulnerable to penicillin. The sailors would have been better off if they had tossed all their money into Shit Creek and returned to the base. Throughout the Philippines crime and corruption was universal with shoot 'em-up Wild West politics. Much of the vast jungle was inhabited by primitive tribes, and was therefore off limits to everyone. Fortunately, most of our port calls before Vietnam were at Naval Station Yokosuka, Japan, because the SIOP commitment kept carriers closer to our targets."

"Like Germany, I suppose Japan had recovered from World War two by 1958?"

"Oh yes, even more so, mainly because it was undivided and there was less to replace. Most Japs lived in tight quarters with their parents and children. Still, like the Germans, the Japs had good reason to feel superior to their relatively weak neighbors. Their level of culture, industriousness, unity, applied intelligence, and island isolation put them far removed and above the other Asian countries I visited."

"You saw no sign of bitterness toward Americans?"

"No. On the contrary, the people were grateful, friendly, and humble. They had been convinced that Americans were vicious beasts who would torture, rob, rape, and murder everyone if Japan lost the war. General McArthur, whatever his ego issues were, was an incredibly popular political genius who was entirely deserving of the highest adulation of the entire population, almost equal to the Emperor. Instead of punishing and humiliating them, he left the Emperor and self-respect in place, and in every way managed the total recovery of that nation. The Japs were greatly relieved that the war was over and took complete responsibility for their own defeat. If there was resentment toward us, there surely was no public sign of it."

"I've always read that Japanese society is pretty much closed to foreigners. Did you find that to be true?"

"Absolutely, so you might ask how much of it I was able to penetrate as a Navy guy during brief port calls. I won't get ahead of myself, so I'll just say that though my observations were shallow in some ways, still, I visited there over a period of nearly twenty years. As for intimate contact, which I expect you may be wondering about, would you like to finish the evening on that topic, Mike?

"Sure. I assume this gets us back to your personal 'fork in the road'?"

"Yes indeed. First, I'll summarize my marital situation again. Aurelie and I got along very well, but after the turmoil, two small children, and an intense new career, there wasn't time for us to recover the level of intimacy we shared before our three year separation and I feared another pregnancy. I settled for what we had, believing that was just the way life was. However, after checking out the veteran 'straight arrows' in the air wing and seeing their lost hollow faces wandering around the ship, I was seeing my future self in an unfavorable light. I did not want to be like them. So, it didn't take many quiet nights aboard in port before I came to the conclusion that I had two options, leave the Navy or go ashore. Since leaving the Navy was not an option, going ashore was the choice. Although I was determined to remain a straight arrow, I knew that my past record of what one psych Prof called a 'stud-like propensity' was going to be a difficult handicap to overcome. There would surely be many birds trying to build their nests in my hair again. It was a risk I had to take. I was not willing to become a hermit out of fear."

"So, what was the night life like downtown?"

"Quite a pleasant surprise, actually. Not at all what I expected. But I didn't jump in at the deep end. I began by signing up for tours. Even though tourist oriented, the bus tours were so pleasant, interesting, and informative that I took advantage of opportunities to have days off the ship wherever we went. Japan in the fifties was a most unique country in every way. The people, clothing, culture, landscape, and cities. The people took the time to 'smell the flowers' by enjoying detailed and refined ceremonial pleasure in the smallest details of their lives and surroundings. I won't dwell on them, but as examples you may be familiar with their tea ceremonies, food preparation, bonsai trees, traditional clothing, and specially grown and elaborately marketed vegetables. Their disciplined and extraordinarily polite public behavior was evident everywhere. They even repeatedly bowed to each other on the telephone! Most impressive for me was their obvious loving devotion to their children. Pre-toddlers were comfortably and securely carried on mothers' backs under outer garments. It was most charming to see a serene little Japanese face peacefully sleeping undisturbed by the noisy hustle and bustle of the streets or markets. Large groups of uniformed school children were common sights, touring parks and cultural sites, marching along in long lines of two abreast with the one in front holding up the guiding flag. The best evidence of the love and attention paid to Japanese children by their entire society was their joyous behavior. I never once saw a Japanese child cry or misbehave in any way. Generally speaking, Japanese women, though rather thin and shapeless, impressed me as being uniquely beautiful, mature, and self-confidant. Young Japanese men, on the other hand, seemed awkward, immature, and unsure of themselves until in their late forties when they suddenly metamorphosed into the most dignified of men. Contrary to Western impressions, Japanese women were far from being subservient. Although a wife would always defer to her husband and never do or say anything to embarrass him publicly, it was well understood that she was responsible for managing everything at home. This is not to say that husbands were kept on short leashes by any means. Frequent 'nights out with the boys' at the bars and clubs were condoned. These occasions were often amusing to observe since Japanese men do not hold their liquor well at all and tend to behave like silly little children -but always in good humor. In other words, social roles were well defined and cheerfully accepted. Free of Western religious constraints or guilt about an 'original sin' Japanese women took genuinely innocent interest in being knowledgeable about sex and pleasing men. Geisha's, of course, are the most refined traditional example of this, though most Westerners have misconceptions about their lifetime profession. Webster, for example, defines geisha as 'a Japanese professional singing and dancing girl'. That definition falls so far short of being adequate that I will elaborate later, but the point for now is that geishas were universally considered by young women, as well as men, to be the epitome of Japanese feminine role models."

"OK enough of the tour guide preamble, let's get to the nitty-gritty. Again, what was it like in 'downtown' Yokosuka?"

"Patience, Mike, I'm getting to that. A typical evening ashore began with 'happy hour' at the Officers Club bar, followed by a steak dinner in the Club dining room, followed by more happy hour to the evening's conclusion, but more often by a short walk to town. The first stop was usually the 'hotsi baths'. This was particularly good sport with a young aviator in tow on his first Japan visit because of the public nudity in front of fellow aviators and young girls in halters and short shorts. Some nuggets who heard stories in advance were very difficult to persuade. The routine at the baths was to disrobe and enter a large brightly lit white tiled room with the teenage girls laughing and jabbering away in Japanese. Because it was said that the girls identified naval aviators by their big watches and little dicks, it was natural to assume that the girls were laughing at you which of course added to the embarrassing 'shrinkage' effect. After some time in a Turkish bath sweating it out, a designated girl directed you to a wooden three legged stool about six inches high right in the middle of the room in front of everyone. Imagine yourself sitting stark naked on a six inch stool in front of everyone trying to look dignified with your knees at eye level and then having a bucket of hot water dumped all over you, followed by having this scantily dressed very young girl vigorously scrubbing you all over with a soapy washcloth. Ah, such a humiliating initiation of an innocent fellow aviator into the ways of the exotic orient was exquisite to observe, Mike. After the scrub down and another bucket dousing rinse-off came the hot tub with your buddies which was about ten feet square, five feet high, and filled to overrunning scalding hot water only one tenth of a degree cooler than causing third degree burns. Then, about the time you begin to hope you might survive the searing heat, your girl leads you down the hall to her private room for a full body massage which included walking on your back in her bare feet. This could be a difficult experience if you were nervous or ticklish, but these girls knew their business and there was no grab-ass involved. The whole experience took only about an hour, but when you stepped out into the cold night with all the nicotine and alcohol sweat out of you, all your muscles totally relaxed, and your skin tingling pink, you were as close as you'd ever get to being a new man again. Now, at last you were well primed for the bars and night clubs."

"Sounds like a perfect start to a night on the town, except if you are a determined 'straight arrow'."

"Yes, true. Well, I was counting on the strength of numbers by being with a group of friends to keep me walking the line, but little did I know what I was getting into. Not surprisingly, there were many typical small grungy bars on 'Thieves Alley' with brightly lit signs, loud music, and girls in the doorway. One I recall was the Bar Monroe which advertised that all the girls had at least thirty four inch busts, huge by Japanese standards then. The girls were mostly gorgeous, highly made up and beautifully dressed in low cut silk gowns, but not at all offensive. Thanks to advanced cosmetic surgery, most of them had their noses and eyes westernized, plus their boobs and butts enhanced. It wasn't easy to judge their age, but in a good light there were signs that some of these girls were probably veterans in their forties. In fact, years later I saw one or two who did not look a day older. The custom at all the establishments was that the managing Mamma-San did the match making. You simply took a seat and the selected young lady sat down next to you. Amazingly, regardless of how casual your acquaintance was, every time you returned to that bar, months later or even the next cruise, the same girl joined you, because there was a strong prohibition against 'Butterflies', men who went from flower to flower, even at a different bar in town. About every fifteen or twenty minutes the girls were automatically served a small 'drink', probably tea, which cost about a dollar. Most of the bars had a small dark dance floor with slow music. Though language was a partial barrier, the girls were skilled at small talk and charming little games. There was no aggressive come-on at all because that's all there was to it. The girls worked at the bars for drinks, period, sex was not for sale. The girls were on their own if they went home with a customer. If all went well, she temporarily quit the bar and you played house while you were in town with never any suggestion of compensation, though the custom was that on the last night you left whatever you could afford in a discrete place she would find later. All in all, Mike, it was a great system, every bit as respectable, if not more so, than dating in the states with added big pluses. As with the tradition of geishas, there were no expectations, demands, guilt trips, or fear of pregnancy. None of these women were into it for love, romance, marriage, or clinging emotional dependence. In fact, these ladies were so honest, practical, and independent that it was sometimes disarming."

"So, are you saying that you failed at walking the line right away?"

"No, but the birds were gathering overhead. It was actually the nature of the culture that helped. Since sex was not for sale and the girls were on the own in their private lives, it was quite possible to enjoy the evening in a girl's company without going home with her. The first time I nearly went astray was when I got overheated dancing with a lovely girl, but when she subtly indicated an interest in me, I blurted out that I was married. I felt like the greenest aviator who ever wore wings."

"How did it happen then that a bird finally managed to nest in your hair?"

"I'm getting to that. Besides the bars, there were two other establishments.

"One was a full blown five star forties style night club with a revolving lit dance floor and revolving band stand featuring three fourteen piece bands with sequin gowned singers featuring forties favorites. Since there is no L sound in the Japanese language, it was quite amusing to listen to a lovely girl sing 'Rove me or reave me, or ret me be ronery. I can't believe that you rove me onry.' A girl I met there let me know up front that she had a boyfriend. The other place had been the wartime Japanese Navy Officers Club. It was unusual in that it was very quiet and informal. There was a record player and an impressive collection of music. If you wanted to hear something, you put it on the turntable yourself. You were allowed to bring your own bottle and charged only for set-ups. You put your name on the bottle and they kept it for you. When you left, they marked the level remaining and it was there waiting for you the next time you were in port. They served meals in small private Japanese style rooms. There were private hot tubs and bedrooms up stairs. If you wanted company, you had to request it, but extracurricular activities were for a price here. I remained on the straight and narrow for most of the cruise, but then providence had other plans."

"Providence in the person of Jean, Captain?"

"Judge for yourself as we go through these many stories, Mike. Our Detachment had been flown off for temporary shore-basing at Naval Air Station Atsugi. One day a group of us went shopping in the Yokohama art district where I bought two famous woodcut prints by Hokusai, Fuji Over Lightning and Great Wave Off Kanagawa. Our boss, Marvin, knew of a good restaurant on the outskirts, so we decided to have dinner there. We stayed on afterward for a few drinks and were joined by girls. This was altogether different from the bars and clubs in Yokosuka. The atmosphere was more of a neighborhood restaurant than a bar. The girls were not gowned, over-dressed, or cosmetically altered, and seemed to be just pleasant typical local girls. My companion, Omiko, seemed quite innocent. She was very thin, plain, and in her thirties. She spoke little English, but there was a special quality about her I found attractive, perhaps because she laughed so honestly when I asked if this was her first time in Japan, the usual first question I got from the bar girls. It was late when we left the restaurant, so I offered to walk Omiko home and she accepted. I had no other intentions or expectations. Her home was a small typical bamboo and rice paper house with matted floors and sliding wall panels which permitted rooms to be sized for different functions. Furnishings were Japanese style that is, almost no furniture at all except a low oversize coffee table. 'Chairs' were large pillows called futons kept in closets, as were the 'beds'. Between the kitchen and bathroom was a hot tub. It became clear that Omiko had mis-understood my intentions when she unrolled the bed. I started to explain, but backed off when I saw that she was hurt and embarrassed. Even though I was totally unprepared emotionally, I was to spend the night, 'play it by ear', and hope for the best. It wasn't easy, Mike, believe me. It was only when she was in tears that I relented. It turned out that Omiko had baggage of her own. She was married to a Japanese man who had recently divorced her, virtually unheard of to my knowledge. Consequently, Omiko felt very rejected, inferior, and unsure of herself. It was time for me to face up positively to the inevitability, so we regrouped and proceeded slowly. For the next week, I left her house only once to go to the nearby Army Post Exchange for supplies. We spent a lot of time in bed and her hot tub. It was a wonderful mutual experience for both of us at a needed time in our lives. That fork in the road was behind me without guilt or harm done. So, let's stop there and call it a night, OK?"

"Sure, but wouldn't it have been even better if you had shared that experience with Aurelie instead of a stranger half way around the world?"

"Yes, Mike, but that did not seem possible for us for a variety of reasons. As my Grampa said, 'It takes two to tango'. I'll see you at breakfast. Good night."

Pilots' day and night views on landing approach.
USS Ticonderoga (WW-2 class, like Hornet)

At night, before the mid 1960's, the only lights were the optical glideslope fresnel lens (left center), and the landing area outlined by three verticle and two horizontal rows of white lights. The red centerline stern verticle lights to aid line up.

F3H "Demon"

Wingspan: 35 ft Height 14 ft 7 in - Loaded weight: 33,900 lb - engine 1 × Allison
J71 thrust: 9,700 lb, with afterburner - max wt 14,750 lb - max speed 716 mph
ceiling 35,050 ft - guns 4 20mm cannons - missiles 4 AIM-7 Sparrow or AIM-9
Sidewinder - Bombs: 6,000 lb - radar AN/APG

Lt Manny

**USS Ticonderoga 1960
cruise book photo**

Demon inflight refueling from a VAH-16 AJ-2
offshore Southern California 1958

The bureau number on the tail of this AJ appears in my pilot
log book ten times from Oct '57 to Dec '58, so it's slightly
possible I was flying this hop.
At that time I had no idea that I would be flying Demons in a
couple of months.

15

SAVAGES TO DEMONS

"Good morning, Mike."

"Good morning, Captain. How are you?"

"Couldn't be no better, thanks. You?"

"OK, but I want to apologize for my dumb rhetorical question last night about sharing your Japan experience with Aurelie."

"Not a problem, Mike. If I seemed testy, it was because I got that same moral judgment when I made the mistake of telling the story to Carin forty years later. Certainly it would have been better if Aurelie and I had shared the experience, but such an event cannot be imposed on someone who is not on the same page. I should have noted that Aurelie volunteered that whatever happened overseas should stay there, she didn't want to hear about it. In any event, if I brought anything home, it was therapeutic and I'm glad for it. There's a fine line for you and me, Mike, between being journalistic or moralistic. The episode wasn't directly relevant to your history, except for whatever characteristics you may have inherited from me, so I'm glad you asked. It's good to have a listener's reflections. It gives me needed perspective and an opportunity to address criticisms. Life at sea as a naval officer and pilot pursuing a career and adventure was quite apart from life at home which demanded different roles and responsibilities as a husband, father, wage earner, lawn mower, handy man, etc. There were broken things needing repair, kids in diapers, shopping, garbage, social obligations, financial chores, not to mention twelve hour work days. We didn't have much time for marriage. Life at sea was high adventure, freedom with my pals, flying airplanes off carriers, exotic port calls, stewards cleaning my room, and meals served with linen and silverware in the Wardroom. It was a totally irresponsible and carefree existence."

"Did you believe that Aurelie was content with her life?"

"She seemed to be. If she wasn't, she didn't complain. After all, things were going her way. She was on her own schedule of priorities, progressing toward having four kids, with financial security, and no job pressures. Her philosophy of housework and child rearing was to do as little as possible, while taking time to read and dabble with arts and crafts. But then I was not very domestic either. In any event, the boys were happy and healthy and she seemed content with no restrictions or demands imposed by me. We got along well and never argued. Still, we were nowhere near the ideals of love we had shared in Munich. As the Chief said, Navy marriages were happy at least half the time."

"It will be interesting to see where that Yellow Brick Road led you in future relationships, Captain, but shall we relocate down Heritage Pines' yellow brick sidewalk after breakfast to continue your Hornet cruise tales?"

Later...

"Recorder's running, Captain. You have painted a rosy picture of going to sea. Was there no down side?"

"Sure, lots of downers. There were no port holes to look through, there was little privacy, and there were no safe places on deck to be during flight quarters. Carriers are so large they pitch and roll imperceptibly most of the time, so below decks there were few clues that you were at sea. We were confined in cramped spaces in a long, gray, noisy, hot, steel building with countless numbers of pipes, conduits, vents, hatches, valves, and machines to bang your head and shins on. Even though jammed with up to six thousand people aboard, life on carriers seems isolated from civilization. During six to nine month cruises, the f-word is used for every other word in a sentence as an adverb, verb, adjective, noun, modifier, exclamation, or as a sentence in itself. This becomes somewhat demoralizing and contagious, making it difficult to clean up language ashore. Although I have not been at sea with the Navy in more than fifty years, I still involuntarily resort to the language sometimes, despite resolutions not to."

"Even with women aboard?"

"After my time. I expect that the presence of ladies on warships had a civilizing effect; however, there was a surviving mariners' myth that women were bad luck aboard ships. As late as the 80's, I know of several yacht clubs which did not permit female membership and many yacht racing skippers did not permit female crew members. There were no women Midshipmen at the Naval Academy until the Class of '80. We'll get to that."

"To some, sacrificing a lifetime away from family and culture in that kind of environment sounds like a terrible waste, Captain. It's hard to understand why men do it."

"It is true that 'A man who would go to sea for pleasure, would go to hell for a pastime'; however, many others manage to waste their lives ashore in far worse ways, don't they? My own life ashore to that point had not been all that productive or joyful. I had attended fourteen schools scattered through the US, Central America, and Europe. I had no home town or extended family ties. I never saw myself spending an ordinary lifetime in a small town as a family man with one boring nine to five job. The positives of Navy life outweighed the negatives for me, partly because of my Army gypsy and only-child conditioning, but mostly because I loved flying and the sea more than the options. I never tired of watching the ever-changing moods of the sky and sea, day or night, across an unobstructed horizon. Everything just as it was since the dawn of creation–the same clouds, sky, sea, storms, fish, birds, sunrises, sunsets, moon, and stars–unaffected by mankind for billions of years."

"How did flying over the ocean compare to sailing on it?"

"Sailing the ocean was a 24-7 meditative life style for weeks or months at a time. Flying over it day and night was more adventurous, but limited to a few hours duration. Unfortunately, we didn't fly much on Hornet. During the remainder of the cruise following Hawaii, January to June 1958, I had only thirteen flights off Hornet, plus eight flights ashore at Atsugi and Cubi Point. The good part was that the ship double or triple-cycled the AJ's for three to five hour flights to clear the flight deck as much as possible. Since we had nothing better to do and lots of time to do it, we ventured quite far away from the carrier on these long flights for navigation practice. In spite of any lack of flight time or cruise experience, I felt quite at home with my crew and flying AJ's. Still, there was a feeling of 'cutting the cord' to fly out of sight from Hornet. As large as carriers are, they look tiny from the air. There are no landmarks to find them again and often nowhere else to land. We were on our own with whatever skills and equipment we had aboard to get home. Whereas the distance to the horizon from the deck is limited to a few miles by the curvature of the earth, the 'as far as the eye can see' view from our altitudes greatly added to the vast empty expanse of the Pacific Ocean and our solitude in it, especially at night, alone, with no signs of life. The experience was awesome and more than made up for the drawbacks. The shore-based flights in Japan and the Philippines were also fascinating. World War Two was fresh in everyone's memory and reinforced for me during my school days in Germany, so it was intriguing to fly a nuclear bomber over Tokyo or Mount Fuji, though there were no remaining signs of a war. The Philippines were primitive jungles, mountains, and islands where there had been fierce fighting. There were no restrictions against flying as low as we dared down the shorelines over bamboo huts in fishing villages. There was one curious event when our Detachment was off-loaded in the Philippines to clear Hornet's decks for their special operations in Indonesia in response to Communist revolutionary activity there. Inexplicably, the aircraft remaining aboard had all insignia and markings painted out -as though there could ever be any doubt about the nationality of Navy carrier aircraft flying over downtown Djakarta! One day when I was on the Cubi Point runway as the LSO for field carrier landing practice, a most unusual silver airplane with long wings entered the landing pattern. I happened to have my movie camera with me, so I got some highly classified close up film of a U-2. The pilot was loaded into a waiting ambulance on the runway and the U-2 was towed to a remote hangar. The pilot was later identified at the O Club, but he was escorted by 'men-in-black' types who permitted no conversation with him. So Mike, where else could a twenty-five year old Buck Sergeant's kid experience so much adventure and irresponsibility?"

"Nowhere, I'm sure. So is it fair for me to observe that escaping family ties explains your drive to fly and go to sea?"

"No. That's too simplistic, Mike. Escape was not a motivator, though being self-reliant made it easier. I was mostly attracted by the unique adventure of it. Nothing less than a trip to the moon could top sailing or flying, and no one expected to go to the moon back then."

"Well, it beat working for a living, didn't it, Captain?"

"You bet it did. I was a 'lifer' for sure."

"I assume 'lifer' is a derogatory term for a career sailor, as in life imprisonment?"

"Yup, except I was a volunteer, not a prisoner. I loved Navy life. But all too soon, it was time to sail home."

"All too soon? Didn't you miss Aurelie and the boys?"

"In fact I did, Mike. Prolonged detachment from life ashore afforded a valuable opportunity to put my personal life in perspective, which I probably wouldn't have done otherwise. Serious introspective reflection began about the third month of cruises and came to me in writing letters home. Unfortunately, Aurelie had no such opportunity to detach. Her plate was full with the boys and the same busy daily routines, only more so with me gone. Her letters seemed newsy and unresponsive, so the old uneasy feeling returned that there was something important she hadn't told me about that stateside summer home from Munich and her traumatic confrontation with her father. So, I raised the question with her again, but without response."

"So, did homecoming go as well as you hoped?"

"Not exactly. I was a stranger to the boys, so they were unsure of me, but I was in charge again. Appliances and machines defiantly refused to function for Aurelie and I wasn't much of a handyman. It was a challenging adjustment for us, though there was no animosity or conflict. There were so many changes and demands on us that by the time we adapted, we weren't far from where we started. I was back at work, flying a lot preparing for the next deployment and Aurelie was pregnant again."

"How did you feel about that?"

"Well, I wasn't surprised or upset or glad. I wasn't anything. Just numb. I tried not to dwell on it, but it did take a toll on my enthusiasm for sex. There was a saying that husbands returning from sea couldn't even throw their hats on their bed without a pregnancy. As the Italian flight student's helmet said 'Que sera sera.'"

"How typical do you think your marriage was compared with other Navy couples?"

"My peers did not discuss their relationships the way women do and who can judge another's marriage from the outside. It's difficult even for the couples in them to understand what's happening. I would say that Aurelie and I were atypical in that we avoided Navy social life. We associated with 'civilians' who shared our hobbies and interests art, modeling, and music."

"OK, so how was life at the squadron?"

"Much improved, thankfully. It happened that we were the final carrier deployment of AJ's the 'Last Bombing Savages'. The jet powered A3D Sky Warriors were replacing us in the Heavy Attack mission. We became an in-flight refueling squadron and we were re-designated VAH-16. We reconfigured our bomb bays with five ton jet fuel tanks with hose and reel for aerial transfer. Many of the old-timers transferred and there was no longer a need for BN's since the Third Crewman operated the refueling package. So, without four carrier Detachments splitting up the squadron, fewer people assigned, and better aircraft reliability, plus being an old-timer myself, everything was looking up."

"But you said you were preparing for another deployment?"

"Yes, but not aboard a carrier. The squadron established a four-plane shore-based detachment at Naval Air Station Atsugi, Japan, to conduct in-flight refueling missions throughout the Western Pacific from Japan to the Philippines and I was one of the four pilots assigned."

"That must have been quite a letdown, going from being a carrier-based Heavy Attack Aircraft Commander to a lowly shore-based tanker pilot and not transitioning to the new A3D?"

"I didn't see it that way. I assumed that I would eventually go to A3D's. Meanwhile, I was happy flying AJ's and wasn't worried about future jobs. As it had been with being a BN, I focused on enjoying flying and doing my best. As one Assignment Officer said, 'There are no bad jobs for Junior Officers, only bad Fitness Reports.'"

"How soon did you deploy?"

"The Hornet cruise ended in June 1958 and I was back in Japan early December."

"How was it?"

"Excellent, Mike. We were home-based in Japan, on lucrative per diem and separation pay, so everyone was glad to be there. Each flight crew had its own AJ assigned. We worked our own flight schedules independently wherever we wished to go, returning to Atsugi only for scheduled periodic maintenance inspections. Two of the pilots liked the Philippines and Okinawa, so I happily chose to operate from various Japanese bases. Our maintenance crew was equally happy and conscientiously productive. We never missed a single mission and gave away tons of fuel to everyone who wanted it, mostly the Air Force."

"How long did that go on?"

"Not long. Someone noticed that we were having way too much fun and that it was time to scrap the AJ's. Two months later I was back in San Diego in time for the squadron's decommissioning looking for a job. Transitioning to A3D's was not offered."

"Were you going to miss flying AJ's?"

"Not at all. A friend told me, 'Once you've proved you can do it, move on.' For me, airplanes, boats and cars were machines, a means to an end. I found that it did not much matter to me how high or fast I was going, or what the mission was, as long as I was the only pilot at the controls of whatever airplane I was flying."

"Then what was the Navy to do with an obsolete AJ tanker pilot?"

"Well Mike, as providence would have it, during the Hornet cruise word was passed to get me fully qualified as a Landing Signal Officer. I'll digress here to elaborate about LSO's. From the beginning of landing airplanes aboard carriers it was obvious that pilots needed supervision from the flight deck during approaches. Someone also had to be in charge of training ashore, plus assume responsibility for assuring that the flight deck was clear and that approaching aircraft were within safe limits for landing. LSO's were positioned on a platform extending over the port side near the stern at flight deck level. They signaled approaching pilots with a pair of extended hand-held paddles to visually signal pilots that they were high or low by holding the paddles up or down, fast with the right paddle down, slow with both paddles touching forward, or lined up right or left of center line by leaning to tilt the paddles toward the correcting direction. For night recoveries, the LSO's paddles, arms, and legs were lighted. If the LSO judged the aircraft to be within safe limits as it crossed the ramp, he dropped his left arm and crossed his right paddle over his chest to signal the pilot to cut the throttle and flare for a three point touchdown to an arrested landing. If the LSO judged the approach or flight deck to be unsafe, he repeatedly crossed the paddles over his head to signal a 'wave off' to the pilot who immediately added full throttle to go around for another try. The pilot could also initiate his own wave off, since he remained in command of the aircraft. Signals from the LSO were advisory, except for wave off and cut which were mandatory. With the advent of jets, the LSO's paddles became obsolete, though the LSO's nickname 'Paddles' stuck. Jets flew much faster and longer approaches which made visual signals ineffective. By the time the pilot could see the LSO, it was too late to make significant corrections, so the paddles were replaced with a radio and a stabilized lighted glide slope—at first a mirror and then a Fresnel lens."

"It sounds like one of the most crucial jobs on a carrier."

"I'd say that it was the most responsible, challenging, and exciting job you could have as a junior officer when you consider the possible catastrophic consequences of a crash and fire on the flight deck which could put the carrier out of commission. Beyond consideration of the hazards, it was important to recover all airborne aircraft as quickly as possible in order to maximize time before the next launch for positioning, fueling, arming, and maintenance. So the interval between landings was normally thirty seconds."

"What were the requirements to be an LSO?"

"Just two you had to be an aviator and you had to volunteer. It was the only voluntary Navy job I know of other than flying. LSO training was all 'on the job' under the supervision of an experienced LSO. Because there were few LSO's and some of those tended to be old-timers who had been passed over for promotion, being an LSO was seen as a career dead end, despite glorification in historical documentaries and films such as 'The Bridges of Toko Ri'. Consequently, there was such a critical shortage of LSO's that their assignments were individually controlled by the Commander of Naval Air Forces Pacific. The timing was perfect for me. I was being transferred to 'Fighter Town' NAS Miramar, San Diego, and given my choice of squadrons. No more bombers, props, bombardiers, or tankers for me, I was going to VF-121, an all-weather jet fighter training squadron as a flight instructor and LSO to fly FllF Tigers or F3H Demons, front line jet fighters. Whoopee! Hallelujah! A real fighter pilot at last. One giant leap for Manny!"

"Amazing. No wonder you believe in yellow brick roads. Gives new meaning to, 'Good things come to he who waits'. Did it turn out as well as you hoped?"

"Even better, though there were one or two glitches, of course. First, was the stigma of having been a multi-engine bomber pilot. Plus, I was an inexperienced LSO. In retrospect, however, these concerns were reflections of my own misgivings. No one gave me a hard time on either count. The saving factor was having made a carrier deployment flying a large all-weather airplane aboard at night. Another leg up I had was having already been in a large disjointed squadron."

"You say that you were a flight instructor in a training squadron flying front line fighters?"

"Yes. That does need explanation. Because sea to shore duty assignment rotations depended on length of time on sea-duty, normally four years, plus accident and retention losses, it was necessary to replace many deployed squadron personnel on an ongoing basis. A Ready Air Group (RAG) was formed, composed of large shore-based squadrons, with instructors experienced in the particular Fleet type aircraft and missions, which greatly relieved the training burden of Fleet squadrons. Not just pilots, aircrew and maintenance men were also trained in the RAG squadrons. The objective was to send standardized and qualified personnel to Fleet squadrons. RAG squadrons also trained entire squadrons which transitioned from other type aircraft. I did not, however, get to fly the airplane I hoped to. The FllF Tigers were breaking their keels on normal carrier landings and were being taken out of service, so I was left with flying the infamous F3H Demon."

"I want to ask you about the Demon, but first, please decipher for me what the letters and numbers mean in Navy aircraft designations. I understand that F means fighter, A means attack, and T means trainer, but what is the significance of the number and second letter?"

"Alright. I'll start with the letter after the number which ID'd the aircraft's manufacturer. For example 'J' was North American, 'F' was Grumman, 'D' was Douglass, 'H' was McDonnell, and 'V' was Lockheed. The number between letters was simply the aircraft sequence model number by that manufacturer. For example, the A3D was the third Navy attack airplane manufactured by Douglass Aircraft Corporation. I should also explain that a dash number was also assigned to identify modified versions of aircraft. For Example, the F9F-8 was the eighth model of the F9F Panther. Sometimes another letter followed the modification number. For example, the F9F-8T was a two place trainer version of the Cougar, informally called the 'Twogar'. In late 1962 the system was changed when some civilian genius in the Pentagon who got paid to make up stuff like this came up with the idea of standardizing US military aircraft designations. The letter for the manufacturer was dropped and a dash was added between the first letter and the model number, and the model number signified the order in which the airplane came into service. The practice of adding the modification dash number was changed to a letter. For example, the first model 'Phantom II' by McDonnell Aircraft, the F4H-1 became the F-4A. Got it, Mike?"

"Sort of, I'll have to review the recording, but thanks. Back to the F3H Demon. In my brief research of the Pukin' Dogs tour in Demons, I read that it was underpowered."

"That's also what I heard and read about Demons before I went to Miramar, so I had some trepidation about flying them. The early models were so underpowered they made national news when Navy grounded them all and barged them to the 'bone yard' for decommissioning. The follow-on much modified F3H-2 had a marginally more powerful J-71 engine, but retained the reputation for being underpowered. Demon Drivers unaffectionately called J-71's the 'Mark Four Converter' which converted JP-4 jet fuel at a high rate to smoke and noise, but little thrust. To make matters worse, J-71's had two annoying traits. First, it had the habit of failing in visible moisture, such as clouds, rain, sleet, or snow -not an attractive characteristic for an all-weather day-night fighter! And J-71's didn't just quit running, they went into spectacular compressor stalls with flames shooting out of both ends of the engine, requiring shut down and pilot ejection. These unexplained failures continued for the service life of Demons without resolution because the engine and aircraft manufacturers only pointed the blame at each other. A second quirk was that occasionally the engine mounts broke during carrier catapult shots, allowing the engine to shift aft over two feet, pulling the throttle off. Apparently J-71's did not produce enough thrust to keep up with catapults! Since Demons did not have ground level ejection seats until late in their service life, pilots had no option but to ride those engine mount failures sixty feet down to the ocean ahead of the ship. Oh yes, speaking of ejection seats, I'm reminded of yet a third Demon problem. A fellow LSO, climbing out after takeoff from NAS Miramar, had a compressor stall, turned back toward the field and rode the plane into the Chiefs Club, burning it to the ground. The accident investigation determined that the pilot had attempted to eject but that a design flaw in the McDonnel seat caused the face curtain to jam 'preventing the seat from firing. The fix for that was to retrofit Demons with the Martin-Baker ground level ejection seat which fired the pilot two hundred feet up with a force of 18 G's. These were the days before rocket powered seats. The glitch with that fix was that the angle the seat had to be mounted in the Demon resulted in certain spinal compression fractures on ejection! What with engine and ejection seat failures, there was a period when a pilot's least chance of injury was to ride the crippled airplane down."

"My God, Captain! Wasn't it enough of a challenge to fly jets off carriers day and night in any weather without the added engine and ejection seat problems? Why didn't the Navy take more positive responsible action to resolve those issues? And why would anyone volunteer to fly such an airplane?"

"I guess you had to be there, Mike. The Demon mockup was completed in 1948, only forty-odd years after the Wright brothers' flights and just a few years following the first jets. The 1950's were a period of major change in aviation. We were on the cutting edge of technology, so the risks were high. According to actuarial tables, the overall life expectancy for all military pilots, not including combat losses, was age forty two, and the carrier aircraft accident rate was very much higher, especially at night. Remember too that Korea and the Cold War pressures were accelerating aviation technological progress beyond limits. As my Granny said, 'You've gotta break some eggs to make mayonnaise'. We were the eggs. Pilots have always been a dime a dozen and airplanes were expendable. Beyond that, two common traits of aviators carried us through. First, the belief that bad stuff only happens to the other guy. Plus, 'Demon Drivers' were viewed with awe by their peers. For us to fly such an unreliable machine into the Valley of the Shadow of Death elevated our status as fearless fighter pilots. You just can't top that kind of esteem. Astronauts hadn't been invented yet, so it seemed worth the risk. Anyhow, Demon Drivers were all doing the same thing, so it didn't seem like such a big deal to us."

"Was there nothing good to say about the Demon, Captain?"

"Oh yes indeed. In some ways it was a uniquely outstanding airplane and it was in every way a far cry from the other single seat F9F-2 jet I had flown for seventy-five hours in flight training nearly three years before. I became a Demon Driver in April 1959 after four transition flights in F9F-8T 'Twogars'. Demons had forty feet less wingspan than the AJ; however, at over 22,000 pounds and fifty nine feet long with the cockpit ten feet above ground, it was as large. Getting into the cockpit without a ladder was a challenge involving climbing onto the port side trailing edge of the wing leaning onto the fuselage and walking forward where three retractable six inch 'goat steps' provided foot holds for the last six feet forward of the wing to the cockpit. The cockpit was very spacious and forward visibility was excellent. A uniquely outstanding feature of Demons was its weapon system. The primary mission of Navy fighters was to protect the carriers by intercepting incoming high altitude Russian bombers, armed with long range air to surface missiles, before they could launch them. Demons' guns were obsolete for the intercept mission and were often removed to reduce weight. The only guided air-to-air missile was the heat-seeking 'Sidewinder' which suffered the disadvantage of having to be launched from behind the target to permit homing in on its engine exhaust heat. Converting a head-on intercept to a rear attack against a high fast bomber was a tricky and time consuming maneuver, so a head-on missile was needed. The solution was Navy's 'Sparrow' missile which homed on the target's reflection from the Demon's radar at ranges up to ten miles. Demons were the first fighters of to have this major advantage."

"What was the Demon Driver's role in this system?"

"A shipboard Controller guided pilots to the target with range, bearing, and altitude information, but the pilot had to have his eyes on the radar in a hood mounted on the scope. Since the Demon's radar range was limited and closing speeds were over 1000mph, there was little time to find the target, lock on it, fire the Sparrow, and maintain radar lock-on. In adverse weather or in a Dog Fight, Demon Drivers more than had their hands full. One flight stands out in my memory as an example. During a week long war game exercise offshore San Diego, I was launched off Ticonderoga at 1 AM to intercept an unidentified incoming, slow moving, low altitude target trying to sneak in under the ship's radar. It was a totally black night- no lights, stars, or horizon. I climbed to just 100 feet so I could search upward with the radar to avoid ground return on the scope while trying to hold heading and altitude. My target turned out to be an unlit 120 knot P5M seaplane at my altitude. Since it was a requirement of the exercise to validate the identity of the target, I had to slow down to his airspeed–which was below my landing speed–and fly alongside to get his numbers. For me, this was 'white knuckle' flying at the extreme limit of my ability. In follow on all-weather fighter and attack airplanes, such as the F-4 and A-6, it was recognized that the complex workload required a two man crew in combat conditions."

"What was life like for you in the squadron, Captain?"

"Damned busy. As one of three LSO's, I was either on the runway day and night at Miramar, San Clemente Island, or El Centro for field carrier landing practice, or aboard various carriers for day-night CARQUAL, carrier qualification, operations for a week at a time every other month or so. CARQUALS were the 'graduation exercises' for new Demon Drivers who often had less than fifty hours flight time in Demons and were making their first ever night carrier landings. The youngsters fresh and eager out of flight training who didn't know any better, generally had little fear of night landings, so they did well. On the other hand, the 'retreads', second tour pilots who often came from shore duty desk jobs and knew of the Demon's reputation, tended to a have less positive attitude toward night carrier operations or being told how to fly by LSO's. So, most of the washouts and our single carrier fatality came from that group. As LSO's we were fully trusted and backed to set high standards and to weed out those we considered unsafe. It wasn't easy to be in the position of grounding senior aviators, including prospective CO's, but all agreed that it was better than letting a potential flight deck catastrophe slip past us. On more than one occasion, I believe those pilots were glad to have someone else decide it was time for them to quit."

"It sounds like a great deal of responsibility above and beyond being an Airwing LSO where you were teaching inexperienced pilots for their first night landings -and in marginal airplanes. Did you enjoy it?"

"Yes, absolutely. And I was good at it. I thrived on making instant life and death decisions every thirty seconds over pilots who sometimes seemed bent on killing themselves rather than go around for another try. You never knew what to expect from them, but I had always been slow to react emotionally, which was an advantage in remaining calm and clear on the radio in dangerous situations."

"You said there was one fatal carrier accident during your time at VF-121. Were you the controlling LSO?"

"No, but I was on the LSO platform when it occurred. The pilot, a second tour Lieutenant Commander, had an attitude problem toward LSO's. Years before, he had been called out to a carrier to make demo landings for VIP's without an LSO aboard or with the glide slope mirror turned on. So he made several landings by just spotting the deck and was therefore very vocal in egotistically declaring that he didn't need our help. It was early in my VF-121 tour. Reg Witthoft was my LSO mentor and the controlling LSO. It was a clear calm day. As the Demon went low in close, Reg waved him off with the red lights on the mirror, but did not back it up on the radio. Obviously, the pilot was looking at the flight deck, not the mirror, because he did not respond. The Demon's landing gear struck the 'ramp' short of the flight deck and exploded in flames with debris nearly hitting us on the platform. The remains of the burning Demon continued down the center line and off the angle deck into the water where it quickly sank. The pilot was not recovered. When I looked around, Reg was gone. He had jumped into our safety net and went below to Sick Bay. He quit being an LSO and never again returned to the LSO platform. We never talked about it, but I believe Reg blamed himself for not using his radio for the wave off. It didn't help that the Accident Board gave Reg 'contributing factor' for the accident; however, the real cause was the pilot's arrogant attitude. As we say, 'There are old pilots and there are bold pilots, but there are no old bold pilots.'"

"Were there many other non-fatal carrier accidents during your tour there?"

"No, not a single carrier landing accident. We ran a tight ship and didn't hesitate to weed out the chaff regardless of pilot rank or experience, even when we trained the first Phantom squadron with a bunch of hotshot test pilots and future astronauts. In fact, in eight years as an LSO, including four years in VF-121 and two tours as Air Wing LSO, I'm proud to say that I waved only two no injury landing accidents, which both happened within minutes of each other.

But I'll get into all that later. There was another benefit of being a VF-121 LSO. I was the Officer In Charge of the CARQUAL detachments I made, which mainly consisted of the maintenance crews we walked aboard with. In writing the Operation Orders for those deployments, I always included myself for day and night refresher landings with the rationale that LSO's should maintain a current perspective. So, I ended up with more day and night carrier landings in VF-121 than I made in AJ's. By the way, I also successfully used that proficiency rationale to get checked out in flying several other RAG squadron aircraft. One of those experiences was the memorable encounter with 'The Screamer'."

"How did you like being a flight instructor?"

"Neither here nor there, Mike. Chasing guys in loose formation, flying head-on intercepts or instrument approaches, was routine flying. Not much like what I expected of being a fighter pilot with lots of 'yanking and banking'. The best part was that I got to fly a lot since many of my fellow instructors were more interested in enjoying shore duty than flying, and since I was also the Schedules Officer, it was easy for me to fill in for the malingerers and get all the flights I had time for About the only times for raising hell, however, were the engine change test flights I volunteered for, where the only purpose was to see if the engine was going to run alright. There was no better place for that than the free for all melees over the Mount Palomar Observatory, sometimes involving a half dozen or more airplanes of different types mixing it up in a huge dog fight. With everyone trying to shoot each other down and all of us on different radio frequencies, there was a real danger of mid-air collisions, so it was pretty exciting flying. These were short flights, so I could afford the fuel luxury of using afterburner as needed–to the surprise of some opponents who assumed the Demon was underpowered. One night I had several hours to kill between LSO runway duties, so I flew an engine change test hop. It wasn't usual or prudent to do this at night, but there was no restriction against it either. So off I went in afterburner and left it there climbing north toward Los Angeles to see how high I could go. I had never been above forty thousand feet in a Demon and had never heard of anyone getting to fifty thousand feet. It was an magnificently clear smog-free night with the entire city of Los Angeles and surroundings beautifully lit up under me when I topped out at fifty one thousand feet with just enough fuel and plenty of altitude to indulge in some aerobatics. One fighting advantage of the Demon was an incredibly high roll rate, so just imagine yourself alone in a cockpit in the inky lonely darkness of fifty thousand feet watching Los Angeles spin around over and under you at 360 degrees a second."

"And you actually accepted flight pay to do things like that? Shame on you. But speaking of engine tests, did you ever have a problem with the J-71?"

"Just once, thankfully. I was chasing a student on a day navigation flight. As we approached Los Angles from the east, I noted slightly unusual engine sounds. Nothing I could detect on the gauges, but I decided to climb for altitude and head back to Miramar. For unknown reasons, rather than follow me, my student broke off and returned to Miramar on his own. I arrived over Miramar at 36,000 feet and got tower permission to make a precautionary simulated flame-out approach, but when I reduced throttle to idle to begin descent, the engine quit cold. Since cockpit pressurization is supplied by bleed air off the engine compressor section, cockpit altitude went to 36,000 feet. Packed inside my seat pan was a one man life raft. Although deflated for packing at sea level, there was enough residual air to partially inflate it at this altitude. So, there I was at 36,000 feet with a dead engine, jammed up against the canopy by the raft, barely able to reach the stick or throttle, and no way to eject or bail out–an awkward and undignified position, I assure you. With little choice, I lowered the nose to keep up airspeed, cut the throttle to shut off, and reset switches to attempt an engine air start. It worked first try at 28,000 feet. As the cockpit pressurization returned, so did the raft return to its proper place and I was back in my seat with no indication of engine malfunction. Nevertheless, I completed an uneventful simulated flame out approach. The engine mechanics found no indications of engine malfunction and were unable to duplicate the failure, so their write off was 'ground checks OK' and the Demon was returned to flight status for a one-time flight to the nearby North Island overhaul facility. I did not volunteer for that flight, but I did volunteer for a cruise in January 1960."

"How and why did that come about? It seems that for an Army Brat you sure did a lot of volunteering, Captain!"

"True, Mike, but I just followed the Yellow Brick Road and this time there was method in my madness. Airwing Five had been working up for deployment aboard Ticonderoga off shore San Diego and was just beginning night operations. The ship had recently come out of the shipyards where a faulty arresting gear restrictor valve had been installed which allowed a Demon on a day landing to pull out the arresting wire to the limits before the wire broke. The Demon went over the side and the pilot was lost. The wire, having been stretched like a rubber band before breaking, snapped back and struck the three LSO's on the platform. A Marine observer was hit in the head, so of course he was OK. Another LSO in training was struck in the kidney and was on the critical list for several days, but he eventually recovered. The Airwing Staff LSO's left knee was shattered and it was going to be some time before he was back in action. This left the air wing without a qualified LSO, so I stepped forward."

"I see the Yellow Brick Road, but what was your motivation?"

"Several factors. First, it was an opportunity to gain carrier flying operational experience–and credibility. Second, AIRPAC agreed to my stipulation that I would return to VF-121 following the cruise, just in time for the delivery of the first F-4 operational Phantoms. Hopefully, I would then finish up my shore duty tour as a Phantom instructor and be in an excellent position to make my next sea duty tour in an F-4 squadron. By staying on as an LSO, I would remain in operational flying instead of getting the usual dreaded staff or ship's officer assignment. Finally, there was the plain old thrill of going to sea again. After all, that's what I signed up for, wasn't it?"

"But is that what Aurelie signed up for?"

"If she objected, she didn't say so—and, truth be told, it wouldn't have stopped me if she had. My eldest daughter, Jennifer, was born April 1959, one week before my first Demon flight, so she was nearly nine months old, David was four, and Christopher three. I had averaged twelve hours a day at the squadron, including many nights on the runway as an LSO for FCLP, and a fair amount of time at sea for CARQUAL cruises. So, there wasn't much of me at home for Aurelie or the kids to miss."

"Aurelie wasn't pregnant yet again, was she?"

"Not yet, so that was another good reason to get out of town. And this is a good stopping point for us this morning. It's about time for your flying lesson. We'll pick up after dinner this evening for the Ticonderoga cruise, OK?"

"Excellent. I'll see you for dinner in the Lodge Dining Room at six."

16

TICONDEROGA 1960

"Hi Mike, how was your flying lesson?

"Well, I didn't break anything and Sam soloed me today!"

"Hooray for you! Congratulations! This calls for a celebration. Dinner is on me and its steak night. Shall we?"

"Lead on, Captain."

"Good evening, Georgie."

"Good evening boys. You're looking cheery tonight. What mischief have you been up to?"

"Mike soloed Sam's Cub today!"

"That's wonderful, Mike, congratulations. Does that mean we have a new Pukin' Dog among us?"

"Hardly, Georgie, but it is a proud and happy day for me even though I still have a long way to go to earn my Private Pilot license and glider rating."

"Please join the celebration with us at dinner, Georgie."

"Thank you, Captain, I'd love to but I've already eaten and there's an issue in the kitchen to tend to."

"Uh oh, not the Health Department again, I hope?"

"Very funny, Captain—just a minor adjustment for a new employee. Perhaps I'll join you for dessert if that's OK."

Later, in the Lounge....

"Well, Captain, whatever the issue in the kitchen was, it sure didn't affect the food. Who would ever expect Beef Wellington for dinner at a retirement home?"

"True, Mike, but this isn't the ordinary old farts' farm you know, thanks to Georgie. I'm glad she joined us for dessert, that's rare. I think she has eyes for you, my boy. What do you say to that?"

"Very flattering, but I doubt it. She is such a gracious, intelligent, and charming woman with everyone, it would be hard to tell.'

"So, I take it you are not ruling out the possibility?"

"If I were one to rule out possibilities, I wouldn't be here, would I Captain? I'll just see where my Yellow Brick Road goes.

"Well said, Mike. Shall we pick up with the 1960 Ticonderoga cruise?"

"The recorder is on, Captain."

"As I said, I joined Air Wing Five as the replacement Staff LSO following the arresting wire break accident which put Carlos Font in the hospital with a shattered left knee, grounding him for a year and a half. The Air Wing had been aboard 'Tico' for initial work-ups for a brief period of day flight ops when the accident occurred, so I arrived just in time for the beginning of night operations. It was quite an exciting challenge for me as an LSO since I had not controlled any of the Air Wing aircraft types except Demons–day or night- and the pilots were strangers to me. At the same time I'm sure the pilots, the Air Wing Commander, and Ticonderoga's Captain had reservations about my lack of experience, not to mention concerns about the arresting gear. Nevertheless, I am thankful to say that all went well and without incident. Although I was assigned to the Staff, I was attached to the Demon squadron, the VF-53 Pukin' Dogs, 'for flying purposes.'"

"How did the Pukin' Dogs react to having a 'staffee' thrust on them to share flight time?"

"Thankfully, everyone was very welcoming. I wasn't a total stranger since I had been an instructor and LSO with some of them in VF-121. Plus, I had as many Demon flight hours and carrier landings as most of them. Fortunately, my Air Wing administrative duties were light, so I was able to spend time hanging out with the Dogs and came to feel included. The best measure of it was that I ended up the cruise with as many flight hours and carrier landings as anyone in the squadron."

"How were you able to get away from the LSO platform to fly?"

"From the beginning I was determined that I would not be 'indispensable', so with my boss CAG Salty Moore's blessing, each squadron was required to have a qualified LSO and another one in training. Surprisingly, it wasn't as hard to recruit volunteers as I expected, once they believed it wouldn't interfere with flying and they were relieved of other administrative collateral duties. We were soon up and running with a merry band of 'Paddles' .If there was something special about carrier aviators' society, there was extra camaraderie among LSO's. There were usually four to eight of us on the platform during recoveries and it became a social center where the competition was to gross each other out with the most vile jokes ever told. There was also a myth, which some claimed was true, that LSO's once competed with each other in 'Two Wire Derbies' in the days when LSO's signaled a cut with the paddles to tell tail-dragger prop pilots to cut throttle and flare his touch down to get the tail wheel on deck for the tail hook arresting wire engagement. It was a mark of expertise for an LSO to cut an airplane for a particular wire because of deviations in air speed, altitude, deck motion, and pilot technique. The only prop tail-draggers remaining in my time were the AD Skyraider squadrons, so it was a special treat to wave them aboard and give them a cut signal with the green lights on top of the mirror. Anyway, the story went that LSO's sometimes competed to see who could cut the most airplanes to the number two arresting wire -'The Two Wire Derby'. The winning LSO's prize, they say, was that he got to bed the other LSO's wife. 'Hi honey, I'm home. I lost again.' All pilots were welcomed to visit the platform to see what landings looked like from our view and it made believers of them. I was alone on the Platform one afternoon when Salty Moore appeared and offered to write my comments in our record book. The first airplane was a big A3D which came aboard a little left of centerline, putting its left wing tip a few feet above our heads. There wasn't anything especially dangerous or unusual about it, so I didn't think much of ducking my head as it passed. When I looked back at CAG, he was white as a sheet. He handed the book back to me, left the platform without a word, and never returned."

"What were the Demon Driver Pukin' Dogs like?"

"The 1960 VF-53 Dogs were an interesting and unusual combination of naval aviators. The Skipper, Johnny Johnson, was a good man, though overweight, a somewhat weak aviator, and an ineffective 'hands off' leader. He owned a liquor store in Coronado and consumed a fair portion of the product. His wife died giving birth to their sixth child and he made the six o'clock news by marrying a widow with six children. He was a great dad apparently, and a compassionate man. Because of his girth and his Happy Hour behavior, he was affectionately known to the Dogs as 'Buddha'. In contrast, his Executive Officer, Claude McCullough, was a short skinny feisty insulting renegade who enjoyed denigrating everyone. Humor to him, but not to us when we couldn't return the sarcasms to a senior. Number three Dog, Gib Kirk, the Operations Officer, was an aggressive and dangerously overconfident aviator. In his mind he was the acting commanding officer and a hotshot pilot. Claude and Gib both disliked LSO's because they believed they did not need our help. The effect of this fractional leadership void on the other eleven. Dogs was that they banded together, probably in a way similar to Buddha's children, to become the most interesting group of individualist aviators I ever knew. Unlike what you would expect of a fighter squadron, however, the flying was mostly routine straight and level at relatively low speed to save fuel for getting back aboard. Since our all-weather interceptor mission was performed single-place, single-engine, and single-plane, there was little operational team unity. We flew little formation, aerobatics, or dogfights with each other, so there was not much overt camaraderie either."

"It doesn't sound much different than flying AJ's, Captain."

"It wasn't. The greatest difference was our pulse rate and blood pressure during night carrier approaches. Although Demons looked relatively stable and steady on the glide slope, if you watched the elevator and ailerons during the approach, it was obvious that there was a lot of pumping and thrashing of the controls going on which contributed to the high 25% Demon bolter rate. Ron Hess, my good Dog friend and fellow LSO, aptly likened it to killing snakes in the cockpit. My marginal eyesight didn't help me either. I could not define the mirror's 'meat-ball' well enough to tell me whether I was above or below glide slope until late in the approach. I was five years away from wearing glasses."

"Good grief, Captain, how did you get through it?"

"Fortunately, Ron was meticulously analytical about Demon carrier approaches. He found that the large indicator near the top of the instrument panel for engine exhaust nozzle position permitted ready reference for small throttle changes. He also worked out the glide slope geometry. At a mile and a quarter from the ship at 1000 feet altitude, we could establish a 600 feet per minute rate of descent which would keep us in the ball park on the glide slope. So, I was able to focus more attention on cockpit instruments for the first half of the approach. Remember, Mike, on dark nights at sea, far from lights ashore, there are no outside visual cues for pilots to judge altitude, attitude, closure speed, nose position, depth perception, or rate of descent except cockpit instruments, three lines of landing area lights, and the mirror's 'meatball' glide slope indicator did not provide sensitive indications to deviations until close in. Orientation required a combination of flying on outside visual contact and cockpit instruments which Ron termed 'construments', which was very conducive to inducing vertigo. We were still years away from electronic glide slope indicators, white flood lighting of the landing area, auto throttle, or the Automatic Carrier Landing System. Carrier commanders still operated with the World War Two mentality of minimizing lights and electronic emissions to evade detection. During some exercises, aircraft made navigation lights off approaches and LSO's were not permitted use of the radio except in emergencies. Those nights were quite challenging on the LSO platform."

"If you couldn't see well what you were doing in the cockpit, as an LSO how were you able to tell what approaching airplanes were doing?"

"That was another LSO 'mystique'. You see, there was a degree of mild friction between pilots' egos and LSO's. It goes against the grain for aviators having someone tell them how to fly and criticize their mistakes. During debriefings, pilots often denied the LSO's observations of pilots' mistakes and declared that LSO's were all blind. For a while I wore a white flight suit, dark glasses and a sailing hat, carrying my guitar case in one hand, and once a red tipped cane in the other tapping my way down the flight deck to the LSO platform before recoveries. Little did they know how blind I really was."

"Tell me about Ron Hess, Captain."

"That's not easy, Mike. Ron was so uniquely eccentric that I couldn't do him justice. He came into the Navy as a NAVCAD–Naval Aviation Cadet. That is, he had only two years of college; however, he more than made up for the other two years with a thorough self-education. Earlier, he had apparently been a hard-drinking, motorcycle-riding hell-raising bachelor, but that changed dramatically when he married the love of his life, Joanne, who was quite tall, thin, and plain. Ron had been in love with Joanne since high school, but she married someone else and had two children before her divorce and marriage to Ron. I have never known a man as devotedly in love or happily committed to his marriage, yet he kept his motorcycle and their only car was an MG sports car. His fighter pilot instincts remained undiminished, yet his domestication knew no bounds–lawn care for example. Ron decided he was not going to have ordinary grass, so he got a Department of Agriculture manual for dichondra lawns, bought the seed, chemicals, and special soil, and rented a cement mixer to stir up the concoction. He had the most beautiful dichonrdra lawn in San Diego for a few years until an untreatable fungus attacked the roots and killed it all. Ron loved flying and was a consummate, nearly compulsive, professional, but family separation on cruises was difficult for him. At sea, he was gregarious and humorous, but in port he was a reclusive loner. One of the few times I saw him ashore he was sitting silently alone at the bar in the Yokosuka Officers Club nursing a drink. I saw the depth of his feelings displayed only once -in a most surprising and uncharacteristic outburst. While we were in Hawaii, Buddha had one of his bouts of heavy drinking on Waikiki Beach which had been reported in someone's letter home and circulated among the wives. Of course the 'code' demanded that what happened ashore on cruises stayed there. So, Claude assembled us all in the Ready Room to chew our asses out. As usual and unfortunately, he said it the wrong way, blaming 'you pussies who write home every day'. In a flash, Ron leapt from his chair in a rage declaring that he was one of those pussies and would not stand for being derided for it or blamed for the event. Claude, of course, was not a big enough man to accept this justified angry response, so Ron probably suffered for Claude's well-earned humiliation in his subsequent fitness report. As I said, Ron's outburst was uncharacteristic, he was mainly known for his odd sense of humor and observations about life. He coined 'Men are led through life by their penis'. Another was, 'Indecision is the key to flexibility–and vice versa'. The one I liked most was, 'Don't fade into the woodwork, let 'em know you were there.' I'll think of others as we go along. Ron created a fictitious pilot in the squadron, Ensign Wicker Kleegan. On his initial radio call on glide slope, 'Taproom 102, ball, state two two', Ron added, 'pilot Kleegan'. Then Ensign Kleegan's name was added to the Ready Room roster board, as well as administrative lists and routing slips. Our very young and naive Intelligence Officer, Ensign Bob Hoffman, a.k.a. 'Bobby Blues Eyes' thanks to Ron, spent his time in the intelligence spaces and rarely visited Ready Room One. One day, however, he was the Squadron Duty Officer during a man overboard drill. Of paramount importance was to determine if someone was actually missing, so all hands quickly assembled in assigned places for an accurate personnel accounting. 'Where's Kleegan?' Ron asked Bobby Blue Eyes. 'Better call his room, he probably slept through the alarm.' 'No answer', said Bobby. By then, Bobby was very nervous, so of course everyone piled on. 'You'd better call the bridge right away, Bobby, and report Kleegan missing.' So he did and shortly after came the announcement from the bridge on the lMC, 'Now hear this. Ensign Kleegan report to Ready Room One on the double'. Everyone except Bobby and the Captain's bridge team appreciated the humor and Ensign Wicker Kleegan achieved everlasting Pukin' Dog fame. Ron and I were together as LSO's for six years. He had more influence on my outlook than anyone I have known. Hardly a day passes without recalling something he said."

"You speak of Ron in past tense, I assume he is not living?"

"No he isn't, but he was in and out of my life for another ten years, so I'll get to that. Now is a good time to relate a composite picture of pre-Vietnam life in the Philippines at the old Cubi Officers Club which you'll recall was essentially nothing more than a screened in bamboo shack with a thatch roof over iron pipes. However, the view of primitive Subic Bay and the high surrounding mountains was spectacular. The Cubi Club was popular because it was close to the carrier pier and the atmosphere was especially relaxed and informal. Since there was no air-conditioning, the dress code was casual–coats and ties not required. Since crime and social disease was rampant in the primitive town of Olongapo outside the gate, many didn't venture off base and so the Cubi Club was one of the few places where squadrons socialized together. Aviators invariably lean or hang on to anything handy and it is said that an Irishman or fighter pilot is never drunk as long as he can hold onto a single blade of grass and not fall off the face of the earth; therefore, those pipe rafters were irresistible to hanging upside down from them by the knees like bats. It takes some practice to down a drink that way, Mike, but many accomplished it with great finesse. Following happy hour, squadrons often assembled in the dining room at long pushed together tables. Sometimes, less experienced junior officers were not able to remain conscious through the meal, so following the meal they were selected to be the 'Airplane' for a little fun called 'Cat Shots and Arrested Landings'. Besides Airplane, others were selected to be the Catapult Officer, Landing Signal Officer, and Arresting Gear Officer. The stronger and more sober were selected as two Wing Officers and two Engine Officers, to provide the needed aerodynamic thrust and lift to Airplane for 'flight'. Seeing what was coming, the waiters would quickly attempt to clear away the dishes, silverware, and glasses from the Flight Deck -but not always successfully in time for the first 'launch'. The semi-conscious Airplane was then taxied into position face down on the 'flight deck' with his 'wings' and 'landing gear' spread and with a 'Wing Officer' and 'Engine Officer' on each side holding on to the Airplane' s 'wings' and 'landing gear', ready for the Catapult Officer's 'launch' signal when Airplane was fired down the 'flight deck' with remaining tablecloths and dinnerware scattered to the 'ocean' and Airplane 'flown' around the 'pattern' by the Wing and Engine Officers. Sometimes, sadly, Airplane would get a 'cold shot' and would leave the 'flight deck' without lift or thrust provided by the Wing and Engine Officers and would join the debris in the 'ocean' -only to become once again airborne, thanks to the renewed thrust and lift of the Wing and Engine Officers to continue around the 'pattern' for a 'carrier approach' and 'arrested landing' under the control of the Landing Signal Officer who gave the 'cut' signal to the Engine and Wing Officers who then ceased to provide 'lift' or 'thrust' to Airplane. Sadly again, Airplane would sometimes land short and have a 'ramp strike'. Or on other occasions, the Arresting Gear Officer failed to engage Airplane's 'hook' and be would 'bolter' off the end of the 'flight deck' into the 'ocean'. Needless to say, all of this good fun was very valuable training for young junior officers in teaching them to pace their drinking properly at happy hour. This little game, however, was becoming a regularly disruptive and destructive event -not to mention dangerous -and had to be stopped somehow. The solution was an ingenious mechanical contraption to replace the tables. I'll describe later... On one of those Cubi Club evenings, Buddha exhibited the finest leadership display of surviving over-indulgence ever witnessed. We expected him to pass out before dinner. Instead, Buddha seemed to go into a meditative trance. His glazed eyes stared into another world. His sweaty puffy face was oblivious to his environment and he spoke only to order the largest T-bone steak. After dinner we adjourned to the main room, leaving Buddha behind totally detached from the task of gnawing on his steak, for the floor show native ladies in folk costume were performing the Philippine national dance, Tinikling. The dance, which originated from a form of punishment for slow farm workers during the Spanish conquest, consisted of clapping together two large bamboo poles against the worker's ankles. Today, the dance is performed on Sundays by women in colorful native costumes and bare feet dancing to the slowly increasing tempo of percussion and string instruments. Four men on the ends of two pairs of ten foot four to six inch diameter bamboo poles, crossed as in tic-tac-toe, kept time by beating them against the floor and clapping them against each other in a complex rhythm. The graceful Tinikling dancers in colorful flowing costumes imitated the movement of the tikling birds walking between grass stems, branches, or dodging bamboo traps. The rhythm began slowly and dance steps seemed fairly simple, as the ladies delicately withdrew their feet in time to avoid injury by the heavy clapping poles. By the end of the dance the beat was so fast it was hard to see how the dancers were able to step out of the way in time. After the performance, the audience was encouraged to give the dance a try. This is no small feat—pardon the pun—which an inebriated aviator should not attempt, for the pole men do not always take pity on fools like us. I describe all this in detail to you, Mike, to set the stage for what happened next. From the sidelines to stage center came the mighty Buddha, walking unsteadily and clutching the remains of his T-bone in his greasy hand with pieces of fat attached, as four beautiful young girls positioned and steadied him between the poles. There he was, our fearless Pukin' Dog leader, eyes glazed, face soaked with sweat and grease as the music began and the men kept the beginning slow beat with the poles against the floor. Buddha made no effort to raise a foot as the poles came together the first time against his ankles from four sides. Amazingly, there was no physical sign of pain in his expression or even a blink in his far off stare. His only reaction was to raise his T-bone to get a mouth full of fat. And so the Tinikling dance continued as the mighty Buddha just stood motionless except for gnawing on his T-bone with no change of expression as his ankles were pummeled by the poles in increasing tempo until several Dogs decided it was time to bail Buddha out. To my knowledge, none of the letter writing 'pussies' ever wrote home about the incident and the subject never came up in the ready room. Apparently, Buddha had no injury or memory of the event. The permanently stationed officers at Cubi Point, however, took great exception to the rafter-hanging, dining room games, and inebriation at their club. In an effort to upgrade the decorum, the dress code was changed to require coat and tie or uniform of the day after 5 PM. Needless to say, arbitrarily requiring dress-ups at an un-air-conditioned grass shack in the tropics did not sit well with us and accomplished nothing to modify behavior except to raise the level of animosity and noise. One afternoon a Marine helicopter squadron assembled in working uniform for happy hour. When they remained past 5 PM, one of the base officers reminded the Marine CO of the dress code. When the Marines failed to comply, the unhappy base officer called the Officer of the Day. Lo and behold the OOD was in working uniform too, Tropical White Short, shorts instead of the long trousers of the uniform of the day. Instead of leaving as requested, the Marine CO took his pants off, as did the rest of his men, so their underwear matched the OOD's shorts. The Marine CO led the OOD to the door and advised him to close the club to more patrons and the Marines had the place to themselves for the rest of the evening without consequence. On another evening, the bar was closed early to dampen our behavior, so one of us called the base CO who earned a prominent place in naval aviator history by coming to the club in his bathrobe, re-opening the bar, and drinking with the boys until daybreak. I am proud to report that CO later made Admiral. In the end though, many decided that if we had to dress up we may as well take our act to the much nicer and more formal family officers club at Subic, or the small informal club with a swimming pool at the family housing area. The Cubi club missed our business and the other clubs' patrons were, to say the least, unhappy with our presence. The situation came to a head when a group young aviators formed a Christmas choir to sing a very foul x-rated version of 'The Twelve Days of Christmas' at the Cubi club. Encouraged by their popularity and the Christmas spirit, the choir took their show on the road to all the clubs, including the Chiefs' and Enlisted Clubs. Shortly after, the Cubi dress code was dropped and life returned to normal. Still, a few of the Cubi base officers continued to be poor sports about our behavior. One evening after happy hour and dinner, a local Lieutenant took great exception to 'Duck' Huey's inebriated behavior. The Lieutenant lost his temper and Duck took his gestures as a physical threat and punched him out. Unfortunately however, Duck forgot that he had a beer bottle in that hand and smashed it across the Lieutenant's face with bloody results. For some weeks after, court martial charges were pending against Duck. Fortunately, largely because of the Lieutenant's own aggressive behavior and unpopularity with his superiors, the charges were dropped. A few years later, the ultimate solution was to tear down the Cubi club and replace it with the most hideous and non-functional Officers Club in US military history. Nevertheless, the tradition of 'Cat shots and Arrested Landings' was occasionally preserved in the dining room by new junior officers, until a 'dirty shirt' annex was built in back of the club with a mechanical contraption with a chair on inclined rails next to a pool of water. The rails were fitted with an arresting wire and the chair was fitted with an arresting hook dropped by the chair's rider. There was an adjustable ramp which caused the hook to skip the wire if dropped too soon, allowing the chair and rider to continue into the pool. At least that's the way it was described to me -I never saw it because most old-timers ever after shunned the new Cubi O Club in favor of the Subic O Club."

"And you say that shore leave was not especially colorful, Captain? I cannot imagine it getting much more rowdy than that!"

"I suppose your right -compared to the life of an Albuquerque attorney. Too bad. I once read a book written by a World War Two flight surgeon titled 'Flying Health' in which he made a strong case for the benefits of happy hour in relieving the tensions of regularly facing death in the air. Perhaps that's where the tradition originated -one excuse is as good as another. Everyone needs some way to relax from the pressures of life. Honestly though, I was never an enthusiastic participant. My father was a tee-totaler who often said that 'The only person who can stand a drunk is another drunk'. Since in his eyes everyone drank, he was anti-social. I suspect he swore off because he distrusted himself. Perhaps it rubbed off on me. It probably would have benefited both Father and me if we had learned to lighten up more in our lives. After all, 'moderation in all things' does not imply being an anti-social tee-totaler, does it?"

"No, but I have seen a few tee-totalers talked into drinking and realized what a mistake it was. Still, that doesn't justify their judgmental wrath against those who can handle social drinking properly. There are times and places like the old Cubi O Club, as you described it, where it may serve a beneficial purpose—especially when alcohol consumption aboard ships is against Navy Regs, right?"

"True, it's against regulations, however, not always strictly observed. I'll get into that more later."

"So what was shore leave like at other ports, Captain?"

"In Japan we tied up at the old Jap Navy base in Yokosuka on the western shore of Tokyo Bay south of Yokohama, where Hornet docked in '58. It was protected by close-in rocky hills which had been extensively tunneled with workshops and storage facilities. Like most things in Japan, the base was in miniature but very well done. The routine for these port calls was much the same every time I visited there, so they tend to run together in some ways. For that matter, so do the cruises. So, I'll recall events that standout in memory without too much regard for chronology. If we were to be in port in Yokosuka for an extended period of yard work on the carrier, the Air Wing was flown ashore to NAS Atsugi so we could maintain flying proficiency. One of those fly-offs was memorable. Because of a late shore basing decision, we were catapulted off Ticonderoga after we tied up to the pier in Yokosuka. It was quite a sight–and damned noisy with us in after-burner in that confined space. I know of no other time where Demons were catapulted off a carrier while docked in port. One night at the Atsugi Officers Club happy hour, Buddha, in a mellow mood, agreed to let four of us fly Demons on a weekend cross country. When Gib Kirk heard about us going over, around, and behind him for permission, he was furious–not only at us for asking, but at Buddha for agreeing because we were due to fly back to the ship the following Monday and Gib was sure that we would have four Demons down for maintenance scattered at USAF bases all over Japan Monday morning. To punish us, embarrass Buddha, by making sure we would have maintenance problems precluding Monday's return to Ticonderoga, Gib demanded that we fly two legs a day to different bases. To Gib's great chagrin, we returned without a single maintenance gripe on any of the four Demons. To this day, Smoke Wilson, Kirby Wells, Roger Harris, and I are remembered as 'HAAC Flight'."

"What does HAAC mean?"

"'House Arrest And Confinement, the non-judicial punishment of an officer being confined to his stateroom by his CO. Happily, HAAC Flight was only confined to flying Demons for three days!"

"Was there some similarity between the Atsugi and Cubi O Clubs then?"

"None. We didn't hang out together much there, because there was nothing primitive or threatening about being off base in Japan. On the contrary, I felt that the Japanese were most culturally refined. Though theirs was a relatively closed society, the people were very tolerant, honorable, and polite to us. Whether aboard ship in port or shore-based, however, normal working hours were maintained. After all, we weren't on vacation and the burden of collateral administrative duties never slowed. Unlike the city of Yokosuka, with all its bars, clubs, and shops catering to the Navy, Atsugi was very rural and quiet. So, we generally teamed up in taxis or trains from there for shopping trips to Yokohama. It was a pretty tame life, really, but none-theless interesting for our glimpses of Japanese life and culture. "OK, Captain, so much for the 'tour', how about your personal 'night life' on that cruise. After the positive experience of the previous cruise, weren't you hoping for another?"

"No, Mike. You'll recall that I wasn't looking for action before either. This cruise was no different. Nevertheless, stuff happens, doesn't it? We had two first tour flight surgeons with us who expressed an interest in seeing what Yokosuka night life was like, so I took them to the ex Jap Navy Officers Club in town which I described before. When we agreed to have girls join us, there were only two. That was fine with me, so I indicated that they should sit with the docs. Then one of the girls said she had a girlfriend visiting from Tokyo who worked at the world famous Queen Bee night club and that she might like to join us if it was OK, but that she could not speak a word of English. OK with me, I was just showing the doctors around town. Nobuko was very tall, thin, and lovely. These ladies were unusual in that they were wearing street clothes and were not as interested in the usual bar conversations or drinks. Instead, they were more intent on having a conversation in Japanese among themselves like a group of wives out for lunch—not that it was annoying, just unusual. When their conversation became more animated and it was apparent that they were discussing us, I asked what they were talking about. They explained that the girl from Tokyo was a virgin and they had agreed it was time to change that condition and that they were debating which of us would be best for her first time. They had settled on me."

"'The Yellow Brick Road' again, Captain?"

"Most assuredly. Here I was, nearly thirty years old, being asked to deflower my first virgin—in Japan of all places. I ask you, Mike, how else does something like that happen? What else could a poor boy do?"

"Of course, I sympathize totally, but first virgin? What about Aurelie?"

"Yeah right, we'll get to that question one day. One story at a time, alright?"

"Sure, so what can you say about how it went?'

"Awkward, but not too badly, considering that we two strangers with no common language or attraction, there alone in the darkness of a strange room with no furniture except a bed on the floor, for the prescribed clinical purpose of a 'first time' induction. It helped that she was in her mid to late twenties, not a silly teenager, and that she was Japanese. In Japan sex isn't complicated by sin, religion, morality, scorn, or laws. It is simply a highly accepted body function fact of life. Unlike American women, who tended in those days to 'sacrifice' themselves on the altar of marriage and knew little of the subject, Japanese women were very curious and well informed of sex. Besides, I was skeptical about her virginity. Anywhere in the Orient, or the rest of the world, it surely had to be a very rare event indeed to be asked by a lovely mature woman to deflower her. Yellow brick road, you ask? Absolutely and undoubtedly. Anyhow, without going into intimate detail, the obstruction was real and there was so much pain and bleeding for her she asked to stop. There was no doubt about her virginity, unless she had some very elaborate way of staging it. So, we took a break and she soon asked to try again. It worked out just fine all around and we became an item for a while. Nobuko became insatiable and demanding. When I was at my limits, she wanted more–and knew how to get it. I reckon she read all the right books. There were just two problems, her drinking and her sister. Her reaction to booze was an unpredictably violent temperament. Unfortunately, it turns out that the private, as opposed to public, behavior of the Japanese is quite like all other humans worldwide. Her older sister had a child and was married to a black sailor in the US who had abandoned her. She became a problem because she was constantly with us and expected me to fix her up with someone. This was not a cherished role for me, especially since she shared the drinking and insatiability tendencies of her younger sister. One night, around three AM, the sister barged into our room, taking a flying leap into bed with us. Nobuko didn't seem too upset about it, so it occurred to me that I was expected to take care of Sis too. Well, Mike, it may be most men's fantasy to have two sisters in the sack at once, but I guess something in my psyche put me off. I took Sis to her room and deposited in her own bed alone and explained to Nobuko that we were not to be a threesome any longer–in any sense of the word. It all finally ended when Nobuko, under the influence, attacked me one night. In the end, I learned a lot about universal female behavior, and it was not a joyful experience. Nobuko was an anomaly, but at least I learned to be less idealistic about encounters in the Orient. Nothing in life is all black or white, Mike. For me, my compromise was the best choice I could live with in the real world. Although I have no regrets, there was a corner in my religious beliefs which acknowledged guilt. I was well aware of the pitfall of the morally corrosive consequences. In my mind, in the end of those days, the only Commandment I hadn't broken was 'coveting thy neighbors' wife', which I dearly clung to avoiding. As you will see later, that conscience nearly did me in."

"What about other port calls? Did your own 'butterfly' rule apply to those?"

"Yes, no more than one flower per cruise. The only other port was Hong Kong which we normally visited only once each cruise for five or six days for a frenzy of intensive duty free shopping for goods from all over the world, including cars and yachts. Especially in the fifties and early sixties, Hong Kong was a most fascinating exotic Asian city. It was a wide open, free trade, duty free, port with the best of Indian tailors and goods from everywhere on earth at truly bargain prices. Some called it 'Sampan Frisco' because of its geographic similarity, as well as its cosmopolitan character. It was a unique mix of the total spectrum of Chinese and British Colonial culture in those days. Steaming into port, it was usual for a junk or sampan to cut across our bow as close to collision as possible to 'cut the tail of the dragon' which represented death to them. As soon as we dropped anchor we were surrounded by dozens of sampans alongside to paint the carrier's topsides from stem to stern with long rollers, as well as water and garbage barges to tend to our needs. Other sampans plied goods for sale to the crew. The harbor was strewn with trash, garbage, and animal remains–sometimes human. Behind the glitter, life was cheap and survival difficult. Nevertheless, the people were industrious, hard-working and honest. Literally thousands of refugees from mainland China were pouring into the territory daily and the Brits quickly constructed dozens of high rise 'resettlement' apartment buildings to try to keep up with the flood of humanity. Still, some chose to live on sidewalks starving and begging for work, too proud to accept government welfare. In contrast, night life was like a 'pajama party' for the many gorgeous teenage girls working at the bars, night clubs, and dance halls. Very unlike Japan, however, those customers who escorted these ladies home at 3 AM, typically discovered that groups of girls shared apartments who also had their escorts present. So then the cards came out and a bundle lost playing poker until dawn when our hung over, discouraged, exhausted, and broke heroes made their retreat back to the ship. I knew of no successes in those quests, so I stuck to the tailors and some of the world's finest Chinese, Indian, and British restaurants to be found anywhere."

"You haven't said much about the flying this cruise. Considering the usual hazzards, plus the Demon's engine unreliability, are there no scary episodes to relate?"

"Oh sure, a couple of them. We lost two Demons to compressor stall engine failures and pilot ejections at sea. Fortunately, both pilots were rescued uninjured. The first was on a squadron fly-off to Atsugi Japan. Since we were to be ashore for several weeks and the was no luggage space in Demons, we consolidated our clothes, cameras, golf clubs, etc in the single 'blivet' we had, which was a purpose converted external fuel tank hung on a bomb rack. So of course you will quickly guess correctly which engine failed and dumped the Demon with blivet into the deep Atlantic Ocean. Ironically, the pilot was Ron Miller, the squadron's Aircraft Maintenanc Officer."

"How appropriately deserving, Captain. Was the second loss colorful also?"

"Much more so–and couldn't have happened to another more appropriate victim. Gib Kirk was climbing out after launch passing through a low cloud layer when his engine went into compressor stall with the usual flames shooting out both ends resulting in engine shut down. Since Gib was above the clouds and wished to be spotted by the rescuers, he turned downwind abeam the ship and glided below the clouds before ejecting. The launch was still in progress and I was on the LSO platform for the following recovery near the four A-1 Skyraiders tuned up awaiting deck launch. Gib's Demon was gliding silently and majestically on its own in a slight turn as though in the landing pattern downwind abeam making a landing approach. Who would ever have imagined that an engineless Demon could glide so beautifully. Surely it couldn't glide and guide itself all the way to the ship? Well, it was making a credible attempt–which caused considerable alarm to all–especially the anxiously observing tied down Skyraider's pilots helpless ly strapped into their cockpits, engines running, props turning."

"I expect you quickly lost interest in witnessing the outcome and left the scene?"

"Lord no, how many lifetimes would one have to live to witness a scene like this–a Demon with no canopy, engine, or pilot silently guiding itself in a near perfect carrier landing approach?"

"Obviously then, since you are here to tell the tale that did not happen."

"But it very damn near did—gliding 100 feet astern at flight deck level across our wake and splashing down gracefully and disappearing into the deep blue sea."

"Didn't Ticonderoga's CO have a few things to say to Gib. This doesn't seem to be an event left undiscussed."

"Gib was admonished for putting the ship in harm's way, but it was hard to argue with success. As my Granny said, 'A miss is as good as a mile'. Or as the Marine Corps says, 'Close only counts in horseshoes, hand grenades, and nuclear weapons' as was the case in my closest call. I had a case of food poisoning one morning with a severe belly ache. I felt a little better after vomiting and went to bed. I didn't mention it to anyone since I was scheduled for a night flight. By the time briefing time came around, I felt well enough to make the flight. Wrong. I got violently sick half way through and barely got my oxygen mask off in time to throw up all over the cockpit. I felt so awful that I could barely fly the airplane, so I turned over the lead to my wing man, Irv Astor, as we headed for the approach marshal point at twenty thousand feet—which happened to be in the middle of a thunderstorm and contributed to Irv getting totally disoriented with vertigo. Let me tell you, Mike, it's a challenge to fly an airplane in a night time thunderstorm on the wing of an aviator experiencing vertigo in lightning and heavy turbulence while puking. And guess what? .It got worse. The recovery was delayed because of rain at the ship and we were going to be low on fuel. It was every naval aviator's dream of a night carrier landing: low fuel, storm, rain, rough seas, and vomit, in an airplane with a twenty five percent chance of missing the arresting wires. And it got worse. Bless his heart, Irv dove for the deck and bent his nose gear fork so badly that he was unable to taxi out of the landing area, so I had to go around while they attached a tow bar and tractor to drag him out of the way, leaving me with only enough fuel for one pass. If I didn't get aboard on my first try, I was going to have to eject. In these seas and rain, there was less than a fifty percent chance of being rescued."

"It terrifies me to hear it. How does an aviator cope with fear and nausea in such dire straits, Captain?"

"At such times you're too busy to reflect on fear. There's only one good way out of these events—concentrate on the task at hand. Looking back now, I marvel that I was able to get through it, but the only consequence was getting my butt chewed for flying sick. Bless the plane captain who had to clean up the mess in the cockpit I left them."

"Amazing. You were truly lucky, weren't you?"

"Some would say providentially protected, Mike."

"Well, Captain, it's getting late. Is there anything else to say about that 1961 Ticonderoga cruise before we wind up this chapter?"

"Just two anecdotes about the homecoming fly-off to home bases. As the 'staffee' I was assigned the 'hangar queen', a Demon which had been grounded for maintenance for months, but had been patched together well enough for a one-time flight home. I was on the port catapult against the hold back with the throttle up when I saw that the safety pin indicator on the right wing showed that the wing was not locked in the spread position and might fold up after launch, leaving my sorry ass in a very embarrassing situation. Airplanes do not fly at all well with one wing folded. After frantically signaling the catapult officer with a thumbs down and got him to suspend the launch, a maintenance man climbed up on the wing and was finally able to stomp the pin down with the heel of his shoe. So, off I went and the wings remained spread. Unfortunately, that was not quite the end of the cruise. A friend, fellow LSO, and Skyraider pilot, Ray Agee, collided with another Skyraider on formation join up and took the prop through his cockpit. It was not a cheerful homecoming on the ramp at Miramar for us to inform Ray's waiting widow and children that daddy wasn't coming home after all."

"I'm beginning to understand what you meant by cruises being completely apart from your domestic life ashore. It must be very difficult indeed to shift gears at homecoming."

"Yes Mike, mixed emotions for all concerned. So, let's call it a night and resume in the morning. I'm going to skip breakfast. I'll meet you at ten at our spot at the end of the yellow brick path, OK?"

"See you then, Captain. Good night."

17

SEA STORY & SAN DIEGO

"Good morning, Mike. Having breakfast alone?"

"Yes, Georgie, I'm meeting the Captain outside later. Can you join me?"

"Thank you, I have some time before meeting with our accountant. I hope everything is going well for you here?"

"Oh yes, excellent. Much better than I hoped possible. I could almost stay indefinitely."

"Almost?"

"Well, I'll stay until the Captain tells his story, if he can stand me. It's not that I have to be anywhere, but I'm not ready to drop this far out of the main stream yet. I'd like to go to sea. My Portuguese heritage perhaps. How about yourself? What brought you to Heritage Pines?"

"My husband Jack died eight years ago after years of slow decline with cardio-vascular complications from smoking and obesity which required full time home care by me. We didn't have children, so there were no grandchildren to mother when he passed. I was retired as Chairman of the Management Science Department at the Charles County Community College, but I needed to recover my financial situation and emotional state. A colleague introduced me to the owners here, and as they say, the rest is history. It has worked out very well for me. Empathizing with the residents and the management challenge suits me; however, I'm beginning to feel it's time to put this transition behind me. Like you, I'm not ready to settle in yet either. Coincidentally, I am intrigued by the idea of applying my management trade aboard a cruise ship sailing the Mediterraean Sea, but I've only sailed once and that was just an inside passage to Alaska. I'm not sure how well I'd adapt to life at sea, plus I've heard that crew members must remain aboard most of the time in port. My age will be a hiring issue too. Have you ever been aboard a cruise ship, Mike?"

"Just once-years ago. From out of the blue, the Captain invited me for a trans-Atlantic repositioning passage from Saint Thomas, US Virgin Islands, to Lisbon, Portugal, aboard Holland America's Wind Spirit, a 400 foot, four mast schooner."

"My goodness, what an adventurous introduction to sailing. Tell me about it!"

"We embarked in Saint Thomas, with eighty two other passengers for a midnight departure; however, we were delayed four hours by the late arrival of our food. Naturally, we all remained on deck to ensure that all went well without more hitches. For as everyone knows, cruise ships are nothing if not about copious quantities of delicious cuisine! In fact, the Captain bet me $20 that he could gain more weight than I could during our time at sea. I took the bet even though I suspect he was counting on me, a mere landlubber, to be sea-sick for the entire passage. Sick or not though, I wasn't going to miss a meal, come hell or high water. There would be no guilt for over-eating on this vacation!"

"Then did you miss many meals because of 'hell and high water'?"

"Not a single one, I'm proud to say. To the Captain's disappointment, the winds and seas were flat calm the first week. What little wind there was so close on the bow that sails were just decoration, so our weight gain game began with great gusto."

"You accent an ample amount of alliteration in your allegories don't you Mike?"

"Yes. Certainly. Sentences expressing something sincere in my soul, stated in succinct and sonorous sounds, sends my sorrows scurrying off, searching for silence and solitude where the sun can't shine nor shadows seen."

"Good grief. Two weeks at sea with you might contribute to mal de mer by itself, Mike. Sorry I mentioned it. Back to sailing. Surely you didn't eat all the time, did you?"

"Pretty much, yes.' But in between meals there was drinking, gambling, massages, sleeping, lounging in the pool, and eating." Obviously, the Captain's strategy, as a highly experienced and accomplished naval aviator, was to drink me under the table into a pool of vomit—and weight loss. But a real lawyer can keep up with an old sea-dog fighter pilot most any day on that score. Of course, the Captain also insisted on constantly reminding me that we were at sea. We spent hours, at all times of the day and night, on the bridge and walking the decks as he expounded his knowledge of the sea and the stories of his two double-handed Atlantic crossings aboard his sloop Wings."

"I take it you weren't impressed?"

"Not much. Remember, this was my first and only 'quality' time with him. I had some respect and empathy, but mostly I regarded him as an old man, though he was younger than I am now."

"Resentment perhaps?"

"I don't think so. Probably no more than my kids have for me. I didn't dwell on it. It goes with the territory of being a father—regardless of presence. Would you agree?"

"I couldn't say. I was an only child raised by my mother after my father was shot down in Vietnam; therefore, I ever after pictured him as a hero, perfect in all ways. I suppose it's easier for girls than boys to be raised by their mothers. But back to Wind Spirit–without the alliteration please."

"Yes, spoil sport–oops. Well, I was the youngest guest aboard and the only first timer at sea. More than forty of them had made this repositioning cruise before. For a few it was an annual event. I wasn't bored by any means, but after a week of flat seas I was beginning to believe that sailing was not such a daring adventure after all. However, I got a much better taste of it the second week as the winds rose to a full gale, with over forty knot winds shrieking through the rigging. The sails earned their keep, crashing Wind Spirit through twenty foot waves, constantly dousing all decks and us with salt spray the rest of the way to Lisbon."

"So were you able to keep down all the galley fare?"

"Yes, in spite of the Captains best efforts at exposing me to the weather above decks, we never missed a course or a chef's demonstration."

"Wasn't there a good deal of deck motion to upset things?"

"Not as bad as you'd think. Pitching motion was moderated by the four hundred foot Wind Spirit's hull, while wind in the sails steadied rolling motion. Plus, like most conventional cruise ships, Wind Spirit had gyro controlled stabilizers below the water line. Nevertheless, there were a few exciting moments. As the Captain explained, the size of waves depends on the wind velocity, the length of time it has blown, and the distance it has blown across the water–called fetch. In addition, changes in wind velocity and direction over time results in waves traveling in different directions and speeds, so that waves will periodically pile up on each other. You may have observed surfers waiting for the big ones. Sometimes this produces giant freak waves large enough to sink ships. The Pride of Baltimore, the city's replica of an eighteenth century Baltimore Clipper, sailing in the Caribbean on a relatively calm night in the 80's, was suddenly capsized and sunk by a single giant wave. Pride of Baltimore went down so fast that only those crew members sleeping on deck survived to tell the tale."

"Heavens, how tragically terrifying! Icebergs, reefs, hurricanes, explosions, fires, the Bermuda Triangle, terrorists, pirates, and freak waves. Going to sea doesn't seem so romantic. Maybe I should re-think my cruise ship ambition! Did you encounter freak waves?"

"We were just finishing the main course at dinner when we were suddenly struck by a huge wave which put Wind Spirit on her 'beam ends', as they say. Every piece of china, silverware, and glassware was swept from the tables along with the food. Most of us also careened across the dining room in our chairs and there was an incredibly loud crashing of pots, pans, dishes and glasses in the galley. Once the ship steadied up again and we realized we weren't capsizing, the galley crew led us all in a raucous cheer. Young Indonesians, who are a perfect combination of cheerful spirits and dedicated professionalism under the leadership of Dutch officers, make perfect crew members. Barely missing a beat, they cleared away the debris and served dessert, coffee and after dinner drinks."

"Well, you certainly earned your 'Old Salt' title on that voyage, didn't you?"

"Hardly. It takes more than two weeks at sea to make that claim. I'd call it 'Freshman Old Salt 101 '. It was a perfect introductory course—much better than Daily Island or port hopping in the Med, Alaska, or the Caribbean, I think."

"Next stop Lisbon?"

"Yes. There could not be a more dramatic contrast of ports of call than Saint Thomas and the ancient capital city, Lisbon. I shouldn't say much about Saint Thomas, since I saw so little of it on the bus from the airport to the dock, but my impression was that it is a poor primitive ghetto, which I'm told is typical of the Caribbean Islands. On the other hand, my lasting impression is that Lisbon is the most beautiful city I ever visited. Holland America booked us into the most luxurious five, star hotel in, the city for three days. We must have walked at least 20 miles, but we saw all the historic sites, parks, museums, restaurants, shops, and bars into the wee hours. A notable restaurant featured a half dozen of Portugal's finest Fado singers performing their melancholy blues traditional music, characteristic of the Portuguese 'happy to be sad' stereotype. Although there only three days, I left with a deeper pride and understanding of my Portuguese heritage which is distinctly different from my Hispanic side."

"Didn't that adventure accomplish a lot to seal a bond with the Captain?"

"Not as much as I hoped. I can't explain why, mostly over his later disputes with my wife, communications between us soured we finally stopped trying."

"Men why do you so often act like little boys, picking fights that way? What a shame, anger is so destructive."

"Yes, true, but that applies to women as well, doesn't it?'

"I suppose so, but by comparison, women are less unforgiving."

"But no less painfully destructive at times."

"Touche, Michael. Too bad, considering all the blessings we have, to actually choose to make ourselves and others unhappy. I hate to end on that note, but I see the accountant has arrived, so I must go."

"OK, I hope we can resume on a more positive plane soon. At least you're prepared to deal with a bean counter now!"

Mike found the Captain at his spot at the end of the yellow brick sidewalk asleep in his wheel chair, covered by his plaid blanket just as he had been the first time Mike saw him here.

"Sneaking up on me again are you, Mike?"

"Of course not, you were expecting me."

"I was last time too, you'll recall."

"You were flying then, but thought you were only dreaming."

"True. So now I'm burdened me with the reality of it."

"Is that a curse?"

"Don't know, might be. It sure keeps me awake nights now."

"Well let's hope you don't sleep all the way through flying again, right?"

"I suppose. I had never considered the possible impractical consequences. Life was a lot simpler when levitation was just a romantic dream."

"Flying airplanes was a romantic dream for you throughout childhood as well and there were consequential realities to deal with when you finally achieved it. Did the realities of aviation dull your dreams?"

"Definitely not, Mike. Not even the realities of people shooting at me. But you must admit that the consequences of levitation could be far more difficult to deal with than getting shot at."

"Not necessarily. We just have to keep it to ourselves and stay out of sight."

"Easy to say, but not that simple. There are eyes and ears everywhere. Just imagine where the temptations to 'explore the envelope', as it were, might lead me."

"Higher, faster, and farther, you mean?"

"Exactly. Who could resist? I would surely be discovered, then what?"

"What's the worst they could do, crucify you? You're ninety four years old. Have you suddenly developed a fear of risks?"

"No wonder you are an attorney. Too bad, you had the makings of a fighter pilot."

"Then I could be a comedian, just like my Dad, couldn't I?"

"Might be an improvement. You know why sharks won't eat lawyers?"

"Spare me the repeat jokes about lawyers, Captain."

"Bet you don't know a single one about fighter pilots, do you?"

"I'll work on that, but wouldn't you like to get back to your sea stories now?"

"That's it, just like a lawyer or a woman, change the subject when you're losing. Where were we?"

"1961, just returning home from flying Demons on the Ticonderoga cruise. How was the transition to the domestic husband and father roles this time?"

"It was good to be home with Aurelie and the kids. Absence does not necessarily make the heart grow fonder, but it does afford an opportunity to put life into perspective and examine priorities, so I had begun to truly miss Aurelie about half way through the cruise. We had been through a lot of emotional chaos over the past dozen years since we began dating and became joined at the hip in Munich. However, the previous five years with the divorce from Emma, three moves, two cruises, and three children had put considerable strain and distance in our relationship. There just was no time for us to repair damages. Still, I felt there was a strong bond between us. I thought things were as well as they could be and that Aurelie was holding up exceptionally well. She easily passed the head of household reigns to me and we resumed being a fairly normal family I thought. The kids were great too. David and Christopher were very close in age and were strongly bonded friends. Aurelie was painting modernistic landscapes in oils and acrylics. I began building RC model airplanes, but radios were so unreliable I switched to RC boats because they didn't crash. I was a founding 'plank owner' and the second Commodore of the San Diego Argonauts, an RC boat club which had exclusive use of the purpose built model yacht basin and club house at Mission Bay. We developed an electronic timing system to measure the straight-away two-way speed averages of our models. My predecessor as Commodore, Ed Hendricks, my closest friend ever, was a Navy Chief Petty Officer radioman stationed at Corregidor when the Japs attacked the Philippines in 1942 where he was captured, survived the Bataan Death March, and endured the war in a POW camp in Japan. Oddly, Ed felt no animosity toward the Japs. In fact, he became friends with the camp commandant who he taught mathematics. In turn Ed learned to read and write Japanese and was allowed to keep his diary in Japanese."

"Ed wasn't tortured? Considering the historic Japanese brutality of the Death March, wouldn't you expect more similar barbaric treatment in camp?"

"Yes I would, but Ed's experience was perplexing to me. He said that the only time he was punished was after they assigned him and the other radiomen the task of designing radio circuits. Then when the Japs made non-functional transmitters from their circuits, Ed was punished by having the left side of his head beaten with a sock full of cotton for thirty minute periods. These sessions were not especially painful, Ed said, but left his ears ringing for hours. Still, Ed and the commandant remained close friends. One day, near the end of the war, Ed was lying on a bench in the compound when a P-51 made a strafing run. The commandant had just come out and as Ed stood to greet him a fifty caliber round went through the bench where Ed had just been. Ed said that the commandant was so overcome with emotion that he hugged Ed in tears. Ed was from the same small west Texas town as Tex Ritter. Faye, two years behind Ed in high school, had a deep crush on Ed but couldn't get his attention. When she learned that Ed was captured, she determined to become a Navy nurse with the expressed purpose of being on hand when Ed was repatriated. And she was. They were married and they had a son named Charles, a quiet and shy genius. When I met Ed, he was working for the Convair test lab where, as a sideline, they developed the first heart machine used in operations. He was very active in ham radio and model building, so RC boats were a natural development for him."

"So how did you come to be such close friends?"

"A 'father figure' for me perhaps, and I was much easier to get along with in those days. Ed was bright, thoughtful, and optimistic. He and Faye were deeply devoted to each other and always pleasant for us to be with wherever we went. The model yacht basin was in the Mission

Bay Park and had a gradually sloping shoreline which made it an excellent setting for our families, unlike RC airplane fields where the environment and middle-aged men are typically less than friendly to women and children. Ed and I shared other interests too. Larry, one of Ed's friends at the lab developed an obsession for the twenty one old gold mines near Hemet and tales of lost gold treasures. Larry bought a mineral and ore detector and honed his treasure hunting skills by having his wife bury silverware in his back yard. At last, he was ready to sally forth to find his fortune. With Larry's friend and son in his Army surplus command car with giant aircraft tires, plus Ed, Charles and I tagging along in Ed's jeep, we set out to find the lost gold 'Treasures of Sierra Hemet'. Our lack of map homework was apparent when we arrived at Hemet before day-break and had to awaken folks in their trailer home for directions. Just as well we did because otherwise we never would have found the road behind the town landfill. With Larry leading in his giant-wheeled command car in a feeding frenzy, it soon became very hairy business to nego-tiate the narrow washed out road on the side of a steep canyon with at least a forty five degree slope. It was doubtful that anyone could have survived that two thousand foot tumble in the Rockies. Still, we pressed on until we came to the opening of a mine immediately adjacent to the road. Encouraged by a strong detector reading on the rocks at the entrance, we charged in armed with one lantern, a pick, and the detector–until we noted that the ceiling had little shoring and some of that had collapsed with debris covering the floor. At that point Ed decided it pru-dent to remain behind so he could call for help on his radio if there was a cave-in. Charles and I continued behind Larry with increasing concern when we saw that there was no longer any shoring of the ceiling whatever, while Larry persisted in picking away at the walls for samples. Finally, Larry got a strong detection on the floor and frantically dug away, only to uncover the rails of the excavation hand cars. Larry's detector registered another strong reading at the end of the mine where there was no shoring at all. So, when he picked away for a sample there was just enough of a cave-in to convince me to get Charles out of there, even though Larry had the only light and we had to feel our way out in total darkness. Thankfully, we made it out and resumed our adventure down the road, sometimes with the command car tires half off the road, hundreds of feet above the bottom of the canyon. Then we spotted another mine; however, it was a steep hundred feet above us with lots of tough sagebrush to chop through, plus it was getting very hot. The climb was at least a thirty degree grade, so it was slow going with Larry chopping away at the dry brush with his machete, declaring in heavy breaths, 'Boy, no one has been up here in a long time.' Then he came nose to nose with a rattle snake about to strike. Fortunately, he had his machete raised for the next slash at a bush and was able to direct the blow to the snake. The going got much rougher as we approached the outcroppings of the mine. Two arduous steps up, one slide back. Ed wisely decided to hang back with the tools. For all of Larry's repeated 'no one has been here for a long time', there was a recently marketed soft top beer can at the mine entrance—and it went straight down. Despite our lust for gold, not even Larry was interested in going down there. Looking across the canyon though, I saw the remains of a miner's cabin and a possible mine entrance. So we slid back down and climbed up the opposite side, thankfully without back-sliding. Ed again wisely chose to stay behind with the picks and shovels. We were disappointed to find that the mine entrance went in only a few feet. Perhaps the miner buried his gold in the cabin? Sure enough, the metal detector picked up a strong return in the corner near the fireplace and excitement ran so high 'gold fever' took hold and we began digging with bloodied bare hands and broken nails until I found a shovel with no handle. After taking turns digging down two feet for a sweaty hour, we uncovered the 'treasure'—about twenty pounds of ancient nails—but there was still a strong return below. Why would nails be buried so deep? Perhaps as a decoy for the gold below? As hot, dirty, and exhausted as we were, not even gold fever could inspire us further. We agreed we had enough. We would return another day."

"Amazing, Captain, that you gave up when you may have been very close to the lost treasure you were seeking. How do you explain that?"

"Speaking for myself, it has generally been more about the trip than the destination. Seeking 'pots of gold' are not realistic motivation for satisfying lust for life, so I intrinsically favored high risk adventure instead of a more lucrative and domestic life. I did not expect to live long enough to need much gold, I was living hand to mouth in the present. I thank God, Jesus, and Jean for forgiving my foibles and getting me through a most rich and rewarding life. What I cherish most now are memories which gold cannot buy, like my friendship and adventures with Ed Hendricks."

"Bravo, Captain. I am proud to share those memories with you—as well as new ones. But didn't any of you return to the cabin?"

"I hope so, but not that I heard about. However, Ed and I did return to Hemet for a different adventure—the International Jeep Cavalcade with over 450 four-wheel drive vehicles, including overseas factory teams, to trek from Hemet down the Juan Bautista de Anza National Historic Trail to the Anza-Borrego Desert State Park. The de Anza Trail was the 1200 mile route from the Nogales Arizona Mexican border to San Francisco used in 1775 by Spanish Commander Juan Bautista de Anza. The segment we did was hardly a trail however. It was more a washed out gully or ravine with large boulders which were a severe axle-busting test for the vehicles, slowing progress to a walking pace most of the way. Ed gave a running account to another ham radio operator in Alaska on his single side-band radio as we slammed our way over the rocks. Without seat belts, we would have been thrown out the top of Ed's jeep several times, so we were pretty banged up and sore when we arrived at the desert rendezvous. That evening around a huge campfire, awards were made and speeches given. The main topic were arguments defending open use of the desert against environmentalists who were promoting legislation to prohibit vehicles in the desert because they were leaving tracks in the sand. Never mind that the tracks were soon erased by wind. Pretty silly stuff, but I expect that off-road vehicles are no longer allowed on the Borrego Desert, nor on the de Anza Trail."

"You will be speaking more of Ed, I hope?"

"Yes, soon."

"What about religion during that period, Captain?"

"I was very grateful for God's constant presence in my life, but I could not abide petty church politics and narrow dogma. However, I agreed with Aurelie's wish to expose our kids to gospel. Since neither of us preferred a particular Protestant denomination, we shopped around for the best minister and found a great one at a nearby Congregational Church. It may be incorrect to compare one church to what little I know of the Unitarian Church, which has a reputation more for being a social hand-holding self- help group therapy facility than an actual Christian 'church'. To whatever degree that is so, I'd say from my experience that the Congregationalists are just a step away from being the same–which I believe is an attractive feature in lieu of the hell-fire damnation interpretations of the Bible I suffered for years in Southern Baptist and Methodist churches. Unfortunately however, this minister was focused on important social issues and in ministering to people who actually needed him, rather than pander to the petty demands of his parishioners. The ax fell when his name appeared on a McCarthy communist list and he was summarily fired without a hearing. That ended our churchgoing."

"A communist preacher? Seems to be an oxymoron!"

"Indeed. In the late 50's and early sixties the long-haired college sociology majors and other scholarly intellectuals known as 'Beatnics', an adopted term from the Beat Generation with heroes like Karouak. White sociology students from Berkely and other universities were leading the way by bearing the segregation cross for Blacks in Southern protest, sit-ins, arrests, and jail sentences. M.L. King only had to take advantage of the political opportunity to lead nonviolent protests. At the same time there was a strong resurgence of campus interest in American traditional music. Coffee houses and folk festivals were everywhere. Southern California or Greenwich Village were the places to be. As noted before, my interest in folk music dated back to the mid-forties, so Aurelie and I fell right into it whole heartedly. We practically lived in coffee houses and attended week long folk festivals at UCLA, Berkely, and San Diego State."

"Sounds like fun, Captain. What were the coffee houses like in those days?"

"Lots of great music and performers, Mike. Actually, 'coffee' house was a misnomer. I do not recall any of them serving anything other than dozens of varieties of tea! The best of them in San Diego was The Sign Of The Sun Book Store which converted a space the size of a living room on weekend evenings. Another one was a motel room with the furniture removed where we sat on floor cushions. Another was a string instrument shop called The Blue Guitar owned by a bluegrass band leader whose mandolin player, Chris Hillman, went on to be the bass player with the famous folk-rock band, The Byrds. Then there was a Navy sailor named Mason Williams playing there whose number one nationwide hit was 'Classical Gas'. The majority were college age kids who were amazingly accomplished musicians, but there were also many authentic and well known old time performers who stopped in San Diego after their Los Angeles gigs. Blues musicians Sonny Terry and Brownie McGhee, who were together over forty years and once performed for the Queen of England, played one weekend at The Sign Of The Sun for $100 apiece. Blind Reverend Gary Davis, an old New York City sidewalk 'holy blues' man, also played there. Sam Hinton, an eminent ethnomusicologist and a professor at the Scripps Institute of Oceanography, who could whistle and hum in harmony with himself, could trace a song like 'The Saint James Infirmary' from London across the Atlantic and the US to Texas 'The Streets of Loredo'. A friend of Sam's, an authentic old time cowboy named Slim Critchlow, who rarely performed in public, shyly apologized for knowing only six chords and two strums on guitar. Inspired by Slim, I dashed off to Sears and bought a $17 guitar, not knowing how hard six chords and two strums could be for a no-talent wannabe and his blistered finger tips. Aurelie took an interest too, so that was my excuse for getting another guitar and launching into collecting folk instruments–eventually including a Mexican 12-string guitar, mandolin, banjo, fiddle, autoharp, and Appalachian dulcimer, plus assorted harmonicas, jews harps, and kazoo's. The banjo, mandolin, fiddle, and one guitar were rare antiques with individual stories I'd like to tell if we can take a little side trip in this, OK?"

"Of course, Captain, it's your story. After all, I'm just the scribe."

"Alright, let's start with an old small Vega folk guitar which belonged to Patty, a friend of Aurelie's. Patty inherited the Vega from her aunt who played with a Salvation Army Band on the sidewalks of New York City in the 30' and 40's. Vega, mostly known for their school band instruments, achieved little popularity with their guitars, but this one was a distinctively beautiful work of art. The body sides and back were Brazilian rosewood–now nearly extinct and prohibited from use. The purfling and neck binding were ivory. Abalone and mother of pearl was used in a tree of life design in the ebony fingerboard, head, bridge, around the sound hole, and the seam on the back. The name Adele was etched in the mother of pearl at the third fret, indicating that this was likely a custom made presentation instrument. Unfortunately, the strings were so high off the fingerboard because of the warped neck that it was hardly playable. The back was slightly scratched, apparently by the aunt's uniform brass buttons. There was also a slight crack in the top's seam down from the bridge. Otherwise, it was in amazingly excellent condition. I tried to convince Patty to have it repaired, but she would only agree to spend twenty five dollars on it. For that price, The Blue Guitar was only willing to lower the bridge slightly and cut the nut string grooves deeper which did help a bit. Although my first impression was that the Vega's inlay put it a bit over the top in ornamentation and that it didn't have a particularly impressive sound, I gradually warmed up to it to the point where I was obsessively compelled to own it, but I had little hope that Patty would part with this family heirloom. Patty's response began, 'Oh no ...' and my heart sank, then she continued 'I couldn't take Manny's Martin' and as Chief Dan George said, 'my heart soared like a hawk'."

"So, Captain, you skinned the poor girl out of her inheritance with a $117 guitar and now owned a fancy unplayable ornament?"

"Hold on thar, pardner. I first did my best to get her to fix it so she could play and I sure didn't hold a gun to her head for the trade. As everyone knows, Martin guitars were the best and most popular acoustic steel-strung guitars ever made and she was rightfully glad to have it. As for the Vega's condition, providence provided a solution. I saw an ad for a string instrument repair shop in Escondido called The Fiddle and Fret, so I took it there for an estimate. To my great surprise, the proprietor was a man named Dopyera, who was one of the Dopyera Brothers who invented and manufactured the acoustically amplified DOBRO guitar in the 20's, popularly used in Hawaiian music before electrical amplification and still widely used in bluegrass bands. DOBRO is an acronym for Dopyera Brothers and this man had forty years of acoustic guitar making behind him. What better place to bring the Vega? After examining the guitar, Dopyera agreed to repair it, but said it would take him several months. No price was discussed. When I returned three months later to pick it up, I was in for quite a surprise. Because trying to take out the neck warp would risk the tree of life inlay, he had removed the neck entirely, as well as the part of the fingerboard on the top of the spruce sounding board. He re-attached the neck tilted slightly down and re-attached the finger board piece with a slight wedge under it to align it with the rest of the fingerboard. The strings were now at the proper height and the warp was hardly a factor. He also made a new ebony bridge with the identical inlay, filled the crack in the top with a tiny sliver of spruce, and re-strung it with new silver wound low tension compound strings. I was all the more impressed when he played it. What a wonderfully sweet soft delicate sound, ideally suited to 'parlor' finger picking and a woman's voice. I was more surprised when Dopyera offered to buy it! Bad timing for Mr. Dopyera, I honestly wouldn't have taken any amount for it, so it didn't occur to me to ask what he'd pay. Then he floored me by saying that this was the most beautiful example of an American folk guitar that he had ever seen–a national treasure. Many years later, another music shop owner estimated its value at over $10,000."

"Well, that's quite an Antiques Road Show tale, Captain. Now what? The guitar is repaired, but it's far too rare to wear out playing or risk ever taking it out of the house. Weren't you back to having an ornament to hang on the wall?"

"To a degree that's true, and pretty much what I did, though I did play it a fair amount when the inspiration moved me, I soon replaced the Martin with a D-18 'Dreadnaught', the most popular of all Martin designs."

"Do you still have the Vega?"

"Yes, but sadly there's more to the story which I'll get to much further down the line. Now for the mandolin story. My very good friend, Ed Fitch, a fellow aviator I'll have much more to say about in later chapters, had a 1916 Gibson F-2 mandolin which he inherited from the family's Italian landlord who played it and sang for him as a child. There was a little damage to the finish and two glue joints had been warped loose because it had been left in its case on top of a radiator. The top 'sunburst' finish was OK and the neck was straight. It was completely playable."

"How did you pinpoint the age?"

"Some time later I found a collectors reference book which listed the serial numbers by year of manufacture."

"How did you come by it?"

"Over my strong protests and offer to buy it, Ed insisted on giving it to me gratis although I told him it was worth over a thousand dollars. Later estimates valued it at over $3,000."

"Some friend! How did that come about?"

"Separate story, Mike. We'll get to that in a later chapter."

"Did you play it well?"

"I never played anything 'well'. I did learn enough tunes to satisfy my justification for owning those fine instruments. I sometimes played the mandolin as a rhythm instrument with groups because everyone played guitar better than I did."

"Groups? You had a 'Sousa Band'?"

"Yes. A couple of strictly amateur old time string bands. Plus, Aurelie and I played publicly a few times. We'll get to all that too. I just want to mention the instruments now. Initially, I thought it would be fun to apply my model airplane experience to making a guitar. So, I bought a book, 'How to Make a Spanish Guitar', and quickly saw what a formidable challenge it would be. Then when the Vega came along, I shifted my thinking to a 5-string banjo project. I'd just have to make a neck and hoop, metal parts were available for the rest. Providentially, I found an ad for 'Frank The Banjo Man', who advertised banjo parts, as well as used string instruments and his own home-made mandolas. Frank's shop was a small barn in the back yard of his home and wife's antique business. Whenever she came across string instruments—mostly violins—tucked away in folks' attics, she passed them to Frank. He had at least fifty violins, banjos, and his mandolas hanging from the rafters. Frank was a wonderful man who was very generous with his time. I spent many enjoyable lunch-time hours visiting with him, learning a lot about the secret art and science of string instruments. Frank played all his instruments every day to loosen up the resin in the capillary tubes of the spruce sounding boards. He said each were acoustic chambers which resonate the strings' vibrations, and that is why close-grained Alaska Sitka spruce is favored for all string instrument sounding boards. On the other hand, the ringing sound of the best Banjos depends on the heavy bell brass hoops around the tightly stretched 'skin' head. Many banjos other than old time mountain banjos have their open back covered with a resonator to amplify the sound. With all that, banjo's sustain notes a relatively short period, so why they are played with many rapidly picked notes to ornament the melody. One day I took my Gibson mandolin to Frank. Without opening the distinctively shaped case, he took it outside to his rocking chair in the sun, put it on his lap and said, 'I don't know what you have in here, but the case is worth $200.' Frank had very high praise for the instrument too, but he didn't offer to put a value on it, so I didn't ask. Like my Vega guitar, it wasn't for sale at any price. When I got around to telling Frank I wanted to make a banjo, he was not encouraging. The parts were custom made and expensive and I would never get my money back from an amateur made banjo. I could do better than waste my time and money by buying one of his old banjos. Knowing that my interest was in old style mountain 'drop thumb' or 'frailing' style picking, he brought down one without a resonator. I recognized it as a Vega by the mother of pearl star logo inlaid in the head and another at the fifth fret of the ebony ivory-bound fingerboard on a blond maple neck, otherwise it was quite plain. The previous owner had removed the fifth string and tuning peg to convert it to playing it as a four-string plectrum or tenor banjo. The neck had a slight warp to the right which did not affect its string action. When I checked the identification on the inside brace, however, I found that it was a Vega-Fairbanks Number 2 'Whyte Laydie'. From the serial number and an instrument collector's book, I later learned that Fairbanks, a highly respected banjo manufacturer, was bought out by Vega shortly before this one was made in 1921. I had never played a banjo and the only one I ever held was a new Vega 'Pete Seeger' long-neck model 5-string. The average quality and steep price were factors inspiring me to make one. Despite their relative simplicity, Banjo's were considerably more expensive than comparable quality guitars! When Frank handed it to me, I was surprised that it weighed a ton. Frank explained that good banjo's were heavy because of the thick bell brass used, necessary to enhance the string vibrations from the bridge and skin to achieve the desired ringing sound. I took Frank's word for it that the witchcraft of the Whyte Laydie's uniquely rich sound was because of the scalloped inside hoop. When Frank said he would replace the pegs with new geared one's and throw in a case for a total of $150, I bought it on the spot. I later learned that Fairbanks Whyte Laydie banjo's were the most favored of all frailing banjo's and that mine was easily worth as much as the Gibson mandolin."

"Some luck you had, Captain. So the usual questions, did you play it much and do you still have it?"

"No and yes."

"With the guitar and banjo building projects by the board, did another instrument inspire you?"

"Yes, the Appalachian dulcimer–and there were several kits available for those. However, as providence would have it, I have one given to me."

"So you never made an instrument?"

"Yes I did. Autoharps were invented and exclusively marketed by Oscar Schmidt for years. My problem with them was that they were inexpensively made of cheap pine. I probably couldn't improve on their sound, but I wanted one made out of decent wood and it wouldn't take a lot of fancy carving to make one. Through a Chicago exotic wood dealer I found a large enough piece of gorgeous Brazilian Rosewood and took nearly three years to make one, but it came out well enough to justify the effort for me. I never played it much, however, because it was a pain in the rear to keep 36 strings tuned up. Unless there's a piano handy, it can drive you crazy. Fortunately, I had bought Aurelie a spinet, in part because I was determined to learn to play Debussy's 'Maid With the Flaxen Hair'. Before you ask, I no longer have the autoharp or piano. While telling tales about instruments, I'll jump ahead and mention the fiddle. I always thought I should add one to my collection since the fiddle and banjo constituted the basic old-time mountain string band -both considered instruments of the devil by southern evangelists who also considered dancing sinful. While I was in Troy New York attending RPI graduate school in 1967, I went to a music shop in search of a fiddle and was shown a very old one which appeared to have been in a fire from the darkly crazed appearance of the finish. Still, it looked right to me at only $40 with case and bow. Later, I noted that the label said it was made by Antonio Stradivarius Cremonensus, 1764–the last two digits were scribed by hand. I assumed it was made by Cremonensus, named after Stradivarius, so I thought little more about it for seventeen years."

"Ah, yet another suspenseful 'we'll get to that' tale?"

"Yup, except to say that fiddling was by far the most difficult instrument for me. Since the fingerboard has no frets, your finger has to stop the string at precisely the right spot to get the note right, though fiddlers may stop the string a bit 'south' of the note and slide up to it since the human ear is more forgiving for slightly flat notes than sharp notes. Another complication, are the many styles of complex bowing action. So, fiddling is like patting your head and rubbing your tummy. Worse yet are the horrible screeching sounds on the high strings made by beginners, Newbies are wisely advised to learn tunes on the low strings. So that's what I did—but only two old time gospel tunes and never played it in public. And no, I no longer have it. I want to add that Ed Hendricks also bought a guitar Whereas I was determined to laboriously teach myself from books and recordings, Ed took formal lessons and each evening afterward stopped by my house on his way home to show me what he had learned. Moreover, when RC radios became more reliable and I went back to building model airplanes as well as boats, Ed did too. How's that for friendship?"

"Surely above and beyond, Captain. How great that you shared each other's rich interests."

"Yes indeed. Sadly, I'll close this chapter by telling you that when the time came for me to go to sea again, Ed's wife, Faye, told me that Ed was having constant severe headaches on the left side of his head. He was taking dozens of aspirins a day but refused to see a doctor. She asked if I would please try to talk Ed into going to the hospital. So I did and he did. Shortly after I deployed to the Western Pacific again, Ed died of brain cancer. Navy doctors concluded that the POW camp beatings were likely a contributing factor. I reckon that's all the fun with memories I can handle today, Mike."

"Sure thing, Captain. Let me just say that I am very happy that we are doing this project together."

"Same here, Mike. It's great to have such an astute captive audience. And we have a lot of flying to do too. As Dorothy often said before we chickened out, 'The best is yet to come.' Fly safely. I'll see you at dinner."

1921 Vega-Fairbanks "Whyte Laydie" #2 5-string banjo

1916 Gibson F-2 mandolin

Early 1900, custom Vega rosewood guitar ebony fingerboard with inlaid tree of life

San Diego Model Yachr Basin, 'Argonauts RC Model Boat Club

18

SHORE DUTY

"Good Morning, Captain. Sorry I missed you at dinner last night."

"You had me a little worried before you called. The flight lasted longer than you expected?"

"Yes, I found several strong thermals, so I tried my hand at soaring with a Cub."

"Good for you, Piper Cubs made fairly good training gliders during World War Two, Army glider pilots were trained in similar airplanes converted to gliders by having their engines replaced with weight and a skid in place of landing gear. In fact, their glide ratio was better than the CG-4A troop gliders flown in Europe. So, how'd you do?"

"Not bad I guess—for a beginner. The cloud bases were nearly seven thousand feet and I managed to center several thermals at around two thousand feet, throttle back to idle, and ride right up to six thousand feet, climbing at better than 500 feet a minute. It was so much fun the time whizzed by. It was nearly sunset when the lift died or I might still be up there."

"That's wonderful, Mike. You could have shut down the engine!"

"I thought about it, but it isn't my airplane and I was too far from an airfield if the engine didn't re-start."

"Yes, Sam's a patient man alright and he has been extremely generous in leaving his Cub over here for you, but an off-field landing after intentionally shutting down the engine would have been difficult news to deliver."

"There's rain in the forecast, so shall we convene on the porch after breakfast and catch up on Passing Through?"

"Sounds good."

"So, where were we, Mike?"

"September 1960. You had just returned from the Ticonderoga cruise."

"Ah yes, and a new training cycle with new people to prepare for the next cruise."

"But weren't you supposed to return to shore duty in VF-121 as an instructor and LSO in time to fly the first Phantoms?"

"Yes, but the Airwing was facing an unusually quick turnaround for another cruise aboard Ticonderoga. Despite my best efforts at training squadron LSO's, I hadn't made myself dispensable, so I agreed to remain for a few more months through the Operational Readiness Inspection off Hawaii. Besides, fleet introduction of the Phantom had been delayed and I was having fun flying with VF-53, so there was no urgent rush to get back to VF-121."

"Were there many new pilots coming into VF-53?"

"No. That was another good thing. Nearly all the Pukin' Dogs were turning around for the next cruise. The greatest challenge was that VF-51 was transitioning to F8U Crusaders. Everyone was new to the squadron from the CO down and early omens were that it was to be the worst squadron I ever knew. The new CO's Ensign wing man, retracted his landing gear and flaps too soon after takeoff on a hot day in Yuma and settled back onto the runway, sliding off the end on the Crusader's belly at better than 100 knots–so the Ensign ejected. At that time, Crusaders did not have ground level ejection seats, so the pilot came down still in the seat with the chute streaming unopened. When the crash crew, and ambulance with several squadron mates arrived on scene, they were astonished to find the pilot standing and taking off his parachute harness. Miraculously, he seemed to be uninjured except for speaking gibberish and not recognizing anyone. Shortly after delivering him to the hospital, however, the Ensign died of internal bleeding from a broken pelvis."

"Wow, quite a beginning for that CO's command!"

"It got worse. A few months later, flying back to Ticonderoga offshore San Diego one clear afternoon, still over thirty miles away, I saw thick smoke rising from the flight deck. My heart sank with the realization that there had been a crash. It was the CO's second Ensign wing man. He had settled far below the glide path close in. The LSO waved him off, but it was too late. The Crusader struck the round down so low that his main landing gear didn't even get to the flight deck. The Crusader, what was left of it, came to a stop in the arresting gear with the left wing broken off and the remaining half of the fuselage laying on its left side on fire. Crusaders were largely made of magnesium which burns like a flare when ignited, so in three frames of the 35mm crash film, the upwind right wing tip went from no fire to melt. The crash crew was quick to get the hoses to the scene, but the foam generators malfunctioned for some time before they were able to get the pilot out of the fire which was so intense it melted the Ensign's helmet visor. Though his oxygen mask and nomex gloves and flight suit did a credible job of protecting him, a burning piece of magnesium penetrated his inside left thigh. Amazingly, two days later Ensign Number Two was taken off the critical list at Balboa Naval Hospital and was well enough to sit up in bed and visit with his squadron mates. But that night he died of a staph infection."

"What a shame. I see you numbered the CO's Ensigns, so there's a story about Ensign Number Three coming?"

"Correct, Mike. Ensign Number Three had a lot of catching up to do before the imminent deployment date, including qualification carrier landings. As was customary, we had the usual Dependent's Day Cruise with the wives and parents invited to spend a day at sea serving flight operations. Of course the best place for an LSO's wife to see carrier landings up close and get an appreciation for hubby's collateral job, was with him on the LSO platform."

"Wasn't that considered dangerous? Weren't flight deck personnel getting hazardous duty pay?"

"Yeah, except not for LSO's since we were already on flight pay. We just took the wives along without asking and no one said anything about it. On those small World War Two vintage carrier decks the LSO platform was quite close to 'the landing area, even with the platform extended out over deck edge sixty feet above the ocean. The only escape route off the flight deck was a mesh wire safety net with mattresses below the platform to jump into, leading to a hatch on the deck below. I'd say that our thinking was that if it was OK for LSO's to be there day and night in weather fair or foul, it seemed worth the risk to have our wives share the experience to gain perspective. Otherwise, I found that mothers raising children tended to see life through kitchen windows with their children's outlook–which sometimes lead to uninformed judgments and unrealistic expectations about the world."

"Why not just say 'bitchy and demanding', isn't that what you mean, Captain?"

"I'd rather not be quoted that way, but if you're going to tell this tale as our conversation, then you can quote yourself. Anyhow, back to the LSO platform. It was the usual calm off-shore San Diego day with light wind and smooth seas. Everything was going well–until the Crusader approaching the ramp suddenly went very low. I immediately triggered the wave off lights, backed up forcefully on the radio. Even the wives could see that the Crusader was in deep trouble and they lead the way clearing the platform, jumping into the net and running through the hatch. Fortunately, the Crusader cleared the ramp by inches."

"I presume that the pilot was Ensign Number Three?"

"Of course. The CO decided to spice up the Dependents Day Cruise by putting up his unqualified and most inexperienced pilot, flying Navy's most demanding carrier airplane, without telling us because he knew damned well what my response would have been. I gave him hell after the recovery."

"A Commander CO had to get permission from a Lieutenant LSO and then take a lot of disrespect for not doing it?"

"Not disrespect, Mike. LSO's are key players with the giant responsibility and authority for safe carrier landings and no one else can do that job for him. The LSO's authority necessarily transcends rank, especially in cases of colossal stupidity which endangers the ship and crew."

"That's a pretty heavy load for a junior officer, isn't it?"

"That's what I liked about it."

"What was Aurelie's reaction to the excitement?"

"Nothing. She didn't mentioned it, so I let it pass. Aurelie had little interest in the Navy or my flying. She had little appreciation for what I was doing and did not socialize with squadron wives functions unless they were command performances. At the time, I chalked it up to having her time taken up with raising the kids and I figured that was just the way it was with women. My mother was the same way about my flying. She persisted in telling everyone I was a bomber pilot until I threatened to tell folks that she was a retired hooker who had worked every whore house from Singapore to Calcutta."

"I can see how that would do it. So, you got through the Hawaii inspection OK and returned to VF-121?"

"There was just one more incident to talk about. You remember that the Pukin' Dog Operations Officer?"

"The aggressive, over-confident marginally talented pilot with a negative attitude toward LSO's?

"That's him. Gib Kirk's carrier landings were too often damned dangerous. One day, after a very close call, I lost my temper and reamed his ass out in the ready room before all, telling him he was going to kill himself–the only time I said anything like that to anyone. I should have grounded him."

"Because?"

"Because later in the cruise he fulfilled my prophesy one night by hitting the ramp and going over the side, leaving his wife and six children behind because of his inflated ego and stubborn defiance."

"Surely you didn't blame yourself. You weren't there, and as you said, the pilot is the one ultimately responsible for flying his aircraft, right?"

"Mostly correct. Still, I saw it coming. I should have had the guts to prevent it."

"How were you effected?"

"Good question, Mike. Remember the old Commander I met in flight training when a classmate was killed, who wept when he recalled all the friends he lost to crashes? Well that was me. The odd thing is though, of all the aviation fatalities I was near throughout my career that was the only loss I took personally. To this day, I choke up recalling that event. For all his shortcomings as an aviator, Gib was a strong leader and a good administrator, which was just what VF-53

Pukin' Dogs needed in the absence of those qualities in the CO and XO. Gib was a role model and mentor to me. Perhaps the most professionally valuable lesson was how to write clear, brief, and concise Navy messages with spare use of adjectives to emphasize important points. To appear busy in the CAG office between landing recoveries, I took to practice by typing letters home on message forms."

"How did Aurelie 'respond to that?'"

"No differently than to other letters. Sometimes I wondered if she read them, but there was such a long period between sending and receiving that I usually forgot what I had written. It's hard to connect when the time and distance is so great and there's little common ground."

"Women often save letters from their men. Didn't Aurelie?"

"I don't think so. I saved hers to re-read periodically until the end of the cruise, and then tossed them. As I said, some of my letters toward the end of cruises were more romantic, but nothing of literary value."

"I imagine the Navy message style didn't exactly enhance love letters!"

"No doubt, Mike. Yet, even in Navy format, some of my letters were more flowery romantic than Aurelie's."

"As you say, she 'had other dogs to pet'?"

"Yes, I assumed so. After all, we didn't have much time together at home, why should she warm up to me when I was eight thousands of miles away for seven months?"

"There must have been some quality time between you. Didn't your youngest, Skye, come along during this shore duty tour?"

"True. When I came home from work one day, Aurelie simply said, 'Guess what? I'm pregnant', the exact same words your mother used in 1955 to announce your happy event. It doesn't take very much quality time' to produce pregnancies, does it Mike?"

"Touché, Captain, it surely does not."

"That is not to say that I did not enjoy being a father. I did. For the time I had, I don't think I was all that bad at it either. Fortunately, the noise level doesn't go up much after two kids. Partly because of Aurelie's 'hands off' parenting philosophy, they relied on each other a lot and got along beautifully. In fact, they were so close that when we took them out they remained tightly together. Once, for example, when we drove up into the mountains to a beautiful panoramic clearing near the woods for a picnic, the four of them remained huddled. It was the same 'joined at the hip' behavior at places like the zoo. They truly loved each other especially David and Christopher. Since the boys were only ten months apart and were such close playmates, they were sometimes assumed to be twins. Skye was a wonder–a totally self- sufficient angel from cloud nine, viewed with admiring awe by her family. Jennifer was distinctly different. My sense of her was that she was directly linked to my mother. From the beginning, Jenny did not see eye to eye with Aurelie's relaxed housekeeping habits and tended to be somewhat critical and bossy -a trait which magnified with age. Still, all was amazingly tranquil at the Sousa home, largely attributable to Aurelie's philosophy that the prime aspect of parenting was to let your children know that you love them. It's fortunate that it worked for her because she otherwise had little interest in mundane household tasks like cooking or cleaning. The kids' appearance resembled ragamuffin orphans and they often had to fend for themselves. One morning I found that Skye, who had only just learned to walk, had climbed a kitchen counter and was reaching to a high cabinet shelf to get a box of cereal down for her breakfast. Obviously, that was not the first time."

"Did that bother you much?"

"No. I wasn't home enough to warrant interference and I was satisfied that the children were happy and healthy. I had been quickly infused with Navy's management emphasis on results, not the manner in which results were achieved. Give people all the authority needed to carry out their responsibilities."

"Your experience as an LSO was a good example of that."

"Yes indeed, and' typical of the Navy way from top to bottom."

"So now you were back to being a Demon flight instructor and LSO on shore duty in VF-121?"

"Yes, it was as though I never left the VF-121 Pacemakers, often referred to as 'The Space Takers' because our aircraft availability was so low. We had a large number of mixed type aircraft assigned with various modifications. Many were aging castoffs which had seen their day at sea and were difficult to maintain. There was also the relaxed attitude that goes with shore duty. During sea duty tours we busted butt twenty four hours a day, so there was a general expectation that the pace ashore was much slower to compensate. Unfortunately, that didn't apply to LSO's in RAG squadrons which was often a more time consuming grind than sea duty with day and night FCLP and regular week long carrier qualification deployments."

"You mentioned FCLP (Field Carrier Landing Practice) before, please explain it in more detail."

"Runway 24 Left had a simulated carrier deck outline and lighting fifteen hundred feet down the runway. The optical landing system was similar to carriers' and the LSO station was equipped with a radio. Pilots made ten approaches during a thirty minute period, and as I recall, each pilot completed around ten day and ten night periods before going to the carrier. It was a very demanding challenge to day and night carrier qualify pilots with less than fifty hours flight time in the Demon or Phantom—especially for 'retreads', mid-grade and senior pilots returning to sea duty from desk jobs. There had been a great improvement in the night carrier landing accident rate, but many retreads had fearful memories of prior experience in the days when night landings were not fully operational, depending on all-weather missions and pilot experience which made retreads more difficult to train. On the other hand, the 'nuggets' just out of flight training eagerly accepted the challenge with much better attitudes because they didn't know better."

"The power of positive thinking, Captain?"

"Absolutely. As Skipper Tiger Lewis told us in flight training, no one should be at the controls of an airplane, especially for night carrier landings, unless he would rather fly than eat. Fortunately, there were only a few who had been initially attracted to the glamour, flight pay, or career opportunities, who, as they matured, realized the grim realities of the risks. When one Demon Driver admitted his fears to me, I asked why he had decided to become a naval aviator in the first place. His reply was that he saw that most Admirals wore the Navy wings of gold! It worked for him. His ambition overcame fear and he later made Admiral."

"I guess you can't argue with success then."

"I can. I didn't want to be in the same squadron, much less the same airplane, with an officer focused on promotion as a prime objective, usually at the expense of everyone near him."

"Were there many Nuggets who washed out in the RAG?"

"No. It was quite rare, the Training Command did its job well. Since carrier qualification was the primary and most demanding function of RAG training, the LSO's were the ones to bite the bullet in weeding out those who just couldn't cut it. We were conscientiously ruthless in these rare decisions because we took our responsibility very seriously not to pass along marginal aviators to fleet squadrons. Thankfully, we had very strong backing in those cases, even when prospective CO's were grounded."

"It seems that night carrier landings required super human flying ability."

"Not so. Most naval aviators are average pilots. Their attitude and motivation, reinforced by excellent training and high standards makes the difference."

"So how do CO's rate pilot ability in evaluations?"

"As one CO put it to his squadron pilots, 'No one else does what you do and if you couldn't get aboard at night, you wouldn't be here.' So, Navy officer evaluations are based on leadership and management abilities in the performance of collateral duties. A very fair and effective system, I believe, since squadron time is limited and there's only so far to go with flying in a Naval officer's career. If all we did was fly, there was little justification for being commissioned officers. Of my thirty-one years, only fifteen were in the cockpit of operational airplanes. Still, I had more squadron time than most since being an LSO kept me from the dreaded ship-board and staff tour assignments."

"But didn't being an LSO eight years make you a 'one trick pony in Navy's eyes?"

"That was a commonly held view, but who knows? I liked the way a Personnel Detailer put it in responding to a question about preferred career patterns, 'There are no good or bad jobs for junior officers, there are only good or bad fitness reports'. So, I just focused on being the best LSO I could be. It worked for me! Ron Hess, Tony Wenzlau, and I were a damned outstanding LSO team in VF-121, thankfully with zero accidents in three years of constant carrier qualification operations with Demon and Phantom newbies. We averaged going aboard every other month for week long landing qualification deployments -and we maintained day and night landing currency ourselves. The Skipper, Flight Surgeon, and I were the first in the squadron to day-night carrier qualify in Phantoms. Besides LSO, I had two other demanding collateral duties. As the Schedules Officer, I was responsible for producing and implementing the daily flight schedule, complicated by individual pilot and RIO training requirements in three different type aircraft, as well as adjusting to aircraft and instructor availability. I was also the squadron coffee Mess Treasurer, which sounds pretty mundane; however, we did $1200 a week in drinks and sandwiches until the Navy Exchange folks complained about the competition and reigned me in. As with many aspects of my life, I can't figure how I was fortunate enough to get through that time successfully and happily."

"What did you think of the Phantom?"

"If 'higher and faster' is an aviator's quest, the F-4 was the dream come true, especially for us old Demon Drivers. In little more time than it took for a Demon to get off the ground, the Phantom could be at forty thousand feet. The airspeed advanced steadily like the second hand of a watch all the way up to the 1500 mph limit. The speed limiting factor was high engine inlet air temperature resulting from the shockwave compression. So, for the mach 2.4 speed record, water was sprayed into the air inlets. Phantoms set world altitude and speed records from sea level to over one hundred thousand feet. No operational airplane today flies higher or faster. Plus, F-4's were by far the highest quality airplane I ever flew. It was truly a Rolls-Royce class machine in every respect. What a thrill it was to pick up brand new F-4's at the McDonnell factory in Saint Lewis where we were treated like VIP's with factory tours, including the Mercury capsule assembly area, and first class receptions, and then blast off in afterburner for a test flight at a civilian airport with Mr and Mrs America watching."

"Exciting business! You got paid for that too. What was it like to fly Phantoms?"

"Fighter pilots say, 'speed is life', as is altitude advantage in aerial combat. But you know from riding the airlines that forty thousand feet at just under mach one can be pretty boring, though I could never understand those at window seats who close their shades so they can just read or sleep through the experience. Personally, I always enjoyed the view from any altitude. Same with speed whether forty knots or mach two, there isn't much sensation unless you're close to the ground or a cloud layer, even then you're quickly conditioned to speed. Truth is, fighters are nearly always flown in the same speed and altitude ranges as airliners, because fuel consumption is extremely high in afterburner and because window shattering supersonic booms are illegal in most land areas. Having said all that, however, I'll give you a more complete and positive answer by describing our 'graduation' flight in Phantoms -the zoom climb to maximum altitude for which we wore pressure suits. The adventure began with being fitted out for the suits and testing them in the pressure chamber. These were the same type single-piece full-pressure suits worn by the Mercury astronauts. Donning the suit required putting your legs and hips into the bottom half through a zippered opening diagonally across the front torso and then curling up in the fetal position to get your arms in the sleeves and your head inside and up through the helmet ring attachment. Next, the gloves and boots were pulled on and zippered up to the suit to form a pressure seal. Finally, the individually fitted helmet went on your head and attached to the collar ring, which was on ball bearings, allowing the helmet to be freely turned from side to side. Oxygen was fed into the helmet through a regulator which also sealed the faceplate and directed flow across the inside of the faceplate to keep it from fogging up. A system of external cables and pulleys on the suit kept your arms and legs from splaying out like a gingerbread man with the suit fully pressurized. To keep the suit bearable on the ground, a small portable suit-case-size air-conditioning unit was carried until you strapped into the cockpit. Then came the live test of me and the suit in a special telephone booth size section of the pressure chamber to simulate an altitude of over eighty thousand feet. A flight surgeon monitored the test from the outside through a thick three inch diameter viewing port. I sat on a small chair with nothing to do as the chamber pressure was reduced. The only item with me was a glass of water on. a corner shelf for demonstration purposes. There was a small pressure gauge on the top left thigh of the suit which read three and a half pounds 'in the green' with the suit fully pressurized. Although you'd think three and a half pounds pressure was trivial, I assure you it was enough to stretch every inch of the suit drum tight to the point of concern for whoever stitched this thing together. Even in a booth size chamber, the altitude ascent seemed to take forever. Then I noticed the reflection of my face on the inside of the face plate, watched my eyes blink back at me and feel my exhaled breath blow back in my face. The only sound was the soft pshhh of oxygen flow. I watched the water in the glass slowly coming to life with little jiggles and contemplated the fact that as altitude increases, the boiling temperature of fluids -including blood -decreases. I looked back at the suit pressure and into my blinking eyes as my blowback breath seems more exaggerated. The water now shows signs of boiling and I reflected on the reason for wearing pressure suits at high altitudes. Without the suit or cabin pressure, blood boils and I die. I checked the suit pressure again. It's still in the green, but the suit fabric seems extremely taut. I looked into my face reflection, watched my eyes blink, and felt my breath. The water was boiling now. I realized that even though I have never before experienced any symptoms of claustrophobia, I will now appreciate what it is like for the rest of my life. Bless the Navy's penchant for developing torture devices. Finally, it was over. The altitude descended as the chamber pressure increased rapidly. The suit and I survived. The next test would be for real in the zoom climb."

"You've got my hands sweating from the chamber, Captain. I'm not sure I can handle the flight!"

"Strange that my most vivid memories of stress in aviation were created on the ground by the flight surgeons, so the flights weren't bad at all–mostly because there were more important things to do than watch your eyes blink. Once I donned the suit and was helped into the cockpit, I felt comfortable and at home. Although turning the helmet and looking down seemed awkward at first, I quickly fell into the routine of bringing the Phantom to life and completing the takeoff check list. The flight profile was to climb to about forty thousand feet where the air temp was lowest–as I recall, around sixty below–and accelerate to mach two. As I said, there is no particular sensation of speed; however, there was a tendency to squish down into the seat and hope something didn't depart the airplane. There was good reason for that concern. For one thing, Phantom wing and tail trailing edges were a sandwich of foil honeycomb material between aluminum outer sheets. At altitude, moisture trapped in the honeycomb would sometimes freeze, expand, and break away large chunks of wing or tail trailing surfaces. Fortunately, the loss was not noticeable in flight. Another more noticeable event while accelerating at supersonic speed was the movement of the engine air inlet ramps. Briefly, the purpose of the ramps movement was to position the shock wave on the forward edge of the engine air inlet ducts on both sides just aft of the front seat. As airplanes accelerate at supersonic speeds, the shock wave angle becomes less acute. Phantom's ramps functioned outward from the fuselage to compensate for the changing shockwave angle. The necessity for this was that air flow behind the shock wave was subsonic, which is required at the engine, otherwise, supersonic air into the engine would destroy it in a rather dramatic way. The thing about the Phantom ramps was that they tended to stick. They would really get your attention when they abruptly unstuck and it was not clear to the pilot what had happened. Another consideration for scooching down in our seats was the very dramatic slow motion thirty-five millimeter film of a Phantom coming apart attempting to set the low altitude speed record in Operation Sage Burner. Since Phantoms were aerodynamically unstable, they had a 'stability augmentation' system. Normally, Phantoms flew OK with STAB AUG off, so the Sage Burner pilot elected to attempt the record with system inoperative. Bad decision. As I recall, the pilot entered the course at well over 600 knots indicated airspeed. In just a few close-up frames, the Phantom pitched slightly nose down and then nose up, whereupon both wings folded over the top and both engines departed the airplane side by side and continued down course straight and level while the fuselage disintegrated in a ball of fire."

"Wow, that somewhat detracts from the 'speed is life' adage, doesn't it, Captain?"

"When you push the envelope that far, bad stuff can happen. That's the difference from flying airliners, though bus drivers do get occasional thrills as well, don't they? So, back to the zoom climb. The profile after accelerating to mach two was to pull the nose up with 3–4 G's into a vertical climb, then just ride it up as far as possible. An aerodynamic note appropriate to this and the Sage Burner story is that a supersonic wing will not stall. For that reason Phantoms had artificial feel applied to the stick in supersonic flight and it took both hands pulling hard to get three G's at mach two. I'll digress again now to tell the story of setting the altitude record as I heard it from the pilot, Tiny Granning. As you might expect, Tiny was a big man who had been an All-American lineman on the Naval Academy football team. Tiny said the engineers were concerned about an expected enlarged engine afterburner flame pattern damaging the stabilator at high altitude, so they limited the amount of forward control stick movement. The engineers also told Tiny that because the limited controls would be relatively ineffective at slow speed and high altitude, he would have to start getting the nose over early. As told, Tiny started the nose over early, which worked OK except that the nose just kept going and the Phantom pitch-poled end over end from ninety-eight thousand feet to thirty-five thousand feet where he was able to recover from a normal departure. He went on in later flights to set the record at over one-hundred thousand feet."

"Did that qualify Tiny as an astronaut then?"

"I hope so, but I don't know if that happened in Tiny's case. If you read books like The Right Stuff, you recall that in the beginning of the competing space programs there was some 'distance' between the test pilot and astronaut communities. But back to the zoom climb experience. Pulling the nose of an airplane straight up and keeping it there is a unique experience anytime, but passing seventy five thousand feet, heading for space in a pressure suit is a special thrill. The sky turns a deeper shade of blue until it begins to lose all color and becomes black. The earth takes on a glow from its atmosphere and the curvature of the horizon becomes more and more apparent. Things are happening in the cockpit too. The engineers didn't figure on the lack of oxygen at sixty-five thousand feet causing the afterburners to blow out; therefore, it was unnecessary to limit forward control stick movement. On the other hand, the engineers were correct about the engines over-speeding and over-temping at the top and had reduced idle fuel flow to gain more engine time for the record attempts."

"What altitude did you reach on these training flights?"

"I don't know. Pressure altimeters are unreliable at those heights, so unless there's calibrated ground tracking radar, it's a guess. My guess is that we probably topped out under ninety thousand. Oddly, it didn't much matter to us. I don't even recall looking at the altimeter, it was more important to monitor engine gauges and observe the spectacular skyscape. In fact, there really was no realistic operational necessity for pressure suits or the zoom climb and I think the exercise was eventually dropped. The important thing was that it was an incredible experience and I'm glad I was flying Phantoms in the era that did it."

"How many times did you go?"

"Just once in the front seat, but I rode along in the back seat as an instructor several times."

"Weren't you inspired to get into the space program?"

"I did make a feeble attempt to get into the astronaut program. But with five kids, being over six feet tall, not a test pilot, and with just a BA degree in psychology, there was zero opportunity for me in those days. Later, when they picked guys like me, I was over age."

"How much F-4 backseat time did you have and how did you feel about it and the RIO's you flew with?"

"One fourth of my flight time in VF-121 F-4's was in the back seat, but I did not mind paying my dues for the front seat time. Remember, I initially trained as bombardier-navigator in AJ's, so I understood the crew perspective. As you know, I had mixed feelings about the need for F-4 RIO's in our interceptor mission. I believed that bombardier-navigators played a role as necessary as the pilot's in the AJ mission. I flew with many Phantom RIO's, rarely the same one twice, but I remember only a few. It's not that I disliked having them aboard, it was simply that they were out of sight out of mind and I just forgot anyone else was in the airplane. They might as well have been surface-based intercept controllers. I might have felt differently if I had flown with a regularly assigned RIO and we were in the same space like the three man crew in AJ's or the side by side seat arrangement of the F3D Druts."

"Were there other aspects of flying Phantoms that impressed you initially?"

"Inflight refueling comes to mind. Plugging a probe into a small basket on the end of a short waving hose close in to another airplane was challenging in any airplane–more so with Phantoms. F-4's were three times heavier than the then current light attack A-4 Sky Hawks. At 220 knots refueling speed, the controls were relatively sloppy and unresponsive -a factor which made Phantoms poor close formation airplanes and cause for both the Blue Angels and Thunderbirds to stop using them. Also, the F-4 refueling probe was above to the right and only slightly forward of the pilot in his peripheral vision, and well behind the bow wave of the airflow at the nose. The procedure was to stabilize position ten or fifteen feet back with the probe lined up slightly above and to the right of the basket, then increase closing speed to the rate of a fast walk. As the basket passed the nose bow wave, it hopefully moved up and out the distance allowed to plug in. After plug in, the hose was pushed in until the tanker's green fuel transfer light came on and then backed off when transfer was complete. That's when all went well; however, there were several complicating factors. If the closure rate to the basket was too slow, the likely result was unsuccessfully trying to chase the waving basket and having to back off to start over. On the other hand, if the closure speed to the basket was too fast, it was possible for the probe to hit the basket off center and flip it off, sometimes across the canopy breaking it out, or else possibly going down the right engine intake. Another possible consequence of a fast closure rate was getting too close to the tanker and getting sucked into its slipstream. In that case, exacerbated by sloppy controls and high weight inertia, pilot induced oscillation, PIO, might be induced, and in the effort to avoid collision with the tanker, might result in breaking away with the basket and hose connected to the Phantom instead of the tanker. It's an embarrassing experience to land with eighty feet of hose attached or with no canopy."

"Did you have any of those experiences, Captain?"

"All of them, except for landing with a busted canopy or a hose. My worst time was one night when I closed .too fast, plugged in and flew into the tanker's slipstream. By the time I was able to slow down, back off and safely get away, I had induced PIO so badly that I hit the stops with the control stick nose down as well as nose up. I was especially embarrassed to have the Airwing flight surgeon in the back seat, but bless his heart, he didn't say a word about it. Al Balciunas certainly earned his flight pay that night. Later, he was also to earn hostile fire pay with me, but we'll get to that."

"At least you remember his name."

"Oh yes, better than any other RIO, for more reasons we'll get to. But that's all I have to say about VF-121. It was a good, enjoyable, rewarding, exciting, and successful tour."

"There couldn't have been much time left for being a husband and father or for hobbies."

"No, but as I recall, what there was of it was quality time. The kids were great and Aurelie and I got along well. We continued with playing folk music, coffee houses and folk festivals, as well as weekend family outings for picnics, trips to the mountains, Disneyland, Knott's Berry Farm, and weekend afternoons at the Model Yacht Basin. I had one notable accomplishment with model boats. The Argonauts got interested in pure speed, so a member designed and built a photocell timer for calculating straightaway speed on a measured 1/8 mile straightaway course on our model yacht basin. Two way averages were used to establish club speed records in various classes. My special interest was in the full size unlimited class three-point hydroplane types, the fastest in all boat racing competition. The challenge with hydroplanes was that they virtually flew and were very unstable. Powered by 1200+ horsepower V-12 aircraft engines, their hulls were airfoils which actually lifted them just off the surface with only the lower blade of the propeller in the water as the sponsons skipped the tops of waves to add lateral stability—which was easily upset, especially in turns, by combinations of winds, waves, and the wakes of other boats. It was not uncommon for hydroplanes to roll or flip end over end with fatal results to their drivers. The effects of wind and waves on small model boats were of course far more magnified, consequently no one had successfully modeled a hydroplane which would 'fly' like the real thing."

"So that's where you came in to develop an RC model hydroplane that could fly. How'd you do it?"

"I found a detailed article with the plans of a 'shovel nose' Miss Budweiser, as well as a Naval Research Lab article on super-cavitating propellers developed for submerged submarines. The plans had all the information I needed, including center of gravity location and sponson angles. It took three months to design it, but only two weeks to build it. Since it was meant to be experimental, the model wasn't pretty. The hull didn't look much like the original and everything about it was homemade and crude, but the hull airfoil sponson angles, and CG were correct. The hull was only thirty two inches long, fourteen inches beam, and made of 1/16 and 1/8 inch aircraft plywood. It was well overpowered by a McCoy 60 model race car engine run at over 13,000 RPM, adapted to this marine application with a homemade flywheel, exhaust pipe, throttle, drive shaft, propeller, and rudder. The radio controls were primitive, even by 60's standards. But by golly, it flew just like the real thing right off the building board. It handled beautifully and I never had to change anything about it. What a thrill to see it come up 'on the step', hauling butt down the course with a two foot rooster tail behind. In two years of running it, the only mishaps resulted from radio failures, wave action, or high winds. Several times it flipped or swapped ends, but it proved to be indestructible."

So how fast did it go?"

"Well, I assure you it looked and sounded a whole lot faster than it was actually going, though the two way average was just under forty miles an hour. Still, it set the sanctioned Western Associated Modelers (WAM) unlimited speed record. Since WAM was the only official sanctioning organization for RC boat speed records and I was in the top class, mine was in fact a world record for all RC boats–which remained unbroken for nearly three years."

"How exciting! How did you follow that act?"

"I didn't. That was my last operating RC boat and I retired from it."

"Once you've proved you can do it, move on, as Ron Hess said, Captain?"

"Partly so, but radios were improving enough to entice me back to model airplanes. Plus, the time flew by at Phantom speed and it was soon 1963, nearly time to go back to sea and to war. Model building was going on the back burner for a long while. A good place to end this chapter, I think. Let's start again after lunch, if you're up for it?"

"Let's do it."

F-4 Phantom II - <u>Specifications</u> - **Length:** 63 ft - **Wingspan:** 38 ft. 4.5 in.
Height: 16 ft. 6 in. - **Empty Weight:** 30,328 lbs. **Max Weight:** 62,000 lbs. -
Crew: 2 - **Power Plant:** 2 × General Electric J79-GE-17A axial compressor turbojets -
Combat Radius: 367 nautical miles **Max. Speed:** 1,472 mph (Mach 2.23)
Ceiling: 60,000 ft.

NOTE: Compare deck size to previous Ticonderoga approach photo

223

19

VIETNAM 1964

"Inside or out this morning, Captain?"

"Looks like the Lodge is setting up for a function in the lobby, Mike. Let's go outside. Fewer interruptions, though we may have to dodge showers later."

"I'll get an umbrella and meet you out there, OK?"

"Sure, but I think you're just avoiding a race against my wheelchair."

"You would have an unfair advantage, but I may still beat you there."

"Let's see Captain, it's 1963. Sea duty and another LSO tour is looming again. Wasn't that a brief shore tour?"

"In a way it was. My time in VF-121 before the Ticonderoga cruise initially counted as sea duty, but then Navy changed its mind and said it was shore duty. So all my time in VF-121 before and after the Ticonderoga cruise ended up being considered shore duty. As the Recruiter said, If you can't take a joke, you shouldn't have joined up."

"You did your time 'in the barrel' as an LSO? Couldn't you have hung it up at that point?"

"Yes, but then I would likely have been assigned to a non-flying shipboard or staff job since I'd had more than my share of operational flying. Either way, I was going back to sea duty. Another tour as CAG LSO was a sure thing for a cruise flying Phantoms."

"With all your volunteer time at sea, wasn't Aurelie a bit discouraged with Navy life?"

"Back to Aurelie again? OK, let me get this said, Mike. Aurelie fulfilled her plan to have four kids and needed financial support in that endeavor. She surely understood my drive to fly and she knew it wouldn't change the course of events if she complained about it now, for I had few options in civilian life. The airlines weren't hiring. Even if they were, I was pushing their hiring age limit. Plus, my eyesight was marginal and there was my history of high blood pressure. Besides, the challenge of Navy flying had squelched whatever ambition I once had to fly a bus

- where there was also lots of family separation, just in shorter periods. Other opportunities in the civilian job market were very limited for an ex fighter pilot with a BA in Psychology. Aurelie's BA and thin work experience, wouldn't help us much either. Now, with four kids to feed, plus child support payments, there were no attractive alternatives. Aurelie had locked in her 'career' choice too. I was doing what I knew and liked best. Navy pay and benefits were excellent, and as my father often reminded me, the US government would be the last to go bankrupt."

"You were stuck in the Navy then?"

"I was slightly hemmed in, but only by my own choices, knowing I wouldn't be as successful or happy doing something else–including other flying jobs. Frequent moves were just below family separation given as a reason for leaving the service. There had been no disruptive family moves for us. Seven years in San Diego and three more coming up was an unusually long time in the service or civilian jobs to be stationed in one place, especially one as desirable as San Diego. Aurelie and I had much to be thankful for."

"What about Ron Hess' advice to move on when you've proved you can do it? You had made four deployments in five years and were now facing more of the same."

"I did feel that twinge, Mike. I had completed a full sea-shore cycle and fulfilled 'obligated service'. The future would be repetitious. Even flying Phantoms wasn't much different than what I had done before, nor was there anything to prove as an LSO. But I had no career ambitions beyond flying. I had no wish to drive ships nor longing for Admiral's stars. Except for dreams of sailing the Atlantic and writing the great American novel, which would not feed a family, I had nothing to move on to just then and I was quite happy with what I was doing. Another important consideration was that I was eight years toward twenty year retirement eligibility. At age forty four, the kids would be nearly grown, so I could sail and write then."

"OK Captain, now I have the picture. Sorry if I focused on it too much."

"Not at all. That period was a decisive now-or-never career fork in the road for me, though I didn't have much time to dwell on it. I had orders in hand to report next door to CAG-14 Staff as the Airwing LSO to fly with VF-142. Phantom squadrons were too space-consuming for the small World War Two carriers, so we were assigned to USS Constellation–one of the new huge thousand foot 'super carriers'."

"At least you were going to a normal size fleet squadron. Wasn't VF-142 an improvement over VF-121 in that respect?"

"Yes, in all respects, plus I felt very welcomed by VF-142. An added factor was that the companion Phantom squadron was VF-143, the 'world famous' Pukin' Dogs."

"Wouldn't you rather have gone back to flying with the Pukin' Dogs?"

"It didn't much matter. I knew all the crews in both squadrons as their instructor and LSO in VF-121. The transition couldn't have been easier."

"But with two crew members in Phantoms, there were now twice as many officers in the ready room than in VF-53, right?"

"Good point. Phantom squadrons then had fourteen crews assigned plus several ground officers. Thirty officers is a crowd in a ready room and there was a subtle distance between pilots and RIO's. So naturally, there was a bit less camaraderie. I am not implying that there was abnormal friction, there was not. Flying off carriers is serious business which levels the playing field for all those engaged, whatever seat they fly in or their rank. There was no room for petty distractions. After all, Mike, Navy is not a flying club or a state legal agency. That aside, since we already talked a lot about the personalities in VF-53 and adventures ashore overseas, I'll go forward focusing more on personal high points and overviews of my eleven years during Vietnam. I will not attempt a historical document. Truth is, it's now difficult for me to sort out the details or chronology of events through five flying Vietnam deployments from 1964 through 1971. Those cruises tend to run together in memory now. My cruise book collection, which was my best reminder, with photos, names, and dates, was washed away by hurricane Ivan in 2004, so I'll leave the historical details to other sources. Hopefully, my personal adventures will hold your attention. If not, I trust you to push me on, Mike."

"OK, push on now, Captain. Let's go to war!"

"Alright Mike, however as some said, 'It wasn't much of a war, but it was the only one we had.'"

"You were there when it started with the August 1964 Gulf of Tonkin Incident, weren't you?"

"Yes, I was at the GOT Incident, but fighting began before that. Like the American Indians who had been busy scalping each other long before the Europeans' arrival in the New World, the brutality in Southeast Asia preceded us by centuries. Before us in Vietnam in the twentieth century were the Chinese, Japs, and French; however, our carrier Navy wasn't strangers there either. We attacked Jap shipping in Saigon Harbor in January 1945 and had since maintained a carrier presence in the South China Sea. The French Army, in another of their consistent string of defeats, was driven out of Vietnam at Dienbienphu in 1954, opening the way to continuation of a thirty year civil war ending in 1975, despite the Geneva Agreements of 1954 which partitioned North and South Vietnam with a Demilitarized Zone, DMZ, on the seventeenth parallel. President Ike Eisenhower apparently believed that it was in our national interest to take up the cause against the revolutionary spread of communism by drawing a line in the sand as was done in Korea. There was obvious truth in the so called 'Domino Theory'. China was sponsoring expansion of Communism by forceful revolution throughout Southeast Asia. If successful, self-disarmed Japan would ironically end up standing alone in the western Pacific as our only ally. However, they too would eventually have had little political or economic choice other than submission to communist domination. Accordingly, US military arms and 'advisors' were assigned to South Vietnam forces ad we became increasingly engaged in direct action against the

Viet Cong. Truth be known, we had little altruistic motivation to 'save' the South Vietnamese, as was propagandized at home. Strategically, coastal Vietnam was a convenient place to fight Communism from carriers and bases in the Philippines, Okinawa, and Guam -without the bitter Korean winters. Naval air action preceded the GOT Incident with soft escalation in Laos, a pacifist nation with an ineffective Buddhist government which gave reign to the Pathet Lao communist rebels under the direction of North Vietnam, to secure the 'Ho Chi Minh Trail' supply line from North to South. Naval Air initially supported CIA assisted gorilla activities against the Pathet Lao by flying unescorted photo missions over the Plain des Jarres in north central Laos which were regularly shot at, finally downing an F-8 Crusader. So, our first Phantom missions were to escort the photo planes, for no practical purpose other than to report shoot downs, for we had no bombs or guns to retaliate with, nor the loiter time ability to support rescue missions. Obviously, the strategy had not been thought through and only succeeded in presenting more targets to the antiaircraft guns."

"Those were your first combat missions, Captain?"

"They were not considered combat missions, since there was no formally declared hostility. There was a request through higher command to activate 'hostile fire pay', but there was no response from Washington. Nevertheless, some prospective 'heroes' were anxiously contemplating career enhancing ribbons and medals."

"So tell me about the infamous August 1964 'Gulf of Tonkin Incident'."

"Constellation had been in port in the Philippines for ten days in July and then sailed on to Hong Kong. As was usual on Hong Kong port calls, we sent an advance liaison group to make hotel reservations and reception arrangements for the first evening at the Hong Kong Hilton with invitations to the dignitaries and staff. Since Constellation anchored out in the typhoon shelter, a thirty minute boat ride away from downtown, squadrons also reserved hotel suites for rest stops, shopping goods storage, and rendezvous. Many of us took leave to stay ashore to avoid the boat rides. My good pal Ed Fitch, whom you'll recall gave me his mandolin, had a British girlfriend there. Overcoming considerable resistance, we persuaded her to invite two Australian girls we had not met to a party at the squadron suite. Australia was highly grateful to the US Navy for saving their butts from Jap invasion in World War Two and the women had a reputation for being sexually aggressive. Australian men, on the other hand, had the reputation for being somewhat rough and crude. So we expected a warm welcome from Australian ladies. But when these two big, hard-drinking, and aggressive Australian ladies appeared, my fellow aviators scurried off for cover. So, out of a sense of responsibility for the girls' embarrassment, I was being hospitable to them when the message came that there was an emergency recall to the ship for all hands. We were to sortie to the Gulf where the destroyer Maddox was attacked with torpedoes launched by North Vietnamese PT boats on the night of August 2nd. VF-53, then flying F-8 Crusaders aboard Ticonderoga, claimed to have sunk one of the PT Boats with strafing runs. Nearly everyone had left the suite as I was taking my leave of the young ladies when further word came that we didn't have to return to the ship until the next morning. Since one of the ladies was then strongly determined and I was suddenly without an escape. Afterward, she asked if I thought she had been too aggressive. I sincerely assured her that she had not, for no young innocent Samurai fighter pilot was ever sent off to war in finer fashion."

"Off to the war then, you scoundrel."

"How about that! A lawyer, of all people, one who was surely no 'lily of the valley', now pointing the scheming finger of scorn at me? You ain't got no couth at all, Mike. Anyhow, we were steaming for the Gulf on the night of August 4th as Maddox, joined by another destroyer, Turner Joy, picked up five high speed surface radar contacts making torpedo runs which missed their targets. Two A-1 Skyraiders from Ticonderoga attempted to provide air cover, but were unable to gain visual contact with the PT boats. I went to the Combat Information Center to listen to the radio transmissions from the attacked destroyers describing the events. Despite claims by conspiracy screwballs, like Admiral Stockdale, that the strike was a hoax staged by the Administration to justify retaliatory strikes, there was no doubt for me or other participants that it was for real. We launched F-4's after the event to cover the destroyers, but no PT boats were detected. Because of the extreme circumstances, I had the LSO duty, so I missed the fun of chasing around at low altitude that night."

"Considering night time and bad weather with aviators on their first combat mission who hadn't flown in weeks, the recovery landings must have been highly challenging."

"It was indeed a circus with some very colorful passes and wild wave-offs which summed up and justified my years as an LSO."

"So, Phantoms were the airplane of choice for night attack missions against boats, despite its lack of guns or a bombing capability? What did you shoot with?"

"Unguided rockets were more effective than bombs or guns in close against small fast boats, though we had almost no experience firing them in the day, none at night. The Phantom's greatest advantage, before the deployment of A-6 Intruders with their specialized all-weather attack capability, was our excellent radar system operated by an RIO, allowing the pilot to focus on flying the airplane in all-weather combat conditions. We had only partially learned from the Japs that we had to be able to fight at night and in adverse weather conditions."

"What happened next?"

"President Johnson announced retaliatory strikes by aircraft from Ticonderoga and Constellation against PT boat bases saying, 'We seek no wider war'. Since Johnson's announcement was made before we launched the strikes, the North Vietnamese were waiting for us. The strikes damaged the bases and destroyed or damaged twenty five PT boats, half their forces. Ray

Alvarez ejected from his damaged A-4 Sky Hawk and became the first and longest held POW of the war, imprisoned in Hanoi for nearly nine years."

"Sounds like Navy got off to a fairly good start with coordinated strikes?"

"Our success had more to do with the enemy's lack of marksmanship. We were in no way prepared for coordinated attacks with a large number and variety of airplanes in a conventional war. Despite the Korean War experience, Air Force and Navy were primarily armed and trained for a doomsday all out nuclear war with the USSR and China with a variety of specialized single-airplane nuclear weapon delivery missions following behind ICBM's. The Marines still trained for conventional ground attack in close support of troops, but were not deployed aboard aircraft carriers or used for strikes against North Vietnam. So, Navy was conducting 'on the job training'. When asked if Phantoms could carry bombs, we had to shrug our shoulders–the 'Reservist's salute' we called it. Soon, however, special teams from weapons development squadrons were sent to show us how to re-configure Phantoms to carry bombs. We had no notion of what mil leads to use in our old fashioned 'iron' sights, but we quickly discovered the benefit of having RIO's call out airspeed, dive angle, and altitude, while also keeping an alert lookout for other aircraft. CAG-14 was composed of four different type combat aircraft: prop-driven, low-slow A-1 Sky Raiders; A-3 Sky Warriors, high altitude heavy attack twin-engine strategic nuclear bombers; A-4 Sky Hawks, fast and agile light attack airplanes designed to carry a single nuke, without radar or all-weather capability; and F-4 Phantoms, all-weather mach-2 interceptors which had not dropped bombs. Therefore, the challenges to coordinate strikes with that mix of aircraft were differentials in airspeed and altitude, bomb delivery techniques, and a lack of training for conventional warfare. For example, the night before my first scheduled mission, we assembled in Ready Room Six with the CO of the Skyraider squadron, a good choice for flight leader we thought, since he was the only aviator aboard with Korea combat experience. But hopes sank when the CO asked our Phantom flight leader, 'What do you think we should do?' The plan's accommodation of the various speed and altitude differentials, believe it or not, was to rendezvous the strike force in a circle near the target, thereby sacrificing the element of surprise and extending our exposure. Surely this would be an excellent training exercise for North Vietnamese anti-aircraft gunners!"

"Did you have a better idea?"

"No one did, though we re-assembled three times throughout the night to try to come up with a better plan. We understood that it would have been far more sensible and effective to attack with eight A-4's, but our flight composition had been decided by higher authority who apparently wanted to make a 'maximum effort' Airwing air show of it, regardless of the pitfalls. Finally, we went to bed with Plan C which was little different from Plan A, so it was just as well that McNamara's Pentagon Whiz Kids cancelled the mission shortly before launch time.

So it went for fifty two days on the line, planning and loading for missions only to have them cancelled by Washington at the last minute, whereupon we downloaded the bombs and flew training missions. Connie's CO, Captain Bardshar's term for these frustrating exercises was 'tactical masturbation' and he warned that steaming in circles risked putting Connie high and dry on our own coffee grounds."

"When did you finally fly your first combat missions and what were your feelings?"

"Oddly, Mike, I cannot give you a clear answer to that question. My only written documentation is my flight log book, which was maintained by ops department Yeomen. Navy pilot log books have a narrow column headed 'kind of flight code' for each flight. There was a number for 'condition of flight', followed by a letter for 'purpose of flight', then another number for 'type of flight' including one for 'not specified elsewhere. For example, lAl recorded '1' for daylight visual, 'A' for unit training, and '1' for fundamentals. For months there was a degree of question, indecision, and confusion about how to correctly log the various missions. Were we in a state of conflict or war in South Vietnam, North Vietnam, or Laos? How were combat flights defined? Were missions flown entirely over the Gulf, well away from opposition, to be considered combat missions? For example, many Phantom missions were Combat Air Patrol, CAP, missions flown entirely over the Gulf out of harm's way between the carrier and Chinese bases on Hainan Island to our east and mainland China bases to the north, as well as North Vietnam bases to our west. These patrol missions were generally flown in race track patterns at low speed to save fuel. Doesn't sound much like combat compared to hauling bombs over well defended land targets, does it? Therefore, my early missions were logged as 1Q5, 'not elsewhere specified' and so, odd as it may seem, I don't specifically recall them now. We always assumed we were being shot at flying over land, so you could say that my first missions were escorting the photo-recce flights over Laos where there was a heightened sense of danger, but little cause for much concern. From the air, there was no visible threat, just a few roads and small villages in a vast expanse of jungle. Aeronautical charts had large blank areas in the mountains which had never been surveyed. As ancient as civilization was in Laos, it had remained primitive and remote, and appeared quite tranquil."

"Did you 'consider keeping a diary?"

"No, and I don't know anyone that did. We were far too busy to even take much time for letters home. Anyhow, a diary would have been repetitious and of little value. One reason veterans don't talk a lot is that there's not much to say that anyone cares to hear. Kinda like what is said about flying in general–ninety nine percent boredom and one percent sheer horror. Suffice to remind you of what the flight surgeons who wired us up learned, we experienced the greatest stress during night carrier landings."

"It does indeed say a lot about night carrier landings for them to rate over getting shot at!"

"But to a degree, I believe the studies compared apples to oranges -physical tension versus psychological anxiety. During night landing approaches, pilots experienced physical stress, but were in command of their fate in a relatively routine, controlled situation where they had confidence in themselves and the environment. Carrier landing accidents had become rare, plus, carrier approaches lasted less than a minute and become instant history. I submit that the more important finding of the studies was that pilot anxiety peaked between flights. Getting shot at by scores of effective cannons and missiles manned by well trained, experienced, and highly motivated gunners doing their utmost best to kill us had little effect on pilot performance during a mission, but became a serious matter which stuck with us afterward. As the war heated up and losses mounted, air crews became reclusive. According to the study, seventy five percent of the pilots believed they would not survive the cruise. That is a truly startling statistic if accurate. As I recall, the highest pilot loss rate for an Airwing during a Vietnam cruise was fifteen percent -a significant number for sure, but one which I think made the flight surgeons conclusion questionable. It's difficult for me to imagine such pessimism by an aviator and I believe it is doubtful that pilots would make such an admission to an authority who might ground him on the spot."

"Really? A flight surgeon would do that?"

"Yes indeed. Example: a fellow Demon Driver in VF-53 who survived a night cat shot into the water when his engine rolled back, was asked by our flight surgeon if he trusted Demons. His understandable answer was no and for that he was permanently grounded and transferred, though he was only along for the short ride and was in no way at fault. For all flyers, civilian as well as military, doctors are a constant threat and there is nothing to gain by trusting one with personal information."

"Amazingly counterproductive it seems. Then tell me more about what life was like from your perspective during those line periods. You say that you were busy?"

"Generally, there were two carriers on Yankee Station, alternating twelve hour periods of flight operations. One carrier conducted flight ops from noon to midnight and the other carrier from midnight to noon. The schedule was swapped every two weeks and line periods often lasted over fifty days. Think about what it does to your daily routine to get up for breakfast at 11PM, go flying in the middle of the night, dinner at noon, and back to bed early afternoon. After two weeks, then switch to the noon to midnight flight schedule. During flight ops there were launches every hour and a half, followed by recovery of the prior launch. Each squadron generally scheduled four airplanes each launch, plus a manned spare in the event of a maintenance problem with a 'go' airplane. Eight launches for a total of thirty two missions per squadron meant the fourteen aircrews were involved in briefing or flying thirty missions a day, plus manning two condition alert Phantoms for two hour watches in the cockpit on a catapult during non-flying hours. Also consider that carriers were often at flight quarters twenty hours a day. In a 'staff study' I was tasked with by CAG, I found that pilots were averaging twelve and a half hours a day briefing, manning, flying, debriefing, or standing alert watches spread out over twenty four hours for up to fifty day line periods. Plus, there were those all-important and demanding collateral duties which left little time for eating, sleeping, showers, etcetera.

"I understand why VF-142 was glad to have you for their flight schedule! There doesn't seem to have been much time for reclusive depression though."

"Periods of reflecting on the dangers mostly followed publication of the squadron flight schedule for the next day when we located our targets in the Intelligence spaces on large slide out panel wall maps with thousands of colored pins to indicate known AAA and SAM site locations. There were usually so many pins clustered around a target that it was impossible to discern the map beneath. Supplemental aerial photos were used to identify targets and plan how best to get in and out; however, there was no way to avoid the barrage fire over targets except to minimize the time flown through them by making simultaneous single pass bombing runs. There is nowhere in the world darker than an unlit steel stateroom to contemplate the dangers of the next mission while trying to sleep through the continuing ship noises of aircraft being fueled, repaired, loaded, and re-spotted for the next launch."

"Are you saying that there was little anxiety in the air during those missions?"

"Initially, there were times when anxiety remained with me right up to catapult launch, but then dissolved as the job of flying took over. Once in the air far above the signs of war, the risks of combat seemed remote, so I felt the peaceful joy of flight and invulnerability. I also felt twinges of guilt for having allowed anxiety to get to me between flights. I believe it was the same for most of us."

"How about the threat of missiles imported from the USSR?"

"SAMs were not as effective as the simple, cheap, old-fashion, and reliable anti-aircraft guns. Nevertheless, SAMs had a significant psychological impact and a definite influence on our tactics. Although it was an impressive sight to see a telephone pole size radar-guided missile rocketing toward you, the SAM's large turning radius made it possible to outmaneuver one if you were warned of the launch and saw it coming. Since we had no radar warning or counter-measures electronic equipment aboard our aircraft then, we had to rely on offshore patrol aircraft radio warnings of imminent missile launches to give us a heads up. Our initial tactic was to fly at four thousand feet on road recce missions which we thought was at the upper range of AAA gun effectiveness. When SAMs were launched, our defense was to dive to lower altitudes in the belief that if SAMs had to turn down to track us, its radar would lose us in ground clutter. The reality, however, was that we were actually flying over North Vietnam at the altitude which put us in both SAM and AAA effectiveness. Since SAMs sites were relatively few and less frequently used, we would have been wiser to fly at much higher altitudes, especially considering the low value of our targets."

"Describe more about those missions and targets."

"Because fighter squadrons' primary mission was to defend carriers from air attack, CAP missions initially required most of our Phantom resources."

"What threat was there to defend against?"

"Carriers in the Gulf of Tonkin were in a small body of water surrounded on three sides by North Vietnam to the west, China's Hainan Island to the east, and mainland China to the north–all within range of aircraft, surface to surface missiles, surface ships, and submarines. China was no happier to have us off their shores than we were to have the Soviets in Cuba. At that time the North's Migs and pilots were still in China for training. Still, anything could happen and Lyndon Johnson was very wary of the escalating consequences of the GOT Incident. When he reiterated that we 'sought no wider war' that turned out to mean that we could never do our job in Vietnam properly. Ridiculous rules of engagement, target restrictions, and detailed mission decisions were centralized under Secretary of Defense McNamara and his smug thirty-five year old 'trees full of owls' pipe-smoking civilian PhD's superimposed throughout the Services chain of command, making operational decisions and reporting directly to him to ensure 'more bang for the buck'."

"Please elaborate on the rules, restrictions, and targets. I read that you mostly bombed trees."

"I may be putting the cart before the horse here with overviews and conclusions ahead of the chronology, but targets and tactics didn't change much during Johnson's administration and my flying tours there, so I'll say it while I'm inspired and you can edit later. Keep in mind that the carrier Navy's missions were virtually all flown in North Vietnam and Laos. Navy flew few missions in South Vietnam, where the environment was relatively 'permissive'. That is, there were no Migs, SAMS, or heavy AAA. Missions 'in country' were mainly flown in close proximity to our ground forces, so precise accuracy and coordination were prime concerns in supporting troops and avoiding friendly casualties. Navy was not practiced in close air support for our ground forces except for the A-1 Skyraider squadrons."

"Where was Army and Air Force flying?"

"Army mainly flew helicopters in support of their troops and only in the South except for a few clandestine incursions into Laos and Cambodia. Air Force flew strike missions in the South, as well as Laos and the North. Laos became a traffic jam of all types of Navy and Air Force aircraft, including many B-52's, bombing the passes and trails to the point where collision avoidance required positive ground control of all air traffic in Laos. North Vietnam was divided between Navy and Air Force into areas called Route Packages. All of the North was considered hostile 'Indian Country', where pinpoint bombing accuracy was not a priority and where we could always assume someone was shooting at us with heavy AAA. It was reported that North Vietnam had the heaviest AAA defenses of any war in history."

"Is it correct to conclude that road recce was the primary mission in Laos and the North."

"I think it would be more accurate to say that our expressed strategy was to slow the flow of troops and supplies from the North to the South. While we flew many road recce missions in search of trucks, we were only successful to the degree that convoys could not move openly and rapidly in daylight hours, nor quickly at night with headlights on. Truck parks, troop concentrations, and storage areas were so well hidden and photos so quickly outdated that our intel could only label those areas as 'suspected'; therefore, they were assigned as secondary targets for road recce missions, since we could not return to the carrier with a bomb load. A suspected storage area, for example, might be several bomb craters with a single full or empty fifty-five gallon drum in each one. So, it is true that most of the damage was caused to the vegetation since most of our targets were in the woods–suspected storage areas, suspected troop concentrations, or trans-shipment points, suspected truck parks, river crossings, mountain passes, SAM sites, and truck convoys. It was difficult to get highly motivated to put ourselves in harm's way to drop six five hundred pound bombs into prior craters or on trees. Yet, those area targets didn't require a high degree of accuracy and there were no 'friendlies' around, so we soon decided that there was no reason to make low runs or repeated passes while worthwhile targets such as dams, power plants, harbor facilities, and railroads were off limits to us. There was a thirty mile ring around Hanoi and a fifteen mile radius around Haiphong Harbor we were prohibited from even flying through."

"What was the rationale for all the restrictions, Captain?"

"Let's see. 'No wider war'? Maybe we didn't want to have to pay for rebuilding the place? Didn't want to risk angering them? Maybe if we did no harm, they would beg for peace? We should do nothing more than slightly impede the flow of troops and supplies to the South? If we let the USSR bring in SAMs and advisors to shoot us down, they would talk the North into quitting? Johnson's concept was allow the North 'save face' and talk peace if he declared frequent bombing 'pauses', which only served to allow them to rebuild defenses and assure them we were admitting failure. Obviously, we never intended to invade North Vietnam, nor even cause it serious harm, so there was no cost to them. Meanwhile, South Vietnam–the folks we were supposedly saving from their own civil war–was in political disarray under corrupt and inept leadership, much like the US. Their Army was unwilling to fight as long as we did it for them. Since we had no plan, determination, or strategy anywhere on our side, there was every incentive for the North to continue victoriously. In other words, Mike, it was a half-assed war with no leadership or support at home, plus weak leadership in our own military. Returning drafted troops were labeled 'baby killers' and spit on. Our cowardly teenagers publicly burned our flag and draft cards and then ran away to Canada, if not gunned down by the National Guard on a college campus. It could all still be going today if Johnson hadn't been run out of town. I may as well say it, I and others believe President Lyndon Baines Johnson should have been impeached for his callous and gutless incompetence as our Commander in Chief, as well as for his totally failed 'War on Poverty', motivated to attract liberal votes by paying poor minorities not to work and encouraging teenage girls to become breeders for child welfare careers, few of them or their progeny ever to become more than a burden to society—while we were meanwhile presenting ourselves in harm's way with no target justification, hope for results, nor plans for victory. Johnson's failures demoralized us at home and abroad. Of all my negative feelings about Vietnam, disrespect for Lyndon Baines Johnson is number one. Considering the heroic bravery and\charismatic leadership of President John F. Kennedy in standing up to the Russians during the Cuban Missile Crisis, just imagine how different from Johnson he would have lead us as a great Commander in Chief and national leader during the Vietnam War."

"Good point, Captain. Too bad it didn't happen that way, so push on. What did happen? Where were the Admirals and Generals on these issues?"

"Where indeed? Well you should ask. From the beginning, the Admirals and Generals, having been displaced downward in the chain of command by the Whiz Kids, became petty and bitchy, turning the war in the South into a body count contest and the air war in the North into a Navy versus Air Force sortie count race, to the point that we flew with partial loads when the bomb supplies ran low. Since we had no one on the ground in the North to count the very few bodies, nor was there bomb damage assessment possible other than aerial photos of bomb craters on top of bomb craters in those areas not covered by trees, there was no way to claim that we had accomplished a damned thing—or ever would. The weak excuse used by the Admirals and Generals was that if they spoke up, they'd be fired like General MacArthur was by Truman during Korea and lose their effectiveness altogether."

"You disapprove of that excuse."

"Absolutely yes, Mike. Johnson totally lacked the courage, integrity, or respect of 'Give Em Hell Harry' Truman. And no officer can have the respect of his men if he lacks the backbone to act responsibly. The thing military leaders should have kept in mind about Washington politicians is that for good reason they are very mindful and fearful of the possibility of military revolts. For example, Ole 'Empty Suit' Obama's security guys ranked US military veterans as the number one terrorist threat in the United States. There have been many successful military coups in history, particularly in the America's."

"Once again I say good point, Captain. Too bad it didn't happen that way. So what did happen?"

"The Hawaii based Admiral in command of Pacific Forces took it on himself to approve retroactive payment of Hostile Fire Pay to all of us just before we made a return port visit to Hong

Kong to pick up all the unfinished tailoring we had left behind when we exited post haste for the GOT Incident."

"Oh boy, you were going to get to see your Australian sweetie again. How great for you, huh?"

"You're a real smart ass aren't you Mike?"

"What's your point, you saw her didn't you?"

"Lord no. No way did I wish to re-visit that event. In fact, I remained aboard the first day. Sure enough, Ed returned to the ship to deliver the message that she was waiting for me on the dock with a car and an apartment, so I asked Ed to deliver my regrets and I stayed aboard the second day as well to be certain. Given her aggressiveness, surely she would engage another playmate by then."

"Well then, after criticizing your fellow fighter pilots for scurrying off for cover after meeting her, the truth comes out that you were no braver than they?"

"There's that saying about something being the greater part of valor. I had at least done my part once and that was more than enough. By avoiding her, she could fabricate whatever ego-saving reason suited her best. In any event, I never saw her again, thank goodness"

"Alright, Captain, if you say so, but others might say that you just knew you'd be unable to resist her charms if you did meet again."

"Whatever 'others' might say, Mike, this seems like a good stopping point and I'm ready for an afternoon nap after all the war talk. I'll see you at dinner?"

"Sure, wanna race back to the Lodge?"

"Yeah, now you want to race because the Yellow Brick Sidewalk is all uphill going home."

"Should have worn your ruby slippers, Captain."

"Let the race begin. GO!"

USS Constellation (CVA-64)

History

 United States

Name:	*Constellation*
Awarded:	1 July 1956[1]
Builder:	Brooklyn Navy Yard
Cost:	US$264.5 million
Laid down:	14 September 1957[1]
Launched:	8 October 1960[1]
Acquired:	1 October 1961[1]
Commissioned:	27 October 1961[1]
Decommissioned:	6 August 2003[1]
Struck:	2 December 2003[1]
Nickname(s):	*Connie*
Fate:	Scrapped

General characteristics [1]

Class and type:	*Kitty Hawk*-class aircraft carrier
Displacement:	61,981 short tons (56,228 t) light
	82,538 short tons (74,877 t) full load
	20,557 short tons (18,649 t) dead
Length:	1,088 ft (332 m) overall
	990 ft (300 m) waterline
Beam:	282 ft (86 m) extreme
	130 ft (40 m) waterline
Draft:	39 ft (12 m)[1]
Propulsion:	eight boilers, four steam turbine engines, totaling 280,000 shp
Speed:	34 kn (63 km/h)
Complement:	3,150 – Air Wing: 2,480
Armament:	2 × Sea Sparrow missile launchers
	3 × 20 mm Phalanx CIWS guns,
	Formerly: Terrier surface-to-air missile systems.
Aircraft carried:	72 (approx)

TOP: VF-143 'Pukin Dog' patch, named by a squadron wife in 1959 for its resemblance. Over time others came to erroneously believe it is a gryphon. According to the 1948 designer, however, it is actually a winged black panther, chosen because the squadron, VF-53, had just transitioned to F9F 'Panther' aircraft.

BOTTOM: The McDonnell 'Phantom Phlyer' patch. They also made patches for the back-seater - 'Phantom Pherret'; maintenance crew - 'Phantom Phyxer"; and the flight surgeon - 'Phantom Phlyer Phyxer"

20

LEVITATION

"Good evening Captain. Did you have a nice nap?"

"Yes, I'll tell you out it after dinner. What are we having?"

"Chateaubriand."

"Didn't we just have that?"

"No Captain, we haven't had it recently."

"Oh alright. Then I won't complain to Georgie. I haven't seen her today. Have you?"

"Yes. In fact, I had lunch with her today."

"Ah ha, I see, a date!"

"Not a date. We had lunch, that's all."

"Maybe you should escalate to real dates, Mike. Time's flying you know and you guys ain't spring chickens–not that it's any of my business."

"I agree with all you just said. Speaking of time flying though, now that I have passed the private pilot written exam and have nearly enough solo hours for the flight exam, Philip has suggested that I spend next week on the Eastern Shore with him to finish building time in his Cub and take the flight exam while I'm there. What do you think? I hate to take a week off from the book."

"Sounds great, Mike. Go for it. It's much better to concentrate your flight time rather than string it out a few flights a week. Then you'll be set to start on your glider rating with the Ximango which shouldn't take more than fifteen or twenty flights. Too bad Philip lives across the bay with all the time and expense of going back and forth. I thought about letting you take the Ximango over there for a week or so but there's no hangar space for it and we shouldn't leave it outside."

"Certainly, and I'd as soon fly out of here to stay close to your expertise and to keep up the pace on your book."

"*Our* book. I'm sorry this has turned out to be a longer project than you expected, Mike. I'm doing my best to clip sentences and subjects down to essentials, but here we are on chapter twenty and only up to 1964 with two-thirds to go. I know you were mainly interested in a fighter pilot's war stories, but I hope you won't be disappointed if I don't dwell too long on Vietnam and Navy life. I'm itching to get on to other adventures more important to me and 'hopefully more interesting to readers.'"

"Honestly Captain, I think your personal story, however you wish to tell it, is what we're after. My situation could not be more comfortable and enjoyable. I'm happy as a clam and free as a bird here, so please don't feel rushed. There's no better retirement vacation for me than being here and flying–not to mention an engaging social life."

"Interesting choice of words. Good luck. You'd sure be getting the better side of that bargain. None of my business, of course."

"Of course, Captain. I see we're having your favorite dessert again, French vanilla ice cream. You must have influence with the management. None of my business, of course."

"I'm ninety-four, but I'm not dead. Have you considered that Georgie may be interested in you because she hopes you might be a chip off the old block?"

"No Captain. Frankly, such a thought would never have crossed my mind."

"Touché."

"Let's convene here on the porch, Mike, I can't think clearly with that lobby TV in the background."

"Suits me, nice evening and a Commander's full moon. I'm anxious to hear about your afternoon lie-down."

"Well, I have been following your suggestion to re-create the original conditions which inspired my childhood dreams of levitation–except of course for the chronic ear ache pains which began it. Although my neck is stiff and sore all the time these days, I have been pushing through it, rolling my head back and forth on my pillow trying to put myself in the kind of semi-conscious self- hypnotic sleep state where I once got to the part of my mind to concentrate very hard on lifting myself off the bed."

"As I recall, you were only four years old and levitation was more or less accidental?"

"Initially, yes. My earliest thoughts of leaving the earth was wishing to see what the severe night time thunderstorms looked like from above the clouds. I had no particular thought of flying. In fact, I recall now that my first experiences with rolling my head were not levitation at all. I saw myself unsupported in a fetal position in the farthest corner of the ceiling looking back at me. Further along, I would be up there looking back down at myself in bed. It was some time after the GI in Father's band began giving me model airplanes and I imagined flying them in the cockpit that the levitation dream experiences began. It was so natural that I took for granted that 'flying' was a normal human capability. I came to believe that if I practiced hard I could fly about whenever and wherever I wished; however, I also learned that if my concentration didn't remain focused, I would fall. Any lapse of attention and I had to begin the mental conditioning process over. So, although I was aware of the physical experience as it happened, I didn't know for certain if it was just a dream, since fully awake, I could not come close to duplicating it."

"Captain, I can assure you again with absolute certainty that your dreams came true, because I witnessed it. You have the ability to actually levitate, even if only while in a semi-conscious dream state. How far have you progressed this time?"

"During today's nap, I briefly achieved lift off–at least in my mind, but I quickly lost focus. So, I'm closing in on where I began as a child, re-learning how to work the magic and not just stumble on it inconsistently in brief random dreams. Whatever develops, even if I progress no further, what a trip it is at this age to now know that there is a place in my mind which frees me of gravity."

"Excellent. I believe you will go on to flying higher and faster–consciously."

"Have you thought of giving it a try, Mike? Your current flying experience should give your imagination a boost and this is an excellent opportunity. What is there to lose but your ties to earth?"

"Quite right, now would be the time, I've been exploring the internet for historic eyewitness reports. The art of levitation still exists in India and Tibet. Many scholars mention the phenomenon of 'flying lamas'. Alexandra David Neel, a British explorer, witnessed the flight of a Buddhist monk who flew a dozen meters in broad daylight, bouncing off the ground again and again, keeping his eyes on a guiding star only he could see. Medieval Europeans achieved levitation too, but unlike the Brahmans, yogis, and lamas, they did not undergo special training. They simply rose in the air after reaching a state of religious ecstasy. Saint Theresa, a Carmelite nun in the Middle-Ages, was one of the first documented levitators. According to church records and her 1635 autobiography, her flights were witnessed by 230 Catholic priests. It is noteworthy that Saint Theresa did not want to fly. She prayed that the Lord would relieve her of her special power and her request was finally granted."

"Isn't that a woman for you, Mike? Complaining about a miraculous gift from God. It reminds me of the Cole Porter lyric, 'Flying too high with some guy in the sky is my idea of nothing to do'. Can you imagine a guy rejecting such a gift?"

"Surely no fighter pilot would. You may enjoy the story of Josef Desa, though it illustrates a down side to levitation. Josef was born in South Italy in the mid seventeenth century. As a boy, he physically tortured himself in order to put himself in a state of religious ecstasy. Later he joined the Franciscans and at times became so ecstatic that he rose into the air. When Pope Urban VIII granted him an audience, Josef was so excited that he floated right before the Pope's very eyes until the head of the Order of Saint Francis brought him back to earth. Men of science observed and documented more than a hundred flights by Josef and news of the 'miracle man' spread quickly. Wherever he appeared, people from neighboring towns stood outside the monastery walls waiting for a miracle. Church officials, however, were apparently embarrassed by Josef's flights. He was transferred from one remote monastery to another at regular intervals until his death in 1653. He was canonized four years later."

"Strange what that says about the Catholic Church, isn't it, Mike? Miracles are central to church doctrines. Christian churches proselytize on the basis of biblical miracles and Catholics canonize those who perform them. So how do they explain hiding away their famous 'flying man' from public verification, in denial of the real thing as though he were a loose cannon?"

"Yes, odd that the Catholics are proud to proclaim that their way is the sole path to sainthood and heaven, yet, Josef's history demonstrates that they themselves did not believe in live demonstrable miracles by one of their own monks, even when the Pope and hundreds of priests were eyewitnesses to them. It seems hypocritical that after hiding Josef from public contact they should then declare him a saint only four years after his death—just because he could levitate?"

"It would be interesting insight into church thinking to read the documents related to Josef's canonization to read their justification to glorify his sainthood. If the records read like the embellished citations for many Vietnam era Distinguished Flying Crosses, they may bear little resemblance to factual truth. Nonetheless, it is significant that the Church did accept and endorse levitation as a historical fact. Did you come across more modern Western levitation reports unrelated to religion and saints, Mike?"

"Yes. The most famous levitator of the nineteenth century, was Daniel Douglas Hewm. An American newspaper editor reported that Hewm suddenly surprised everyone in the room by lifting a foot above the floor, with a twinge from head to foot in a state of fear and rapture, unable to speak. He came down some time later and rose again. On his third ascent he went up to the ceiling. He eventually learned to levitate of his own free will and showed his ability to thousands of spectators, including such celebrities as William Makepeace Thackery, Mark Twain, and Napoleon III, as well as many politicians, doctors, and scientists of note. Hewn was never accused of hoaxing an audience."

"What explanation do today's scientists offer?"

"There is much controversy, of course, regarding the physical nature of levitation. Some researchers, like Alexander Dubrov, Doctor of Biological Sciences, have theorized that it is a product of a biogravitational field created by a special kind of mental energy emitted by the human brain which can be deliberately created and manipulated by a levitator to change the height and direction of a flight. Amazingly, scientists have more recently pinpointed the particular part of our brains which functions to produce out of body experiences which they have consistently induced in subjects by stimulating that part of the brain. Having achieved it, what do you say, Captain?"

"I believe that many reports of levitation are factual–not fables, hoaxes, or illusions. I concur with the common thread in the reports that levitation is derived from the ability of human brains to control interaction with gravity. I do not know whether this ability is a holdover from our creation or if it is evolutionary in the development of our intelligence in applying willpower. I do not think it is a special gift. I believe that all humans may be capable of levitation."

"Why do you allow for it being a holdover from creation?"

"During the social revolution of the sixties, I heard about a religious group who believed that humans came to Earth as space travelers, but fell from a state of grace and lost the ability to leave–a sci-fi variation of the Garden of Eden story."

"An appealing theory, Captain. Do you side with the Creationists view then? "

"For me it comes down to 'God works in mysterious ways' through both creation and evolution. It doesn't have to be one way or the other, does it? For the sake of discussion, suppose God created 'humans' elsewhere? A planet named Heaven, for example. Suppose beings had the ability to teleport anywhere in the universe, found themselves on this beautiful blue planet and lingered too long, ate the forbidden fruit, and fell out of a state of grace, So now the descendants are Earth bound until able to elevate ourselves through as many lifetimes as it takes to regain the state of grace to return to planet Heaven."

"I see, Captain, the 'forbidden fruit' being that the space travelers perhaps mingled with Earth's native beings. Kinda like fighter pilots consorting with corseted Australian ladies in exotic Asian ports?"

"OK, for the sake of discussion I'll buy your chiding analogy, since you got the point for a change. After all, that's how evolution works, isn't it? There's no denying that all God's creatures continue to evolve."

"But the evidence does not as clearly support biblical miracles or sci-fi theories of creationism, does it?"

"Au contraire, Mike, the more discoveries scientists make, the closer they come to understanding and believing in a Master's grand plan of creation. How can anyone seriously believe that the intricate workings of life and the cosmos occurred spontaneously from a vacuum without a Creator? I've read that eighty-seven percent of Americans believe in God. So, can it be a great stretch of reason, evidence, and faith to acknowledge the possibility that He created the universe and everything in it with a Big Bang and evolution? Isn't it truly miraculous that we are even alive?"

"Do you think that mankind may once again achieve a state of grace and return 'home'?"

"I believe it's possible, absolutely yes. We have been blessed with all the tools on earth to make it so and the ascent of man is accelerating exponentially. If we can imagine it, we can do it. Suppose fish came out of the ocean, developed lungs and crawled on the land looking up to the sky, wishing to fly. So they evolved wings and flew! We looked out in space toward 'home' and built rockets to begin the journey back. Some imagined they could levitate and did it. Can teleporting be out of reach when ordinary people achieved it? Our only limitation is our capacity to follow up on inspired dreams."

"You paint an optimistic picture of the future, Captain. Unfortunately, isn't it also very possible that mankind will exercise its God-given option to turn this beautiful blue planet into a nuclear fireball? Too many peoples, cultures, religions, and societies are so primitively ignorant, hateful, greedy, and cruel that they place no value on life whatever. The poor and oppressed are easily mesmerized and enslaved by charismatic, articulate, and insane gurus who lead them like lemmings to self-destruction."

"Very sad but true, Mike. It is amazing. Even many civilized, bright, and educated people, in advanced God fearing nations, too often behave in mass like utterly deranged idiots to their own demise. The only hope for us beyond the best efforts of those who are willing to sacrifice their lives to defend against those forces is our prayers, 'Thy will be done on Earth, as it is in Heaven.'"

"With God on our side, Captain?"

"Yes, Mike, just as George Washington believed that we could not have won the Revolutionary war without God's direct intervention, there have been many times in history when the margin of victory was so slim that there is no better explanation of the miraculous outcomes. Suppose, for example, that the Nazi's had succeeded, as they very nearly did, in developing nuclear weapons before they were defeated?"

"Perhaps those people are the ones to be left behind on Earth by the Travelers and eventually perish in their own nuclear holocaust."

"Perhaps so, Mike. As the Bible says, it won't be water, but fire next time. Anyhow, I've had all the fun I can stand for today, so I'll call it a night. Are you flying tomorrow?"

"No. So I'll see you at breakfast?"

"God willing and unless I'm off doing some flying of my own."

"Good night and good luck, Captain. Happy landings."

2I

VIETNAM 1964 & '66–RPI '67

"**G**ood morning, Captain. I see you finished breakfast early. Couldn't sleep?"

"I slept so soundly that I woke up early and hungry."

"Yes, but science and medicine have come a long way to compensate for some things. Many of the hearing aids you see here are likely high sensitivity spy ware listening devices. You can't trust old farts at all. Go on with your breakfast and I'll meet you down the brick road in a half hour."

"You look so comfortable in that wheelchair, I should get one.. This bench is good for an hour or two at most."

"I thought lawyers and judges toughened up their butts with years of sitting on benches?"

"It doesn't work that way- just as years of being a smart ass doesn't make one more humorous."

"OK, enough chit chat. Where were we before we got off track into tales of levitation?"

"You were back in Hong Kong after the Gulf of Tonkin Incident to finish up shopping with your hostile fire pay, while trying to avoid another tryst with the Australian honey."

"Oh yes. Then we went right back to Yankee Station for more of the same type missions against the North and Laos. Most memorably, the CINCPAC Admiral who authorized hostile fire pay got his wrist slapped for it and was ordered to collect it back from us, inspiring an impromptu hootenanny in the Wardroom one evening with appropriate songs and poems. A recited old soldier's poem I recall was, *'You're paid to stop a bullet. At least that's what they say. So you stop a bullet. And then, they stop your pay!'* The outcome was that the Carrier Division Commander stuck up for us against the chain of command and shamed them into canceling the recall. It was an unusual and gratifying example of telling Washington to stuff it and the episode turned out to be a morale boost for us. We were going to need one. Missions were relatively routine, but the long line periods and extended hours of flight operations, not to mention getting shot at, was wearing us down. At least we would be home for Christmas–we thought. Meanwhile, short port visits to the Philippines were small compensation. The colorful fun and games at the Cubi 0 Club had tamed. Still, there was lots of drinking at sea. The A-3 Sky Warriors now had no mission except in-flight refueling since Naval Air was relieved of nuclear attack SIOP commitments, so their large bomb bays were used for oddball shopping trips such as picking up tailored flight suits in Thailand, lettuce in Japan, ceramic elephants in Saigon, and most importantly, booze from Cubi Point with open sales on the hangar deck until it went quietly underground. My room was closest to the wardroom and I had the only stuffed olives, so it became the spot for happy hour with friends before dinner vodka martinis to mask the odor of alcohol. When I ran out of vermouth and olives, we added the olive juice to the vodka. One evening matters went a little over the top when Magoo slipped us an unannounced bottle of 150 proof vodka which had us reeling as we stood hanging onto our chair backs during a long-winded grace by the Chaplain. Nevertheless, we mostly managed to keep the lid on the drinking without consequences. Flying combat missions off carriers has quite a sobering effect."

"Mostly managed to keep a lid on it, you say?"

"Matters nearly got out of control on Halloween. As we sometimes did, my pal Ed, who gave me his mandolin, Tom, and I had been playing and singing Harry Belaphoney, as they called him in Trinidad, Calypso songs with Tom on harmonica, Ed on an olive can 'drum', and me on guitar. After running through 'Kingston Town' and the others several times, plus two bottles of Courvoisier until the wee hours, we retired toward our rooms. Some folks, however, were going room to room playing trick-or-treat for drinks. So Ed, who was in no shape for it, was inspired to visit CAG. Unfortunately, CAG failed to find humor in having Ed bang on his door at three AM shouting, 'Open the door you sonofabitch, I know you're in there!' It took a good deal of persuasion by Tom and me to talk CAG out of taking official action against Ed."

"You said you were scheduled to be home for Christmas–you thought. What happened?"

"We were to be relieved by Ranger, but it had a major power plant casualty inbound to WESTPAC and nearly had to be towed to the Subic Navy shipyard for lengthy repairs. Coincidentally, Ranger's CO was Burly Grimes, the VAH-6 skipper who put me in the AJ left seat for my first cruise aboard Hornet. Unfortunately, the breakdown cost Burly his Admiral promotion. To add insult to injury, America, the follow-on carrier after Ranger, also had a delaying engineering casualty. So, December came and went with a dreary Christmas at Cubi Point and New Year's Eve back on Yankee Station. Disheartening day to day speculation on Ranger's progress dragged on through January and we finally arrived home in February1965. A nine month deployment was difficult enough, but the extension also shortened the turnaround time for our next deployment in November. "

"The brief time at home must have had special family value for you."

"I remember little about those hectic days, so things must have been pretty much as before at home. Aurelie remained a good mother to the kids and they were great with each other, though Aurelie otherwise had little interest in being a homemaker and no concept of the value of money. She bought a small reproduction bronze Ming Horse statue for a month's pay. Our '53 Studebaker had been parked for weeks after the engine was run without oil. Though the kids were happy, bright and healthy, they were so unkempt they looked like ragamuffin orphans."

"Did you express disapproval to her?

"No. Aurelie was doing the best she could and that was not the time for me to assert myself. If she was to bear the responsibility, it was best to let her do it her way. As we had done from the beginning, we kept the peace and made the most of matters. We still shared an interest in traditional music and hung out at coffee houses and campus folk festivals; however, the social cause had shifted from racial integration to anti-war protest. The music therefore had less musical value or interest to me. Also, my age and military haircut made me conspicuous in coffee houses and on campus. In any case, I was back on a heavy training schedule with deployments to Yuma, Fallon, and carrier ops. I hadn't stopped to ponder shore duty–after all, we were at war. Nevertheless, I filled out my Preference Card, just in case my Assignment Detailer in DC was interested. One part of the card had a choice of 'do' or 'do not' desire graduate school. Although I had no motivation to return to school and my undergraduate GPA was dismal, I thought better of showing lack of ambition by checking the 'do not' block, so I also had to select which graduate program I preferred. I found few choices for someone with a BA in psychology. The simplest would have been the Navy Post-graduate School at Monterey, except that it was a two year program at Navy's 'company' school which was struggling for accreditation by flunking out many officers to demonstrate phony academic standards in lieu of having a viable institution with a qualified faculty. Instead, I found a one year Management Engineering program at Rensselaer Polytechnic Institute with no thesis requirement. A safe choice, I thought. Surely, neither Navy nor RPI would select me after reviewing my pitiful academic records. Besides, everyone knew that Preference Cards were rarely considered by Detailers, so I put it out of mind as deployment time approached. Then to my horror, I was notified to take the Harvard Business School entrance exam at San Diego State College. It was the toughest reading comprehension test I had seen and I saw a bunch of them in testing courses as a psych major. I felt totally humiliated, certain I had done miserably, so I focused on deployment preparations. Other than the 'Hanoi Hilton', Graduate school was the last place I wanted to be, so I took some comfort in failure. But soon came the real horror–orders to detach in May and report to Rensselaer Polytechnic Institute, Troy, New York. Meanwhile, Joan Baez and her followers promised to blockade San Diego Harbor with yachts to prevent Ranger's departure. Flyers were also mailed to Ranger's 'occupants' encouraging sailors to protest the war by deserting and taking shelter in a Mission

Bay church. Then, one morning as we were loading aboard, we learned that Ranger's CO was ill in Bethesda Naval Hospital. Reliable scuttlebutt, however, was that the CO was not ill, but was being confined to his hospital room with Marines guarding his door. Reportedly, the CO had ordered the Ensign assigned as Ranger's Postal Officer to not deliver the desertion flyers. When the Ensign protested that it was an unlawful order to interfere with the mail, the CO confined him to quarters–also an unlawful order. So the Ensign called his Senator and we had a new CO just days before deploying. Had the real story of the CO's 'illness' become public, the protestors might have taken some satisfaction in getting him fired; however, he was not heard of again."

"Amazing. How successful was the Baez blockade and desertion campaign?"

"Whatever advance publicity value the threats had, the blockade was a flop. The Harbor Police and Coast Guard easily cleared Ranger's way and arrested the crews of the few yachts that showed up. The prospect of the looming bow of a one thousand foot aircraft carrier bearing down was apparently too much for the spineless draft-dodging liberal protestors. As Ranger cleared the coast unhindered, the few sailors who took shelter in the church were rounded up into helicopters and flown to Ranger where they were confined to the brig under marine guard to await courts martial, far from the media and civilian courts.. It was a proud day for me to be in the Navy, as was every other day."

"So how was it to return to Yankee Station again?"

"SOS–same old 'stuff'–just as we had left it. Ludicrous rules of engagement, restrictions against bombing high value targets or mining harbors, and no plan for victory. However, there was a significant improvement in our aircraft with the installation of effective radar detection and electronic jamming equipment defense against SAMs, which permitted improved tactics. Since we became equally safe from SAMs at any altitude, there was little reason to fly low within AAA effective range. With the slow prop-driven A-1 Skyraiders and unadaptable A-3 Sky Warriors out of the mix, we developed 'Alfa Strike-' group attack tactics by twenty or more compatible aircraft simultaneously rolling in on the same target from various directions which dispersed AAA gunners' aim and limited our exposure time. Thus, three golden rules of survival arose which greatly improved our chances! 1. No repeated runs on the same target. Deliver all weapons on the first pass and get out. 2. No low pullouts. There were no pinpoint targets, so there was no need to get down in the weeds for accuracy against low value area targets. And 3. No dueling with AAA sites. It was an utterly foolish risk to dive a four million dollar airplane straight down the barrels of four thousand dollar guns manned by four men when we were very likely to be unsuccessful in placing a bomb inside a revetment."

"Sounds reasonable, Captain. Why then were so many shot down?"

"Several reasons. Since we attacked the same areas repeatedly, the AA gunners learned that they didn't have to track us. With 150 guns ringed around the area, they could just cross their fire over the center and let us fly through it! Another factor was that some chose to disregard the three golden rules. Senior aviators, including CAG's and CO's, were especially remiss, perhaps because they felt it necessary to set examples of fruitless bravery. Other 'heroes' were simply going after medals."

"Where were the MIGs?"

"Training in China at first, then when they returned to home bases they flew training missions northwest of Hanoi and were not a threat. Actually there was little reason for them to employ the Migs since their AAA was more effective. Because we were doing little damage on the ground and our fighters were largely burdened with boring CAP missions flying 260 knot circles over the Gulf, everyone in Naval Aviation, from the Admirals to the JO's, was obsessed with shooting down Migs. It nearly became the purpose of the air war! There was even a kind of 'Shoot a Mig, win a Silver Star' suggestion contest to find ways to draw out the Migs. I facetiously suggested circling a flight of Phantoms low in Laos, below radar detection, to await a Big Look early warning aircraft notice that the Migs were taxiing out for takeoff. Then the Phantoms could pop over the mountains and blast the Migs on takeoff before they even retracted their landing gear."

"That seems hardly fair, Captain. Weren't there rules of chivalry in aerial combat, as in the days of King Arthur's knights?"

"That's the romantic image of gallantry that some fighter pilots may like to project; however, the reality was that most often, victims were sneaked up on from behind and didn't know they were being shot at until it was too late. Plus, many targets were lumbering bombers or outdated relics."

"Silver Stars were awarded for that?"

"Absolutely, without question. Quite unjustified when compared with the true acts of bravery by real heroes doing the less glamorous dirty hand to hand business of killing on the bloody battlefields, but that's the way it always was since World War One. No other warriors have ever captured public adulation as well as the romantic charisma of fighter pilots."

"How did you feel about yourself as a fighter pilot at that time?"

"Mixed emotions. On one hand, I was proud and honored to be one and to fly cutting edge airplanes. Otherwise, I recognized that we tended to be undeserving immature egotists who were no better aviators than others. When I left Ranger in May 1966, headed for RPI, Troy, New York, I was of course relieved to leave Vietnam behind, but I was also not unhappy to be leaving 'Fighter Town' and San Diego behind, despite the awful prospect of graduate school."

"Still, after nine years in San Diego, it must have been a traumatic transition for you and the family to move all the way across the US to a totally new life as a graduate student at a civilian university in an old small New England city."

"True, Mike, I liked Coronado and La Jolla, but I never cared much for San Diego itself. It was a Navy town and commercial port like Pensacola with the floundering Convair aircraft factory. Surrounded and hemmed in by the Mexican border, Pacific Ocean, desert, and Los Angeles, there was no escape. I never looked back."

"So, how was the move and transition to your new life?"

"Not bad. I had made military moves all my life and they were surprisingly smooth since all packing and unpacking was well done for us. If you forgot to empty the trash cans, you'd find them the same when you unpacked. Thanks to a Navy predecessor at RPI, we rented a house seventeen miles out of town in Avirill Park, population less than 1,500. It was a lovely home built in the late eighteen hundreds with several acres and a stream in back. Thankfully, we settled in quickly, for my fears of academia were well founded. The outgoing class indicated that we would all make it if we made a team effort and the faculty felt we were giving it our best. But for me, that meant twenty hour days with thirty minute naps. In addition to lectures, each course had a 'lab' and we had many group study sessions, so I was constantly driving to and from campus. In the experimental six week computer introductory course using a primitive IBM processor and mark sense punch cards, we wrote programs in the three earliest computer languages—machine language, all zeroes and ones; Assembly; and FORTRAN. Though one of my predecessors had advised me to simply skip any problem requiring calculus, as he had done, I had to face my math deficiencies with the calculus required to write a computer program for artillery shell ballistic curves. The one other naval aviator in our group was also deficient in math, so we had to attend a special 'dumb bell' class taught by a math PhD who had never left school longer than it took him to wash out of Navy flight training and who could not fathom our ignorance. Unfortunately, he also taught all of the many math based courses in the program which focused on 'scientific decision making', probability, statistics, and word logic problems. Since a B average was required for the master's degree, my C in a math course meant I needed an A to balance it, not an easy challenge at Rensselaer 'Probability' Institute. We were trapped in an environment we had no control over, competing with very bright kids highly motivated to maintain their draft deferments and scholarships, while we were also treated, as all students regardless of age are by faculty, like children."

"What was the campus attitude toward Vietnam?"

"Surprisingly positive. Instead, of anti-war protests, student groups even invited representatives of the military-industrial complex, like Dow Chemical, manufacturers of napalm, to conduct well attended seminars. RPI was truly a brain factory like a lesser MIT with an academically dead serious student body. Once, going between classes on a Saturday, I noticed a football game in progress with the stands virtually empty. No one cared that RPI was playing Harvard."

"All work and no play, Captain?"

"No time for play at RPI, Mike, though there was one memorable light spot. Against the wishes of the administration and the community, the Student Union invited Timothy Leary for a stage presentation in the auditorium. To make the event palatable, however, the New York State Narcotics Commissioner had to be given equal stage time to balance Timothy's 'Drop out, Turn on, Tune in' LSD message."

"Wasn't the phrase 'Turn on, tune in, drop out'?

"That's one of two versions from later in 1967 at a San Francisco Golden Gate Park 'Be In' gathering of 30,000 hippies."

"Refresh me on Timothy Leary. I only recall that he was a Harvard PhD psychology professor who conducted laboratory experiments with mind altering drugs."

"I don't want to get side-tracked much beyond Leary's RPI show, so I suggest consulting the internet where I found this Wikipedia quote last night which I'll include here as it pertains to that point in time.

"In 1966, Leary founded the League for Spiritual Discovery, a religion declaring LSD as its holy sacrament, in part as an unsuccessful attempt to maintain legal status for the use of LSD and other psychedelics for the religion's adherents, based on a "freedom of religion" argument Leary spoke at the 1967 Human Be-In, a gathering of 30,000 hippies in Golden Gate Park in San Francisco and uttered his famous phrase, "Turn on, tune in, drop out" which came to him in the shower one day"

"Did you attend Leary's RPI event?"

"Oh yes, I can replay much of it in memory. Leary's followers occupied the front rows when the lights dimmed to total darkness and silence. Then Leary lit a single candle on the stage floor as the house lights came up dimly to reveal him in a white Nehru jacket and pants, sitting cross-legged on a rug before the candle and a glass of water. He began by saying that water and fire, as well as mind altering methods, including psychedelic drugs, have been used in religious practices throughout history, yet we understand that those elements can be dangerous if mis-handled. While it is possible to experience spiritual awakening with drug use, it not necessary, he explained. It's possible, for example to achieve the same effects by 'dropping out' of society and fasting on a mountain top and 'tuning in' for forty days. Facilitating the experience with drugs is only a passing phase, he said, which may one day evolve into having the proper area of our brains wired up to a battery and switch in our pockets whereby we can 'turn on' anytime for as long as we wish. After 'dropping out' of society and going to the mountain tops to 'turn on', it is necessary to return to 'tune in' to society again to share the spiritual awakening with others."

"So, Leary was promoting the use of LSD as a religious leader, since it had been made illegal otherwise?"

"Yes, however he also strongly warned others against it. He compared our usual lives to being actors in a TV studio with our scripted actions manipulated by directors for episodes of 'cops and robbers' or 'cowboys and Indians'. In the corner of the TV studio, though, is The News Room where we are never allowed. For the Directors knew that if we dropped out of the studio and tuned in there we would learn the truths which would permanently alter our outlook. We could never again fit into our former roles in the studio. He also warned that it was essential to have reliable close friends surrounding you during LSD experiences."

"I suppose Leary was a major guru for the counter-culture revolutionaries?"

"To a degree he surely represented the 60's generation's rebellious rejection of all the conflicting, inconsistent, and outdated institutional laws, values, ideals, and morality fed to them by their parents, teachers, preachers, and politicians. Instead, the hippies were re-inventing American culture from the ground up on their own with re-investigation of the world's religions and philosophies through drugs, sex; rock and roll, and lifestyles whether at Haight-Ashbury, the concerts, dancing, 'happenings', or communes. But I wouldn't say that Leary was as important as other elements. In my opinion, the poetry of their creative music was the major uniting and motivating factor of the 60's culture and social movement."

"How was rock and roll that important?"

"In this context I wouldn't use the term rock and roll because it includes throw away music played on the radio, Most serious music of the day generally wasn't aired on the radio because it was over three minutes long and wasn't considered 'commercial' enough."

"Well they certainly played all of Elvis' records and still call him 'The King of Rock and Roll', Captain."

"Exactly, Mike, thank you for making my point. Elvis was a 'Rock a Billy' star. Sixties' serious pop music evolved from American Black Country blues which was admired and preserved in England and then re-introduced to the US by white British bands like the Beatles. Then Bob Dylan and many other singer, song-writer musicians who grew up in coffee houses, added to traditional music with electronics and mind-blowing sound systems to create a unique blend of great poetry and melodies. Concert attendance rivaled any other event in human history and made the sixties movement world-wide–though it was nowhere else as well understood as it was in its California origin, which had also given birth to the surfers' unique culture and musical contribution. For me, the music was as effective a psychedelic or social motivator as any drug or fasting on a mountain top could have been."

"And you know that how? Did you go to those big concerts or Haight-Ashbury yourself?"

"I went to a number of concerts and clubs in California and made two very memorable trips to San Francisco. We'll get to that in 1969. I stayed far away from drugs because they were much too dangerous for an aviator to experiment with–especially LSD because of its long-term severely disorienting flashbacks."

"Yes, it surely wouldn't do to trip out during a night carrier landing approach, would it? So it wasn't all work and no play for you at RPI, was it?"

"No. In spite of the pressures and twenty hour days, I have fond memories. Though it began snowing in November and didn't stop until May that year, which provided exciting commuter driving challenges, the kids had a ball with their first experiences in it, especially sledding down the great hill on the vacant property next door. The retired RPI Philosophy Professor who lived across the street was relatively tolerant of ignorance during our lively happy hour discussions. Because he suffered with advanced emphysema, he extended his heated swimming pool season to year round with a large inflatable rubber enclosure. With outside lighting and rising mist, the effect inside was quite eerie at night. He also had a large collection of antique black powder flint lock pistols and rifles which we occasionally fired in the wee hours -thankfully without me putting a hole in his pool enclosure. What's more, the pastor of the church we attended was into traditional music and had coffee house programs at his church Saturday evenings and he convinced Aurelie and me to perform twice for our first time in public. The challenge of playing an instrument and singing at the same time required hours of rehearsal. It was traumatic for me and we were awful, but the thing about coffee houses and amateur folk talent was the tolerance of audiences."

"Very nice. I suppose the year passed quickly and you were anticipating a tour with the Air Force flying the brand new F-111. Didn't you feel honored?"

"I should have. If I had given it any thought I might have realized that the RPI assignment and this one to fly our newest fighter might indicate that I was being 'fast tracked' for a bright Navy future, but I just never figured it out. I was totally unprepared and shocked to receive orders to an A-7 'Corsair Two' squadron at NAS Lemoore California. Not only would I be going back to Vietnam for the third time, I was leaving fighters to fly subsonic attack airplanes based at the worst joke of an air station in Navy history. Three calls to my Detailer proved futile. The airlines were hiring, so many pilots were bailing out of the military. Plus, Navy was suffering heavy combat losses, particularly attack pilots. Moreover, Navy had successfully stuck USAF with the F-111after modifying it so extensively that it was no longer capable of flying off carriers and had quickly developed the A-7 to replace it and the A-4's. Recognizing the wall's handwriting, I pleaded for return to F-4's having been out of the cockpit only a year. The Detailer's response was memorable, 'We've got a lot more fighter pilots than attack pilots, Manny, carry out your orders.'"

"But with an RPI master's degree now, your civilian options had broadened considerably. You could tell the Navy to stuff it."

"It's true that the degree opened many new career doors to me, but there was a 'Catch 22'. Along with the RPI tour came an added three year active duty obligation. By that time I would have over sixteen years invested. The college tour was a Navy retention device to get mid-term officers into the 'retirement pull'–one reason I didn't feel all that special. So, once reality set in, I resolved to make the best of it, as I had tried to do with previous disagreeable events. I did take satisfaction in achieving a master's degree in a more useful field from a top university, to be flying Navy's latest war bird, pin on Lieutenant Commander oak leaves, and retire from my LSO career. Nevertheless, as a wise man once observed, 'It takes a lot of 'atta boys' to make up for one 'aw shit'. So let's break for lunch now and reconvene after your flight for dinner."

"Suits me, Captain. Want to race back to the lodge?"

"Hell no. You know very well you'd win with me pushing this wheelchair up hill and I'd be too out of breath to have dessert. You know the story about the old rooster, don't you?"

"Tell it, Captain."

"There was an old rooster nearing retirement, so the farmer bought a young one. The old rooster was standing at the top of a hill in the chicken yard perusing all the hens when the young rooster introduced himself. 'I guess you know why I'm here?' 'Sure', said the old rooster, 'the time comes for all of us but I'm not done yet.' They stood in silence for a while, gazing at the hens, then the young rooster said, 'So let's run down there and knock off a couple of them.' The old rooster replied, Let's walk down and knock them all off'."

22

NAS Lemoore–Vietnam 1968

"Good evening Captain"

"Hi Mike. How was your flight?"

"Good. I'm feeling more comfortable in the Cub."

"Ready for the flight examiner?"

"Hopefully tomorrow morning."

"Great! Then what?"

"A few more solo hours in the Cub, then on to your Ximango, if that's agreeable?"

"Sure. How does Phil want to work it?"

"He suggests that he could get some Ximango time with you while I am flying the Cub. That way he can fly the Cub back and forth and kill two birds with one stone. How does that sound?"

"Perfect. Fun for me too. I see we are having pork roast."

"Good! Do you want to convene on the porch afterward?"

"Sure."

 Later...

"Where were we, Mike?"

"How was your RPI graduation ceremony?"

"No idea- missed it. We were stampeded back to California, so I had the degree forwarded to VA-122 NAS Lemoore, the A-7 training squadron we were headed for. Earning the MS was professionally anti-climactic since academic credentials do not enhance pilots' combat abilities, except perhaps in improved mental discipline. Although long term career options opened, Catch 22 was that Viet tours made future plans tenuous at best. If I survived, the Navy 'promotion enhancement' advantages of the degree were pretty much lost on me, already a Lieutenant Commander and determined to retire at the twenty year mark- should I be so lucky. So, the best of it was that I felt proud of myself and very grateful to the Navy for an education and for the well spent year off from the other stuff."

"You said NAS Lemoore was a joke?"

"Yes. If 'location is everything', as a Naval Air Station Lemoore had nothing. Forty miles south of Fresno in the San Joaquin Valley without a house or a tree as far as the eye could see in any direction except for mountains to the east. The vacant scene reminded me of our arrival at Albuquerque in '52, except here it was huge farms instead of desert. One of those giant corporate farms made the news for being paid four million dollars in government subsidies NOT to grow anything in 1967. The largest town within miles was Hanford with a population of 4,500 cowboy farm worker families. There was one bar with a card room in back and a whore house upstairs staffed by underage Indian girls from the nearby reservation. Combat losses were high, Morale was dismally low. The worst of the joke, however, was the weather. Zero-zero ceiling and visibility in fog frequently curtailed flight operations for days on end, so squadrons in training had to deploy to Fallon Nevada or Yuma Arizona to make up for lost flight time, while most other squadrons were deployed to WESTPAC. The Officers Club, the only show in town, was therefore virtually deserted. Those irresponsible politicians and incompetent DOD pencil .pushers involved in approving that site should have been publicly thrashed and locked up in stocks for that fiasco."

"Were there no redeeming features about Lemoore?"

"It made San Diego look good and Vietnam less bad! Nevertheless, there were several memorable experiences to welcome me. The road map showed a large lake not far away which might allow for some sailing, so, I set out to find it in my '66 VW Bug one afternoon with the map in my lap. The lake was harder to find than expected because many of the farm roads were not identified or mapped. Although I was sure I was in the vicinity and had crossed the area several times, there was no water anywhere. Then I drove down a straight road which appeared to go to the horizon. Driving along, studying the map in my lap, I heard a steady distant humming sound. I was in the only vehicle on the road, so I went back to my map. But the sound continued and it was getting louder. Perhaps a helicopter approaching from behind? Nothing I could see in front or behind, so back to the map. As the sound continued getting louder, it sounded more like a truck air horn. But there were still no vehicles up or down the road. As the sound became very close indeed, I bumped over some railroad tracks at an unguarded crossing and in my rearview mirror saw a train cross left to right, inches behind me so close I believe that if I had seen it at the last minute and even taken my foot off the accelerator, I would have been rammed."

"Pretty amazing, Captain. A VW Bug wouldn't have done much damage to a freight train, but didn't the engineer even attempt to stop?"

"I don't know when he applied the brakes, but he did stop the train a quarter mile past the intersection and step down from the cab. I stopped too and got out of the VW as we both just stood and stared at each other for a minute or two."

"Were you badly shaken?"

"It had all happened so suddenly and without consequence, I felt only embarrassment for being unaware of the danger. So, the engineer and I returned to what we had been doing."

"A miss is as good as a mile?"

"Right. Or as the Marines say, 'Close only counts in horseshoes, hand grenades, and nuclear weapons.' Up to that time in my life I was very slow to react emotionally to confrontations or crisis–a characteristic of sociopaths, I suppose, but a decided advantage in my line of work and personal life."

"Did you find the lake?"

"I kept searching until I approached a small settlement and saw that the train was also approaching. No way did I wish to encounter that engineer again, so I quickly exited the area and gave up the search. Just as well since there was no real lake at all, just a flood control basin which contained no water during the five years I was stationed there. So much for sailing at Lemoore."

"How about the squadron and flying the A-7 Corsair Two? No joy there?"

"I got off to a cheery beginning with the check-in flight physical. While waiting for the Corpsman to check my eyes, I saw that the ancient memorized eye chart had been replaced. I had time to walk up and look at it only briefly before the Corpsman entered, told me to cover up my right eye and read the fourth line from the bottom. I couldn't read a single letter, so I made up a line. Then he told me to cover the other eye and read the same line backwards, so I made up another one. As I left, he handed me my check-in route slip with the entry 20-20!"

"How fortunate! Why do you think he let you slide by?"

"I have n no idea, but I was very thankful. I wasn't enthusiastic about returning to Vietnam, but I had no wish to be grounded."

"How were you hoping to get through future eye exams then?"

"It so happened that the eyesight minimums had been lowered to 20-50 because of the pilot shortage. It was now alright to fly with glasses and use them for eye charts, which I did thereafter."

"So, you were home free after all those years of skating by with disqualifying astigmatism!"

"I thought so."

"There's more?"

"Yup, we'll get to it."

"How about the flying? Any difficulty getting back in the saddle after just a few hours in 'Bug Smashers' during the year at RPI?"

"No. As they say, like riding bicycles. Even instrument flying under the hood in the back seat of a TA-4 seemed easier than ever and the A-7 was a joy, though underpowered and low-tech as a bomber. The A-7 had been built in a rush to replace the A-4 Sky Hawk and lacked electronic sophistication. The advantage was that the A-7 had better range and bomb load capacity. The Navy F-111 had been cancelled, but we were stuck with the engines procured and had to put them in something without the afterburners, since the A-7 was not supersonic. Nevertheless, the engine proved very reliable and miserly with fuel consumption. A-7A's were capable of two and a half hour operational flights without in-flight refueling, but were underpowered with a significant weapons load aboard and lacked maneuverability."

"Were subsonic attack airplanes loaded with air to ground weapons expected to also function as fighters?"

"Defensively, as necessary. The air battles over the North had heated up in 1967. Migs were making single pass slashing runs through Alfa Strikes. A-7A's were armed with guns and Sidewinder air-to-air missiles, but were also heavily loaded with bombs and air-to-ground missiles."

"How were attack pilots trained for dog fighting?"

"Marginally. There was little time to train for our primary missions, much less fighter tactics as well. Nineteen A-7's were lost in VA-122 Aerial Combat Maneuvering, ACM, training because they were subject to 'departing' in high G turns at any airspeed with zero warning, resulting in rapid uncontrolled loss of altitude. More agile A-4's were used as 'aggressors' in ACM training and low time A-7 pilots, looking over their shoulder in tight turns, naturally pulled too hard. Because the rate of descent in recovering from departures was so high, pilots were directed to eject if they had not resumed level flight passing ten thousand feet above the ground, so we didn't lose any pilots."

"As I recall, the full aerodynamic term was 'departure from normal flight', but it sounds like you are describing ordinary accelerated stall-spin events?"

"That's right, Mike. 'Departure' was a generic term. Different aircraft types behaved so differently 'outside the envelope' that conventional terms and recovery techniques often didn't apply. Aircraft designs are compromises, depending on their purpose. Light attack and fighter aircraft designs emphasize maneuverability over a very wide range of speed, altitude, weapon loads, and G forces. The tradeoff for maneuverability is reduced flight stability; however, bomb delivery accuracy also requires a fairly stable platform. So, tactical aircraft are not as unstable as aerobatic airplanes."

"The loss of nineteen A-7's in ACM training must have caused considerable alarm. What was done to get around the departure problem and still meet training objectives?"

"We leveled the ACM playing field by using A-7's in place of A-4's as aggressor aircraft. Ground training was intensified, of course, but departure avoidance and recovery training in single seat A-7's without an instructor was impractical. Instead, we acquired four T-28's for stall-spin training."

"The second airplane you flew in flight training? A slow, straight wing, prop-driven trainer? How could T-28 spins have any value to an A-7 pilot?"

"Hopefully, flying a variety of aerobatics would improve pilots' situational awareness and sensitivity to flying on the edge of the flight envelope. Inverted spins, which we thought would be most useful were disallowed, considered too dangerous because of engine oil starvation risk with sustained negative G's. Nevertheless, some instructors got around that restriction by having students begin loops at slow entry speeds. Pilots with little T-28 flight time were more likely to run out of airspeed or pull too hard on top and fall off into an inverted spin."

"Were the efforts successful?"

"Yes. We stopped losing A-7's in ACM training and I don't believe MIGs ever shot down a single A-7. For that matter, A-7's never shot down a Mig either, mostly because the F-4's did their job."

"Any other highlights for you during training?"

"Dive bombing on target ranges near Fallon and Yuma was a hoot. We launched in four plane flights for scheduled thirty minute target times with a load of ten twenty-five pound mark-76 reusable inert practice bombs with smoke charges for spotting and we made single bomb runs spaced around the target in a race tracking pattern. We rolled into the target for a forty-five degree dive angle, accelerated to 350 knots, released at four thousand feet, and pulled off straight ahead with four or five G's, and then climbed back to pattern altitude taking interval on the plane downwind ahead. To keep each other informed of where we were in the pattern, we transmitted radio call sign, our number in the flight, and position -'Mace One In', 'Mace One off', and so on. Ground spotter reported bearing and distance of each bomb hit. We often refueled and reloaded without getting out of the cockpit for a thirty minute turnaround and another session. So, it was a hard clay's work, constantly pulling 3 to 5 G's around the pattern. But it was satisfying fun."

"As an old heavy bomber and fighter pilot new to dive bombing in competition with experienced attack pilots, weren't you a bit out of your element?"

"Bless your heart for asking, Mike. As a matter of fact, I earned the Top Gun bombing award! Somehow the news got to NAS Miramar 'Fighter Town' and to my pleasant surprise, Diz Laird, the XO of VF-121, flew to Lemoore to attend the award ceremony just to rub it into their noses that the attack community had been whipped by an old Phantom Phlyer."

"That's great, Captain. Maybe your master' degree did some good!"

"Not in that instance; however, it might come in handy for my next administrative job. I was assigned to VA-27, a brand new squadron formed in December from scratch with all new airplanes, people and paperwork, to be deployed aboard Constellation five months later in May '68 for the second deployment of A-7's. Our CO was Commander George Pappas, a short temperamental Greek. In contrast, the XO, Commander Lynn Felt, was tall, thin, and reserved, and from a family line of Admirals. Because of the pilot shortage, with JO's bailing out for the airlines or just literally bailing out! Seven of the other sixteen pilots in the squadron, including myself, were Lieutenant Commanders. Where there would normally be three of us as department heads, it was an unusually top heavy distribution of rank to have half the squadron that senior. Since I was a fairly junior LCdr and longtime LSO, I was surprised when George asked me to be the Maintenance Officer. Bear in mind, Mike, only one squadron before us had deployed with A-7's, so significant maintenance personnel and material complications were 'likely, especially in a new squadron. My lack of experience in aircraft maintenance, management or leadership was not enhancing."

"So why were you chosen?"

"I was not George's first choice, I learned, but others had asked to be excused from the job."

"Isn't it unusual for an officer to turn down responsibility to his CO?"

"I would say so. That's why I accepted and glad I did, as it turned out."

"You mean that hot new master management degree of yours paid off?"

"Hell no, I had the great good fortune to have an outstanding mustang Lieutenant as my Assistant Maintenance Officer, John Whidden."

"Mustang?"

"A commissioned officer who came up through the enlisted ranks. Quite rare at that time in the Navy. In fact, I should note that John Whidden was the finest naval officer of any source or rank I ever knew–period. If my education and experience was of any benefit, it was that I was smart enough to give John full scope, keep myself informed, and consistently back him up. Plus, LTV did a fine job of designing and manufacturing the A-7. I believe there were very few Navy jet aircraft which had a more trouble-free history."

"So, you were smelling like a rose at work. How were things at home with you, Aurelie and the Kids?"

"The strains of previous cruises, RPI academics, and isolated off base life in Hanford were harder on Aurelie than I had time to notice. Our disinterest in Navy social life further isolated her and she became more detached and distant. She had good reason to feel the same about me I suppose. No doubt Aurelie's sustaining hope for our future was a quiet and restful shore tour on the East Coast. Now we simply had very little time together and the outlook was bleak for as long as the war continued. Fortunately, David and Christopher were as close as two brothers could be, nearly like twins. Beautiful David, very bright, innocent and good natured, was truly his brother's keeper. Christopher, being a year behind David in school, had a hard act to follow with David's teachers, so he capitalized on his clown-like face and charm and didn't do as well academically. I regret the one time I lost it with Christopher about his poor grades and told him he was going to wind up digging ditches. I had never made such a harsh remark to the kids, so Chris was truly shocked and hurt. But I didn't try to fix it, recognizing that he was a 'chip off the old block' and recalling the negative effects of my parents' lack of interest. Jennifer and Skye were quite separate and different. It wasn't hard to see that Jenny did not approve of Aurelie's house-keeping style and was planning her escape as I had done. She didn't make a fuss about it, nor did she take an active interest in being close to Skye. So, little Skye from cloud nine was pretty much on her own."

"Aurelie still made no objections to you about your relationship?"

"Not in a way that got my attention. Mind you, I wasn't a totally happy camper myself. Although there was no open conflict, physical as well as emotional intimacy was largely absent between us. Four births, two within ten months, Contributed to physical and emotional stress between us. Since there seemed to be no point in railing over unresolvable issues, I maintained a 'that's life' attitude. On to Yankee Station in mid-1968. The war had escalated considerably in 1967. The Christmas Truce, another Johnson naive diplomatic move to bring the North to a peace agreement was used by NVN only to move thousands of vehicles and troops south unhindered by air attacks for the Tet and Khe Sanh offensives to begin their invasion of the South, but in the end, NVN suffered major defeats. More than thirty two thousand enemy troops were killed and six thousand captured, with no territorial gains. More importantly, NVN failed to rally the South Vietnamese populace to their side. We, on the other hand, had long ago learned that the South Vietnamese were to let us do their fighting for them."

"Didn't they appreciate the fact that we were there to help them save themselves, Captain?"

"I doubt it. The South Vietnamese population was mainly focused on survival, not their government. The truth for us, of course, was that we were there in our own national interest to prevent forceful Communist expansion–just as was our purpose in Korea."

"So you guys were fighting your own separate type of war in the North to help defend your GI comrades in the South?"

"McNamara's February '67 statement to the press was that our objectives were to raise South Vietnamese morale, reduce the flow of supplies, and make the North understand the futility of trying to subjugate South Vietnam. The facts were, however, that there were more than 50,000 North Vietnamese troops in the South, five times as many as two years before, at the cost of over 500 fixed wing aircraft costing 1.1 billion dollars, and the loss of more than 200 airmen– without results."

"What were the US military leaders saying?"

"The Administration and military commanders came to realize that the North could continue to fight indefinitely as long as population centers, port facilities, air fields, and agricultural facilities remained off limits. Nevertheless, the prohibition remained against bombing inside a ten mile circle around Hanoi and the major ports could not be bombed or mined. So, in January 1968 some target restrictions in the North were lifted to permit strikes against bridges, railroads, storage depots, and airfields. Nevertheless, the North's determination to fight on was portrayed in propaganda film of them walking bicycles with five hundred pound loads around bomb craters. On the diplomatic front, LBJ and McNamara's continued concept of 'oriental face' was that US bombing pauses would bring them to peace negotiations."

"I still don't get it. Tell me again. What was the Administration's rationale?"

"Simply that if we played nice with them and didn't humiliate them by bombing the hell out of them, they would play nice with us too. Whereas, all that was achieved in North Vietnam's view was that we were admitting we were wrong and they were winning. All the while giving them the time to re-deploy SAMs and AAA, repair the trails, and move great quantities of supplies and troops southward unhindered, totally defeating all we had risked and accomplished before. In addition, the supply of WW2 five hundred pound bombs ran so low that we often launched with half bomb loads, keeping the same number missions because the Admirals were playing with us like boats in a bath tub, competing with the Air Force Generals for sortie rates. Needless to say, the effect on morale and loyalty was devastating, so the exodus of junior aviators to the airlines accelerated, while some undertook crusades with letters to the media and congressmen to no avail. Meanwhile, we paid a high price for our limited effectiveness."

"I recall you saying your squadron lost five of twelve A-7's?"

"Correct. Jim Lee was hit by AAA pulling off a bomb run in the North, but he made it out to the Gulf where he ejected and was rescued safe and sound. He was flying NK 513, the A-7 with his name on it. Someone suggested that thirteen was an unlucky number, so we numbered its replacement 514."

"Was that sort of superstition prevalent in naval aviation?"

"Not more than in other professions, I think. I guess we all tend to have our own good luck charms though. Retiring the 513 number wasn't taken seriously, but the next loss got everyone's attention in a different way. Also pulling off a bomb run in the North, Skipper Pappas took a small round hit near the right wing fuel vent which ignited a small fuel fire, so he was bingoed to Danang rather than risk a larger fire on the flight deck. As he slowed for landing approach, however, the flames grew and during rollout on the runway the fire engulfed the airplane, forcing George to eject. The ejection was successful and George was uninjured, but the airplane continued off the end of the runway into an Air Force hanger destroying it and several airplanes. George was flying 501—with his name on it."

"Wow, two downed planes in a row—like bullets with the pilots' names on them! I don't suppose anyone proposed retiring the names, did they?"

"Not hardly practical to retire the Skipper's name, was it Mike?"

"If I remember correctly, you explained before that squadron aircraft were traditionally named and numbered according to pilot seniority with the first of the three digits assigned to all squadron aircraft. In other words, all VA-27 aircraft were five hundred series with the CO 501, the XO 502 and so on down the line. I think you also said that there was no special significance to it other than the prestige of having your name on 'your' airplane, and there was a one in twelve chance on any given flight that a pilot flew 'his' airplane. Therefore, the odds of losing two airplanes in a row flown by their namesakes must have been astronomical!"

"Agreed. Not even an RPI statistics professor could compute those odds. But it gets better, Mike. Suppose I told you that all five of the A-7's we lost on that cruise were being flown by the pilot with his name on it and that the same thing happened to the A-6 Intruder squadron aboard?"

"I'd say that such an occurrence was way beyond coincidence and downright providential. It had to be some kind of omen or message from the Almighty, but what was the message? How did you all feel about it?"

"It's hard to say how the other aviators felt since it was not discussed much beyond acknowledging that it might be 'bad luck' to fly your airplane."

"No kidding! I should say so. It is truly astonishing to me that a Ripley's 'Believe it or not' event didn't even inspire discussion, if not a policy against assigning an aircraft to the named pilot."

"I'd say that we put the odds in the category of a catapult or arresting gear failure, a highly unlikely event which we had no control over. Other threats involving some degree of pilot skill were more likely and if you were going to be shot down it didn't much matter whose name was on the airplane, did it? Still, I believe that an effort was made by our maintenance crews and Duty Officers to help us avoid flying our named airplane."

"What was your reaction?"

"One stormy night I was the spare for a four plane launch and the way the aircraft were spotted on the flight deck left no choice but to assign me to 'my' A-7, NK 506. After start up, I noted that the standby compass light was out. Stand by compasses were primitive wet magnetic compasses mounted high over the instrument panel for use only as a backup for several other electronic and gyro compasses. So, although the burned out light was a legitimate down gripe for a night flight, it was highly unlikely that any pilot would abort a flight because of one. Nevertheless, when one of the go airplanes cancelled for a maintenance discrepancy and I was to be launched in its place, I did not hesitate to follow suit and gave the plane captain a thumbs down. I was very lucky to dodge a lot of close calls in life, but I couldn't see going up against this one. I felt no guilt for canceling, then or now. The only interpretation of the omen I needed was, don't fly the airplane with your name on it into combat."

"Did anyone consider removing the names from all the airplanes?"

"I doubt it. It just wouldn't have been an acceptable or effective reaction for us to try to hide."

"Other than that, how was life in an A-7 squadron compared to the F-4 squadrons you flew with?"

"Quite different in important positive ways. We were closer because there were half the number of aircrew members. We flew single-crew single-engine airplanes, often in four plane formations in coordination with eight or twelve other attack airplanes and we 'moved mud' instead of grinding around in circles in spread out pairs. We were less colorful, but more professional and there was less rancor among us. Of course in the JO's eyes, Lieutenant Commander department heads, were set apart in the mid-grade 'menopause' career phase, although my prior F-4 combat experience gave me some credibility. Even so, it's not so simple for them to be friends with officers who are writing your fitness reports."

"Did your A-7's hold up well?"

"Very well indeed. John Whidden's leadership and the A-7A's excellent reliability allowed us to fly an amazing average of thirty-one missions a day on the line for the entire cruise still flying noon to midnight for two weeks then midnight to noon."

"So with eighteen pilots you were averaging one point seven flights a day, including briefing, debriefing and manning spares, plus time with demanding collateral duty responsibilities. Doesn't sound like much time for relaxation?"

"True. I don't recall the line periods being as long. Our night road recce tactics evolved to working with the more effective A-6 'TRIM' aircraft which had low light level TV and infra-red sensors, in addition to moving target indicators on their radar. Because the A-6's were not highly accurate bombers, they were armed with cluster bombs, CBU's, which scattered hand grenade size bomblets over a wide area. The tactic was for single A-6's to patrol the roads at low altitude while the A-7's in pairs orbited in assigned areas at high altitude. If an A-6 located a truck, a CBU was released. Even a single bomblet hit was enough to stop a truck and start a fire, bringing the convoy to a halt and marking their location for the A-7's to follow up with five hundred pound bombs."

"Sounds good, did it work?"

"Although the A-6 sensors' effectiveness was limited by high humidity, trees, and slow movers, I believe they limited truck convoy movement at night; however, I heard of only a few instances of bombing success. CBU's might have been better used by A-7's against troops, supplies, and anti-aircraft sites, but they were too expensive and scarce for allocation beyond the A-6's which needed the CBU's scatter."

"What did you do on those night missions after milling around for an hour without A-6 success? You couldn't return to the ship with bombs, could you?"

"We were assigned secondary targets—trans-shipment points, river crossings, road intersections, and suspected storage sites to bomb on our own before returning, but we gave little credibility to these stale assignments. We regarded all sparsely populated areas in North Vietnam to be hostile 'Indian country' where a bomb was equally unlikely to cause damage wherever it was dropped. So, I occasionally pickled off a bomb just to wake 'em up."

"Is that all the success you had, Captain?"

"Yes, as far as I know. We had little bomb damage assessment. BDA, especially at night in the North since we had no one on the ground to provide feedback. In coordinated strikes we were in and off strikes so high and fast we scarcely saw targets, much less discern the damage. Aerial photos just showed craters on top of old craters. I was credited with eight KIA's by a forward air controller on a strafing run against NVN troops in Laos, but I discounted it as part of the political emphasis on inflated 'body counts'. Except for the AAA, SAM and Mig threats, the whole business was entirely impersonal for us and with the low value targets became simply a survival exercise. The only time I know for certain that I caused any damage was on one of those night road recce flights with the A-6's. It was a rare occasion where A-7's carried seven hundred and fifty pound bombs with air burst fuses which were normally allocated to the B-52's for Laos strikes. As usual, there had been no road action that night and it was time to return to Constellation. It was a clear starlit night with no moon, so I just looked for an aim point, not a target, and saw stars reflected on a sharp bend in a river outlining a peninsula. So I rolled in on it, released all six bombs and pulled off to the right, heading east for the ship without bothering to watch the bomb bursts. Soon, I saw a bright orange flash in my left rearview mirror and turned to see a series of huge explosions visible all the way to the ship sixty miles offshore as well as by all the other A-7 pilots who also rolled in on it. Obviously, by pure blind luck, I had bombed an ammunition dump!"

"Good for you, Captain, that must have made you quite a celebrity?"

"Not quite, Mike. For the most part, the naval aviators I knew were honorable men, but not all of them. The XO landed before me and took the credit."

"How could he get away with that? Didn't the others in the air know better?"

"I had made no voice transmissions whatever about the event, nevertheless, it was surely obvious to Lynn that someone had preceded him in setting it off. But who could say? He simply seized the opportunity and I wasn't going to be the one to publicly humiliate my boss. The satisfaction was mine, though I hadn't done anything extraordinary, so I saw nothing to gain from it. I was disappointed in Lynn, but not surprised. I suppose he was under pressure to follow in his daddy's footsteps. I later collected a lot more than I would have gained by making a fuss over nothing."

"More to come on that, I assume. Are there other war stories to tell about this cruise?"

"Just one more. Johnson declared that we were to stop bombing north of the twentieth parallel. So, all our efforts and losses for the past four years were flushed. With the restrictive Rules of Engagement imposed on us which severely limited our effectiveness, it was just as well to cut our losses if we were not seriously going to try to win this half-assed war. Johnson added the face saving provision that we would continue to fly reconnaissance missions over the North and by God we would make them sorry if they shot at us? Another of the many of LBJ's grossly stupid mistakes guaranteeing the humiliation of the US Presidency and US failure in Vietnam. What sane person could believe that the North would be persuaded to talk peace by such a weak dumb-ass President?"

"But weren't you greatly relieved to stop flying bombing missions further north?"

"Not greatly. To a degree, I had become emotionally callous to the threats. Missions had become almost routine and I sometimes lit a cigarette. I recall once launching before dawn during monsoon season. My wing man was delayed, so while I circled waiting for him to join up I looked out across the limitless ocean to the east at daybreak. The sky, clouds, and sea were as pristinely beautiful and peaceful as on the dawn of creation with no evidence of man's strife. The contrasting view over land to the west was one of darkness, storms, lightning, explosions, chaos, destruction and death. To the East, beauty, hope, love, elation, innocence, and faith. To the West, despair, horror, hate, depression, and anger. Then my wing man joined, so we dove into the storms to the West and made our contribution to the chaos and destruction."

"A dramatic contrast between the dawn of God's creation and of man's modification which I suppose stunned many combat aircrews over the years. World War Two bomber crews launching before daybreak in England must have watched the sun rise serenely in the Channel before all hell broke loose over Europe, with little hope of surviving the mission. Did you believe you would survive?"

"It had stopped being a conscious factor for me, not that I felt invulnerable. I suppose I felt my fate was not in my hands, other than making night carrier landings safely. But back to my war story. It was the last launch on a midnight to noon schedule. My wing man and I were RESCAP, Rescue Combat Air Patrol, for an RA-5 Vigilante photo plane, escorted by four F- 4's for a mission over Vinh. We were armed to the hilt with guns, bombs and missiles which significantly handicapped flight performance, but we were to hold offshore with two A-3 tankers unless the A-5 or an F-4 was downed. The pilot of the RA-5 was Ernie Stamm, a past acquaintance from the Ticonderoga '60 cruise. The ship was well south of the usual Yankee Station near the

DMZ, so we joined up on Ernie to have our picture taken as we all headed north in the Gulf. RA-5's cruised so fast in basic engine at low altitude during their photo run that the F-4's had to use afterburner to keep up. So, fuel capacity was a limiting factor for the fighters. Vinh was an inland town in the southerly part of the North in a flat densely populated agricultural area heavily defended by three SAM sites and more than 150 37 and 57 millimeter AAA guns. I don't know why Vinh was considered important by either side, but many Navy aircraft were shot down there. That day was no exception. Ernie was hit by AAA and immediately went down very near the town. We heard an emergency beeper, indicating that at least one of the two of them had ejected, but it seemed hopeless that they could escape capture or be rescued that close to population and without cover. The F-4's quickly declared bingo fuel and beat feet for the ship, leaving me in charge as the On-scene Commander with my wing man, now the only two US airplanes airborne over the North for this rescue mission. Since there was no follow-on launch scheduled, we could not expect backup. Although rescue seemed hopeless, I felt there was no choice but to try as long as we had a beeper, so I told the search and rescue destroyer to launch the hello and hold him just offshore for further direction. As we went 'feet dry' at the coast, we clearly saw the smoke of the A-5 wreckage rising straight up to 35,000 feet on that clear windless day. Suddenly, I recalled my 1950 conversation with God in the Bavarian woods near Augsburg when I agreed to sacrificing my life for a fellow aviator in combat in return for ten years of flying. 1956 to 1968, I got a two year bonus but I realized today was payback time."

"How did that effect you?"

"If anything, the thought committed me to pressing on. I had been so blessed, how could I refuse? Like the Italian flight student's helmet, *'Que sera sera'*. To build speed and get down to where we could see Stan and his crewman, we descended to four thousand feet, the altitude where he had just been shot down and in the middle of the AAA envelope. As we passed over the wreckage in a right turn, wing man on my left, I heard a loud whoosh and saw the smoke trail of a SAM pass directly between us, close enough to blow us both out of the air if it had fused. I rolled out of the turn and saw the second SAM coming up. The only maneuver left to us was to roll hard right to near inverted and pull as much as I dared for the ground. This meant getting down in the weeds into the AAA guns and losing sight of the SAM and just waiting for the outcome. It missed us, thank the Lord. We then climbed out for the coast unscathed. Since we had no SAM radar warning or jamming, we concluded that the SAM's had been optically guided. Why the fuses had failed was purely providential. We still heard a beeper when we reached the coast at twenty-five thousand feet, which meant going back for another try. As we returned with the helo still standing by offshore, the beeper went off the air and we heard Big Look give a Bandit (Mig) warning southeast of Bulls Eye (Hanoi) on guard channel. I disregarded it, but my wing man suggested that the warning was intended for us; however, the South SAR destroyer controller said it was not. The next transmission from the Big Look EC-121 offshore was very clear, 'Two A-7's over Vinh, you have five Migs fifty miles northwest, closing fast'. I asked our controller if there we had fighters airborne, but the reply was 'wait one'. Then our SAM warning and jamming gear came alive indicating a SAM launch. My alert wing man fired a radar homing Walleye missile and we broke hard right as the controller issued a 'recall' directive to confirm my decision to abort further rescue attempts and get the hell out of Dodge. There was no way two heavily loaded A-7A's were going to win this battle alone. Apparently our radar jamming or wing man's missile worked, the SAM went stupid and self-detonated high above us. In dodging it, however, wing man became detached and we were switched to new frequencies. By this time we were too low on fuel to get home, so we were depending on the two A-3 tankers. However, they were also recalled and switched to a different radio frequency and were hauling butt ahead of us for the ship, leaving us unable to speak to them or find them. Somehow, we each separately found an A-3. Initially, neither of them was willing to slow to refueling speed, but frantic hand, thumb and finger gestures got our messages across and we landed safely."

"What a day, Captain. I expect you had a few questions at the debriefing about the poor planning, fighter support, or coordination?"

"No, there was no debriefing or review, at least not at my level. I was unaware of any discussion of the fiasco whatever. I hope that at least the press back home made enough of an announcement to rub Johnson's face in the dirt, as he so well deserved for his spineless stupidity. Personally, I was so grateful that the SAM hadn't fused and God got me through it without calling in our ten year agreement that the rest seemed insignificant to me."

"I understand, kinda like your near train collision incident what's done was done. Do you know what happened to the A-5 crew?"

"We only knew that at least one of them ejected and was presumably captured. The NVN probably kept the beeper operating to lure us in for more target practice. It wasn't until repatriation of the POWs in 1973 that we learned that the crewman did not eject. Ernie was captured, but he was so badly burned that he was transferred to a Hanoi hospital. According to their report, two weeks later Ernie insisted on shaving his burned face with a rusty razor blade and died of a staph infection."

"What a shame. Were there no improvements incorporated in subsequent photo missions?"

"I don't recall, but I think the number of missions tapered off. A-5's were unsuccessful, unreliable and accident prone airplanes which occupied more deck space than they were worth. Plus, photos were of marginal value, since the bombing halt the North made no secret of building up troops and supplies southward toward the DMZ which allowed them to divert some of the traffic from the long haul in Laos and devote more large AAA guns to defend the trails. In other words, the North had succeeding in pushing us back, while political deterioration continued in the South, assuring our humiliation in everyone's view. Naturally, the South remained content to let us do all the fighting, failing and dying for them."

"Well then, Captain, would you care to shift to a more cheery subject like life ashore?"

"Good idea, but let's close this chapter and start afresh tomorrow after your flight, alright?"

"Yes, I probably won't be back until late, so can we plan to meet after dinner?"

"Sure Mike, Call to confirm."

"The weather forecast is favorable, so wish me luck."

"Happy landings, Mike."

VA-27 'Royal Maces'

STATUS: established as Attack Squadron (VA-27) on September 1, 1967
Ling-Temco-Vought A-7A Corsair II (1969-70)

DEPLOYMENTS: May 1968 - January 1969 with CVW-14 aboard USS Constellation (CVA 64)

A7-A Corsair II, was the first version of the A-7
VA-27 was the second A-7 squadron deployed to Vietnam, 1968

The initial contract, N0w-0363f, specified a total of 199 airplanes to be designated the A-7A. Design work began immediately and first flight took place in September 1965, only 18 months after the winner was announced. This is a record unequaled by any other modern military jet aircraft program. To add to its fine performance in the design program, LTV delivered the first A-7A to an operational Navy squadron in September 1966, only 12 months after

first flight, another record which has never been equaled and is not likely to be.

Powered by the Navy-chosen Pratt & Whitney TF-30P6 non-afterburning engine which delivered 11,350 pounds thrust an weighed a mere 14,857 pounds, this sturdy little "bomb truck" could carry as much as 10,200 of pounds of fuel, which would allow it to stay in the air for over 12 hours! The normal weapon load was around 15,000 pounds, which was carried on eight store stations, but the A-7A demonstrated the capability to carry 20,000 pounds of ordnance. An incredible mix of weapons and fuel loading produced varying radius-of-action capabilities within its 42,000-pound gross weight

23

VIETNAM 1968: LETTER FROM HOME

"Hello, Mike. Cheated death again I see."

"Please, treat a fellow pilot with more respect!"

"Congratulations! How did it go?"

"There was such a strong gusty crosswind, no one else was flying, but the Examiner didn't suggest canceling, so I pressed on with the briefing. Of course, he caught me on a few academic items during the briefing, but the takeoff was OK, considering that the wind conditions were the worst I have flown in. There was a lot of turbulence as we climbed out, so it was challenging to plan the cross country flight he surprised me with and fly the airplane too, with a pencil in my mouth and charts and calculator falling off my lap–all the while, as you say, 'fighting snakes' with the stick against the turbulence. I figured the Examiner was testing my multitasking ability and remembered you saying that flying the airplane is always the first priority. So I dragged out the flight planning until he finally cancelled the task. After a few stalls, he asked me to demonstrate a slip. I admitted that I had never done one and asked him to demonstrate. After I did several and really got into it with nearly ninety degrees of bank and full top rudder for a five hundred foot altitude loss, he had enough and we headed back to the field for touch and go landings. If the crosswind and turbulence was bad on takeoff, it far worse when we returned. I was literally hitting the stops with the controls on the first approach and the Examiner asked if I would like to terminate the flight and try another day. I replied that whether or not we completed the flight exam, as long as we were airborne it was a million dollars' worth of experience for me to continue with him aboard. He said he appreciated my spirit, so we completed the flight without breaking anything and he signed me off!"

"Atta boy, Mike. Good show, well done. Thanks for making me proud of you. I'm happy that one of my decedents has finally shown an interest in aviation."

"Thanks, Captain. If you had been there seventy years ago, I would have had an earlier start."

"Perhaps, Mike, but seventy years ago I couldn't have been around much and my life was so tumultuous I might have been little value to you."

"I believe that takes us back to the 1968 cruise and personal domestic developments? From what you have told me, you may have denied the cumulative traumatic effects of your missions. The significance of the Vinh SAR mission with the SAM near miss trauma had to have taken an emotional toll. No one can simply brush off years of combat. Plus, weren't you at the ripe age for a mid-life crisis?"

"Maybe, Mike, but I was more conscious of feeling that nothing we were doing in Vietnam had any support from home. Not just the politicians and protesters, I mean my home! By then, it was obvious that Aurelie had no positive interest or concern with anything to do with aviation, Vietnam, or the Navy, and I was nearly a stranger to my kids. So what the hell was I doing there? An answer came in the mail."

"A letter from Aurelie?"

"Yes. As during prior cruises, I had once again pleaded with her to explain the significance of her family's 1950 US visit. On returning to Munich, she was an emotional basket case, but would never discuss it. I only knew it had something to do with a confrontation with her father."

"That's all she would say?"

"Yes, except that she would never see him again."

"That was eighteen years before, five years before you were married. Why was it so important for you to dredge that matter up?"

"It's true we weren't married then, but we were very seriously engaged. I just intuitively knew it was an important missing element in our twenty year relationship–and I was right."

"The recorder and I are all ears, Captain."

"Aurelie's explanation was so lengthy that she took two letters to tell it, but receiving part two before part one greatly magnified the devastating effect on me. The 'punch line' arrived twenty-four hours before the joke! Anyhow, here's the story in proper order. After these many years of family damnation caused by Aurelie's version of the truth after the split, I want my day in court. You'll understand why in future chapters."

"Fair enough, Captain. You have my promise, but why have you waited fifty eight years to speak out?"

"What would have been the point? I was out of the picture and Aurelie was going to have to raise the kids, who were too young to understand anyhow. Besides, there were to be other extenuating developments. I'm telling it now because it was a major event in my history."

"So what was in the letters?"

"First a brief review to put it in perspective. In Munich, Helen, believed I wasn't worthy of her brilliant daughter, so she tried to break us up by telling my parents I was 'seeing Aurelie too much' and asked them to discourage it. My father, bless his heart, blew off Helen by telling her that was a matter between her and Aurelie. I was angry with Helen, but thought little more about it. All during our six year courtship, Aurelie and I refrained from sex by mutual agreement, nor had I with anyone else before your mother in 1955.Since Aurelie's stepfather, Clayton, was a high grade State Department official in the provisional government in Munich, the family was entitled to annual summer vacations in the US. Aurelie's letter about the 1950 summer revealed that Helen arranged for Aurelie and her first cousin to have a car for the two of them to tour New England for three weeks–screwing their brains out. The crisis came at the end of the trip when they visited Aurelie's father, where to her astonishment, the cousin declared his love for Aurelie and asked for her hand in marriage!"

"I take it Daddy did not react kindly to his daughter's marriage to her first cousin at age sixteen?"

"Evidently not. He reportedly went into extreme rage, calling Aurelie and Helen whores, plus every other name he could think of, and threw them out."

"Aurelie blamed her father for being upset?"

"Sure, that's what women do, isn't it? It's always men's fault."

"Of course, but why wait twenty years to tell you?"

"Exactly, Mike. She probably figured that for me that would be the finish of our marriage.

"I'm not quite following you. Your own infidelity could hardly qualify you to judge. I don't understand why such an ancient event was to be a marriage-ender?"

"That's what others said, Mike, so I gave up explaining. No one except the two people directly involved can make valid judgments about what happens inside marriages.

"The crucial factor for me had nothing to do with infidelity. The issue was honesty. If Aurelie had leveled the field with me when I married Emma, Aurelie's episode would have been long forgotten. Moreover, I recognized that Aurelie finally revealed the story to me as her way of initiating the divorce she wanted. I was being dumped."

"Then why wait until you were eight thousand miles away in the middle of a war?"

"Why do you suppose?"

"She didn't have the guts to confront you directly in person with a divorce request before you left?"

"Isn't that the way it goes? Don't wives typically find indirect ways to motivate their unwanted husbands to leave while making him appear as the villain to the kids, court, and neighborhood? To contain the event, Aurelie had isolated herself socially at Lemoore and waited until I was far away. Society might be unsympathetic to a mother of four small children who would voluntarily abandon financial security without reasonable justification, right?"

"Still, how did she know what your reaction would be?"

"Ah, an insightful question, Mike. It went back to when I told Aurelie that Emma was pregnant and that I had no choice but to marry her. Despite my father's advice never to see Aurelie again because she would hold Emma over me ever after, I felt compelled to deliver a personal apology. When I saw her, however, I was overwhelmed by Aurelie's positive attitude and steadfast devotion. All was forgiven and she was going to Pensacola too!"

"Weren't you a little uneasy with that turn of events?"

"Of course. I should have asked her to wait until I was free, but I expected to be single shortly after your November birth, as your mother promised since the marriage was only for the sake of legitimacy, she said. Besides, we had already waited six years and I had put Aurelie through enough, including weeks in a psychiatrists care when I married Emma. Plus, there was no suggestion that we would live together in Pensacola and I couldn't stop her from going. My purpose in reviewing those events with you was that I had faced the music with Aurelie, so that was the time Aurelie should have been openly honest with me about her affair, instead of letting me bear the burden of guilt all those years. The only difference between us was that Aurelie hadn't become pregnant by her cousin. Instead, she chose to let me believe she was a forgiving saint, worthy of the high pedestal I put her on for fourteen years of marriage."

"All that while placing your unworthy self at her feet. So, having deceived you through the years, despite your repeated questioning, and was in fact far less than the saint she let you worship, you felt the worst kind of deeply dishonest betrayal."

"Good, Mike, I am glad you understand my "point, even if you don't sympathize."

"Didn't you express all that to Aurelie?"

"Of course, over and over in twenty page nightly letters for the rest of the cruise with no attempt on her part to engage in a dialogue, much less acknowledge my feelings."

"What do you suppose Aurelie's side of the story would be?"

"I believe she would say that I was away too much and not really there when at home. She'd say that we had never been close since we were married and that the sex was infrequent and lousy. She'd say that she hated the Navy moves to Florida, Texas and California and she missed New England. She'd say that she had nothing in common with Navy wives and that the Vietnam Conflict was wrong. She'd say that the affair with her cousin was personal to her, not my business, and that I only told her about Emma because it was unavoidable. She'd say that what happened before we were married was irrelevant. She would most surely re-invent history, as she did to the kids, and say that I abandoned the family to run off with a Chinese whore."

"Where did the whore part come from?"

"Providence stepped in on our next port visit to Hong Kong. To escape depression aboard ship, I took leave and shared a hotel room with Mel, my shipboard roommate. I was treating myself to a Hilton hair cut the first afternoon when a Chief Petty Officer took the barber chair next to me. Something about him reminded me of myself. He seemed to be quietly alone, out of place in a bubble just passing through life. It struck me that there was something to the meno- pausal image JO's had of guys our age. The sad realization of what I recognized in the Chief was that I was out of place -not just overseas but at home too. I was in a dangerous tunnel with no light at the end."

"Then how did providence step in?"

"Mel, a reserved and dedicated family man, and I stood on the sidelines of the Hilton recep- tion that night and returned to our hotel room before midnight and poured ourselves scotch on the rocks. Our room faced an apartment building close across the back street where a good bit of activity attracted our attention. Hong Kong residents seemed to never sleep or stop eating. Each apartment was brightly lit with no curtains, so we had a clear view of Chinese home life, as though we were watching a dozen TV soap operas. It was a pleasant relief for us to be away from our eight by ten windowless steel Connie stateroom, so we enjoyed the distinctive outdoor sounds and smells of Hong Kong by opening our windows and blinds. It was so warm and humid, however, that we turned off the lights and stripped down to our skivvies."

"What scenes did you Peeping Toms spy on?"

"A boisterous mahjong game was going. Movement of the tiles is so noisy and the players so loudly emotional that there was a law prohibiting the game after midnight; however, it was so popular that the law was routinely ignored and rarely enforced. There were several other apart- ments with families gathered around watching television. Two other apartments attracted most of our attention though. In one, a girl in a negligee sat before her vanity mirror brushing her long black hair. At another apartment, a young girl made repeated entrances at about thirty minute intervals to change clothes and leave again."

"Fascinating. What do you suppose she was doing?"

"Our best guesses were that she was either a model or a hooker, but there was no conclu- sive evidence either way. In any event, our conjectures were interrupted by our telephone. Mel answered and a girl said, 'Why are you two guys standing in the window with your clothes off!'"

"Busted! Who was it? How did she know your room number?"

"Mel had no luck getting answers, so he passed the phone to me. I had no more success and she hung up. We put our pants on and went back to the window looking for clues, but nothing had changed across the street. The girl didn't seem to have a Chinese accent, so we wondered if the call may have come from an adjacent room in our hotel. We finally gave up and went to bed"

"That wasn't such an overly providential occurrence, was it?"

"Patience, my lad. There's more. The next morning I went shopping and returned to the room at noon. Again I opened the windows and blinds to watch the busy street activity below and peruse the apartments. Behold, the girl on the sixth floor was still in her negligee brushing her hair, so I chose to linger awhile. In a few minutes she came to her open window and leaned out to watch the street activity too. The distance between us prevented a valid assessment, but she seemed to be an attractive young lady, so when she glanced my way, I waved, but she ducked back into her apartment. After a while, she returned dressed and I waved again. This time I held her attention and with hand signals asked her to telephone my room, 406. When I answered, I was surprised to hear a different voice and accent than the previous night's caller, but the conversation went so well that I invited her to lunch. She said it was well past lunch time and I noted that my watch had stopped. The bedside clock indicated it was midafternoon. I was fumbling for ideas when she asked where I was going for lunch. Just the hotel dining room, I said, still struggling for plan B when she floored me by suggesting that I should go to lunch and then come up to her apartment."

"Now I'm seeing the hand of Providence, Captain, but since you were getting dumped by your wife and feeling over the hill, I don't suppose you followed through, did you?"

"I had read Carlos Castaneda's 'Journey to Ixtlan' about his adventures in the Arizona Desert with a Yaqui Indian shaman named Don Juan Matus who taught Carlos about 'nagual' non-ordinary reality and awareness of the omens and messages which constantly surrounded us. Though Casteneda's books are now presumed to be fictitious, the Indian's lessons rang true to me in the 60's and raised my own awareness of spiritual signs of direction in the events of my life–most recently my encounter with the SAM over Vinh recalling my Munich conversation with God, plus my fifteen year quest for Aurelie's explanation of her 1950 summer. In lesser ways too. My fellow LSO's said I could 'smell one coming before a landing approach became dangerous. I had therefore learned to take messages and omens seriously and I generally followed their road signs. It wasn't the event itself, but the timing was surely not a coincidence"

"All this by way of rationalizing why you accepted a strange lady's invitation to her apartment?"

"You bet, Mike. I damn near choked on a club sandwich before running across the street and didn't notice the elevator before rocketing up six flights of stairs. The astonishing sight that greeted me when the door opened took my remaining breath away. There, standing before me in a skin-tight slit-skirt turquoise embroidered silk cheong sam dress was the most gorgeous and perfectly formed girl I ever saw firsthand. I say 'girl' because she had to be in her teens. She was obviously Eurasian, combining the most attractive features of both cultures. As I struggled to get my breath and regain composure, I introduced myself. She said her name was Maria Chan. As her elderly Chinese housekeeper served us tea at the couch, I noted that her spacious apartment was first class by any standards. Maria was obviously doing very well for herself, so of course I wondered how such a young Hong Kong girl could afford such luxury unless she were a 'working girl'. Yet, there was nothing about her appearance or manner which suggested that she was a bar girl. If she were a 'kept' mistress, it was unlikely that she would have invited me up. Unless she was in show business, there were virtually no other professions open to women, much less teenagers, in oriental cultures in 1968. Though English was not her first language, nor did she seem well educated, her exceptional grace and charm more than compensated. Above all, the genuine innocence and warmth of her sparkling eyes and bright smile lit up her perfect complexion and beautiful face. After I apologized for my forward behavior, explaining about the prior evening's event, I risked asking her what she did. Maria beamed when she explained that she was an actress at Shore Brothers studio. Maria Chan was her stage name, her real name was Nazira Begum. She said she'd had the lead in four feature films. I must admit that I was skeptical, so I told her I was in the movies too, that we were shooting a James Bond film and I was a stand-in stunt man for Sean Connery. I meant to be facetious, but she bought it! 'Oh yes, I see', she said, 'You look like him and the hair on your arms is the same.' Then she proudly showed me her album of studio still photos, as well as an issue of *Cavalier* magazine with a featured fold-out full length reclining nude portrait of her! She said the Shore Brothers studio had asked her to sign a twelve year contract to do a series of television Mandarin traditional soap operas, which meant a 24/7 cloistered studio grounds dormitory training regimen to teach her the classical Chinese theater moves, dances, and acting styles."

"So, Captain, you were the phony actor, not Nazira."

"Yeah, my act didn't translate well, so I asked for her gracious acceptance of my apology and explanation of why I was really in Hong Kong. She was easy on me."

"So, since you were old enough to be her father, you did the honorable thing and took your leave?"

"Somehow my age and depression didn't seem so severely oppressive, so I invited her to dinner. What harm could come of that? After all, what interest could she have in a guy my age in town for only a few days? Plus, she was seeing stars with a bright acting career ahead. Anyhow, I had more than enough on my plate already."

"Sounds like ripe conditions for a mid-life crisis to me, Captain."

"Perhaps Aurelie's mid-life crisis? I was seeing faint light at the end of my tunnel. At dinner Nazira explained that her father was from Pakistan. Her mother was Portuguese and Chinese from Macao, a Portuguese colony near Hong Kong. Nazira was the youngest of four daughters who were driving their traditional Muslim father crazy in the rapidly modernizing and fast-paced cosmopolitan life of Hong Kong, especially with so many Vietnam GI's in town on R&R. Nazira's mother, on the other hand, was having a wonderful time living vicariously in the lives of her girls, all four of whom were equally as gorgeous as Nazira, though in much different ways. The eldest, Hameda, had been married to a Dutch ship-broker in Singapore and then married into one of the four watch-manufacturing families in Switzerland. The second, Rashida, managed a jewelry factory in Hong Kong and was married to a British civil servant in the Colonial Government's Special Branch, an intelligence agency somewhat similar to our CIA. The third daughter, Sukina, was engaged to an Air Force Major F-4 pilot West Point Graduate. Nazira said that she was considered the 'black sheep' of the family. Her show business career began at age eleven as a magician's assistant in an Australian's night club act. When the Australian indicated that he wanted to take Nazira with him on the road throughout the Orient, her father believed that Nazira intended to run away with him. Somehow, her father succeeded in having her locked up in a juvenile facility, even though she had committed no crime. Nazira explained that she was devastated since she didn't know what she had done wrong or why her parents never came to visit her. So, she escaped and survived on the-rooftops of Wan Chai, the most depressed district, for several months before she was captured and returned to the facility with an extended sentence. Soon, however, she escaped again- with the same results and spent over five years in jail before finally being released only a little more than two years before."

"What a story! Nazira must have despised her parents for locking her away and ignoring her during those most formative years."

"You would think so, nevertheless, she loved her parents very much. I didn't detect a trace of lingering resentment. Still, Nazira did have mixed feelings about signing over twelve more years of her freedom to a movie studio, regardless of the enticement of glamorous rewards."

"But what were her options? As you say, other than marriage or the bar girl life, there were no other choices open to her."

"Nazira's experience in Won Chai taught her that at best the economic life of a single girl did not extend past age thirty- no longer marriage material and left with no marketable skills. She had the same concerns about a movie career. Few Chinese or Muslim women age well, so she recognized that she had to cash in on her looks quickly."

"But didn't it seem a bit odd that she was doing so well financially after only three films?"

"Yes if did. I wondered if perhaps her parents were well off and were compensating for the jail time they had subjected her to, but Nazira said her father was a chauffeur for a wealthy Chinese widow and her mother did not work. Part of the mystery was explained after dinner when Nazira took me to her bar."

"Her bar? She was a bar girl after all?"

"No, a bar owner–actually, only half owner. Nazira's explanation was that she had been given half ownership in exchange for her regular appearance there only to attract customers and lead the other girls, nothing else. Keep in mind, Mike, that girls worked for the bars to earn commissions from the drinks they sold. They were on their own with their private lives, except the bar had to be paid for the girls' absence from work, either by the boyfriend or herself. Nazira was a special case, not only for her beauty and personality, but moreover because she was 'Eurasian."

"Why did that make her so special?"

"In those days, Hong Kong women who had the slightest trace of something other than Chinese ancestry claimed that as their nationality. This was typical if there was any Macao

Portuguese blood in the family history, no matter how far back. Nancy Kwan, a beautiful Eurasian actress in the 60's, made a movie with William Holden set in Hong Kong, 'The World of Suzie Wong'. The story line was an Oriental girl's hopeless romance with a Westerner, typical of every bar girl in Hong Kong. So Suzie Wong remained their all-time favorite heroine. Nazira had all the right stuff to soon become the next Suzie Wong."

"I see, she was wise enough to know that her best long term option was be married and out of Hong Kong while in her prime, as her sisters had done, probably with a lot of coaching by their mother. Didn't you see yourself as a potential candidate, Captain?"

"No. I was just a burned out, battle weary, rejected, and depressed fighter pilot who wasn't thinking with his brain."

"Well, this wasn't so much different from your prior escapades. From what I remember of being thirty-six, you may be exaggerating, except for the brain malfunction. I see that you are not going to tell me that you bade Nazira farewell after dinner and returned to the ship, are you?"

"Sure I am, except you skipped over a couple of parts. Nazira asked if I would like to visit her bar. Out of curiosity, I accepted. After all, how often does one get an insider view of such places? It was a small plain dimly lit bar with just room for the bar, eight booths and four tables. From the warm excited greeting she got from the eight very presentable girls in their twenties, it was plain to see that Nazira was a very popular and in-charge partner. Since it was early evening and there were no customers, we pushed the tables together and I had the gang to myself. Big Spender bought the drinks and Mona,' the mama-San bartender, joined us. I could see that the ladies were genuinely having fun. Nothing could have cheered me up more."

"Great, Captain. So what was the second part I skipped? You say that nothing could have cheered you up more?"

"Oh, you're a sly devil, Michael. OK, so when I escorted Nazira back to her apartment, I saw that her house-keeper had turned her bed down, which seemed to be a sign of approval, so what else could a gentleman do? I didn't make it back to the hotel until ¢he next morning."

"Didn't you tell her you were married?"

"Yes, though it was obvious. I had removed my ring in reaction to Aurelie's mail, but the fourteen years of wear was plain to see. Plus, it turned out that Nazira was an incredible fortune teller. Using Tarot cards that evening, she recounted amazing details of what had happened with Aurelie, as well as the obstacles ahead."

"What were your expectations?"

"I had no idea, but it was a more serious encounter than I anticipated. I had to return to the ship in the morning for the day, so I told Nazira I would call her later. But when I called late afternoon, there was no one home. Dinner time came and went and I ordered room service. It was after midnight when the phone finally rang. It was Mona and she was with Nazira. Mona explained that Nazira feared her developing serious feelings for me and felt it best not to see me again. Mona, however, was encouraging her to hang on to the chance that things might work out and asked if she would bring Nazira to see me, if that was agreeable."

"Agreeable, meaning that you was willing to take a chance on the future too. How could you make such a major and risky decision with someone you had known less than twenty-four hours?"

"Snap life or death decisions were not new to me. Divorce seemed certain, whether I liked it or not. My gut reaction was to go for the gusto since there was more to be gained than lost with far less risk than I was facing in the skies."

"What in the world were you thinking? Weren't you conscious of the distinct religious, cultural, language, and educational chasms between you, not to mention the age difference? What if she wanted children? Were you prepared to spend the rest of your life raising kids? What about Navy's reaction? Would you and a Hong Kong teenager who apparently broke up a marriage with four kids be acceptable in NAS Lemoore Navy society? I cannot imagine anyone making life more difficult for themselves, Captain."

"I wasn't blind to the obstacles, Mike, nor was I blinded by love. I had been around the block before in matters of the heart. I also recognized that Nazira was very pragmatic and probably had even less notion of love than I did. I was inspired by the revolutionary spirit of the 60's. Remember the ending of the movie 'The Graduate' where Dustin Hoffman's character swings the cross in church at his girl's wedding with everyone hatefully screaming at him? That was me, see? I didn't fear the chasms and risks. I was willing to accept my challenges. This time I was doing it 'my way', not as a lamb led to the holy alter of matrimony because of pregnancy. As I saw it, there is no end of second thought excuses for those who avoid the Yellow Brick Road and live out their lives dreaming of what might have been, missing out on happiness, fearing what strangers might think. Whatever the Navy's or society's opinion was going to be, it was theirs to ponder. Regardless of my choices, I was likely to be judged for the divorce, but the fact of the matter was that Aurelie was the one opting out. So, what Nazira and I chose to do with our future was no one's business but our own. I had faith in Nazira's extraordinary maturity, common sense, humanity, and determination."

"But weren't you leaping way far into the future for such a commitment? How could the relationship develop after you sailed out of Hong Kong with less than a week together? Surely, such a short courtship in the emotional condition you was in wasn't going to seal your choice was it?"

"Bless her heart, on her own initiative and expense Nazira met me at every port for the remainder of the cruise. First stop Japan, where she met the rest of the squadron and immediately became the belle of the ball with everyone. All the Japanese girls loved her dearly as well, since they were highly advanced in cosmetic surgery to straighten their noses, round their eyes, and pump up their curves to look more western. Nazira's immediate popularity was the same in the Philippines. She was a true 'Star' in every sense—not just her incredible beauty and figure, but her warm-hearted shining personality, mature grace, poise, and self-confidence which endeared her to men and women of all ages everywhere we went. The skipper said, 'You can get away with this, but I never could.' I expected the squadron wives to be less hospitable and welcoming, but they weren't going to be writing my fitness reports."

"How could Nazira's parents allow their eighteen year old daughter to chase around Asia after an old married fighter pilot who was likely to get his butt shot off? After all, they had her locked up for five years to avoid a stunt like this."

"Nazira was as successful in charming her father as she was everyone else. Her mother was obviously an enthusiastically supporting ally. She seemed to love managing her beautiful daughters and living vicariously through them."

"Didn't they understand your marital situation?"

"Absolutely. Nevertheless, I somehow passed muster for they seemed to have no hesitation about me. Nazira's amazing fortune telling ability apparently helped her credibility with them in her faith in me and our future."

"What did Nazira foresee about the resolution of your marital crisis?"

"Other than what I anticipated–the time and difficulty of it–she said there would be two men blocking the way. One a friend my age trying to help, the other an older man with evil intentions. There were many other details I can't recall now. Some made little sense at the time, but I do remember them all amazingly coming to pass."

"So the future was fast catching up with you as the time to go home approached. I don't imagine you was looking forward to it."

"Can't say that I was, Mike. Some events are as hard to face as war; however, I had been selected for promotion to Commander and screened for a squadron command which meant that if Vietnam was still dragging on, I would be going back for two more tours, one as XO and then CO."

"But maybe Nazira would be with you next time?"

"Perhaps–if she could wait me out."

"You lived in exciting times, Captain. Unless you have more to say about the cruise, would you like to end this chapter on that note and resume tomorrow morning?"

"Good idea, we'll pick up with home front combat."

"OK. See you at breakfast."

24

BREAKING UP

"Good morning Captain. Sleep well?"

"Oh yes, thanks, Mike. Did you?"

"Indeed yes. I had the most amazing dream I've ever had."

"Great. Tell me about it."

"I was soaring."

"How was that amazing? What were you flying, the Ximango?"

"No. I was flying me!"

"Hey, now that is amazing. Where were you? How did you do it?"

"I was in the middle of the grassy area east of the runway at the Saint Mary's Airport on a bright sunny afternoon with scattered cumulus clouds and calm wind. Somehow, I felt inspired to just spread my arms straight out and a passing thermal very gently lifted me off. It wasn't like levitation, I was actually flying with my arms as wings, not flapping at all, just soaring like a hawk."

"How did you feel about that?"

"Beyond surprise or elation, but I was concerned about how to use my 'wings' and how much strength it took. When the thermal lifted me to several hundred feet, I wondered how long I would have the strength in my arms to stay up. When the thermal weakened, how would I control my descent? I was more concerned when little I did with my 'wings' helped control the flight and I was tiring. Then I flew into another thermal -a strong one which quickly lifted me to three or four thousand feet. As you know, it's a fascinating experience to soar in a glider at that altitude, but it's an entirely different kind of adventure to do it with only your weak and inexperienced arms to keep yourself aloft. I may as well have been looking down from a hundred thousand feet–vulnerability redefined!"

"Well I see you landed safely, so you must have learned."

"I remembered what test pilot Tony Levier said, 'Fly the airplane as far into the crash as you can', but the dream ended just as I began a rapid decent by bending my arms to shorten my wing span. The added speed, however, added to my wing stresses, so I doubt I would have had the strength to make it. I knew it was a dream I could end and apparently that's what I did. Still, it was a completely realistic experience, quite frightening but very exhilarating to say the least."

"I'm happy for you, Mike. Would you do it again?"

"Of course, but I'd like to grow more muscles and feathers first, wouldn't you?"

"Sure, but we'd look pretty silly going into the dining room with feathers growing out of our arms."

"Yeah, and just think what the Porch Pilots at the airport would say if we just walked out of the terminal and flew away."

"No doubt they would find something critical to say about our flying skills before one of them called the FAA to report a flight violation. You say that you were soaring, not levitating, so you were dependent on thermals to gain and sustain altitude?"

"Yes. To truly fly like birds, wouldn't humans have to evolve a protruding breast bone and strengthened muscles to have the leverage, strength and endurance to flap wings?"

"True, but that would take eons. It's more likely that we would develop some kind of strap-on machine."

"Like a Ximango, Captain?"

"Exactly, but from the weather forecast it appears your dreams of soaring may have to suffice for the next few days. So, shall we convene in the lobby to record the 1968 homecoming events?"

"As I recall, Captain, we left off at the end of your 1968 Vietnam tour. You were sailing to an unhappy homecoming with Aurelie, while also leaving a very young hopeful Nazira behind in Hong Kong."

"Correct, Mike. Months of daily letter writing had accomplished nothing to resolve issues at home; however, the delay allowed me time to recover from the shock and I hadn't entirely given up hope for reconciliation 'for the sake of the children'. On the other hand, if Aurelie persisted with leaving, future deployments with Nazira was a growingly attractive alternative. Traveling WESTPAC with Nazira underlined how Aurelie's lack of interest and support had been an increasingly missing factor I could do without."

"So how did it go?"

"Not as badly as I expected. Not all that different from prior homecomings -I was something of a stranger to Aurelie and the kids. The only surprise was that Aurelie had just spent six weeks in bed recovering from surgery to repair the long before muscle damage to her birth canal. Clearly, Aurelie was prepared in earnest to hit the road. All that was left to do was conclude the details as painlessly as possible; therefore, emotions were pretty much put aside. As Aurelie put it, there was no need to consider staying together for the sake of the children. They would soon grow up and move away and we would be left sitting across morning breakfasts too late to start over and hating each other for it."

"Is that the way you felt too, Captain?"

"Not really, but Aurelie's determination was set in cement. 'It takes two to tango', so my feelings were irrelevant. Nevertheless, we had 'one for the road' to test the surgery's great success and I continued to try to get Aurelie to give in a little in seeing my side of the story–to no avail whatever. So then, the challenge was to conclude the details as agreeably as possible."

"How were your parents reacting to the news?"

"Calm and understanding, as they had been about your mother. Unknown to me, Aurelie had declared her frustrations to them after I sailed away on the last cruise. She explained that she could no longer tolerate my Navy career and wanted me to quit. My father correctly reasoned that I would find it impossible to support the family and that I had too much time invested in Navy retirement."

"I don't recall you saying that Aurelie asked you to quit the Navy."

"No, because she did not."

"Why would she burden them without having discussed it with you?"

"I don't know more than what I already said about how Aurelie engineered the breakup. The important point is that Aurelie had made the final decision independent of debates with me at least a year before."

"What was Aurelie's mother's reaction?"

"I had no direct contact with her, but Helen was undoubtedly giving Aurelie a lot of encouraging but impractical advice. Nevertheless, Clayton, Aurelie's child-molesting stepfather social worker, came to stay with us for a protracted and uninvited visit which I considered unwelcome interference. Apparently he didn't understand that the split was Aurelie's initiative and that I had little to say about it, since he offered the bribe of the family's sailboat 'Mandalay' to me if we remained married. To add insult to injury, he propositioned Aurelie in front of me after dinner one evening. Oddly, Aurelie was not put off by Clayton's advances and I had the feeling she might have consented under different circumstances. It seemed that Clayton was the older man blocking matters of whom Nazira foretold."

"Pretty bizarre, Captain. I'm sure you were glad to see him depart. That reminds me of Nazira's other person, a friend, who Nazira said would interfere."

"Yes, that turned out to be my pal Ed Fitch who was between marriages then and had a drinking problem. Perhaps to try to make me jealous and romantically assert myself with Aurelie, Ed also tried to seduce Aurelie in my presence. Whatever his motive, Aurelie and I both laughed him off."

"As they say, 'with friends and family like that, who needs enemies'. Were there other outside disruptions?"

"Aurelie answered the phone one evening when Nazira called to confirm her status. Needless to say, Aurelie was upset and became obsessively demanding that I promise never to marry Nazira and also agree to marriage counseling, which further confirmed the finality of Aurelie's long-standing divorce decision. Seeing a shrink was not a small consideration for me by any means. In order to get a referral for counseling, we had to discuss our relationship with the Navy Flight Surgeon. That was especially hazardous for me because, as a squadron XO/CO and our nuclear mission, I had to have the highest top secret security clearance with no questions about my mental stability, so I was risking my flight status and career. By that time, however, those considerations were secondary to resolving my personal life, so I agreed. Thankfully, the Flight Surgeon was entirely sympathetic. He was amazed that I was able to go through our breakup while in the middle of a combat tour. He further said that the Navy's primary concern was that I was happy. So, he referred us to weekly joint sessions with a civilian psychiatrist, which proved to be an unproductive delay. The only good that came from seeing Dr Papadopolous was that he reinforced my naturally hostile reaction to Aurelie's revelation, whereupon I thanked him and terminated further counseling."

"How were your kids standing up to the turmoil?"

"Wonderfully well. While they knew something very serious was happening, they stayed close, supported each other beautifully, and stayed out of the rough stuff without adding to the difficulties. Aurelie had apparently prepared them thoroughly for coming events. Still, as you can imagine, it was a very sad and insecure time for them. The best I could muster was that at their age, I could recall believing it might be best for each of us if my parents parted company."

"What about the settlement and attorneys. Didn't events heat up between you there?"

"Surprisingly, no. Aurelie and I were able to settle property and finances between us amiably without legal interference or bitterness. With her agreement, I contacted the Albuquerque attorney who represented me in divorce from your mother and he agreed to represent both of us if we signed joint settlement agreements."

"Amazing, Captain. That certainly confirms to me more than anything you have told me that Aurelie was very anxious indeed to bail out of the marriage, perhaps even to the point of disregarding what may have been best for her children's security."

"Right, especially on your last point. As you will see in future chapters, she was thinking too much about herself and not very bright about financial matters."

"So, that was it then, marriage dissolved?"

"Nearly, Mike, not quite. The stage was set for the most significant event of my life and the central reason for me to tell my story, However, I'd like to separate it from the unhappiness with Aurelie and take a break before we go on to the next chapter."

"Good idea, Captain. I have some errands to run and catch up writing to do, so how's if we meet at dinner and happier events afterward."

"Excellent. All these memories are hard on an old fart, so I'm ready for an afternoon lie down. See you at dinner, Mike."

"Until then."

25

1969 Conversation With Jean

———————————————

"Well Captain, wasn't that a fine dinner?"

"The best part was having dessert with your girlfriend!"

"Georgie isn't my girlfriend, Captain."

"Well, she seems to consider you a close friend. That qualifies her in my book."

"In my book, your definition leaves out vital qualifications."

"Qualifications change with age. Seniors don't have many golden opportunities."

"Well I understand you did pretty well in your dotage."

"We'll get to that in about twenty chapters. Sorry to butt in."

"Considering how much I am butting into your life, turnabout is fair play!"

"Atta boy. Shall we reconvene on the porch?"

"I believe you are going to relate a significant event in your life?"

"Yes, though the significance of it will take the rest of my story to elaborate. You may discount the beginning as only a parlor game. Ouija boards are little used these days. Nevertheless, many households still have one put away."

"I've heard about them, but please enlighten me about their origin and use?"

"I believe they began as 'Talking Boards' in Europe which supposedly enabled private contact with the spirit world without mediums or séances. The boards were introduced in the US in the late 19th century, named 'ouija' after an incorrect Egyptian word for good luck. The later promoter claimed ouija was a combination of the French and German words for 'yes'. Ouija boards have the letters of the alphabet arced in two rows across the top, the ten numbers in a line below, plus the words 'yes', 'no', 'goodbye', and 'maybe' in the corners. Two players sit facing each other, knees touching, with the board on their laps. A triangular three-legged 'planchette' pointer has a hole and pointer in the center. The small legs of the planchette have felt tabs, so it slides across the very smooth board with almost no effort. Using both hands, the players each touch the planchette with just their fingertips as lightly as possible, elbows out. One asks a question and the planchette responds, indicating responses with the letters, words, or numbers."

"Do folks seriously believe they can communicate with the spirit world in this way?"

"Some do, believing that the planchette's movement is entirely independent, Others accuse the other player of moving it. Sometimes, however, the depth, insight, wisdom, or prophesy may be very convincing, even to skeptics. Other folks even believe that such activities open the door to the devil or evil spirits which could be harmful. Nevertheless, ouija boards were very popular in the forties while we were staying with the Guinards in Portland after evacuating from Panama. After dinner we often gathered around to ask the board about our futures. Some responses were humorous or relevant, but always light-hearted. I cannot recall any catastrophic forecasts or personal information from the spirit 'speaking' to us."

"What was your belief about ouija boards, Captain?"

"As a psych major, I would of course say that players control the planchette responses themselves, though unaware of it. On the other hand, my spiritual experiences give me an open mind to omens, messages, and events beyond coincidence. After all, Mike, isn't it possible that the players' hand movements may be spiritually guided? Some say every question contains its own answer. Buddhists say, 'Inquire within.'"

"Don't your religious beliefs also allow the possibility that a spirit may guide actions? Christ said, 'Where two or more are gathered in my name, there shall I be also.'"

"Yes, and since I believe in God, that includes the 'other side' as well. Although Ouija sessions are not religious rites, anything is possible. God works in mysterious ways. I'm glad you allow for that, because it is a strong factor in the credibility of my tale."

"Did you and Aurelie use your ouija board much?"

"No. I can't recall the times or any notable revelations. Nevertheless, she insisted on using it then, perhaps as a relief from trying to entertain my parents in that difficult situation. Recall that Aurelie believed she was a witch—though she was low key about it."

"So much for background, Captain, what happened?"

"Nothing much at first. I was reluctant to ask questions and the planchette movement was excruciatingly slow in giving one word responses to Aurelie's routine inquiries. I found it boring and tiring to hold my arms suspended for such long periods, but I did feel tingling sensations in my fingertips. Mother watched nearby, but Father read his newspaper."

"Now before I get into the details, I must explain that we had three successive evenings of three hour sessions on the board. Spelling out responses is a very tedious process which can take more than a few minutes. So, to aid continuity, I'll compress the sessions into a continuous narration. Although sixty years is a long time for an old guy to remember, I am certain of the accuracy of the Ouija board responses I'll recall, so back to what happened."

"I finally gave in to Aurelie's insistence and asked the board if anyone wished to speak to me. After a long wait, the planchette slowly moved to. "Yes"

"I asked why. The planchette spelled out. "You need me."

"I recalled the turmoil of circumstances during the divorce from your mother and Aurelie's pregnancy, so I facetiously asked where this spirit was in 1955". "I was away, I'm sorry." The seriousness took me aback.

"I asked if this visit was voluntary or assigned. "You need me"

"I asked where she was." 'Ether' "defined as an imaginary substance regarded by the ancients as filling all space beyond the sphere of the moon, and making up the stars and planets."

"An oddly archaic term if Aurelie was manipulating the responses, wasn't it, Captain?"

"I thought so too. This was not the Aurelie personality I'd known for twenty years, and the spirit was responding in first person, so I asked who was speaking to me.". "Jean". "I asked if this were someone I knew in life?" "Yes"

"Then it struck me—was this was my mother's deceased sister Jean?" 'Yes.'

"To recall the realization chokes me up even now. This couldn't be Aurelie's work, she had not known Jean or my feelings for her."

"Is this a good point to review your prior history with Jean, Captain?"

"I suppose, but I'm having an old man's teary spell reliving the event, so I'll go slow."

"We can come back to it later if you wish."

"Let's press on. From my earliest memory as a small boy there was something very special about Jean to me which I was not able to define. Not that we were close, I only saw her on the rare family gatherings, then there were so many people and I was just a 'seen, but not heard' kid. I don't recall speaking to her."

"How much older than you was she?"

"About eight years, I think."

"What was there about Jean that impressed you?"

"She was very attractive in a plainly honest and serene way. But there was more to it—a feeling of familiarity and recognition. It wasn't until my late seventies that she revealed our connection."

"That should be exciting, but what happened to Jean?"

"Jean had been married and divorced with a baby girl. When I saw her last, just before we went to Germany in 1949, I was sixteen, so Jean was in her early twenties and living in Boston, dating the shady owner of a night club where she worked as a cigarette girl and photographer. She and her boyfriend came to Portland for the family reunion and we all drove to the old Hoyt family farm in Magalloway where she, Mother and I had our picture taken together. That was as physically close as we got."

"Of course. How was it that you didn't see her after that?"

"We were in Germany a year later when Jean was found dead in her Boston apartment, in bed with the unlit gas stove turned on and the door unlocked. The police investigation ruled it a suicide, but the family believed it was homicide. Jean was not the kind to take her own life. So much for the review, unless you have questions, let's return to 1969."

"OK, where did your Ouija board conversation with Jean go then?"

"I asked her if she was to remain in Ether. 'They will decide.' I asked who 'they' were 'I can't say.' I asked if she had seen her mother there. 'Yes'. Would she be one of those to decide? 'Yes'. To me, this lent credibility to the possibility that we go through multiple lifetimes with some of the same people over again. When we rendezvous on the other side, there may eventually be a judgement about when and where we go next—perhaps to remain in the void of ether, reincarnation, or admitted into Heaven."

"Does Jean's description of her circumstance in ether seem similar to Purgatory to you, Captain?"

"That depends on your Catholic definition of Purgatory, Mike?"

"I'm not a religious scholar, nor any longer a member of the Catholic Church, so I can't speak authoritatively. But Purgatory is believed by many faiths beside Catholicism, often without using the name, to be a process of purification or temporary punishment in which the souls of those who die as baptized believers are made ready for Heaven. What is your definition?"

"I concur with yours and I agree that may well be what Jean calls ether, including her further revelation that 'they' may decide we need to try again on Earth. So, I asked if I have been here before. Her response, 'Stone Age, Crusades, and 1898'."

"Fascinating. I hope you asked for details?"

"No. At that time I felt it was not practical to ask Jean for lengthy, laboriously spelled out, detailed narrative responses to questions. Instead, out of the blue, I silently asked if Nazira had been here before. 'No, she is new. She is fickle.'"

"Fickle?—another archaic term. So if Jean answered a silent question, it could not have been Aurelie's manipulations. If it wasn't Jean speaking, you moved the planchette! Did you ask many other questions silently?"

"No. I stopped doubting Aurelie's motives and Jean was so enthusiastic that the planchette nearly flew out of our hands, even before asking a question at follow-on sessions. 'Hello Manuel dear'. It was clear that neither Aurelie nor I were in charge of the planchette."

"What next?"

"I asked Jean if she committed suicide. 'No. It was an accident'. Had God spoken to her? 'Yes'. What did He say? 'I can't say, but He loves you all very much.'"

"I guess Ether isn't a bad place then! What next?"

"I asked if she could see my future." 'Yes, but you can change it'.

"Some say that eighty percent of our behavior is programmed at birth, so I was glad to know that the program could be changed. I asked if she could influence my future." 'Yes'

"I asked how". 'If I told you, it wouldn't work.'"

"Very interesting Captain. What did you take that to mean?"

"That she had limitations which would be too obvious to me if she explained. Nevertheless, I came to recognize thereafter that Jean's influence and communications were indirect, through 'coincidental' events, omens, challenges, opportunities, obstacles, and agreements, plus channeled behavior through birds as long as I was roaming, then cats when I settled down. She never interfered with my free will in any way, so I trusted her completely and my life's direction has often been a matter of 'following the yellow brick road' which, as in the OZ story, was fraught with fearsome dangers, trials, and tribulations. Recall, for example, that when you came to visit me in 2013 while Carin was in the hospital. Four hours later we were called to ICU to be with her minutes before she unexpectedly died–four days before our twentieth wedding anniversary. Having you there was Jean's manner of loving supportive influence, not a coincidence, Michael. I have a strong feeling that my mission now is to tell this story for the purpose of inspiring or encouraging other believers to more consciously recognize and easily welcome similar spiritual experiences."

"I pray that I may be one of those inspired others, Captain. So has Jean not verbally communicated with you since the Ouija sessions?"

"Correct. Although Jean has been a constant companion and I have regularly spoken silently to her, she has verbally communicated only a single word audibly to me since then."

"Why, do you suppose?"

"I believe she agreed with me."

"Are you saying you thought it best? That seems like the nun's prayer to God to take back His levitation gift. What was your thinking?"

"Our Ouija sessions had been such a powerfully emotional, and intense experience, I feared the distracting consequences of continuing at that level."

"Have you never wished to ask more?"

"Only about my lingering question about the nature of our relationship. Were we together in a former life? Thankfully, Jean dramatically eventually answered that question, as well as the mystery of her 2010 visual appearance to Richard, standing next to me."

"I hope I won't have to bear the suspense of waiting until we get to that point to know the answer."

"Well Michael, since the event is so much further down the Road and I have told this much of it, it seems appropriate to relate Jean's answer now as a profound example of her manner of communicating with me. So here it is. First, recall that when Jean appeared to Richard standing next to me with her left hand on my right shoulder, pointing up with her right index finger and miming 'Mom', I initially assumed she meant that my mother, her sister, would soon go to heaven. But Mother did not pass until many years later, so Jean's message was a mystery."

"Until?"

"Twenty plus years ago I bought a clock I still use which projects the time with rounded digits on the ceiling at night. It won't show well in print, but some numbers resembled letters, for example–number one, the letter I–zero, the letter O–five, the letter S–three, a backward E. Then I saw that 252, 525, and 629 resembled two opposing hearts, one upright and the other inverted, with the left heart containing a colon marking seconds, the right side heart empty. 629 was especially intriguing since the 6 and 9 could represent the Yin and the Yang, 'complementary, interconnected, and interdependent forces.' When I regularly awoke at 2:52, 5:25, and 6:29, I understood them as omens of Jean's re-assurance that she was with me."

"Amazing, a good example of your receptive cognizance and Jean's inventive way of communicating her love. I see that the left beating heart in 2:52 is inverted, whereas it is upright in 5:25 and 6:29. Did you see significance in that?"

"At first I wondered about it, but came to discount significance, since I often remained awake for all three omens, speaking to Jean."

"Were there words as well?"

"Infrequently, but the first one was alarming, 5:05–SOS, the maritime distress call, an acronym for Save Our Souls–in morse code as ... —- ... "

"What did you take it to mean?"

"At first I took it as Jean's warning of coming dangers, but when it repeated over time without connected events, I came to recognize it as a call to worship to literally Save Our Souls."

"*Our* souls? Jean's as well?"

"Yes. It seemed to reinforce the Yin and Yang interconnection of our relationship symbolized in the 6:29 omen."

"Was that Jean's answer to your relationship question then?"

"In part, the rest of her answer came one night when I was suddenly awakened by her voice emphatically saying loud and clear, 'HERE!' I looked at the ceiling and saw that it was 5:15–SIS."

"Wow, how incredible–SIS–sister! Jean was your sister in a previous life–Stone Age, Crusades, or 1898. So she was the sister you missed when you came into this life."

"Yes, which explained the mystery of her appearance to Richard with her hand on my shoulder, pointing up miming Mom, to mean that we once had the same mother."

"In which of your previous lives?"

"I pondered that question for years, but clues suggest The Crusades. Because I was born into the church, raised and lived as a warrior, and have a deep emotional reaction to Gregorian Chants, it seems possible that I was a monk or soldier."

"Or perhaps even a knight. I see your reasoning. Do you have any clues about how you and Jean related in that lifetime?"

"In fact I do, Michael, mainly from how we relate in this lifetime since my birth. I feel such a deep and abiding bonding force between us that I believe we must have shared much of our lives together, culminating in a major life-threatening event, perhaps with a life sacrificing end."

"So you feel that perhaps Jean has dedicated herself voluntarily to your life out of her loving bond from the events of your prior life as siblings?"

"Yes, that is my feeling. Remember her response to my early question in our Ouija sessions, 'Why are you speaking to me? Answer 'You need me.' 'Did you volunteer or were you assigned?' answer, 'You need me.' Indeed I did–and still do–in every aspect of my life this time around."

"So Jean is still with you?"

"I wouldn't still be living to tell you this story if she weren't, Michael. It is no coincidence that you are here, is it?"

"No coincidence–life on the 'Yellow Brick Road', Captain. Then is this a good point to close this chapter?"

"Yes, it's time to move along to three more Vietnam tours and many other assorted adventures with Jean. When you return from flying tomorrow afternoon give me a call."

"Aye aye, Captain. Good night."

"Pleasant dreams and happy landings."

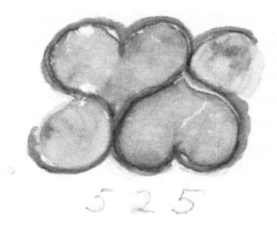

525

294

L-R Jean, cousin, Mother, Manny, Magalloway ME homestead 1949

26

Bachelor Life

"Hi Michael. How was your flight?"

"Excellent. No lift but what a joy to fly your Ximango. Thank you again for entrusting her to me."

"Most welcome. It's nice to have one of my kids show interest in flying. I don't blame them though, there's little romance in aviation now. Old hat. Life's all happening on the internet."

"Well the joy of soaring is new to me and I am thankful for the opportunity. I wish you would fly with me."

"I'll spare you my back seat driving until you get your glider rating and more solo time. I'll bet Georgie will be happy to fly with you too—at least until the knot is tied."

"Cynical to the core."

"Just vast experience. There's not one in a million women genuinely interested in flying or sailing. Just as well, I think, we need those spaces to ourselves. Speaking of spousal experiences, shall we return to the tale at hand?"

"Sure. Where we left off, you still hadn't yet actually split up with Aurelie. Is there more to say?"

"Not much. Aurelie's half-brother Jeremy came to help with the two car drive East. Aurelie and I hugged good-by, the kids waved back and they drove off. That was it. I guess we were all drained of emotion and relieved that it was over. Twenty years done and gone without a whimper. I turned in the keys to the house, drove to the BOQ and called Nazira with the news."

"How could you be ready to jump into another marriage so quickly?"

"Good question, but didn't I answer it already? I had married your mother and Aurelie because of pregnancy. My fault too of course, just not my choice. Nazira was my crusade. Despite the odds against, I was committed. After all, there were greater risks to come. With many risks from her view as well, bless her heart, she couldn't be asked to wait forever. Nazira was also committed, but I felt it would be best to introduce her to the USA as a tourist if she could get a visa."

"Did Nazira want that?"

"She was OK with it. Even if it didn't work out for us, she would at least be out of Hong Kong and in the USA for keeps if she wished."

"Did you believe that was part of her motivation?"

"Of course. Nazira was nothing if not frank in saying that her future prospects in Hong Kong were nil past her twenties. Plus, the British lease was running out and it was certain that China would not renew it. No one expected that the open free-port capitalism and democratic lifestyle would continue under China's rule. At worst, I was a Godsend for her and her parents, as was she a Godsend for me–or Jean sent."

"Beyond coincidence, you think?"

"In looking back, absolutely, and very much consistent with later providential events. As Jean said, she could influence my future, but I could change it. In fact, there were several other future changing opportunities in celebrating my current bachelorhood. First, when I called my idol Dorothy with the news, she shocked me by asking me to come to Pensacola and rescue her from her marriage to Adrian!"

"Hold on, Captain, update me on Dorothy."

"After her husband George split, Dorothy returned to Pensacola with her baby Anne and made good on her pledge to marry the most eligible man about town and bore him Adrian the third."

"How could she have seriously asked you to rescue her?"

"I didn't believe she was serious, except that Dorothy was very frank. She told Aurelie several times over the years that she intended to steal me away from her, but we didn't take her seriously–though Aurelie did know of my admiration. I had not seen Dorothy other than the time I flew a Demon to Pensacola. There was no reason to think she was attracted to me, so I discounted Dorothy's request as nothing more than expressing her frustration stemming from the loveless nature of her marriage of convenience. In any event, I had no wish to risk becoming involved in another's unhappy marriage, so I passed."

"I should hope so. Was that the last of Dorothy in your life?"

"Lord no, not by a long shot. Our next encounter was ten years later, so let's try not to review our history each time Dorothy re-enters my tale."

"So what other of Jean's 'opportunities' presented themselves?"

"For unexplained reasons, the U.S. Embassy in Hong Kong refused to issue a visitor's visa to Nazira, perhaps because of her juvenile detention record or her Pakistani passport issued in Peking. Also, there was official interest in hampering GI's from importing Asian 'war brides'. So,

I enlisted the services of an immigration attorney in Hawaii who had worked in the Hong Kong U.S. Embassy for fifteen years, so this was going to slow things down. Meanwhile, my social life consisted of happy hours at the gloomy NAS Lemoore Officers Club. I had been detached from VA-27 which was deployed again and 'stashed' as an A-7 flight instructor and Maintenance Officer in VA-122 pending promotion to Commander and assignment as Executive Officer to VA-146–so there was time to get into trouble. One afternoon at the Club I was approached by the wife of one of my deployed squadron mates who asked me to be the fourth in their bridge game. My bridge experience was limited to the Wild West variations we played at sea, but I was still dummy candidate, so I reluctantly agreed. When the game adjourned for dinner, there was no graceful way for me to leave, nor was there a polite way to decline the wife's invitation to dance to a juke box tune. When she asked me, 'Would you mind?' there was no doubt what she meant."

"So that's what life back home was like for the wives you guys left behind?"

"Apparently–news to naive me, so my reaction was to say that I had just come out of a failed marriage and didn't wish to be involved in someone else's. She persisted, however, and I relented. She gave me directions to her house and told me to come by at 10. On the drive there, I chickened out and pulled off to a payphone at a quiet intersection to call it off. Incredibly, at that moment two cars crashed into each other at the intersection. There didn't appear to be injuries, but of course I had to attend to the scene and said I wouldn't be coming."

"Another amazing coincidence. Courtesy of Jean?"

"No doubt, though it didn't occur to me. I simply felt relieved."

"Why didn't you connect the dots with Jean's car crash message intervention?"

"I hadn't yet realized that the consequences of the Ouija board communication with Jean would extend beyond then in such direct and dramatic ways."

"OK, what was the other 'opportunity'?"

"I don't remember exactly how it came up, but the fallout from my trips to Albuquerque and your mother's advances led me to ask her to visit me in California."

"I remember that well. I was surprised and hurt that you two pretty much ignored me in pursuing your carnal lust."

"Guilty as charged, Judge Michael. I was as surprised as you, but this was an opportunity for me to fulfill lingering vengeance against a hateful woman who, for no rational justification, had done her best to trash my life."

"Fourteen years later? Good grief, had you really harbored such a grudge for so long?"

"Yes I did, Michael, Emma did everything possible to maintain her attacks for years after our divorce. On the other hand, I'll admit that Emma remained a very attractive woman to me and our physical relationship had been so brief that we had not gotten our money's worth. So, truth be told, when I invited her to come to Lemoore and she said she would not come unless there might be a 'chance for us', I was not entirely dishonest in saying I would allow for that."

"You may not have considered my feelings of hopeful anticipation that I might finally have a father in my life."

"Oh no, Michael, you're not going to lay a guilt trip on me now when you know as well as I do that your mother engineered the entire event. Do you think she was considering your feelings?"

"Ok, quite right. Sorry, but you were an easy target of blame from the way Mother saw it all."

"From the way she said she saw it, you mean. Never mind the truth. It's easy for women like Emma and Aurelie to ever-after play the victim's part of an abandoned mother to her kids when the father cannot defend himself in absentia. I certainly did not intend to do something everlastingly stupid to myself in a futile effort for your sake. Reading between the lines in what I know of you, you know very well what a lost cause that would have been. So which first, the good part or the bad about her visit?"

"Let's try good for a change of pace."

"It may make you uncomfortable to hear it, but good it was. We had an absolute ball, enjoying the best of the 60's California social revolution. We removed the top from my '59 Austin Healey 100-6 and roared through the 90 mile lonely two- lane mountain road to Morro Bay with our hair waving in the breeze, removing every stitch of clothes on the way. One shocked truck driver passing us nearly went off the road. Then dinner at a waterfront fisherman's café with Joan Baez on the juke box providentially singing Bob Dylan's 'Love is Just a Four Letter Word', followed by a night of lust in the dunes at the isolated beach. Next, San Francisco for three days with all the hippie rock and roll abandon it offered. I was amazed how well Emma fit right into the lifestyle, bless her heart."

"Sounds ideal, what went wrong?"

"Too much too soon and too late. Negative frictions could not be erased with a brief encounter. Though we kept up a congenial front and got through the visit, the underlying bitterness proved there was no question of a future together for us, as indeed there never was. So, after putting her on her plane home, I wrote a final letter saying so. Her response was a simple agreement -'I'm OK'. That was our final written communication."

"Were you glad to have evened the score somewhat?"

"No, but I was glad that we had buried some of our past. I believe she felt the same. Now, with Aurelie, Dorothy, and Emma resolved, I was in positive spirits to face the future with Nazira; however, there was one more 'opportunity' I nearly forgot."

"Not another lady in your life!"

"Not directly. It was more about my pal, Ed Fitch, who was living at the BOQ too since he and Pat had divorced. I bumped into him after breakfast when he was on his way to fly. His harried and fatigued appearance was explained by the fact that he was entertaining three ladies in town at the same time without either knowing about the other. Pat-ex and his kids were staying with Ed's parents, who were trying to resurrect the marriage. The two other ladies–a nurse from San Francisco staying at a nearby motel, plus Gloria, a PhD Oceanographer nymphomaniac, who was at that moment in his BOQ room. Keeping up with the three of them had been quite hard on Ed and his car. So, he suggested that if I went to his room and introduced myself, Gloria would probably welcome me to his bed and give him a break."

"Good grief, you went?"

"Hell no, but I joined them for dinner. Crowded between Ed and me in the front seat of his car, Gloria explained what a lousy lover Ed was when she met him in Hawaii and then detailed the improvements she had made. Since Gloria re-enters this tale several times, it's worth reviewing how they met. When Ed was transferred to Hawaii, Pat refused to go, supposedly because of their fancy La Jolla home and the kids school, as well as Pat's modeling career and social ambitions, but Ed refused to take no for an answer and Pat finally joined Ed for a visit in his high rise apartment. One night after his usual alcohol over-indulgence and sitting on the john, Ed saw an open letter in the trash can which was a love letter to Pat from an old friend of Ed's in La Jolla. It was obvious that their affair was nothing new–except to Ed. Still sitting on the john, Ed screamed to Pat and confronted her with the letter. When Pat admitted to the affair, Ed demanded that Pat bring him his .38 pistol–which she did! Still sitting on the john, Ed declared he was going to blow his brains out. According to Ed, Pat simply closed the bathroom door and flew home to La Jolla."

"Well that has to be an effective way to dilute the dramatic effect of someone committing suicide!"

"Ed's life was a series of colorful events, so Pat's action was appropriate. Though understandably shocked and depressed, Ed managed to recover. One evening as he contemplated a leap from his high-rise apartment balcony, he noted a lovely lady on a balcony below him. Rather than put on an aerial display for her, he struck up a conversation and the rest was history–it was Gloria."

"Did she follow him home from Hawaii?"

"Not exactly. Ed explained that Gloria was a PhD oceanographer at Scripps Institute in La Jolla, temporarily assigned to a project in Hawaii and since returned to California and was just visiting Ed for the weekend. Pat and the nurse were surprises, nevertheless Ed pulled it off somehow without repercussions. Not too long afterward they were married."

"What a combination–a nymphomaniac and a recently divorced fighter pilot about to re-deploy to Vietnam. Surely he would have many more important issues to contemplate than getting shot down, but then you and Ed were pretty much alike, weren't you, Captain?"

"You could say that, Mike. There I was, a thirty-six year old divorced battle weary aviator facing two more deployments, engaged to an eighteen year old Hong Kong jail-bird bar-owner actress. What were the odds?"

"Well, you're still alive and kicking, so as they say, don't argue with success! What's next?"

"Let's stop here and resume after dinner, OK?"

"Suits me Captain."

27

MARRYING NAZIRA

"OK Captain, we left off with you as a new bachelor fending off romantic entanglements and trying to get a visitor's visa for Nazira to enter the US. How was that resolved?"

"In fighter pilot fashion, of course. Impatient with the diplomatic blocks, I decided to fly to Hong Kong to be married. Before that, however, I drove to San Diego to bring my parents up to date."

"That must have been interesting."

"It sure was, but not because of my parents' reaction to the news about Nazira, they were totally calm and accepting about that. The visit became notable when my mother insisted on bringing out the Ouija Board I had given her."

"Didn't you feel that you saw no further need for Jean to speak directly to you?"

"Correct. I felt that we had covered my questions and Jean would probably not respond since I was not in a crisis, so I was reluctant to agree to a trivial pursuit. But Mother persisted and I relented on the condition that she would ask the questions. As expected, there was no planchette movement whatever in response to Mother's inquiries, perhaps because we lacked the power. I remained quiet despite her pleas to ask questions and there was no action. Eventually my mind drifted and I wondered if Jean would be nearby if I needed her again. Outside, a bird was making an excited fuss which went on so long I decided to step out to see what was happening with my parents following a good bit behind. From the middle of the front yard, I saw an agitated mid-size bird standing on the front edge of the roof squawking at a baby bird on the ground about ten feet away which seemed to have failed its first flying lesson out of its nest. The baby bird fixed its gaze on me and mother bird went silent. For some mysterious reason I was inspired to reach out toward baby bird with my right arm, my index finger extended, and took a few steps toward it. Mother bird and baby remained still. At a distance of about six feet, baby bird flew up onto my finger and just looked into my eyes fearlessly while mother bird remained still and unprotesting. Time stopped for what seemed like several minutes, though it was probably less than fifteen seconds. Then time resumed and baby bird simply flew away without difficulty. Mother bird followed."

"How amazing. How did you feel? What were your parent's reactions?"

"I was of course very deeply moved and overjoyed almost to tears that Jean had responded in such an obvious, miraculous, and loving way. Since my parents did not know I had been thinking of Jean, they were amazed but unaware of the spiritual significance of the event, so they said little about it."

"Didn't you explain about Jean's presence?"

"No, probably because I didn't want to be in the position of defending the experience to my father's skepticism. Years later when the subject of Jean came up again with Mother I explained the significance of the event; however, none of my experiences with Jean ever really seemed to impress her, even though Jean was her sister and she had witnessed my conversations with her, as well as the bird incident."

"How can you explain that your parents blocked the reality of those experiences?"

"Both of my parents' religious beliefs, though quite different, were solidly based on church interpretations of the Bible. Neither one had strong personal spiritual experiences and both were simple country people who I believe basically feared confusion or damnation if they strayed from church dogma."

"So they sided with the view that Ouija Board communications might be the work of the Devil and the bird incident was just a natural event?"

"Basically, yes, and I wasn't going to risk reawakening the traumatic religious fights between them which had been dormant for many years. For me, however, that event was solid confirmation of Jean's continuing powerful benevolent presence in my life."

"It wasn't your typical kind of ghost story, was it, Captain?"

"None that I know of, as you will see further. So, now shall we resume with my trip to Hong Kong?"

"It's not surprising that you lost patience with visa delays. How did the wedding go?"

"When I arrived, I noted that Nazira had gained a few pounds on her mother's meals. Bless her heart though, it was understandable that she would compensate for uncertainty with home cooking. I had been away over a year with minimal communication, so for her the outcome might be the old story of a Yankee sailor disappearing after promising to return one day. It must have been especially difficult for Nazira to believe that a middle-aged father of four small children would end a fourteen year marriage to marry an uneducated oriental half his age."

"Still, Nazira was financially independent and a prominent 'Dragon Lady' was sponsoring her promising movie career. So, for her to give up those options, she surely must have had strong feelings for you, as well as great trust and faith, wouldn't you say?"

"Of course, Mike, that plus my steadfast feelings for her were what carried us through. So, a few pounds were not a significant concern, besides, Nazira carried them quite well. She was more charming, radiant and beautiful than ever. Moreover, she had proven to be a highly efficient take charge manager in making the wedding arrangements, especially complicated by the many unique family, legal, religious, citizenship, and military aspects of our union. I had limited time on leave and there was so much to accomplish there was hardly time for renewing romance. Although Nazira's parents favored the marriage, her father's consent for his under-age daughter was conditioned on my conversion to Islam, which required academic training by a Muslim priest."

"As a Christian, how were you able to reconcile that with your beliefs?"

"Recall that I was no longer a member of a church, nor did I intend to impose my personal faith on Nazira. So, I viewed the process as an academic opportunity to learn about Nazira's religion."

"Didn't you think religion might be an issue between you, as it had been between your parents?"

"No. Nazira seemed to be a genuinely spiritual and religious woman in a low key and pragmatic way, combined with her mother's Portuguese Catholic and Chinese superstition background. Besides, as it was taught to me by the Chinese priest, Muslims were closer than Jews to Christianity. Christ is accepted on the same divinity level as the other biblical prophets. Neither Jesus nor Mohammed are considered to be the sons of God. So, I didn't find cause for religious concern or conflict as much a factor as other imminent challenges."

"Such as?"

"My prime worry then was Nazira's social acceptance by the wives in my next squadron which I was about to become the Executive Officer, then CO. On the positive side, I was fortunate that my CO would be my old LSO buddy from the 1960 Ticonderoga cruise, Wayne Stephens, a true prince of a man."

"Sounds like a good start. The CO writes your fitness report, doesn't he? So what was the worry?"

"Wayne and Sally had ten children and theirs was the 'all American family' with Sally as the superb epitome of a model mother. Therefore, there was reason to anticipate a cool reception by such a 'queen bee' to a mid-life crisis father who appeared to have abandoned his four children to marry a who-knows-what oriental movie queen. It wasn't just Sally's reception, every wife on the base faced the same threat in their marriage -if not POW, MIA, or KIA next of kin. Might not their men find inspiration in my example?"

"I see your point, Captain your fellow aviators might be tolerant or perhaps even admiring of your defiant anti-social adventure, but who could blame the wives for feeling less than sympathetic with welcoming a husband-stealing Arab into the club?"

"It was a hard test to impose on a new wife, wasn't it? I was determined to press on regardless of the professional or social consequence to myself, but it would be damned unfair for anyone to make Nazira suffer for my decisions."

"I agree, that's as it should be, just not always the way it is. How did the wedding go then?"

"I followed the script. I completed the Islam indoctrination and Nazira's father gave me the name 'Mansur'. I remained quiet and polite, smiled a lot, and posed for our formal wedding photo looking like a hayseed kid while Nazira was beautifully radiant—obviously far more self-assured and mature than I. I don't remember the ceremony, so I guess it went well. The reception and dinners, however, were memorable in several respects. I met one of Nazira's sisters for the first time. Sukina, like Nazira, was gorgeous but in a different way—taller, thinner and more sophisticated with little trace of her Pakistani or oriental background. Sukina was joyously celebrating her imminent marriage to an Air Force Phantom pilot Major by having a last fling with another Major, plus she was being inappropriately forward with me. Nazira was rightly upset, because Sukina had a history of stealing her boyfriends."

"Right there in front of the entire family at Nazira's wedding reception? How did you deal with that?"

"Like I said, I remained quiet and polite, and smiled a lot—until the fight started and deflected everyone's attention."

"A fight? At your wedding reception? Who? Why?"

"Nazira's father and his brother had a long standing feud, in part because the brother sold his youngest daughter into Singapore prostitution, which was still not unheard of in those cultures then. The serious shouting erupted when the argument reduced to trading insults and Nazira's father criticized his brother's wife's obesity. When it appeared that violence was imminent, I made the dumb mistake of trying to break it up. Fortunately it worked long enough for the bride and groom to escape the scene."

"Great start! You said dinners, was there more than one?"

"Yes, we had a second great Chinese banquet with the girls from Nazira's bar in a private room at a restaurant."

"Just the two of you with the girls?"

"Yes, except there was also a man seated by himself at a table apart from us in a dimly lit area. Nazira said that he was Mr. Seng, a friend who was hosting the banquet, so I should introduce myself. So I did. It was clear that Mr. Seng was a very distinguished and dignified elderly Chinese gentleman whose presence and manner suggested great wealth and importance."

"Did Nazira offer further explanation later?"

"She said she met Mr. Seng at a May Smith social function. Recall that Nazira's father was May's chauffeur and she was the 'Dragon Lady' who arranged Nazira's introduction to Shore Brothers movie studio. Nazira told me that she had arranged meetings between Mr. Seng and one or two of the girls, so this banquet was his wedding present to her."

"I see. So part of Nazira's function at the bar was to arrange 'company' for distinguished clients?"

"I believe Mr. Seng was a special case. Anyway, I never grilled Nazira about her past or make judgments based on assumptions. After all, my own past wasn't pristine. However Nazira came to be who she was, the result was all I needed to know. Our plate was full of future."

"An ideal attitude, Captain. Were you able to sustain such a 'Judge not, lest ye be judged' outlook?"

"Yes, I can say without reservation that I did. By the way, does the name Hang Seng ring a bell?"

"Well yes, now that you mention it. Isn't there a major Hong Kong bank with that name which posts their financial index?"

"Excellent Mike, indeed there is."

"Was Nazira's Mr. Seng related to the bank?"

"Not related, he was the Mr. Seng."

"Impressive! No wonder Nazira owned half interest in the bar. What did she do with her share after you married?"

"I have no idea. I never asked. I assume she cashed in and put it aside for safe keeping in case we or I didn't make it. She may have participated in the condo her parents bought, which would have been a good investment during a very lucrative building boom."

"OK, what next?"

"USA bound! We flew to Manila and bussed to Clark Air Force Base where we had a relaxing breather for ten days awaiting a space available flight to San Francisco where we went to China Town for dinner and then to Philmore West."

"Refresh me on Philmore West"

"It was the west coast version of New York City's famous Philmore East rock concert club in the days when bands were paid up to $25,000 per concert. Although there were several uni-formed Rent-a-Cops present, the three floor stairway served to screen out those too stoned to climb socially. Other than a band stand, there were no chairs or tables. Everyone stood or sat on the floor. In the sixties, the kids all wore the same uniform–levies, plaid shirts, and hair to the waist. From behind it was impossible to distinguish male from female, nor was it much easier from the front. The smell of marijuana was so pungent that lighting up was unnecessary, yet the ambiance and behavior was notably calm and well ordered. Then the music began with Country Joe and the Fish doing their 'Give me an F' with a shouting audience F response. 'Give me a

U'–and an even more enthusiastic crowd response and so on to 'Give me a C' and 'Give me a K' in a powerful crescendo. 'What's that spell?' 'F—k'. Over and over, 'What's that spell?' 'F—k'. And a final roof blowing response to 'F—k who?' 'F—k you!' and then the music began. It was magic, Mike, or as called then, a 'happening'. After Country Joe and the Fish, the legendary blues man B B King came on and lifted everyone as high as they could go."

"Well, Captain, what a first night in the USA your new Hong Kong bride! What was her reaction?"

"I was glad she had that introductory exposure to the USA's rock scene, because outside California the impression was warped–nowhere more so than Hong Kong where the interpretation and imitation was little more than hoodlum gang behavior with no social or intellectual credibility. Nazira's reaction, however, floored me when she observed, 'They are not interested in sex.' She was correct. For the Hippies sex had become so casual and meaningless in this rebellious drug society that it had little more spiritual value than shaking hands. If so, then what else could have significance for these lost, mindlessly drugged out, draft dodging children in 'uniform' whose most enthusiastic cry in the end only amounted to 'f--k you'? For all the personal emotional and social upheaval I experienced in the sixties, sympathizing with the so-called Cultural Revolution, Nazira had suddenly re-ordered my perspective and I realized that we were as well adapted to each other as we could have been to face our next chapter together in the real world."

"On to Naval Air Station Lemoore, Captain?"

"Yes, we were ready for anything. 'The Graduate' had nothing on us! But let's re-start in the next chapter tomorrow morning, unless you are flying?"

"Not tomorrow, strong cross winds are forecast. Shall we continue after breakfast?"

"See you there, Mike. Good night."

"Good night, Captain."

Nazira & Manny, 1969

28

NAZIRA IN THE USA. GUANTANIMO, CUBA. 1970

"Good morning Georgie, has the Captain been in?"

"Yes, he came in for breakfast when we opened. He asked me to tell you he would be down the Yellow Brick Sidewalk."

"Was he OK?"

"He seemed a little excited, but didn't explain. Why do you ask?"

"Only because it's unusual for him to make impromptu changes in our meetings. Can you join me for coffee?"

"Thank you. I expect that stirring up nostalgic memories for places, events, and people by reliving one's life stories might disturb sleep sometimes?"

"Yes, its one thing to occasionally recall brief stories from a distant past out of context, but it is quite an different adventure to share one's entire autobiography in chronological order. Everyone believes they have rational reasons for their actions which may seem odd to others unless their life experience is shared, explored, and challenged, especially with an attorney-son playing Devil's Advocate to inspire additional insights. For example, the Captain is at a challenging and happy time in his story, but his actions are better understood with a review of the years of pertinent background which significantly influenced those actions. Looking back can inspire deeper understanding and altered perspectives—especially true for me, since I had only sketchy second hand information about him through the years."

"Well Michael, I must tell you that even from my distance, it has been an enlightening experience to observe your close relationship. I'm sure the other residents are envious of your father to have a constant companion. There is no better therapy for the elderly than sharing memories with someone close who cares to listen. I admire you for what you are accomplishing."

"Thank you, Georgie. In truth, my motives are less altruistic than selfish. Meeting you has been a pleasantly surprising added attraction. If my slow progress on the book and my flying diversion makes it appear that I am extending my stay, you would be partly true. I hope you won't be moving on to new horizons soon."

"Well Michael, my plans are on the back burner, perhaps until I see 'how the book turns out'. Now, please excuse me. I have to show rooms to a prospective resident. For a change of scenery, how about if I treat you to dinner at Fisherman's Inn tomorrow evening?"

"Sounds great. I'd be delighted, thank you."

"May I confirm it in the morning–in case something interferes?"

"Of course. I am very flexible if you need to re-schedule."

"Good morning Captain. Georgie said you were up early. Didn't sleep well?"

"A dream kept me awake most of the night."

"A dream? Or THE dream?"

"Clever boy–THE dream."

"How was your 'flight'?"

"Much better than yours would be with this wind today. The forecasters were right for a change."

"Yes, glad I cancelled. I take it there was no cross wind on your 'runway'?"

"Nope. Not even spider webs were disturbed."

"So, are you going to tell me about it?"

"OK, OK. It was like when I was four, beginning with rolling my head back and forth on the pillow to put myself to sleep, then seeing myself in the far corner of the ceiling floating unsupported in a fetal position, looking back at me. Suddenly, I swapped places and saw myself on the bed."

"You said that as a child during those experiences you were consciously aware and only half asleep. Is that how it was last night?"

"It was dream-like at first, the same as when you found me on your first visit at this spot, floating above this wheelchair. I have a clear memory of the entire experience, but I can't say where the conscious reality of it began–perhaps with transition from an out-of-body state to finding myself standing and concentrating hard to find the place in my mind which allowed me to lift off. As I rose up several feet, I became aware that I was no longer in a dream. It was difficult for me to control my elation and remain focused, but after bumping between the ceiling and the floor several times without injury or losing concentration, I learned to more-or-less control my altitude within a couple of feet. To keep it simple and avoid flying through the window out of control, I did not attempt lateral movement."

"Amazing, Captain. What a break through. How long did the flight last?"

"Not long, less time than it seemed. After just a few minutes, my concentration faded and I settled back to terra firma."

"Did you feel like you was standing on something or supported in some way?"

"Not at all. Unlike your bird-like dream of using your arms as wings, I was in a zero gravity state, as though I was in space. The difference from space-walking was that I could control my movements without touching anything- albeit awkwardly. It was a once in a lifetime 'Kodak moment', for sure."

"No doubt! After all those years, what do you think helped you to finally break through consciously this time? Practice makes perfect?"

"Some Buddhists say 'practice *is* perfect'. Practice was a factor, but I think my mental boost came from re-living my past. Before we began, I was settling into giving up. Our recent exchanges about my experiences with Jean and Nazira were particularly illuminating and uplifting. I had never fully recognized what an especially critical high point the time of Nazira's entry in my life was, especially contrasted by the negative experiences of divorce and Vietnam, and accented by my reaction to the sixties' social upheaval. For this 'shazam' breakthrough, your help was invaluable, Mike."

"Thank you for saying so, Captain. That means more than other rewards this visit has brought me. I hope you will have many more successful flights. You must be looking forward to 'exploring the envelope'?"

"For now, I'm just reveling in the joy of having made it to the top of my mountain for the first time, for I have learned in life that the first time thrill of such events can never be recaptured."

"Yes, I remember the Corsair squadron C.0.'s report of his first combat victory being 'better than my first piece of ass'."

"Crude, but a fair analogy, Mike, but I was thinking of a more lofty personal achievement for comparison."

"Really! What might that have been?"

"Let's say it in unison -We'll get to that."

"Alright, Captain. I should have known. Since you touched on Nazira's entry to your life, would this be a good time to return to your story?"

"Yes indeed. We rented a duplex off base and furnished it sparsely, knowing we would be there only while the squadron transitioned to the brand new and much improved A7-E for our imminent re-deployment to Vietnam."

"How was Nazira received by Navy society?"

"Way far better than I ever dreamed possible, thank God. Nazira received an open arm welcome by everyone. There was not the slightest trace of hostility or hesitation by anyone in accepting her completely. I was astonished and greatly relieved by my most surprising and uplifting experience of humanity."

"That is wonderful to hear. How do you account for being so wrong in anticipating the worst from the wives, Mister Psych Major?"

"Hell, I don't know. Maybe it was my 'prepare for the worst' outlook Obviously, however, I had misjudged and underestimated Navy wives."

"Might you have been projecting a negative attitude toward women?"

"I'll just say, 'You can't live with them or without them', but don't presume that I was too biased. After all, I demonstrated a positive view of marriage by jumping right back into a third one, right?"

"That's one way to look at it. But even with the fine reception, Nazira must have been under considerable pressure. She certainly had no experience to prepare her for the challenges of being a senior officer's lady or a housewife, did she?"

"Well, no and yes, Mike. Although her formal education was minimal, hard knocks in the 'School of Life' had taught her a level of street wise common sense and wisdom beyond most people's maturity. Matched by her great beauty and self-assurance gained in show business and many levels of human interaction, Nazira's demeanor and personality seemed equal to any social challenge. Consistently charming in all situations, everyone loved her without reservation. She did not need a degree in English Literature to succeed in Navy society."

"Was that also true at home? I imagine that having earned her independence, success, and freedom after her formative years in confinement and on the run must have made it difficult for Nazira to settle down to become a wife and home-maker, particularly after having her own live-in housekeeper to care for her."

"Bless her heart, Nazira did her very best—and did it well. She tried to learn the rudiments of cooking from her mother while she waited at home, still she could scarcely boil an egg. Neither could I, so culinary progress was slow, but our small townhouse was an easy challenge."

"I assume you were away a good bit of the time, didn't she find it boring to be home alone in a strange land? Lemoore wasn't exactly anything to compare with one of the most cosmopolitan cities of the world, was it?"

"We took advantage of every opportunity to drive the Austin-Healey to the coast and mountains for many pleasant weekends, so time passed quickly. I do not recall that Nazira showed signs of home-sickness or boredom."

"So, are you saying that all went well between you and there were no issues?"

"I didn't say that, but thankfully none of the likely factors which had concerned me before we married—age, education, religion, language, and cultural differences—materialized as issues. I recall only two minor concerns. First, Nazira was still a bit overweight, though still what was considered buxom, so that was only a matter of subtle attention to it. Another adjustment was that I got over-zealous with her cultural indoctrination, especially with my love of American folk music. When she, made it clear that she was not interested, I was disappointed, but backed off. There was, however, one very serious issue between us and it was totally unexpected. Nazira was extremely jealous of my children because she greatly feared that out of guilt I would abandon her to go back to them. So, she adamantly demanded that I cease communications with them."

"What an unreasonable demand. I can see what an unpleasant surprise that must have been for you. You refused to comply, I assume?"

"Of course that was my immediate reaction, but I could see that Nazira felt genuinely threatened and that I was at least partly responsible, but the trigger had only been my few letters to the kids, who were three thousand miles away in Boston. I was firmly anchored to Navy obligations and WESTPAC deployment, so it must have been clear that there was no possibility whatever that I could consider taking responsibility for the children. There had to be more to her fears."

"Was she worried about Aurelie?"

"If so, her concern was unfounded. I never stopped being angry at Aurelie's impractical and selfish disregard for the kids' welfare."

"If so, that narrows it down to one cause, doesn't it?"

"Yes, Nazira' s bottled up stress was greater than I recognized. I had over-estimated her composure and erred in not seeing the limits of her self-assurance. I discovered then, however, that there is virtually no way for a westerner to have a rational meeting of the minds with an emotional Muslim. Nothing I could say was going to alter Nazira's conviction. With time, perhaps she would grow to accept my kids and realize that Aurelie was out of the picture, but the only short term action I could take to reassure her was to bend to her request."

"It must have been a difficult decision, whether to choose to deny your children and open the door to Nazira's future repeated unreasonable demands on one hand, or to close your mind to Nazira' s feelings of insecurity for the sake of maintaining communication with your distant children."

"It was very hard, Mike. Either way, there would probably be undesirable long term consequences which I might regret ever after. My aviator's gut response would have been to refuse to back down to Nazira. In sleeping on it however, I realized that Aurelie was correct in her rationale to not remain married 'for the sake of the children' because they would soon grow up and be gone, too late for her to begin life over. If I survived and our marriage lasted, there would have to be compromises."

"Except that Aurelie would have the self-defense evidence that you 'abandoned' the kids, right?"

"True, however, since she had chosen the task of raising them without me, she was going to need every advantage she could make. Because of the distance between us, the kids weren't going to see me for a number of years. Letters would be of little interest or value to them, so my involuntary absence would have the same consequences regardless. My first priority had to be my commitment to Nazira."

"So you agreed to Nazira's demand and stopped communicating with your kids?"

"Yes–for the time being."

"And the consequences?"

"We moved on. Nazira did not take up the habit of being demanding and the kids made no effort to communicate. My decision would have been different if I weren't making back to back cruises or if we lived closer to the kids."

"Your parents were relatively close by in San Diego? When did they meet Nazira and how did that go?"

"Soon and well, happily. Nazira was at her most lovely and charming self. They both loved her immediately–in Father's case, literally, I think. Whereas, Aurelie tended to alienate herself to Father as a somewhat plain New England 'artsy-craftsy' liberal with anti-military sentiments who lacked home-maker or career interests, Nazira endeared herself to them masterfully."

"Endeared–masterfully? Meaning intentional manipulation?"

"Yes Mike, but honestly, with great skill, and the best intentions. Nazira didn't want me to be involved with my children, but she absolutely did want to be accepted by my parents as a welcomed close member of the family. While Nazira was physically attractive, much of her beauty came honestly from within. Plus, the Arab, Chinese, and Portuguese elements of her heritage were an excellent combination which served her personality beautifully well."

"How was that?"

"Hard to describe briefly; Portuguese genuine inner warmth; Chinese honesty and wisdom; and Arab salesmanship talent. Her sisters said she was a 'Chinese Jew' because of her uncanny business sense and ability to 'sell refrigerators to Eskimos.'"

"An amazingly unique combination, Captain! Little wonder everyone loved her so dearly. Jean picked you a peach! So, what next?"

"The rest of the training cycle went well. Our transition to the new A-7E was a welcome upgrade to the A-7A with many cutting edge improvements, including a more powerful engine, an inertial navigation system, a terrain following radar, a color moving map display in the same scale as the radar scope, and an extremely accurate computer controlled bombing system."

"What was your impression of the squadron?"

"It's a strange thing that some Navy squadrons went through many evolutions of airplane and personnel changes, yet retained a constant reputation. In its early years, VA- 146 was stuck in a rut of low morale and performance. Then a C.O. came along whose efforts to alter that heritage included forming a four plane formation flight demonstration team he named The Blue

Diamonds which boosted morale and helped transform VA-146 ever after into one of the very best Navy squadron, still formally known as the Blue Diamonds. I had made several cruises in which the Blue Diamonds were part of the Airwing, so I was familiar with their excellent all around reputation. I could not have been more fortunate and proud than to be a member with a former Blue Diamond and friend, Wayne Stephens, as its C.O. and the most competent, cohesive, and professional group of Naval Aviators and men I have known."

"Wonderful, Captain. Since you had to return to Vietnam for a fourth tour, it was great that you were doing it in such good company. I hope that tour went well?"

"There were a few interesting and exciting times, though many mundane routine memories of it blend with other cruises. We were assigned to USS America which was based on the East Coast. For some reason it was decided that the two attack squadrons would fly our twenty eight A-7's across the US and down to Guantanamo Bay, Cuba, to load aboard the carrier in port. However, when we all arrived together at Guantanamo, we encountered heavy showers and thunderstorms with a broken overcast to over thirty thousand feet. There was just one very wet runway, no traffic control, no alternate airfield, marginal fuel remaining, and no airborne refueling available."

"That sounds like a bad beginning for the cruise."

"Indeed—made worse when we discovered that wet runway braking action was poor, so we would probably have to put the hook down to engage the mid-field chain link arresting gear—which required thirty minutes to manually reset- or risk going off the end of the runway."

"Twenty eight airplanes- one runway- thirty minutes to reset the arresting gear- computes to possibly fourteen hours to complete the recovery with how much fuel remaining?"

"You have the picture, Mike. It was a Navy disaster in the making. The A-7E had anti-skid braking which prevented blown tires, but if there was no braking action at all in standing water from heavy rain, anti-skid was useless. Furthermore, because the arresting gear was installed half way down the runway, the pilot's decision to lower the hook had to be made at touch down, since an airplane off the end of the runway would endanger the next one if it failed to stop. So, if we weren't going to run some airborne airplanes out of fuel, some had to land without the arresting gear."

"What happened?"

"Needless to say, there was quite a scramble on the base- especially since it was a weekend and after normal working hours with most of the Airwing at the O Club bar celebrating Happy Hour. We were out of options, the only help was that a radar operator was found to man the station's only search radar. Considering its limited capability, the operator did an outstanding job of sorting out and controlling the traffic. Those airplanes with the lowest fuel state landed first. Those who touched down between the heaviest showers kept their hooks up. A few of those turned off their anti-skid when they sensed it wasn't working and blew tires rather than go off the end of the runway, but were able to clear the runway. Most, however, had to use the arresting gear because of no braking action in heavy rain. So it dragged out until there were only two airplanes airborne which had so little fuel there was no time to reset the arresting gear used on the previous landing."

"You're not going to say that you were one of those two, are you?"

"Yup, you win a cigar, Mike. How'd you guess?"

"Because it's *your* story, Captain. It just more fun that way and you can *say* anything."

"Easy, boy. Would I embellish a story to falsely glorify myself in a book which you *say* will be published, thereby giving the Pukin' Dogs cause for mercilessly hoisting me on my own petard?"

"Sure, if you believe it won't get published in your lifetime and it would get the Dogs to remember you at Happy Hour. Didn't you say, 'Any publicity is good publicity'?"

"Nah that was my Granny- one smart lady I never disagreed with, but it doesn't apply here, because I didn't do anything heroic. My wing man had less fuel so I sent him down first, but he was going to have to clear the runway in a hurry for me."

"So now you're going to say that he went off the end of the runway into the mud, so there was no way for you to land."

"Damn, Mike, that's right! You're good. A chip off the old block. So, what happened next?"

"You ejected and landed lightly on the O Club patio to join the gang for Happy Hour and bought the house a round."

"Love it, but I like my story better. There was an old runway across the harbor which had been out of use because it was far too short for any current aircraft except helicopters. Although it also had mid-field arresting gear, it was rejected for our use because the runway was on a point of land with water at both immediate ends. If the hook skipped the arresting gear, the airplane was certain to end up in the harbor. So, Mister Cigar, what's your version of what happened then?"

"That's easy, Captain. You ran out of fuel on touchdown, your hook skipped the gear. You went off the end and ejected just before the airplane splashed into the harbor and exploded. The pressure and fire from the explosion lifted you in your chute high over the surrounding hills. An hour later, you landed on Castro's patio and joined him for Happy Hour."

"I knew you'd lose it. No more cigars for you. You had only one correct fact in your version. My hook did skip the arresting gear. Care to guess what really happened then?"

"You went to full throttle, barely managed to get airborne again, and caught the arresting gear on your next approach just as the engine flamed out. Then you were hailed as the hero of the day at Happy Hour and the house bought you drinks into the wee hours?"

"Close, but no cigar. You were right about catching the arresting gear, but not about the flame-out and Happy Hour. In fact, in good Navy fashion, there was never any official or informal discussion of the entire event. We handled it without a catastrophe. Case closed."

"Still, that was quite a colorful introduction to the Airwing the for the A-7 squadrons and you, wasn't it?"

"I guess it might have been, had it been peacetime. But events like that get lost in the clutter of war."

"So you loaded twenty eight A-7's aboard American and set sail. Which port next in-route to Vietnam?"

"Rio de Janeiro with its Valhalla of beach babes."

"Did Nazira fly to Rio?"

"No. We put everything in storage, turned in the house keys, and Nazira flew home to stay with her Parents in Hong Kong. Let's pick up in Brazil after lunch. Want to race up to the Lodge?"

"No way, Captain. I'm not racing a man who can fly!"

USS America 1970 cruise book photo

MEET THE SKIPPER AND EXECUTIVE OFFICER

Commander Wayne L. STEPHENS, the Blue Diamonds' [sk]ipper, lends a helping hand to the Executive Of[fi]cer, Commander Manuel B. SOUSA. No longer able t[o hi]de his age, CDR SOUSA allows himself to be booste[d in]to an A-7E aircraft. Three combat cruises have [ag]ed him mercilessly, yet he presses on despite cre[aking] bones and wrinkled skin. Bless him!

1970 VA-146 Squadron newsletter

29

Rio, Sydney, Manilla, and Vietnam. 1970

"This would be your second Brazil visit, Captain?"

"Yes, my first Midshipman cruise seventeen years before was to Sao Paulo, so I didn't visit lpanema Beach. I don't think it was topless then."

"There were many social changes almost everywhere by 1970, but nowhere more famous than Rio de Janiero's Carnival. Did the planners time your visit to that?"

"If so, it was to ensure that we were not in Rio for Carnival. For whatever political reasons, the USA was unpopular in Brazil as far back as our 1953 visit, so we were briefed to keep a low profile. The hotels denied squadron suite reservations and restaurant hospitality to our groups was chilly. The carrier hosted a diplomatic reception where the guests behaved with amazing rudeness. The non-Portuguese Europeans we spoke with were outspokenly critical of economic and political conditions. The road along Ipanema Beach was torn up for construction, blocking access for long sections, so there were few bikini's to be seen. Two blocks behind the beachfront hotels were slums. Beyond that were jungles. So, recalling Rio reminds me of the couplet we filled in the blanks with to tailor our regards for various ports of call to recite on departure: 'Farewell to thee Rio, we're leaving you at last. Take your hotels and beaches and shove 'em up your ass'."

"What about the countryside and people, was there nothing good to be said?"

"Yes there was, Mike, I'm glad you asked. What little I saw of the wild mountainous jungle on a bus tour was incredibly gorgeous. The population was largely Portuguese immigrants from the Azores Islands where my father was born, so they were very glad to have gotten away from the stifling depression of their homeland. Absent was the traditional Portuguese 'happy to be sad' characteristic. The unbridled and liberated Brazilian Portuguese were bright, joyous, and full of energy, accounting for their Carnival pagan rejection of repressing Catholic dogma and

Portugal's backward politics and economics. Of course, those were only my impressions from a brief visit almost sixty years ago, no longer valid observations."

"Where next, Captain."

"A long passage around the Horn for a port call at Sydney, Australia."

"Isn't the Horn famous for shipping losses in some of the roughest weather on the high seas?"

"Yes, many ships have been damaged or wrecked trying to round South America. At that southern latitude there are no land masses to interfere with weather systems circling the Earth, so the unobstructed wind has unlimited fetch to build waves of enormous heights which can overwhelm any vessel."

"Surely a thousand foot warship like America was safe in those seas?"

"Not necessarily. Even modern aircraft carriers have been severely damaged in high seas encountered there. Early aircraft carriers had their forward flight decks ripped off their mounts as the bows plowed through high seas. When Ranger rounded the Horn bound for California in the fifties, its flight deck was cracked mid-ship. The passage was completed safely, but it was in the yards quite a while for repairs and design alterations. As a sailing enthusiast with aspirations for a trans-Atlantic to Europe, I had read Joshua Slocum's 1898 account in 'Sailing alone Around the World' which he accomplished with a forty foot ketch he rebuilt from a wreck. In the book he describes two unsuccessful attempts to round the Horn before succeeding. Twice he was forced back through a narrow strait between rocks by high seas and winds. On his second attempt his rudder came loose, so he had to launch in his dingy to repair it."

"I read the copy you sent me, Captain. As I recall, it was at night in a storm and Slocum was washed over the side from his dingy during the repair -and he did not know how to swim!"

"Right. It was a miracle that he recovered and sailed on. That's why I had a special interest in viewing the Horn for myself."

"Yes, rounding the Horn is an adventure not to be taken lightly! What was it like aboard America?"

"We had a morning low overcast, smooth seas, and clear visibility with a good view of the Horn from several miles offshore. The overcast was signaling coming weather and gave the seascape shades of silver, blue and gray. I can still picture the awesome scene."

"Did you fly at all during that passage?"

"No. Everything was securely tied down the entire time from Guantanamo to the Philippines. The Horn was the only land sighted after Rio until we reached Sydney."

"Life aboard America those weeks without flying must have gotten a little tedious. As you quoted, 'A man who would go to sea for pleasure would go to Hell for a past time'."

"True for some, I'm sure, but going to sea was always an adventure–a pleasure similar to riding a bicycle, driving a car, or flying an airplane for many hours -all forms of meditation for me."

"The brief time I've had flying your Ximango has given me a glimpse of what you mean and why aviators love 'the hard way to make an easy living'. I understand how sailing is similar to soaring."

"Actually, we kept quite busy with briefings, games, reading, and movies. Plus, I had my guitar along as usual. Then someone came up with having a beard growing contest, so I decided to participate."

"Now there's a fine old sea-going pastime–watching your hair grow! I suppose you're going to tell me you won the competition?"

"No Mike, better than that."

"I feel a long story coming on."

"Hey, don't you want to prolong your visit-and get closer to Georgie?"

"What makes you say so?"

"Don't you have a date with her tomorrow night?"

"You couldn't possibly know that. She just asked me at breakfast this morning."

"It's true then!"

"I'll be darned, you just guessed?"

"Of course not. I have certain psychic powers, you know. Like when I saw through the phony alias and disguise you introduced yourself to me with on 1arrival."

"Psychic powers my foot. You called Fisherman's Inn and got my name from Reservations before I arrived."

"That was just to confirm it. Anyhow, I'm not being nosey, I just can't help having these insights. Let's go back to talking about watching hair grow."

"OK, but somehow I'm going to expose your 'psychic power'. Were beards legal in the Navy in 1970?

"Yes, Chief of Naval Operations, Admiral Zumwalt, authorized them in one of his many revolutionary 'Z-Gram' personnel policy directives; however, there were a number of old guard senior officers and Chiefs who dragged their feet complying with Z-Grams because they considered the drastic changes as threats to their authority."

"Since you were growing a beard, I assume you favored the Z-Grams?"

"Absolutely, fully and whole-heartedly. The Old Navy was burdened with 'chicken shit' administrative regulations and procedures, reflecting demeaning attitudes toward enlisted men which harkened back to the days of wooden ships and command fears of mutiny. It was commonly believed that sailors had to be treated like animals to maintain discipline and their weapons locked up until imminent battle to prevent mutiny. With the end of the draft, however, Navy recruiters were going to find it impossible to meet their quotas. The Z-Grams were not some liberal do-gooder's feel-good program, there had to be a major overhaul of practices and attitudes to improve public image and re-enlistment rates. Otherwise, ships, submarines, and airplanes would not be manned. Admiral Zumwalt was selected to be CNO ahead of many more senior Admirals specifically for the task and he did a very effective job of it."

"From what you said about your father, I expect he must have had some strong old guard Army sentiments against Z-Gram reforms too?"

"Yes indeed. Like many seniors, he argued that Navy leadership was becoming too soft. To get around that kind of intransigent resistance in the chain of command, Admiral Zumwalt got first hand feedback from the fleet, bypassing Navy's Washington Palace Guard and stubborn recalcitrant's were subtly weeded out."

"I remember how silly it was that hair length became a major social issue for the 'establishment' elders who were enraged by the long-haired Hippie 'freaks' social rebellion. The more the adults were reviled, the longer grew the symbolic 'freak flags'. So, I expect that hair length was a Navy issue which attracted more emotional attention than it deserved."

"It was absurd, Mike. Even the simple matter of permitted sideburn length generated debate and weekly Z-Gram modifications. The truth is that few junior officers and enlisted men cared all that much about hair styles, but the debacle made their the seniors look foolish."

"Was the resistance to Z-Grams wide spread among senior officers?"

"Those who supported Admiral Zumwalt tended to keep a low profile, waiting out the storm, but those opposed to him were hard to miss. For example, the NAS Lemoore C.O., Commodore Tully, refused to allow flight jackets away from the flight line or permit beards, nor did he permit working uniforms to be worn driving to or from home and the base. All specifically allowed by Z-Grams."

"So your participation in the beard contest indicated that you had a dog in the fight?"

"Not to my mind. I had grown a moustache on previous cruises, so I thought it would be fun to try a beard. The event was well in keeping with sea-going tradition and became a highly popular and successful morale boost. Then inexplicably, the announcement came from Captain Hayward that 'Officers are not expected to participate in the competition.'"

"Was that taken to mean that officers were not to grow beards at all?"

"Not to my mind, but many interpreted it that way and shaved. As it happened, my beard was coming along well and Wayne did not tell me to shave it off, so I pressed on."

"But you didn't participate in the contest, did you?"

"Sure I did."

"How could you, Mister Salute-and-obey?"

"The Captain's statement -'not expected to participate'–was weasel-worded, and non-specific. If he meant to order officers not to grow beards or compete in the contest, he should have clearly stated it so there could be no question that he was issuing an order -albeit an unlawful one. As I saw it, 'expected' was not a substitute for 'will not' in a direct order. Was 'participate' supposed to mean that officers were not to act in support of the contest in any manner? My understanding was that formal Navy policy permitted beards, but that the officers were not to compete so it would be solely an enlisted event."

"How did you participate then?"

"The contest judging took place on the hangar deck the evening before entering port. The enlisted judges were seated behind a long table. Contestants were paraded before the judges one at a time, each escorted by his Division Officer. For squadrons, the term Division Officer was subject to interpretation, so Wayne appointed me to act in that capacity to escort all the Blue Diamond enlisted contestants. For the occasion I wore my leather flight jacket and replaced the grommet in my bridge cap with a flexible surgical tube to give it a 'fifty mission crush' similar to German submarine commanders hats."

"So, you defied Captain America's suggestion against growing a beard and participating in the contest, and you did it out of uniform? I can hear your father's admonition that you were too rebellious to succeed in the military."

"I didn't see it that way. I participated in a leadership support role in the spirit of the event. Besides, as you noted, Wayne was writing my fitness reports, not Captain America. I had fifteen years service and I was a Commander with every intention of retiring on twenty without need for further promotion. Best of all, I was a squadron XO screened for command on the next tour. So how could Navy punish me–ship me to Vietnam? If there was ever a time for me to loosen up and enjoy my success as a naval aviator, this was it."

"Lord knows, after getting away with marrying Nazira, growing a beard was small potatoes indeed. Good for you. Did you keep the beard?"

"No. Captain America decreed all beards shaved off on the weak pretext that we were to be the Carrier Division Commander's flag ship. Earlier, Wayne and an enlisted plane captain staged a few gag photos with me in a silk scarf, leather helmet, goggles, and cigar being boosted up to an A-7 cockpit, presumably because I was too decrepit to climb in on my own. After the contest, as I stood at my sink to shave with just the light over the sink, I took a close up photo with my flight jacket, crushed hat, and lit cigar."

"Was that the end of the beard issue then?"

"Not quite. When the Carrier Division Commander came aboard, he reportedly asked why there were no beards. I don't know what lame explanation he was given but the prohibition stuck–with a lone exception. A Lieutenant in the WF squadron, who was soon to be released from active duty, defiantly retained his beard even after being specifically ordered via the chain of command through his CO to shave it off. The incident grew to be a significant focus of Wardroom conversation as it dragged on and escalated. The Captain shifted his pretext for the beard ban as a flight safety issue—an oxygen mask could not seal on a face with a beard. Still the Lieutenant refused, countering that aircrews did not wear oxygen masks on WF aircraft. Finally, Captain America ordered the Lieutenant to the bridge with his CO for a formal Captain's Mast judicial action, but the Lieutenant, bless his heart, stood his ground. So Captain America only publicly humiliated himself throughout the episode."

"Why would the Captain of an aircraft carrier be so incredibly dumb as to put his career on the line against a lone junior officer short-timer and the Chief of Naval Operations' formal approval of beards?"

"Your answer was contained in your question, Mike—dumb. I can only add that Captain America was a 'water walker' blond country club tennis pro type who was groomed to be the CNO since he was a Lieutenant. Plus, Admiral promotions and assignments were not made by CNO. Zumwalt wouldn't be around long."

"How was Sydney?"

"Very different than I expected of a new world California style city, Sydney and its population were very similar architecturally and culturally to an old world western European seaport -with two interesting cultural distinctions. One was the many soap box speakers in the city parks. Old men literally stood on boxes and ranted away for hours on social and political issues to passersby who stopped and listened awhile. It was quite a refreshing and fascinating display of old fashion democracy in action. The second distinction was the stereotypical Australian behavior of men and women. Compared to other nationalities I've observed, Australian men gave the impression of being distinctly rough and crude, whereas the women were sexually aggressive."

"I recall that you noted that trait in Australian ladies in 1964?"

"Noted then in just a single example, confirmed now only by observation, not 'hands on' experience. Being happily accompanied by Nazira radically altered my outlook on port calls in a most positive way. Besides, we were in Sydney for just a few days nearly sixty years ago. Surely, things have changed."

"Do you think it would be interesting to re-visit Sydney and Rio to find out how much has changed?"

"Maybe, but both are way off the beaten track and too far and inconvenient to get to from nearly anywhere."

"You could fly there yourself, or you might learn to transport yourself instantly -like Jonathan Livingston Seagull did."

"Hmmm, that's a thought. Some flight that would be. But if I got that far, I'd just continue the circumnavigation -an unsurpassable world record. I'll put it on my bucket list."

"List the Moon and Mars too. Anything is possible!"

"Meanwhile, my destination was Cubi Point, Philippines, via conventional surface transportation."

"Did Nazira meet you there?"

"No. The Airwing would be flying a lot in preparation for our first line period, so we planned to meet in Hong Kong during the following in port period. Our first line period went well. The A-7E proved to be all we hoped for–a highly reliable and effective attack airplane. On those rare occasions where we had pin point targets, such as a bridge or power plant, we could be certain of destroying it on the first mission. Not having to go back for repeated strikes to drop a heavily defended bridge was a major advancement, particularly since we were achieving that accuracy without precise regard for altitude, dive angle, airspeed, or maneuvering to avoid AAA. The Blue Diamond pilots and maintenance crew proved to be superbly competent professionals in combat and Wayne's relaxed low key Nebraska rancher father of eleven persona was a perfect combination for the ideal CO. He enjoyed his role so much that he seemed glad for me to leave him to it."

"It sounds like your Executive Officer duties were not very demanding."

"True. I was pleased to be just another pilot in the squadron, free to take time off with Nazira in port, so I wasted no time getting to Hong Kong as soon as we returned to Cubi Point. Leaving the Kowloon Ferry terminal to meet Nazira, I was astonished to be greeted by life-size full length photographs of her in a bathing suit prominently displayed in many of the store front windows."

"What was that about? Did she return to the movie studio?"

"No. She was competing for the Miss Hong Kong title in the Miss Universe contest."

"My my, you two just had to be in the public eye every minute, didn't you?"

"Sure, why not? As my pal Ron Hess advised, 'Don't fade into the woodwork. Let 'em know you were there.'"

"How did Nazira accomplish that publicity campaign? She must have had very strong promotional support."

"I didn't ask, but it became obvious that Nazira was such an enormously popular candidate she was a shoe-in to win the title -except for one detail."

"Her weight?"

"No. Admirably, she had trimmed down to her early centerfold figure. The obstacle was that she failed to mention that she was married."

"How could she conceal that? Nazira's promotion must have come from someone who didn't know her well."

"I assumed that she was such a well-known popular beauty in Hong Kong that the businesses wanted to be identified with her without asking too many questions."

"How did you feel about the surprise?"

"I was glad for Nazira. She had suppressed her movie ambitions and submerged her prominence to marry me, so competing in the contest would be a lifelong boost to her self-image, even if she didn't win."

"Did she win?"

"Expectations were over the top when she became one of the six finalists. Her photo was so prominent in the media that it seemed she had been pre-selected to be Miss Hong Kong of 1970. But then one of the other finalists told a judge about Nazira's marriage"

"Oh my gosh. With all the grand media publicity she received, that must have been a terrible embarrassment for Nazira and the pageant promoters to toss her out at that point."

"You gotta hand it to the Brits for the way it was handled, Mike. After Nazira freely admitted her marriage to the chief judge in a private conversation, she was told that she was to remain as a contestant through the final judging, but of course she would not win or place."

"How did the media handle it?"

"There were no public announcements of Nazira's disqualification. She simply did not win, so that was the end of the matter as far as I know."

"What were the effects on Nazira?"

"I wasn't in Hong Kong for the event, so I don't know what her immediate reaction was, but by the time we met again, she seemed quite alright. She didn't dwell on it, so I didn't either. We never discussed it further."

"How do you think she was able to get over it so easily?"

"I believe it had to do with a cultural aspect of her mentality. Muslims tend not to let guilt for lying spoil their day -a trait that facilitated Nazira's ability to 'sell refrigerators to Eskimos'. She was glad she had made the effort and could have won. I think the experience was a satisfying rite of passage for her out of Hong Kong and into adulthood. Meanwhile, I had a different cause to make."

"How had the war changed since your last cruise?"

"As I recall, not much at all—same missions bombing the same trees and road intersections. I have to admit, however, that I was somehow very fortunate to miss out on the years of the hottest and heaviest air action with large Alfa strikes on Hanoi or air battles with Migs."

"So, still no DFC's for you?"

"Nope. My feeling was expressed in the World War Two song, 'Distinguished Flying Crosses do not compensate for losses', nor were they worth lying for. Early in the war, DFC's were handed out so generously that the flow had to be restricted. The new criteria specified that there had to be elements of documented opposition, bad weather, darkness, and bomb damage assessment, BDA. Over the North there was usually bad weather, AAA, and half our missions were at night; however, BDA was very difficult to document because there were so few permitted targets of value and so many bomb craters. So, the criteria was nearly impossible to meet with truthful citations. First drafts were consistently bounced back down the long administrative chain to squadrons for more details, which meant elaboration, exaggeration, fabrication, delays, and mountains of paperwork for squadron administration which was generally assigned to those with the most 'creative' writing talents. The peculiar thing was that medals seemed to be most important to those who did the least to earn them–fighter pilots. Generally speaking, it was refreshing to see that the 'heavy hauling' junior attack pilots were the least motivated by medals. Instead, their satisfaction came from the 'psychic income' of doing their jobs well and surviving without dumb heroics or fabrications for medals."

"How was the Blue Diamond pilots' morale? On early cruises you said that seventy five percent of all carrier aircrews believed they would not survive."

"As I saw it, morale was excellent at all levels in the squadron and throughout the ship. I don't know of follow-on studies of aircrew fears by the Flight Surgeons, but my perception was that early fears were greatly allayed by better equipment, training, and tactics. Whatever negative opinions we had about the war and the way we were fighting it -and we had many -they did not affect our professionalism and camaraderie. I was always amazed that such complex and dangerous flight operations were accomplished without disaster in all weather conditions and twenty hour work days on the flight deck by such skilled and dedicated teenagers. It was truly heartening to see in all my time aboard aircraft carriers, especially on Yankee Station during Vietnam."

"Weren't young sailors influenced by the Hippie anti-culture revolution and protests?"

"If so, it seemed to only harden their professional resolve. The Z-Grams were an effective morale boost because Navy policy reflected genuine humane concern at the highest levels."

"For Navy's practical reasons though, right?"

"Zumwalt's revolutionary changes went well beyond necessity and the Navy has been the better for him ever since. Remember too that Navy always was an all-volunteer service, so sailors tended to be more inspired by patriotism, whereas the drop-out draft card and flag burning anti-war protesters who bailed out to Canada were motivated by cowardly fear of death, not idealistic anti-war zeal. Moreover, everyone engaged in carrier flight operations was constantly conscious of the crucial importance of doing their vital jobs to the best of their ability. So morale was sky high."

"What other highlights do you recall?"

"Because of the pyramid rank structure, the necessary formalities of command, and the social distance between junior and senior officers, friendships become less common with seniority. As they say, 'it's lonely at the top'. Though Wayne was a friend, as my CO, now we were more formal. On the other hand, my counterpart XO in the other A-7 squadron, VA-147, and I shared common personal interests in sailing and music. Bill was an extraordinarily charming, personable, and popular man—especially with the ladies, who invariably found him completely irresistible. Bill also found the ladies equally irresistible—so frequently that he came to be called 'Mandrake the Magician' since he often made himself disappear ashore. Ordinarily, Bill loved 'em and left 'em without complications; however, he fell hopelessly in love with an incredibly beautiful and highly intelligent Philippine queen of a young lady. Since Bill was encumbered with a wife, children, Saint Bernard, sailboat, and a Jaguar, he was greatly in need of a shoulder to lean on as he struggled miserably with deciding what to do. Since I had recently been through a somewhat similar experience and was equal rank in a different organization, I was the shoulder of choice."

"Wasn't that a lot for Bill to ask of you -and much more than you should have become involved with, Captain?"

"Ordinarily yes; however, I had a convenient 24/7 ear, felt genuine empathy, had some training in counseling, and we were under war time pressures, so I felt inclined to at least listen sympathetically."

"Isn't that what Chaplains are for, Captain?"

"You must be joking, Mike. How can you think a Chaplain's predictable judgments and counseling would be helpful for guys like Bill and me in family situations? As I said, I had the best available shoulder in this instance."

"I trust you just listened and held off giving advice?"

"Surely you jest, Mike."

"Oh damn. Poor Bill to have a friend like you at such a crucial time in his life. I suppose you advised him to follow your example, all would go well, and he would live happily ever after."

"Wow, Mike, you're really good! How did you know?"

"I'm psychic, like you of course."

"A good sense of humor too!"

"So?"

"So nothing. Bill knew better than accept advice from someone like me. He kept dithering and suffering, as I expected."

"Any other notable events during that cruise?"

"One more. Our Public Affairs Officer, Lieutenant, Al Junker, without our knowledge, used the pictures of me with the beard, leather helmet, goggles, and cigar being helped into the cockpit by Wayne for a 'Meet the XO' article he wrote in the squadron newsletter to the families. The wives' were reportedly astonished and some questioned 'Is that really our Executive Officer??' Next in the mail came a personal letter to Al from the editor of the Lemoore newspaper, The Golden Eagle, enclosing a copy of his article captioning my self-portrait photo. According to the editor's letter: '.'Nearly everyone liked it because it was unusual. The beard, the look in his eye, the shadows,–everything caused (to me) favorable comment. With our CO, however, the story is quite different. He's been taking it in the ear from the clean-shaven Navy regulations guys and has made a simple, direct statement. 'No more beards in the Golden Eagle!' Maybe you don't know that beards have been authorized at NAS Lemoore with an overabundance of furry faces around. The real career people are totally upset, etc., and spend a good deal of time talking about it. Cdr Sousa's picture isn't the total cause by any means but was timed just right to set things off again. Anyway, my congrats to you for getting me something interesting but I guess no one else will be able to follow your lead. Remember in future releases -no more beards. Drop lots of bombs. Rus."

"Well, unlike Captain America, you had to at least credit Tully for knowing how to give a direct order, didn't you? It's a good thing you were twelve thousand miles away! Were there any repercussions for you?"

"I'm sorry I missed the celebration with the sailors at home who posted every single copy of the photo and article, including the archives issue, on all the bulletin boards. I'm sure the photo and reports also made it to Admiral Z's desk, so it was all in good spirits as far as I was concerned. However accidentally, I was glad to be on the right side with the sailors and CNO in making a difference by contributing to a social revolution in the Navy. Although there were to be later repercussions, as we'll see, none affected me personally. Thanks to Al, that still wasn't the end of the photo. On return from one of my many trips to Hong Kong to see Nazira, there were 'Wanted, Manuel B Von Sousa, notorious WW II German submarine commander' posters with my picture in many places around the ship."

"Wanted for what?"

"The caption read, 'for desertion, sinking three German destroyers, two hospital ships, and the Good Ship Lolly Pop. Reward: 20,000 old Cruizeros or Abat, or 9 Pesos, or a VA-147 A-7E. Last seen hiding in Hong Kong.'"

"Al sure earned his keep as your PAO by keeping you in the limelight. Since he was doing all that on his own, without your OK, were you concerned that he was overstepping a bit?"

"Not at all, I was a fair target. Moreover, I felt that it was hopefully an indicator of a spirited open channel of camaraderie for me with the officers and men. I was rightly grateful to Al for doing a perfect morale boosting job of using me to promote The Blue Diamonds. I was especially proud of the Navy for letting me get away with all that stuff."

"What told you that the men were with you and it wasn't just Al's show?"

"I just felt good about it and I was unconcerned with consequences—which I believe the troops sensed. If I had been orchestrating Al's actions, everyone surely would have seen through it all as a personal ego trip. Providentially, events came about naturally with no contrivance on my part, which leads me to recall Captain America's farewell party. The squadrons and divisions were tasked to come up with skits to perform for the occasion in the Wardroom. My guys came up with a long poetic narration and musical accompaniment by four of them singing and playing guitars and a banjo. They asked me to be the narrator."

"I see where you saw that honor as positive validation of your leadership. How did it go?"

"The Captain's departure date was advanced to the last day of our line period when he was to fly off to Hong Kong in the ship's COD. Our 'band'–now named The Gross National Product– were the only ones ready to perform, so we had the show to ourselves the evening before his departure. Our performance went off without a hitch and was a real crowd pleaser. Bright and early the next morning I was awakened by a call saying that the Captain was offering me a ride to Hong Kong with him if I could get to the flight deck in thirty minutes. I threw on a flight suit and cap, packed a bag, and made the flight with time to spare. During the flight, I sat with the Captain and had a pleasant personal conversation about his career. He said that having all his tours cut short for 'fast track' advancement left him feeling that he had missed the best parts of squadron flying. When we arrived in Hong Kong, I quickly called Nazira to surprise her, but her mother answered saying that Nazira had flown to Manila, as we had planned. So, I ran to the mens room, changed into civvies, and ran to the ticket counter for a ticket to Manila, but was told that I had to have a passport–which I did not have. In those days we could travel using only our military ID cards, but what I didn't know was that we had to be in uniform for that. Thankfully, the clerk agreed that my flight suit and cap would suffice, although it was somewhat odorous from perspiration. By the time I changed again, the plane was loading–and there, six passengers ahead of me in line, was Nazira! It was too late to cancel, so we flew to Manila. When we checked into the hotel, I pondered what to do with my $800 cash. The Philippine's were notorious thieves and there was no secure place to keep valuables -not even with the hotel management–so keeping the cash with me was the least objectionable option. That evening we made reservations at a five star Spanish restaurant and dressed to the hilt. Street-wise Nazira arranged for a cab driver to be with us all evening who was waiting for us when we left the restaurant and she asked him if he knew of a nice night club. As we drove, it became obvious that we were leaving the city. When we finally stopped we found ourselves in a sparsely settled rice paddy countryside, parked at the one small two-story building with six men standing outside. We were in deep shit. Without discussing it, Nazira and I jumped out of the cab and it drove away. We ran as fast as we could across the rice paddies and didn't look back or slow down until we were back in civilization. The next morning I re-donned my flight suit and we flew back to Hong Kong. Fare well to thee Manila, We're leaving you at last, Take all your cabs and clubs and shove 'em up your ass."

"What an adventure. You were very lucky to escape. Did you feel that Jean was guiding you through the event?"

"I don't recall that occurred to me, but looking back I see that she was very much involved. Most of the time I was like a ball in a pinball machine and Jean was working the flippers and bumpers—with never a harmful downside."

"How was it that Philippine's were so dishonest?"

"I'm not sure. Generally, they seemed to be peaceful, warm-hearted, devoted Catholics. Religious statues, medallions, and crucifixes were displayed everywhere."

"Perhaps as some say, Catholics are so easily cleansed of their misdeeds at confession that they feel free to begin over without remorse, whereas Protestants are burdened with guilt which drives them to repent."

"Could be, you know Catholic behavior better than I. Some sociologists point out significant cultural and legal system distinctions based on religious differences between Protestant and Catholic countries. On the other hand, Nazira's Brit brother-in-law, an intelligence officer in Hong Kong Special Branch, claimed that Philippine criminal behavior came from American gangsters who taught them everything they knew from the time the Philippine Islands were a US Possession."

"How typical for a snotty Brit to blame us. He should have known that the Spanish governed the Philippines long before the US, and that they schooled us and all their colonies in barbaric behavior."

"Well said, Mike. I wish I had thought to come back at him with that. My opinion is that their head-hunter mentality was simply not far enough down the road of human development to adapt to Western civilization. I don't think the people were basically evil, that was just their primitive way of life. Neither us, the Spanish, nor the Church were responsible for their own backward culture and choices. We will return to that subject with another adventure in the next chapter."

"Are there more adventures to relate in this chapter?"

"More like a post script. The new Captain America noted to the chain of command that it would be as short a passage home if we completed our world circumnavigation via the Cape of Good Hope rather than return the way we came around the Horn, and it was approved."

"So much for your fourth Vietnam tour?"

"Yes. Thankfully, we did our jobs well, lost no pilots or airplanes, and the time had come to move up to C.O., but for unknown reasons Wayne asked to delay our change of command until we returned to Lemoore. Considering his kindnesses to me, I had no objection. On the way, we stopped at Sydney again and the new Captain America hosted a ship visit by the Mayor and his wife. When the Captain greeted them on the Quarter Deck the wife pointed to the beard photo of me on the roster board which Al had substituted. 'Who is that? I want to meet him', she exclaimed. Just as well that I was already ashore, I'm sure she would have been disappointed."

"Considering your beard's brief life, you certainly got a lot of mileage out of it, didn't you?"

"Yes indeed, or at least Al did."

"How did the Cape of Good Hope compare to the Horn?"

"In my experience, quite similar. The seas were fairly calm and the visibility good. Passing just a few miles offshore, the earth's curvature can significantly obstruct the horizon, so there wasn't much to see. Still, it was an impressive landmark because of its remote geographic significance at the southern tip of the African Continent. Of course, there's always a special grateful feeling of completion in sighting any landfall after a long ocean passage."

"Since Nazira had been with you throughout, I suppose that homecoming was re-defined for you?"

"Yes it was–for the better–especially compared to the previous cruise when I came home to face a divorce. Yet, there had always been an overriding tenseness, if not pain, in all my countless numbers of farewells and reunions, regardless of whatever sense of relief may have accompanied either. Nazira was to follow after I set up housekeeping, so this homecoming was a welcome non-event for me. Nearly one third of the squadron was moving on to new assignments and half those remaining for another tour went on thirty days leave. Plus, a number of our A-7's were transferred to other deploying squadrons or overhaul facilities. So the Blue Diamonds hangar was peacefully quiet when Nazira re-joined me. A month later, the Airwing Commander, Bill, and I had a three way change of command which everyone on the base attended because flight operations were cancelled by fog. Even Commodore Tully and my parents attended. Following the ceremonies, everyone drove to the Officers Club for our reception, which required passing under a taxiway overpass. There on the overpass for all to see was a huge banner saying 'WELCOME ABOARD SKIPPER SOUSA'. In the middle was the 2 X 3 foot enlarged photo of Wayne boosting me into an A-7 cockpit with beard, goggles, leather helmet, cigar, and silk scarf–into the cockpit."

"Good old Al, what a guy. Do you suppose that Commodore Tully thought highly of Al's work too?"

"I'm sure the bastard had an extreme dislike for both of us, but he was not writing our fitness reports and I never spoke to him. So, let's leave it there tonight and continue tomorrow, OK?"

"Sure, Captain. You had a long night last night and I have a flight and heavy date tomorrow. So, shall we take a day off?"

"Good idea. Best of luck to you on both counts, Mike.

CDR MANUEL B. SOUSA — executive officer of Attack Squadron 146 "Blue Diamonds," flew his 200th combat mission in July. For the mission, CDR Sousa led an interdiction strike against the Ho Chi Minh Trail from the Seventh Fleet Attack Carrier USS America (CVA-66). A veteran of three previous combat cruises, CDR Sousa is well versed in combat aviation. On his first two combat cruises, he flew the Navy's foremost fighter aircraft, the F-4 "Phantom." His third cruise saw him flying the A-7A, which at the time was the Navy's newest attack jet. CDR Sousa joined the Blue Diamonds in December 1969 as they were completing transition to the A-7E, a vastly improved version of the A-7. As one of the first two squadrons to receive the A-7E, the "Blue Diamonds" were tasked with its initial combat employment. CDR Wayne L. Stephens, the Blue Diamonds' Skipper, congratulated CDR Sousa upon returning from his 200th combat mission, noting that CDR Sousa has been instrumental in p ving the superiority of the "Echo" as the Navy's most ad-   ced attack jet. This was CDR Sousa's second milestone while flying the A-7E, as earlier on this cruise he logged his 600th carrier landing.

333

30

COMMAND

"Good morning Captain, you look chipper!"

"Thanks, Mike. I feel fine, but you look a little pale. Tough flight? Or were you up late?"

"Neither one. As one with psychic powers, you already know about my excellent day and evening, so I won't elaborate–and I am not pale. Thanks for your concern."

"My powers and eyesight have become fuzzy over the years. Details need clarification."

"I discovered the secret of your 'psychic powers' yesterday. Your eyesight was apparently good enough the day before to read Georgie's desk calendar restaurant reservations for us. Do you snoop around in her office on a regular basis?"

"Of course not. I just stopped by to pay a bill. She wasn't in, so when I left my check on her desk I couldn't help but notice your name on her calendar for Fisherman's Inn reservations. I am not a snoop."

"I see, you just stopped by and couldn't help notice? I believe you, but there are millions who wouldn't."

"So, Mike, what were you doing in Georgie's office last night?'

"I'll leave the details of the evening to your snoop power. The flight went well, though there was no lift, so I landed early."

"Sure–to have more time to shine, shave, and shower for your big date!"

"Shall we move on with your story and adjourn to the park?"

"I suppose so, but your story has become more interesting."

"For someone who has achieved levitation, that is an amazing comment."

"Shhh, hush up, Mike. Remember, there are some real snoops in here with their hearing aids. I hope you haven't whispered our little secret into Georgie's ear?"

"No, of course not. Would I want her to shift her spotlight to a naval aviator who can levitate?"

"Good point. You wouldn't stand a chance. So, let's keep it that way and I'll stay out of your flight path. If anyone is to be let in on my flights, I want to be the one to do it."

"Unless you lose control and go streaking across the sky over Heritage Pines some Sunday afternoon during a garden recital."

"If that happened, I'd just keep going over the horizon. Let's go to the garden.

"So on with your 1970 story, Captain. Did you find a cozy off base apartment and settle down to life ashore again with Nazira before beginning the business of training for the next Vietnam cruise?"

"Pretty much that way. My command tour got off to a slow start because we initially had only six A-7's assigned and a limited fuel budget."

"Budget? You had to manage a budget? I thought DOD wasn't bothered with such trivia during a war."

"Few appreciate that DOD is one of the best managed organizations in the world, despite its size and complexity. Although Navy squadrons are junior cost centers, financial management, along with authority and responsibility, is delegated to the lowest command levels."

"Without airplanes or money, what did you do about training?"

"I figured we could fly our budget with four day weeks, so rather than sit around, I gave everyone Fridays off and suggested they spend weekends with their families somewhere away from Lemoore. After all, they were going to be away and working 24/7 for nine months in a combat zone, so there was no question of Navy getting its money's worth out of them."

"You had the authority to shorten the work week?"

"Probably not, but no one objected. Amazingly, the maintenance crew volunteered to work the number of people necessary over the weekends to get our planes ready for the Monday flight schedule. It worked out that morale and aircraft availability was very high. Of course, as our deployment date approached, we soon enough had a full complement of airplanes and funding. The pace picked up with training deployments to Nevada, Arizona, and Constellation. Three day weekends were history, but no one questioned that either."

"Did you have other leadership challenges?"

"I explained to the men why what we were doing in Vietnam was important and correct. If nothing more, we were defending the lives of our comrades in arms on the ground. I offered to excuse from the squadron anyone who disagreed. I probably didn't have the authority to do that either, but bless their hearts and thank the Lord, there were no takers. A few weeks later, one of my senior First Class Petty Officers got in trouble after drinking too much at the Enlisted Club, called the Black manager a Nigger and pulled a knife on him. So, some level of Navy judicial procedure was called for–possibly a Court Martial. The Petty Officer was a dynamic high profile leader in our Maintenance Department, so this was a test in the men's eyes. As a Z-Gram supporter, how lenient would I be?"

"I remember that your father, like many old-time Sergeants, believed in physical and verbal abuse instead of formal judicial punishment."

"True, my father had a unique way of terrifying men with just words and looks which worked for him. There were stories of men being taken out back and roughed up in the old days, but I never heard of that during my service. Formal Non Judicial Punishment, NJP, procedures were time consuming, formal, and complex, so they took more patience and intelligence; however, it was far more even, fair, and understood. Modern sailors were more educated and enlightened than their predecessors, so physical discipline was counter-productive, not to mention illegal."

"So what did you do?"

"Lacking Father's temperament, I called the Petty Officer before me at Captain's Mast which was the least formal level of NJP with just the CO and the accused, plus selected witnesses."

"No lawyers?"

"No, but the accused had the option of declining Mast in favor of a Court Martial where legal representation was optional; however, punishment options were more severe–including incarceration. The Captain's Mast advantage to the accused was the limited degree of punishment permitted–fines and/or reduction in rate. The Petty Officer, who had a nine year clear record, admitted to the charges and was appropriately apologetic; nevertheless, I fined him $60 and reduced him in rank to Second Class Petty Officer which removed him from his authority and leadership position in the squadron–severe humiliation for one of my more prominent men, but I felt that threatening the Club Manager with a knife using the 'N word' was unacceptable–especially for a senior Petty Officer in a squadron leadership role."

"What were the effects of your decision?"

"My sense of it was that the men agreed that the Petty Officer deserved to be taken down a notch. Several months later when he asked me to restore his First Class stripes, I declined. To my knowledge, that was the end of the matter. There were no other judicial proceedings during my tour. If we had been aboard ship, NJP, along with much of the squadron CO's administrative authority and responsibility, would have shifted to the ship's departments. So I was glad for the timing of the beginning my command tour after the cruise. Indeed, I am way out of date now, I believe that all judicial procedures are administered externally by JAG officers. By the way, I want to mention that my father had once been busted in rank for an offense early in his career and there was no doubt about the lasting lesson that was for him. Another bump in the road for the squadron during my CO tour was failing a nuclear administrative inspection. Somehow, a routing slip attached by a paper clip to a top secret document had gone missing which had the signature accountability of everyone who had handled the document. The Chief Petty Officer inspector aggravated the issue by going out of his way to be excessively nasty and gratuitously aggressive with me -gesturing to poke his finger in my chest exclaiming that there wasn't a damned thing I could do to him. Apparently, it pissed him off that I wasn't upset by the incident. After all, it was only a routing slip which was no doubt somewhere in the pile of documents. The document itself was intact, so there was no cause to consider the matter a major breach of security. In other words, the Chief was such a pedantic piss ant, puffed up with authority, that it even seemed possible he removed the routing slip himself. So I waited several months to distance myself from the emotions before I sent a personal letter to his boss, Commander Naval Air Pacific, documenting the Chief's disrespectful behavior and recommending his reassignment from inspection duties. Apparently mine wasn't the only complaint -he was fired."

"That must have been a well written letter to not sound like sour grapes, Captain."

"It was, but I can only take credit for initiating, editing, and signing it, since it was masterfully drafted by my crackerjack Admin Officer, Rex Wolf, who witnessed the incident. Rex was a perfectionist with paperwork, so we made a game of it. He bet me a martini for each document prepared for my signature which was error free. I agreed, providing he would owe me a martini for each error I found. When the score became forty two martinis in my favor, Rex threw in the towel to preserve his Yeoman's' morale. Rex was also a colorful aviator who had a penchant for lighting farts at social functions -which of course would have been applauded in fighter squadron society. His writing talents were also handy for drafting our bids for squadron awards. The Blue Diamonds were a shoe-in for the Safety Award since we had completed three combat deployments, including our transition to A- 7E's, without an aircraft accident. We also completed the mission training requirements with high scores for competition in the 'E' for excellence award; however, we did not receive either one. Since my admirer, Commodore Tully, was in the endorsement chain, I believe he sabotaged our nomination."

"Hard to believe that a senior officer would be so petty as to punish such an outstanding squadron because of an unjustified personal gripe with the CO."

"Not if you knew Tully. Later, I wasn't sorry that I inadvertently pissed him off once again. Lemoore A7-E's began having bombing errors out of limits. I was certain that the avionics people had learned incorrect maintenance procedures in training, but there was little chance of tracking down the problem before our imminent Operational Readiness Inspection without stirring up a lot of defensive denials. I proposed getting LTV factory assistance with Bill. He did not want to be involved, so I proceeded on my own. LTV was working hard to sell A-7E's to the Swiss Air Force, so I pointed out that when our inspection bomb scores were publicly revealed to be no better than earlier model A-7's, sales would be difficult. The effect on LTV management was immediate. Their electronic 'Sweep' team was upon us en masse that weekend. Tulley had not been informed because he was in the midst of moving and was enraged that thirty factory civilians were descending onto the base without his approval. Tulley's attitude was that DOD contractors were untrustworthy and up to no good, albeit he chose not to convey his anger to me himself. If he fussed at my boss, Gus Egert, CAG did not pass it along, perhaps because the desired results were achieved -our outstanding bomb scores resumed and no one got their toes stepped on for faulty maintenance procedures. Only a martinet like Tulley would ignore the positive results. Fortunately, I encountered few other naval aviators like him."

"A good thing you weren't working directly for him, considering how determined be was to get at you."

"You're right, Mike. As it was, pissing him off told me I was doing something right."

"It's really fortunate that your somewhat cavalier short-timer attitude toward your Navy future worked out so well for your squadron tour."

"You could say that, Mike, but the attending risks that went with the job made long term planning unrealistic, so my focus was independent of future intentions and more about the job at band. I readily went down the Yellow Brick Road with the opportunities Aunt Jean presented and enjoyed being in a position with the authority to make a difference. For me, there was no higher achievement for a naval aviator than to lead a squadron into combat. Moreover, after having struggled along with just average flying ability for fourteen years, I found my stride. Flying seemed more natural, comfortable, easy, and fun—even though I was thirty eight, a ripe old age for a carrier pilot going off to war for a fifth tour. For example, during the Airwing deployment to Fallon Nevada prior to carrier ops aboard Constellation, I had the good fortune of winning the Airwing Top Gun bombing competition trophy."

"Practice makes perfect? Or was it Nazira's positive influence?"

"Both. I bad a sense of well-being and accomplishment above my highest hopes. Nazira was a jewel. Other than getting over the rough spot about my kids, she was totally charming, adaptive, and supportive, shore-based or on cruise. I should mention, however, that during that Fallon deployment CAG had a mid-air collision with an A-3 tanker while in-flight refueling during a thirty plane practice Alfa flight formation I was leading. CAG ejected and was picked up without injury and the tanker landed safely with minor damage to its right wing tip. Gus bad flown along as an observer to grade my flight for 'E' competition at my request. On his own he decided to take advantage of a rendezvous delay by the A-6 flight for his unplanned refueling. The accident board gave me contributing factor because I hadn't briefed him for that."

"How ridiculous to be so obvious in making excuses for CAG."

"Of course, Mike—so obvious that Ray Charles could have seen it. As usual, however, nothing was ever said about the accident to me and Gus later made Admiral anyhow. So I put the accident out of mind entirely."

"You were very fortunate, Captain. How was the Airwing transition to life aboard ship? If my count is right, that would be your third deployment aboard Constellation, so it must have seemed-like old home week for you."

"There is little distinction between Navy ships below decks and there's nothing about conduits, pipes, and gray steel walls which resemble anything you would call 'home'. Still, I had spent so much time at sea and Connie was such an excellent carrier that it felt comfortable to be aboard again. The move back must have gone well because I remember little about it except a few incidentals. I was at lunch in the Wardroom in port in San Diego when Chaplain Schmidt, briefed the ship's Executive Officer on a forthcoming burial at sea for the remains of a retired officer. The family was to be present with a number of friends and wished to have the ceremony conducted from the flight deck. Schmidt reminded the XO that since offshore winds in Southern California were typically light and fluky, it would be difficult to maneuver the ship to be certain the ashes would drift away from the ship; therefore, it would be prudent to conduct the ceremony from the more sheltered hangar deck, closer to the ocean. After weighing the options, however, the XO decided in favor of the family's wishes."

"Uh oh, I can see where this story is going. Did you observe the event?"

"No, but it must have been quite a sight. At the exact moment of scattering the ashes, a zephyr softly and gently enshrouded the assemblage with the remains and drifted the length of the flight deck."

"Ah yes, 'The best laid plans of mice and men oft times go astray'. The dearly departed must have relished giving the family an unforgettable farewell from the other side."

"Good for him. His kin should have known better. It is no small matter to put an aircraft carrier to sea for the sole purpose of such a minor event. Burials at sea for retired members should not be a permitted option, just as the practice of taking up valuable real estate in perpetuity with grave yards should cease, not to mention the primitively painful ritual of viewing remains."

"I agree. Cremation is much more simple, practical and inexpensive. A friend once told me his interesting experience of witnessing a cremation. May I share his account with you?"

"Sure, let's hear it, Mike."

"My friend Jim, once had an ex-Navy fighter pilot friend, Fred, who was living alone in Colorado dying of cancer. So Jim went to be with him for his final three months and stayed on afterward to tend to the cremation, memorial service, and estate settlement. Fred, had been devoted to Indian lore and wished to be cremated with his bear Totem. That led Jim to gain permission to witness the entire cremation procedure. I can't do justice to Jim's very detailed and moving description, so I'll just relate the highlights as I recall them. At the appointed time, Fred's remains were delivered in the heavy cardboard casket which was to be put into the crematory. When Jim asked if the Totem was inside, the mortician opened the box to let him see for himself. Jim said Fred's eyes were open, as clear blue as ever, and the bear was in his arms. The box was closed, placed in the oven, and Jim was allowed to turn up the flames. After several hours, the flames were turned down and the doors opened to remove ashes and consolidate the larger remaining bones, including most of the skull, in the center for further burning at a greater temperature which Jim initiated by pushing a button ironically labeled 'Afterburner'. Thus, Fred was launched up the chimney into space that night for his last flight."

"Did Jim dispose of the ashes too?"

"Yes, I'm glad you asked. Even the afterburner did not reduce the large bones to fine ash. Those were pulverized to smaller bits and were later scattered by Fred's girlfriend from his horse at his ranch high in the Colorado mountains in the company of other close friends."

"Thanks for telling me that story, Mike. It makes me appreciate that cremation is much more appropriate for aviators than burial. I had the honor of participating directly in the memorial airborne scattering of cremains for an aviator friend, but the background is involved, so I'll wait to tell it. There is also an option offered by The Neptune Society which has undersea artificial reefs on both US coasts for deposit of remains. The society also offers the option of offshore ceremonies for scattering remains from small boats."

"Those sound like excellent options for a crusty old sea dog naval aviator, after-burner up a chimney in smoke and his remains stored in Davey Jones Locker. What could be better?"

"Right you are, Mike, so I hereby charge you with making it so when my time comes. You may consider it compensation for inheriting the Ximango!"

"More than fair, Captain. I shall be honored on both counts, in the event that I do not pre-decease you, of course."

"Well then, you better start taking better care of yourself. Georgie can probably shape you up. But let's try to finish this book before we go to Davey Jones Locker. I saw Nazira off on her flight to Hong Kong and Constellation set sail for our readiness inspection in Hawaiian waters. The Blue Diamonds did well in the inspection; however, the rest of the Airwing and ship departments' marginal performance resulted in a generalized 'shotgun' message of criticism from the Commander in Chief Pacific Fleet directed to all hands aboard Constellation. Since the Blue Diamonds had done well on the inspection and were unjustly included in the blast, Rex Wolf and I once again drew our poison pens to draft a personal protest message response directly to the Admiral, inviting his attention to the Blue Diamonds' excellent performance on the inspection and outlining VA-146's other outstanding accomplishments."

"You say that you responded directly to Commander in Chief Pacific Fleet, bypassing CAG and Connie's CO?"

"That's what I said. It was my personal response to an injustice which did not involve others. Rex arose to the occasion in superb form and we drafted a brilliantly balanced masterpiece message which I did not discuss with anyone. If my response was to have dire repercussions, I would take the brunt alone. We were as good as any squadron ever got and dammit we were going to war. It was my responsibility to not take some staff desk jockey's unjustified shot gun criticism without calling him down for it."

"Well, Captain, I have to say that you were extremely fortunate to have an outstanding writer like Rex to 'interpret' your words to higher authority for you! What happened?"

"The immediate response from CINCPACFLT was that he cancelled his blast message and ordered all copies destroyed. Then I received the Admiral's sincere personal message of apology. I surmised that the blast message had been drafted and released by his Chief of Staff without clearing it with his boss. I heard that CAG and Connie's CO were highly pleased with the outcome which accomplished some good in restoring morale throughout the ship. But of course they said nothing about the matter to me."

"You were sort of sailing off with your own Navy, weren't you, Captain?"

"As I saw it, I was a team player enjoying the authority and responsibility entrusted to me without having someone holding my hand or looking over my shoulder. In other words, I enjoyed the independence, but understood the risk of having been given all the rope needed to hang myself. The only mild chiding comment I ever got was from CAG, who ribbed me once about a lack of humility. As a: fighter pilot, I considered that a complement. The humble folks I've known had a lot to be humble about."

"But the Good Book says the meek shall inherit the Earth!"

"Yes, and it also says that the Earth will be destroyed by fire next time, so inheriting it may be the reward to those who don't go to heaven. In any case, I soon demonstrated an abundance of humility. But that's a long story and it's near lunch time, so let's save it for the next chapter when Constellation reports to Yankee Station again, OK?"

"Sure, Captain.

VA-146 'Blue Diamonds' over Mt Fuji, Japan

Attack Squadron 146 (ATKRON 146)
VA-146 'Blue Diamonds'

A-7E Corsair II (VA-146 / CVW-9) embarked on USS Constellation (CVA 64) - 1974 (National Naval Aviation Museum)

A-7E CORSAIR II SPECIFICATIONS

Manufacturer: LTV Aerospace Corporation

Type: Light attack aircraft

Crew: Pilot

Powerplant: One 14,250 lb. static thrust Allison TF41-A-2 turbofan

Dimensions: Length: 46 ft.,1.5 in.
Height: 16 ft., 3/4 in.
Wingspan: 38 ft., 9 in.

Weight: Empty: 19,490 lb.
Gross: 42,000 lb.

Performance: Max Speed: 693 mph
Ceiling: 43,000 ft.
Range: 980 miles

Armament: One 20mm M61-A1 Gatling gun; AIM-9 Sidewinders; 10,000 lb.
ordinance

31

FINAL MISSION

"OK Captain, it's September 1971 and you are steaming from Hawaii to WESTPAC aboard USS Constellation as the Blue Diamonds skipper on your fifth Vietnam combat deployment. What were your feelings?"

"Relaxed and happy, Mike. Glad to be there with the best officers and men I could ever have wished for. Our heavy-hauling bombing mission–then mostly into Laos–was at the core of aircraft carriers' last link in diplomacy and the A-7E was the best plane for the job. Even the challenge of night carrier landings had been reduced to a more tolerable level with the installation of indirect white flood lights on the flight deck landing area, plus auto-throttle linked to angle of attack. The airwing became a ship's division with many of the squadron administrative responsibilities assumed by the ship's departments, so CO's were little more than one of the boys, coasting on whatever imprint I accomplished during the training period ashore, except that now the buck stopped with me if there were performance issues within the squadron. Vietnam was winding down for lack of society approval and political leadership. The claim of 'they shall not have died in vain' was utter political crap yet again. Nevertheless, my personal life with Nazira had relieved me of the burden of feeling that Navy life at sea was pointless. So yes, relaxed and happy are the right words."

"Your year as CO was nearly up already, wasn't it?"

"Yes. Since I gave up a month as CO to Wayne, I was to have just eleven months as CO, which meant my change of command was less than three months and two line periods away. So there was little opportunity to make a lasting impression."

"Were there no notable events highlighting those few days?"

"Only trivial things, but precious memories to me. One day at dinner, Bill told me that Chaplain Schmidt invited him to read a Bible passage at Sunday service which Bill declined, so

344

he was warning that I would also be asked. I commemorated my response with a poem which was distributed throughout Connie by my inventive PAO, Al Junker.

THE CALL OF THE CLOTH

At dinner one day in Wardroom Two
Sat two squadron Commanders, a lusty crew.
One spoke loudly, his face stuffed with steak,
The head Jason named Bill, known as 'Mandrake'.
For Wardroom etiquette, he gave not a hoot.
His mouth nearly fit his Wellington boot.
Sex, religion, and politics all took their turn,
But on religion Bill had something to learn.
For he was speaking to Manny, the head Busy Bee.
To watch Bill take the bait was something to see.
The Chaplain had asked Bill To read from the Good Book,
But his only response was a horrified look.
He feared the worst if to church he went.
The mark would be on him, he'd have to repent.
"Watch out Manny, he'll be after you next
To stand up in Church and read from the Text."
"I'd do it with pleasure", Bee One replied.
"Bullshit", said Bill, for he thought Manny lied.
Then with his Wellington firmly in place,
Bill took the bait with a smile on his face.
"If you do that," Bill said quite amused,
I'll go every Sunday for the rest of the cruise.
Whether in port or far out to sea,
When there's a service, it's there I will be."
The Sunday has come and the Sunday has gone.
Manny read the Good Book and sang all the songs.
Now Bill we all know you're a man of your word,
So if you don't do it, you're just a big turd.
See the light. Go like a moth.
Get down on your knees, Heed the call of the cloth!

"When I told Chaplain Schmidt about Bill's promise he had a folding chair with VA-147's logo and Bill's name on it placed on the front row of every Sunday service thereafter–empty."

"Good show, Captain–at Bill's expense. Was he a good sport about it?

"Though he didn't complain, he seemed cooler. In any event, humor was scarce on Yankee Station and as providence would have it, I was about to be the rightful butt of a poem myself, chronicling a widely publicized event."

"At your expense?"

"You may judge that. Whenever we were in port at Cubi Point, I took advantage of sailing Special Services 'Lido 14' sailboats in Subic Bay. My Executive Officer, Jack Miller, asked to go along for some sailing lessons. I'll leave the story to the Navy message report and the A-6_ Intruder squadron poets with some interjected explanations by me."

291015Z (29 Oct '71) FM: COMUSNAVPHIL TO: CINCPACFLT INFO: CINCPAC, COMSERVPAC, AMEMB MANILLA, USS CONSTELLATION UNCLAS COMUSNA VPHIVSITREP SAILBOAT BOARDED/013/290700Z OCT 71 J: AT 290700Z RECREATION SAILBOAT USED BY COMMANDER M.B. SOUSA AND CDR J.A. MILLER OF USS CONSTELLATION RAMMED BY BANCA BOAT AND BOARDED. OCCUPANTS ROBBED AT KNIFE POINT OF WALLETS, WRIST WATCHES. APPROX 73 DOLLARS TAKEN. FOUR OR FIVE PHIL NATS IN BANCA BOAT. INCIDENT OCURRED 100 YARDS WEST OF GRANDE ISLAND.

THE SAGA OF THE PUEBLO II

This is the story of two sailors Had themselves quite a day
Skipper Sousa and his XO, Jack Miller And their experience on old Subic Bay.
Early one Thursday morning The Pueblo II set sail
That really wasn't her name you know, but it goes quite well with this tale.
(Pueblo was the Navy destroyer, captained by Cdr Loyd Bucher, captured by North Korea in 1969)
A dapper man was her skipper, a man born and bred to the sea.
He was taking out the XO to qualify him as O.O.D. *(Officer of the Deck)*
He peered at the sea through bloodshot eyes–There was a party the preceeding day.
Then he called to the XO, "Set the mainsail." And the small craft began to make way.
It should be mentioned at this point the overall size of this craft.
Her overall length was two fathoms and her beam was her length by one half.
They gracefully left the small harbor and sailed into Subic Bay.
The skipper told the XO, "I'll surely qualify you today."
The skipper delivered his lectures, as back and forth he did walk.
And the XO said to himself, "Gee, I like that kind of talk"
All that nautical terminology streaming from Manny's mouth.
Things like port and starboard, fore, aft, jibing, and coming about
Yes, the skipper was having a ball that morn ', teaching Jack how to sail.
And Jack was wondering silently If he could he ever do so well.
Suddenly on the horizon a small boat began to appear.
The skipper put on his glasses to make the blurred object more clear.
(My prescription sunglasses had not gone un-noticed)
"What is it, can you make it out?" The XO did emote.
"It may be a PT or sub chaser–Hell it's only a banca boat."
(A 30 ft sea-going dugout canoe with an outrigger, powered by a lawnmower engine)
So they promptly forgot about it and returned to the business at hand
When they looked again, the boat was right there. "My God, we're going to be rammed!"
(At the last minute I told Jack to tack, hoping the pirates would overshoot us. Instead, we were rammed broadside, cracking the hull to the centerboard and knocking Jack to the bottom of the hull, breaking the tiller off short, leaving us without steering)
'Away all boarders' ordered the other CO, but he said it in Tagalog. *(native language)*
So when the first one jumped into their boat, Manny thought he wanted to frolic.
But the pirate made clear his intentions with his great big knife.

Pricking the XO's stomach, he said, "Your money or your life."
(The pirate slipped and fell on top of Jack who had the presence of mind to hold up his hand and calmly say that he would give him the money.)
The thought raced through Manny's mind in about a second or so,
If I try to be a hero I could lose my XO
(I was forward· at the mast as the second man boarded, also armed with a machete. Since three more men were still in the boat, probably armed, and Jack's man had calmed down, I discarded the thought of using my Navy switch-blade survival knife.)
So surrendering his ship and his money, Jack's Acutron and ring as well,
He watched the bandit return to his ship and sail away fast as hell.
(After the second man took my $15 cash, he returned my wallet. Since Jack's fat wallet contained his family photos and addresses, he asked for his wallet too as they began to motor away. Instead, his wallet and contents were scattered into the water and Jack dove in to save what he could as the boat and I drifted downwind away from him with no steering and a torn sail, watching helplessly as the pirates circled back and nearly ran Jack over before turning for the north shore. I managed however, to note the banca boat's registration number.)
"Ah shades of North Korea", he thought, "And shades of Commander Lloyd Bucher,
If I'd had a gun, by God, I'd have shot those little f-ers." *(Not likely)*
After a time their nerve and their pulse Returned to their normal rate.
So they slowly turned their vessel around and returned to the base.
(The piracy had been reported to the base by alert sailors on nearby Grande Island. A Navy helicopter and Swift Boat were dispatched to intercept the banca boat; however, the banca reached the north shore first, motoring up a creek too shallow for the Swift boat and too overgrown for the helicopter to penetrate. Thankfully, the poets didn't know that we had to be towed back to the marina, defeated and humiliated.)
Now Manny was fuming, and so was Jack, and they didn't know what to do.
"If you won't tell on me", Manny said, "I won't tell on you."
"To be caught losing my ship at sea "Would make me out a clown."
"Especially to lose it in Subic Bay,"
"Well, that's a big put down."
"I can't agree with that, Skipper", The XO did retout
"We both escaped with our lives, and that's the important part."
"Yes, we can be thankful that we both escaped with our skin.
Our wives might find it hard to replace us as next of kin."
"Sailing, sailing over the bounding main,
If given a choice next time, we won't go out again."

(During our de-briefing we were told of a similar sailing piracy three months before when an NCIS agent and his twelve year old son were boarded. The agent was stabbed, but his son saved him by beating off the pirate with an oar. In another recent incident a Marine Captain was fatally shot during a night amphibious raid on a Navy Exchange warehouse. The most colorful incident was a broad daylight Sunday afternoon raid where two brand new crash trucks had been offloaded at the docks. After starting the trucks, the thieves roared toward the main gate with all the bells, horns, whistles, and sirens sounding full blast. The guards, assuming there had been a crash nearby, stopped all traffic and waved the crash trucks through the gate at top speed. Since it was common for stolen vehicles to be re-registered and licensed, one of the crash trucks was put in service at the Manilla International Airport. The other truck disappeared–perhaps dismantled for parts. Jack and I were shown a photo album with 3 X 5 mug shots of men who lived at the pirates fishing village and noted that some photos were marked over with a broad black X and "R.I.P." beneath. The explanation was that the village chief was befriended with a regular supply of Johnny Walker whiskey and was said to have executed some of those identified in crimes against the base. Accordingly, Jack and I positively ID'd the first man aboard and agreed on four others for good measure. The last we heard, a man was arrested for selling Jack's Acutron watch, so perhaps the first man aboard became an "R.I.P." in the Subic NCIS photo album)

From the poet's authors
Now Manny, we meant no harm by these lines, but admit it, it is kind of funny
to see two Navy Commanders Get taken that way for their money.
One other thing we'll mention, not meant as a dig,
When you get taken in Subic, You really do it up big.
Manny, it's good you're a pilot. When airborne you'll always get by,
Though they did it in Subic, They can't board you in the sky.
The Boomers would like to help you, but we can't afford an Acutron.
So we'll make a mount for your boat to carry your Mini-Gun.
The Boomers know you're a shit hot stick and not afraid of a duel,
But we recommend you restrict yourself to sailing in the BOQ pool

"Well you sure topped yourself with that little adventure, didn't you Captain? I'll bet your PAO Al Junker had a ball with it."

"Oh yes. Al and others were inspired to launch into a rancorous exchange of poetry with little literary value; however, they may give you insight into the nature of Yankee Station carrier operations. So let's include some, you can delete them later. Here's our response to the Boomers poem, prefaced by explaining that their A-6 Intruder had a two man crew, could carry half again the A-7 bomb load, and supposedly had a more capable all-weather weapons delivery system. Unfortunately, the accuracy and reliability of those systems left a lot to be desired. Plus, the A-6 was the ugliest airplane the Navy ever flew. All of which made the Boomer (their radio voice call) poets vulnerable to Busy Bee (our voice call) retaliation."

BUSY BEES BROADSIDE BOOMERS

Rub a dub dub, two men in a tub were sailing the mouth of Shit River.
(The common name of the sewage creek at the base main gate)
When o'er the horizon a boat did appear, but THIS crew would NEVER quiver.
With a tiller over and smart put-about, Skipper shouted, "XO, look alive.
Only five hoods in that boat, they can't possibly survive!"
But alas, the next thing heard Was the XO exclaim, "I'll be damned!"
And then the Skipper said, "Horse shit, we've been rammed!"
The boarding party clashed in battle. Hey, our boys are quicker,
But the fracus ended with the XO's belly surrounding a pig sticker.
Their money gone, their boat damaged, our valiant crew sailed home.
Their only thought at the time, Was "Here comes a damn Boomer poem."
Only pilots who need a crew could attack with such glee
A close call for our skipper which will live in history.
And what has our XO done to warrant such an attack?
You lousy BOOMERS won't give us no slack!
But there's no hope/or you, as you shall soon see.
You're in trouble now, you pissed off the head Busy Bee.
As VFR bombers, we proved our point, CAG recognized us as best.
So there's that all weather stuff. Let's have a real contest.
Consider what follows herein, a leather glove in your face.
We'll use your weapons at your time and place.
Outnumbered two crew to one, our challenge is issued, we'll wait.
For all you uglies and your uglies to bite at the bomb derby bait.
To radar bomb, Commando Nail style, whatever target deemed fit.
While you search with your Blip, We'll be the ones who hit.
The Busy Bees

"Very cute, Captain. What a loyal crew. How did the bombing competition come out?"

"It didn't, of course. Vietnam was a lot of things, but it was not an occasion or location for competitive bombing derbies. Nevertheless, as bad as the poetry was, our exchanges with the Boomers inspired the F-4 squadron poets to join the frey."

From the F-4 Poets

There seems to be a trend nowadays for writing lots of verse.
At first the poems were horrible, but now they are getting worse.
Who is better between Boomers and Bees? The point is really senseless.
If we depended on either one, Connie would be defenseless.
A-7 pilots may be good, but they live inconstant fear
Of watching their plane hit the water a mile beyond their nose gear.
With A-7's on stand down, you'd think the Boomers would shine.
But check out their mission count since we've been on the line.
Gentlemen, the facts are clear. You really have been shirking.
Come to Ready Rooms one and two to meet the guys who are working.
You Attack Pukes say the F-4J is an aircraft with no mission.
But look who's doing the bombing while you sit around wishin'
It's plain to see the Phantom II Is the best bird all around.
Whether strike, CAP, or escorting the Vig, There's none as good to be found.
We'd like to end this little poem by presenting a modest proposal.
Place you're A-7 Corsairs In the nearest garbage disposal.
If you convert A-6's to tankers we may let you stay

"Ironic wasn't it, Captain, for you to taking gas from the Phantom squadrons?"
"Yes, but you can see how defensive they were about their fighter mission."
"What was their reference to the A-7's nose gear failures? Wasn't that resolved in '68 after yours fell off on cat shot?"
"It so happens that an A-7 maintenance department poet recorded the recurring problem."

First Period Line Report

The A-7 hangar queens were all crowned.
The Diamonds and Jason were all tied to the ground.
"That nose gear's a menace", said HQ,

'And there's an inspection we want you to do."
Pull card 48 of the conditional deck.
There may be more we want you to check."
So Airframes was Jackin' and paint they were strippin '.
The inspection they pulled was really a pippin'
Let's fly 'em. Let's go!" yelled Manny and Bill.
The Boomers are sayin' we 're over the hill.
"Hold it", says SYSCOM, "wait just a minute."
"Inspect it again as if I were in it."
"There's another Bulletin we want you to do."
"Do One Seventeen and then you'll be through."
So Airframes was jackin' until they got blisters and warts.
They zygloed, fluxed, and wrote many reports.
"We're through, we're done! As they let down the jacks,
But alas and alack, they had to face facts.
"Not yet", said SYSCOM, "Those pilots you're doomin ".
"Those struts are like paper instead of aluminum."
"We'll send out our team of Vic, Dave, and Ski.
They'll inspect 'em again, this only makes three."
So out of the heavens and in on the COD,
Came the wide awake team—well maybe a nod.
"To jacks", cried Chief Wade, "Let's get this thing done."
"No sweat", said the team, "You'll like this, it's fun."
So off came the drag links, the paint and the struts.
They even inspected the big packing nuts.
"Everything's smooth, it's going like glass.
If you think it's over, hang onto your ass.
That nose gear's unstable, let's look at the barrel."
Said SYSCOM HQ, which brought on a carol.
"We looked", cried the team, "But an amendment we're lacking."
You guessed it again—go back to jacking.
Corrosion is found and bushings replaced.
But facts are facts and have to be faced.
More messages flew and new designs tried.
Then came the word, Ski's fit to be tied.
The bushings we sent you were not right.

"You've gotta replace 'em. Be nice, don't fIght."
Now everything has quieted, as they always will
And the Diamonds made it over the hill.
To NavAir Rework and SYSCOM HQ
We wish to convey our thanks to you.
For the words you passed, instructions so clear,
Set us back much more than a year.
But when it counts and bombs are dropped,
When all the scores are taken,
The Busy Bees won't be stopped,
We'll bring home the bacon.
"We didn't let the Phantom Phlyers off unscathed either, Michael."

THERE'S A MIG IN THE AIR, I THINK

A couple of days ago, From Connie's mighty deck,
We launched some birds to North Vietnam, Some photographs to take.
This gaggle of CAG 9 aircraft Had a Vigi in the lead,
(RA-5 Vigilante photo plane)
Also flak supress and Iron Hand In case there was a need.
Proceeding from the coast descending, The Vigi called "feet dry".
The Phantoms stayed high to protect him, those warriors of the sky.
They violently jinked at twelve thousand feet, while at the ground they intently did stare.
Suddenly a voice called on UHF. "There's a MIG in the air."
"Holy shit, I don't believe it", Thought the crew of the RA-5C,
I don't dispute their vision, but I think that MIG is me.
It's all too true I'm afraid, The Phantoms had made a bad guess.
Instead of an enemy fighter they nearly laid our Vigi to rest.
We see how in the heat of battle, When the flak is bursting so near,
How judgement might be impaired And one's vision not clear.
But it wasn't so bad that day, the enemy had fired hardly a round.
Shouldn't Phantom Phlyers have exams to see if their vision is sound?
It's not that we think that the Phantoms should change their primary mission.
We just wish they'd take a course in aircraft recognition.

The Attack Community

"Captain, in my limited experience I've seen that another airborne airplane can be very difficult to see. Even with the Ximango's traffic detector telling me there's another airplane less than a mile away, there have been times when I could not find it. So it's easy to understand how hard it must be to sight high speed targets in a hostile environment."

"True, Mike, still there's nothing to motivate one's vision like the threat of imminent danger in combat."

"This was another short combat tour for you again, wasn't it? Similar to your 1966 tour aboard Ranger when you detached early to go to RPI."

"Yes. Some might think it misleading for me to claim five flying combat Vietnam tours, so I reviewed my flight log books last night to get an accurate count of tour lengths and combat missions. When the number of months on the line are tallied–seven months in '64, six months in '65, seven months in '68, ·seven months in '70, and three months in '71–thirty months, an average of six months in WESTPAC for five deployments–two and a half years over a six and a half year period. Normal deployments before Vietnam were for six months, so everything considered, I think it's fair to say five tours."

"No argument there, plus for good measure, a sixth twelve month tour ahead to end it all in '75. What did you come up with in your logbook review of missions? It seems that for the number of tours, you had fewer missions than I expected."

"In reviewing my log books last night, I was reminded that in '64 there was much uncertainty about defining and logging combat missions. Before the '64 GOT Incident we flew just a few photo escort missions into Laos. We were shot at and paid 'hostile fire pay', but we weren't formally at war or even necessarily publicly admitting to being there at all, so the 'flight purpose codes' in our pilot logbooks did not accurately reflect the missions."

"Would this be a good point to review those codes?"

"Not again–too lengthy, technical and boring. Suffice to repeat that even the Ops Yeomen who kept our logbooks initially had a hard time dealing with the challenge of daily redefinition of the terms, conditions and purpose codes. I should have kept a diary, but there was no time for trivia. I really didn't care about the numbers–and still don't except others have been curious, so I thought I should address the numbers for the book. The bottom line guess is three hundred and sixteen 'missions', but I'll be the first to say that some of those could barely be considered combat except for the threat areas flown in. There's no doubt that any flight over North Vietnam was a genuine combat mission because you could be sure of being shot at, but there were wide variations in threats depending on target locations, weather, day-night, and opposition. In any event, with rare exceptions there's little to say about missions which wouldn't be repetitious.

Nevertheless, I told the pilots that I believed they each deserved the Medal of Honor for repeatedly putting themselves in harms way in very hazardous conditions to save the lives of our comrades in arms on the ground in South Vietnam by destroying or slowing North Vietnam supplies and troops. I was pleasantly surprised that several spoke up to deny their worthiness. I did go on to say, however, that because of the administrative burden of writing award recommendations, plus the fact that I needed Rex's poison pen for drafting nasty-grams up the chain of command, individuals would have to initiate their own awards and do most of the 'creative' writing themselves, taking personal responsibility for the embellishments required to meet specified elements of weather, opposition, and damage assessment. To my knowledge, the Blue Diamonds did not seek any DFC's that cruise. I was proud to be in such good company. In fact–though I cannot take personal credit–I am extremely thankful and fortunate to be able to say that there were no training or combat pilot losses in any of the squadrons I deployed with throughout my Navy flying career–before or during Vietnam."

"Which ended all too soon?"

"I have to admit, Mike that I was ready to move on while I was ahead of the game and at the peak of my flying career. I had been very lucky and it couldn't last forever. My final mission was leading a flight of eight A-7's against a storage site in Laos which turned into an embarrassing screw-up when I absolutely could not locate the target and had to turn the lead over to the second division leader."

"Was the target something you should have seen in the open?"

" It was hidden in mountain jungles with no distinctive landmarks, but I hadn't done enough pre-flight preparation to pinpoint my search. It wasn't that it was a high value target, it was simply humiliating that it pointed the finger at me for being an old fart with failing eyesight. At least that's how I felt. It was brought further home to me the following day–the last day before my change of command. I was scheduled for two Alfa strikes leading thirty planes against a highly defended target. For unexplained reasons, CAG took me off the schedule. I assumed because he didn't want me getting shot down on my last day as CO, still I wondered if his confidence in me had slipped. In any case, Mike, I simply felt relieved that it was over–not just Vietnam and my command tour, but likely my Navy flying career as well. There was slim probability of being selected for CAG; otherwise, there were no further flying assignments on the horizon. I felt that I had flown my last flight. While I was very gratified that I had done a credible job and survived, I wasn't prepared for the powerful wave of nostalgia which swept over me for the change of command ceremony, December 7 th 1971, the 30th anniversary of Pearl Harbor when I was age nine at a Panama Canal Army Air Corps Base. I stayed in my cabin for three days waiting for the COD flight to take me off the ship bound for my next assignment to the DC Bureau of Naval Personnel POW/MIA office–not in any way a cheerful prospect. That brings me around to pointing out that if your mission was to chronicle the life and loves of a fighter pilot, then you may wish to wrap up your research at this point and call it a day."

"The end of Vietnam flying is over for you Captain, so this seems to be a good point to conclude Part One of Passing Through. We can launch into Part Two with your POW/MIA Affairs Office tour, then back to WESTPAC on Seventh Fleet Staff for the Mayaguez Incident and on scene for the Evacuation of Saigon, the dramatic conclusion of the Vietnam Conflict in 1975."

"True, followed by ten wonderful years at the Naval Academy, Northwestern University, and the Naval Historical Center. Concluding with high romance, flying, and sailing adventures on the Yellow Brick Road to 'Emerald City' in retirement with Jean and several ladies along: the way to seek the wonderful Wizard of OZ, 'because of the wonderful things He does.' It's going to be much longer, but more fun telling, than Part One. Are you sure you want to continue, Mike.?"

"In for a penny, in for a pound, Captain."

I am most sincerely and eternally grateful for you being here and getting me going with writing, flying, and sealing our relationship. I just don't want to tie you down with more than you bargained for in coming here."

"Well, I surely got more than I bargained for, thank God. This has been a way far more joyously rewarding adventure than I imagined possible, so why in the world would I want to bail out in the middle of it? It's not that I have some place urgent to go or I wouldn't have come here to begin with, would I? So, shall we press on tomorrow morning with telling the world about your continuing adventures with Jean down The Yellow Brick Road?"

"Bless you, my son, you're a glutton for punishment."

"I guess it runs in the family"

"Like father, like son."

"Think we've shot our wad on cliches for the topic?

"Naw, just the tip of the iceberg."

"Good grief, Charlie Brown. See you in the comics."

"If the creek don't rise."

"I give up. Good night."